THE JUDGMENT OF
THE DEAD

The Fall of Jerusalem and the Christian Church
Time and Mankind
Man and his Destiny in the Great Religions
Creation Legends of the Ancient Near East
History, Time and Deity
Jesus and the Zealots
The Judgment of the Dead

THE JUDGMENT OF
THE DEAD

The Idea of Life After Death
in the Major Religions

S. G. F. BRANDON

CHARLES SCRIBNER'S SONS
NEW YORK

A–1.69 [MC]

PRINTED IN THE UNITED STATES OF AMERICA
Library of Congress Catalog Card Number 68-57077

CONTENTS

ILLUSTRATIONS

ACKNOWLEDGMENTS

The publishers wish to thank the following for their courtesy in providing illustrations for this volume: the Bibliothèque Nationale, Paris, plate 10; I. A. Brandon, plate 5; British Museum, plates 1 and 2; the Executors of W. Y. Evans-Wentz, plate 11; John Rylands Library, Manchester, plate 7 and figure 4; the Mansell Collection, plate 3; F. C. Morgan, Hereford, plate 6; Musée Guimet, Paris, plate 12. The publishers also thank Messrs. George Allen and Unwin, Ltd., for their kind permission to quote from *The Principal Upaniṣads*, by S. Radhakrishnan.

PREFACE

The task of the historian of religions is basically the same as that of the historian of any other form of human activity. He is concerned to understand ideas, actions and institutions of a specific kind of past generations of men and women. Although his subject matter is often very various and complex, he seeks to elucidate it by employing the same methods and techniques of research as are used by his colleagues in other fields of historical inquiry. However, while his approach and presentation of his findings must be as strictly academic as those of the political or economic historian, the historian of religions is ever aware that he is dealing with issues that have more than academic interest. To give just two obvious examples by way of illustration: in studying the origins of Christianity or of Islam, the historian of religions will be keenly aware that he has to do with two historical persons, namely, Jesus of Nazareth and Muḥammed, whom millions, respectively, have regarded, and still regard, as the divine Saviour of mankind and the Prophet of God.

The subject of this book has similar overtones of significance. The idea of the Judgment of the Dead, as it has found expression in the various religions of mankind, has represented a belief about human nature and destiny in the light of which men and women have lived and died. And although we may look with curious detachment at the ancient Egyptian belief in a judgment after death, the idea itself provides the ultimate vindication of the moral values of the various religions still powerfully effective in the world today. Indeed, it is soon evident on analysis that the notion of a *post-mortem* judgment also constitutes the ultimate authentication of the traditional ethic of Western society.

My purpose in writing this book has been to trace out the various manifestations of the idea of the Judgment of the Dead from its earliest conception in ancient Egypt some four thousand years ago. The undertaking has naturally stemmed from my earlier study entitled *Man and*

Preface

*His Destiny in the Great Religions.** For in surveying the various ideas which man has had of himself and his place in the scheme of things, it soon became evident that the concept of a *post-mortem* judgment was a topic demanding its own special study; especially since it represented a remarkable linking up of ethics with eschatology.

The religions selected for study here provide, with the exception of the religion of ancient Mesopotamia, the most notable expressions of belief in a *post-mortem* judgment. The considerable attention given to ancient Egyptian belief in this connection has been necessary for two reasons, namely, that it constitutes both the earliest and the most elaborate presentation of the idea. That lesser space, by comparison, has been given to the Hindu and Buddhist conceptions, despite the immense importance of these faiths down to the present day, is due to the fact that in them judgment has been viewed rather as an unceasing process through countless lives than as a definitive act consequent on death.

This book is essentially an historical and comparative study of the subject, and it is hoped that it will be of value in showing how so potent an idea has found expression in different cultures and at different times. No attempt has been made to evaluate the metaphysical or theological credentials of the concept; but some comment has been added at the end on the relation between belief in a *post-mortem* judgment and the moral code of the Western world.

I wish to record my gratitude to Mrs E. Ettlinger for her valuable advice on certain matters of early mediaeval art, and I am indebted to Miss E. A. Lowcock of the Department of Geography, Manchester University, for her skill and kindness in providing the line drawings. The Director of the John Rylands Library, Manchester, and Dr F. Taylor, Keeper of Manuscripts, kindly placed MSS at my disposal and arranged for their photographing, and to Mr G. A. Webb of the Arts Library, Manchester University, I owe the reproduction of other photographs. I thank Mr N. Thompson of the House of Weidenfeld and Nicolson for his original encouragement to undertake this volume, and Mr J. Shuckburgh for his co-operation in its presentation.

S. G. F. Brandon

The University of Manchester,
30 June 1967

*Manchester University Press, 2nd ed., 1963.

x

ABBREVIATIONS

Ae.R.T.B. *Die ägyptische Religion in Texten und Bildern*, by G. Roeder, 4 Bände, Zürich/Stuttgart, 1959–61.
A.N.E.T. *Ancient Near Eastern Texts relating to the Old Testament*, ed. J. B. Pritchard, Princeton University Press, 2nd ed., 1955.

B.A.R. J. H. Breasted, *Ancient Records of Egypt*, Chicago, vol. I, 1906.
Bilderatlas *Bilderatlas zur Religionsgeschichte*, hrg. H. Haas, Leipzig/Erlangen, 1924–30.
B.J.R.L. *Bulletin of the John Rylands Library*, Manchester.
Bonnet, *Reallexikon* *Reallexikon der ägyptischen Religionsgeschichte*, by H. Bonnet, Berlin, 1952.
B.S.O.A.S. *Bulletin of the School of Oriental and African Studies*, London.

C.A.H. *Cambridge Ancient History*.
C.E. *Chronique d'Égypte*, Bruxelles.

D.C.C. *The Oxford Dictionary of the Christian Church*, ed. F. L. Cross, London, 1958.
D.T.Z. *The Dawn and Twilight of Zoroastrianism*, by R. C. Zaehner, London, 1961.

E.I. *Encyclopaedia of Islam*, new edition, Leiden (from 1960).
E.R.E. *Encyclopaedia of Religion and Ethics*, ed. J. Hastings, 12 vols. and Index vol., Edinburgh, 1908–26.
E.T. English Translation.

G.J.V. *Geschichte des jüdischen Volkes in Zeitalter Jesu Christi*, by E. Schürer, 3 Bändle, Leipzig, 1898–1901.

H.G.R. *Histoire générale des religions*, ed. M. Gorce et R. Mortier, 5 tomes, Paris, 1947–52.

I.L.N. *Illustrated London News*.

J.E.A. *Journal of Egyptian Archaeology*, London.
J.N.E.S. *Journal of Near Eastern Studies*, University of Chicago Press.
J.S.S. *Journal of Semitic Studies*, Manchester University Press.

Abbreviations

Kleine Pauly   *Der Kleine Pauly Lexikon der Antike*, Stuttgart (from 1962).

L.R-G.   *Lehrbuch der Religionsgeschichte* (Chantepie de la Saussaye, hrg. A. Bertholet u. Edv. Lehmann), 4. Aufl., 2 Bände, Tübingen, 1925.

N.T.S.   *New Testament Studies*, Cambridge University Press.

O.C.D.   *The Oxford Classical Dictionary*, Oxford, 1949.

P.T.   *Pyramid Texts*.

P.W.   Pauly, A., Wissowa, G., Kroll, W., *Real-Encyclopädie d. klassischen Altertumswissenschaft*.

R.A.C.   *Reallexikon für Antike und Christentum*, hrg. T. Klauser, Stuttgart (from 1950).

R.G.G.   *Die Religion in Geschichte und Gegenwart*, 3. Aufl., hrg. K. Galling, Bände I–VI, 1957–62, Tübingen.

R-G.L.   *Religionsgeschichtliches Lesebuch*, hrg. A. Bertholet, Tübingen, 1908; 2. Aufl. 1926–9.

R.H.R.   *Revue de l'histoire des religions*, Paris.

R.S.V.   American Revised Standard Version of the Bible.

S.B.E.   *Sacred Books of the East*.

S.O.   *Sources orientales*. A series comprising seven volumes by various contributors from 1959 to 1966, Paris.

W.B.   *Wörterbuch der ägyptischen Sprache*, hrg. A. Erman u. H. Grapow, 5 Bände, Leipzig, 1925–31.

Z.A.   *Zeitschrift für Assyriologie*.

INTRODUCTION:
The Dawning Problem of Death

It has been said that man created death.[1] Great percipience lies behind the obvious paradox of this statement, and the truth it embodies profoundly concerns all attempts to evaluate the significance of human life. The biological causes, which terminate the existence of the individual members of every known species of life, operate insidiously and irresistibly in the same general pattern to produce the same result, whether it be in an insect or in a man. But, so far as can be observed, the other species are unconscious of the mortal significance of this process, being aware only of the pain or discomfort it may cause; for them the culmination of the process occasions only the degree of physical suffering that is then inevitable, accompanied perhaps by some unidentifiable fear. Man, however, by his rationality, is conscious of his mortal nature; his time-consciousness causes him to look forward into the future and anticipate his own demise. This knowledge of his mortality profoundly affects his evaluation of both life and death. Man is unable to live wholly existentially, immersed in the here-now experience of each passing moment; for he can never long forget that time is ever passing, and that it is relentlessly bringing nearer the moment of his demise.[2]

This preoccupation with death is evidenced from the very emergence of *homo sapiens* in the archaeological record. For the earliest representatives of our race are found burying their dead, which is a custom practised by no other species, although man's precursor, the so-called Neanderthal Man, had anticipated him in so doing.[3] But this burial of the dead signifies something much more remarkable than a reverent disposal of the dead bodies of members of the family or community. The corpses were not only carefully laid in specially prepared graves, but they were equipped with tools, ornaments and food. The significance of the custom is plain: the dead were thought still to be in

I

need of such things.[4] The idea is crude, but for the evaluation of man its meaning is profound. It shows that at the very dawn of human culture death was not accepted as the definitive end of the life of the individual. Although these primitive peoples were well aware of the phenomena of death and of the change death wrought, they evidently believed that there was a *post-mortem* existence for which provision had to be made. In other words, death was already invested with a significance that ranged far beyond its biological reality.

The idea of a judgment of the dead, which is the subject of this study, is clearly a sophisticated concept, in that it presupposes familiarity with an established judicial process. But the idea itself is based upon a prior supposition, namely, that the dead survive the experience of dying, being fully conscious of their past life; for judgment would have no meaning unless the person being judged was intelligently aware of what was at issue. Now, in our quest for the origins of the notion of a *post-mortem* judgment, we may rightly be curious about the manner in which the earliest peoples, so far known, conceived of the after-life of the dead. The evidence, dating from the Upper Palaeolithic era (*c.* 30,000–10,000 BC), is necessarily wholly of an archaeological kind, and we can only make inferences from it.

Generally the burial customs of the Palaeolithic peoples attest an established belief that the *post-mortem* life would be a kind of continuation of the life before death. That it could not be quite the same must have been obvious to them from the fact that they buried the dead below ground, which suggests that they would have thought that the habitat of the dead was subterranean.[5] The equipping of the dead with things they had needed in this life is probably to be interpreted as due to a natural inability of these primitive peoples to envisage a life after death in any way other than as they knew it here. Certain differences in burial practice suggest some variation of idea about the condition of the dead, but the evidence would seem to have no significance for our particular theme.[6] There is, however, other evidence of a different kind which, though highly problematical, merits consideration.

A distinguished French prehistorian has interpreted certain curious anthropoid, but headless, figures, engraved on rocks at Mineteda in eastern Spain and dating from the late Palaeolithic era, as representations of spirits.[7] His reason for so interpreting them is that they are depicted in too animated a form to represent decapitated corpses. The inference is justified; but we may ask why spirits should be shown as headless? A more likely interpretation would seem to be that these figures are meant to depict dead persons who had been decapitated. If this deduction is sound, the question naturally follows of the cause of their decapitated state. An obvious answer is that the persons so depicted had

Fig. 1   Palaeolithic headless figures, from Minateda.

been beheaded, and as evidence of such a practice a well attested cult of skulls can be cited.[8] But why the victim of such a cult should be represented in a *post-mortem* state as headless affords a topic about which it would be idle to speculate. The most that we may reasonably conclude for our purpose is that already, at this early stage in human culture, belief in survival after death had led to the idea that the *post-mortem* state could be affected by what had happened before death – in the case discussed, that those who had suffered decapitation would be headless in the after-life.

Whether, in the light of this possibility, these Palaeolithic peoples thought that the dead might be punished for evil deeds committed in this life, is a question beyond our ability to answer, or even usefully to speculate about. We have no knowledge of their social organization or values. We may reasonably assume that there must have been some accepted code of behaviour, with penalties for its infringement. There is also some possible evidence of the practice of 'black magic' which, if it could be substantiated, would tell us much about human relationships in the community concerned.[9] But beyond such surmises we cannot justifiably go. However, despite such paucity of information, it is clearly evident that at the very dawn of culture, so far as it is documented archaeologically, death already constituted a matter of profound concern, demanding much effort of thought and practical action.

The tantalizing intimations of the significance that death had for Palaeolithic man recur when we continue our quest into the Neolithic period. Still interrogating preliterary societies, we are obliged to cull what information we can from archaeological data. Funerary practice continues to bear witness to preoccupation with the problem of death and belief in *post-mortem* survival.[10] Of the conception of the after-life some remarkable, though essentially enigmatical, evidence has recently come to light. Excavations at Çatel Hüyük in Anatolia have revealed a settled community, with a well developed culture, going back to the seventh millennium BC.[11] In the remains of a sanctuary unearthed there, dating from about 6150 BC, mural paintings were found showing headless human figures menaced by huge black birds of prey.[12] These pictures have been interpreted as representing human corpses being

Fig. 2   Headless figures menaced by large black vultures, from Neolithic shrine of Çatel Hüyük.

devoured by vultures.[13] Such an interpretation is very reasonable; but, if it is right, the purpose of such representations is beyond comprehension. The sanctuary appears to have been dedicated to a Mother Goddess, and rites concerned with fertility and death seem to have been performed there.[14] This being so, it is impossible to imagine why so gruesome a subject as the eating of corpses by vultures should have been deemed appropriate for the adornment of the walls. Moreover, it is strange that these corpses should all be shown as decapitated. But it may well be questioned whether the figures do indeed represent corpses; for, like the headless figures of the Palaeolithic period, which we have just discussed, these at Çatel Hüyük seem to be depicted in a manner

4

too lively to be representations of dead bodies.[15] It may, therefore, be legitimate to wonder whether they, similarly, may be intended to portray the *post-mortem* state of dead persons, possibly of those whose skulls were found in the sanctuary.[16] If this should be so, then it would appear that the pictures were designed to represent some sinister experience after death, but whether by way of warning, as the Doom paintings in mediaeval Christian churches,[17] can be a matter for speculation only. However that may be, the horrific nature of these pictures at Çatel Hüyük eloquently attests the fact that already in the seventh millennium BC, in this Neolithic community, death was a subject of fundamental import in religious faith and practice.

Some rather curious evidence of preoccupation with death comes also from the approximately contemporary culture at Jericho in the form of so-called 'portrait skulls', i.e. skulls upon which the facial features have been modelled in plaster and painted. They were found buried in the walls and floors of houses.[18] Whatever their purpose, they surely bear witness to some mortuary ritual implying a complex of belief concerning the meaning of death.

The evidence, which we have surveyed, although it is essentially of an inferential character, since it documents preliterary societies, has a unique interest, for it concerns the earliest intimations of man's preoccupation with the problem of death. The problem, however, does not seem so much to have inhered in the achieving of a *post-mortem* existence, as in making provision for the imagined needs of that existence. Whether, in crudely conceiving of this after-life as a kind of continuation of life here, it was expected that the social conditions of this world would be reproduced there, including the operation of any moral codes that may have existed, there is no sure information. However that may be, the history of religions, as we shall duly see, provides ample evidence that belief in survival after death has not also necessarily involved belief that the dead would be judged on the quality of their previous life. In the religions concerned, the absence of such belief has resulted from the particular conception held of the constitution of human nature and the effect of death upon it. It will, in due course, be our task to investigate the factors that have led to such a variety of eschatological belief among the great religions of mankind. But now, from this introductory survey of the earliest evidence of man's concern about death and its aftermath, we must pass on to examine the earliest known evidence of belief in a judgment of the dead.

ANCIENT EGYPT:
Man's First Confrontation with Conscience

It is in Egypt that the earliest evidence is found of the idea that judgment awaited a man after death. This distinction is not due merely to the fact that the first literate society emerged on the banks of the Nile; for in Mesopotamia written records date back to a like antiquity, yet the belief was never current there. The Egyptians, however, were not only unique in being the first to conceive the idea, but with them it also attained a far greater degree of elaboration than with any other people of the Ancient World. This peculiar distinction in the history of ideas merits, therefore, a detailed investigation of its nature and the causes that produced it; for Egyptian priority in conceiving and developing the notion is of the greatest significance for a comparative study, such as we are undertaking, of a belief that has so profoundly influenced the evaluation of life of so many peoples over many centuries.

The earliest adumbrations of the idea of a *post-mortem* judgment in Egypt have to be sought in that great corpus of religious texts known as the *Pyramid Texts*, which also constitute the oldest written documents we possess of Egyptian life and thought. These *Texts*, in their extant form, date from about 2425–2300 BC, but they clearly incorporate much older material. Inscribed on the interior walls of the pyramids of certain pharaohs of the Fifth and Sixth Dynasties, the *Texts* had been compiled by the priests of Heliopolis to assist the dead monarchs to reach eternal beatitude in the after-life. The material used in the compilation is of varying kinds and it comes from different sources; prayers and incantations, hymns and myths, have been worked into the structure of the *Texts*.[1] It would seem that the Heliopolitan priests were prepared to lay any traditional matter under contribution, if they thought that it might have some relevant virtue; they sometimes acted, as we shall see, with little circumspection, and included material that was inappropriate for royal use.

In the *Pyramid Texts* two distinctly different conceptions of the after-life find expression. What is clearly the official view, or rather that propagated by the priesthood of Heliopolis, conceives of what might be called a solar hereafter. Political interest doubtless inspired the propagation of this doctrine. Heliopolis, or 'Iwnu as it was known to the Egyptians, was an ancient centre of sun-worship, its local god Atum being identified with Rē, the sun, under the designation of Atum-Rē. A close association of patronage and support existed between the kings of the Fifth and Sixth Dynasties and the priesthood of Heliopolis, and it found doctrinal expression in the exaltation of the kings as the incarnate sons of Atum-Rē, who at death would return to their divine father and enjoy eternal beatitude with him in traversing the heavens each day in his company.[2] The other conception of the after-life was linked with a divine hero, Osiris, who was believed to have risen from death.[3] This belief expressed itself in an elaborate mortuary ritual, which was based upon the legend of the death and resurrection of Osiris.[4] Both the legend and the ritual were evidently very ancient and constituted a long established tradition in Egypt, which the priests of Heliopolis had to recognize and incorporate into their solar funerary ritual, despite its obvious contradiction to the view they sought to promote.[5] These two different conceptions of the after-life, as we shall see, were destined to produce two distinct traditions concerning a *post-mortem* judgment.

Considered generally, in terms of the conception of the divine king-ship which finds expression in the *Pyramid Texts*, the idea that the deceased king should face judgment was inconceivable. As the representative, on earth, of his divine father, Atum-Rē, the pharaoh had himself been a judge, and it would be natural for him to expect to continue in this rôle in the next world. The only suggestion of his having to undergo a test after death takes the form of an obligation to prove his divine birth, on ascending into heaven. Such a test is obviously conceived as the establishing of a hereditary right, and it involved no idea of moral qualification.[7] There are, however, a number of passages which obviously contradict this conception of royal privilege. The following is a most notable example:

N (i.e. the deceased king) is a member of that great company who were born at the beginning of things at Heliopolis. (He is) of those who will not be seized in the name of the king, nor taken in the name of the magistrates; (he is) of those who are not punished and not found guilty of crime. Such a one is N. He is not punished, he is not seized in the name of the king, he is not taken in the name of the magistrates and the enemies of N are not proclaimed as justified. N has not been made poor; his fingernails have not been *torn out*; no bone of his has been broken.[8]

Another brief declaration of innocence, also obviously inapplicable to the king, may be quoted for further illustration: 'This N has not reviled the king'.[9]

The evidence of these two passages, together with others that could be quoted, is clear. The priests, who compiled the *Pyramid Texts* for the royal mortuary use, must have utilized certain material that derived from the mortuary rituals of ordinary persons, who could, of course, have been accused of crimes against the pharaoh or punished for other offences under the civil code.[10] It would, accordingly, appear that already, in Egypt, there was some expectation that, after death, a man would need to affirm his innocence. No indication is given in these passages as to whom such affirmations would be addressed, presumably in the next world; but clearly the existence of some judicial authority is implied. So far as the form of the judicial process, which is envisaged, can be made out, it would seem that it was rather of the order of the deceased's having to defend himself against any accusations that might be brought against him. This appears even more clearly in the following passage: 'There is no accuser (representing) a living person against N; there is no accuser (representing) a dead person against N; there is no accuser (representing) a goose against N; there is no accuser (representing) a bull against N'.[11] In this formula, with its quaint reference to animals, a kind of comprehensive affirmation of innocence from accusations preferred by either the living or the dead, and even beasts, seems to be implied. The judicial process presupposed is doubtless modelled on that then current in Egypt, and which is attested by the Middle Kingdom writing known as *The Complaints of the Eloquent Peasant*.[12] The underlying presumption is that the condition of a dead person, in the next world, will be well, unless a complaint is brought against him. The moral implication in this would seem to have been of a rather negative kind, namely, that the ideal was not the active practice of virtues, but a mode of conduct that gave no offence; we shall see, however, that there is some evidence against the drawing of this conclusion.

Before we proceed to the consideration of this other evidence in the *Pyramid Texts*, it would be well to reflect upon the significance of the material which we have been examining. If we are right in assuming that the *Texts* concerned really reflect popular mortuary belief at this time in Egypt, it would appear that, survival of death being taken for granted, attention was centred on the nature of the *post-mortem* life. Some basic uneasiness, stemming from the experience that one's position in this world could be imperilled by the accusations of those whom one had wronged, existed apparently in relation to the next life, owing to the fear that cognizance might also be taken there of similar complaints.[12a] Whether such complaints would concern offences already dealt with here, or secret offences which would then be revealed, is unknown; but what is quite certain is that the belief was already current that one's behaviour here could decisively affect one's condition after death.

The *Pyramid Texts* also indicate the existence of what may have been a tradition concerning a *post-mortem* judgment which stemmed from the Osirian mortuary cultus. The following passage concerning the deceased king is of especial interest: 'He desires that he may be justified (*maā kheru*) through that which he has done. For *Tfn*, with Tefnut, has judged N; for the Two Truths (*Maāty*) have heard; for Shu was witness; for the Two Truths have pronounced the verdict' ... 'N goes forth to Truth (*Maāt*); he bears her before him'.[13] The imagery involved here, despite the strange terms employed, clearly implies a process of judgment from which the dead king has successfully emerged. Moreover, in contrast to the passages considered previously, a more positive moral note is sounded. Instead of an assertion of innocence, attested by the absence of accusations, the deceased bases his claim to justification on the deeds which he had done, thus implying that there was a code of recognized virtues. The passage has a further significance. Although *Tfn*, one of the two judges which judge the dead man, cannot be identified, the other, namely, Tefnut, was a cosmic deity who had an important rôle in the myth of the creation of the world which was taught at Heliopolis.[14] Shu also had an important place in this cosmogony, being the divine personification of the air or atmosphere.[15] Accordingly, two cosmic deities are regarded as having had decisive rôles in the judgment of the dead king. Then, the reference to the Two Truths (*Maāty*) is significant, because in the later presentation of the judgment of the dead in the *Book of the Dead*, which we shall discuss at length, the trial takes place in the Hall of the Two Truths. This judgment, moreover, is closely associated with Osiris, as the ruler of the dead.[16]

This suggestion of an Osirian connection is confirmed by, and in turn illuminates, the first statement in the passage just quoted: 'He desires that he may be justified (*maā kheru*) through that which he has done'. The expression *maā kheru* means literally 'true of voice',[17] and, as we shall see, it later became the traditional designation for every dead person who had been buried according to the Osirian funerary rites, and who had presumably been vindicated at the *post-mortem* judgment. Now, this designation derives from the legend of Osiris; for, after his resurrection, Osiris's cause against his murderer, Set, was tried before the tribunal of the gods at Heliopolis, with the result that Osiris was vindicated and Set was condemned. An allusion to this classic verdict is made in the *Pyramid Texts* (1556a): 'Guilty is Set; Osiris is just'.[18] These associations are significant; for they suggest that the legend of Osiris was already exercising a formative influence on the idea of a *post-mortem* judgment. That it should have done so is easily intelligible; because the Osirian mortuary ritual was modelled, as we have noted, upon the Osirian legend. The whole process of embalmment was a ritual enactment of what was believed to have been done originally to preserve the body of Osiris from physical decomposition and to raise him to life again.[19] In these mortuary rites the dead king was so closely assimilated to Osiris that the name 'Osiris' was actually attached to his own name.[20] Now, it is understandable that, as it was thought that the dead king was one with Osiris in his death and resurrection, so it was also assumed that he shared in the deity's *post-mortem* justification and could be accorded the title *maā kheru*. In other words, it is likely that the Osirian mortuary ritual, through the legend that constituted its *rationale*, provided a formative pattern for the otherwise vague belief that, after death, a man might be accused of misdeeds done in this life.[21] However, if a suggestion of such a pattern was there, as these verses from the *Pyramid Texts* seem to indicate, its influence was only felt gradually, for we shall presently study evidence of the conception of a *post-mortem* judgment which appears quite unconnected with Osiris. Nevertheless, as a stimulus to imaginative thinking about a judgment after death, the story of Osiris's *post-mortem* vindication before a divine tribunal could not but have had a great influence, especially with the increasing Osirianization of the mortuary cultus.[22]

Before leaving our examination of the evidence of the *Pyramid Texts*, it will be useful to consider the idea of *maāt*, which appeared at the end of the passage quoted above. There the dead king's intimate association with truth (*maāt*) was emphasized. The importance of this concept at this time in Egyptian thought is amply attested in the *Pyramid Texts*. *Maāt* is associated with the sun-god Rē (1774b),[23] and the deceased king is described as having put truth (*maāt*) in the place of error (265c; 1775b).[24] The word had a wide but related connotation; for it could mean truth, order, justice, right.[25] In hieroglyphs its determinative sign was an object resembling a chisel; the identification of the sign is uncertain, but it seems to express the idea of straightness.[26] Other Egyptian documents reveal that *maāt* was conceived of, mythologically, as a goddess, the daughter of Rē, and also the food on which this supreme deity was nourished.[27] In art *maāt* is represented as a seated female figure, with a feather on her head;[28] the feather was peculiarly her symbol, and sometimes it appears alone, most notably, as we shall see, in one of the scales of the balances at the Osirian Judgment of the Dead. For the Egyptians *maāt* represented the fundamental law of the universe, and, as such, was essentially associated with the sun-god, Rē, the chief state god, whose incarnate son ruled the land in the person of pharaoh.[29] From being the principle of cosmic order, similar to the Indian concept of *ṛta*, the Iranian *asha*, and the Greek *logos*,[29a] *maāt* also came to be regarded as the principle of social order, finding expression as justice, truth and righteousness, as we shall see. Opposed to *maāt*, as the *Pyramid Texts* show, was disorder, exemplified in error and injustice.

From our investigation of the *Pyramid Texts*, it appears, therefore, that already by the middle of the third millennium BC a complex of ideas existed concerning the after-life. Although these *Texts* are exclusively concerned with the *post-mortem* destiny of the pharaohs, it is evident that the Heliopolitan priests drew upon the mortuary beliefs of ordinary folk in compiling this corpus for royal use. Accordingly, we may infer that the Egyptians at this time were not content with the knowledge that they possessed, as they believed, the ritual means of securing immortality; instead, they were troubled lest their conduct before death might adversely affect their well-being thereafter. They seem to have had some conception of a social order, administered in this world by the king as the representative of his divine father, Rē, who embodied *maāt*, the basic order of the universe. From the *Texts* which we have examined, it would, accordingly, appear that offences were deemed to constitute an assault on *maāt*, as exemplified in the social order, and such assault would merit punishment, if it were established against an individual after death. We noticed, however, one indication of a more positive approach to morality, namely, that good deeds done on earth would secure justification at some *post-mortem* tribunal. All these ideas are, admittedly, only adumbrated vaguely: no indication is given of the mode of this assessment after death, of the identity of the judge or judges who would make it, or of the consequences of condemnation. However, the important fact is established, to wit, that, in the earliest documents of this very ancient culture, some tentative belief in a judgment of the dead is attested.

The *Pyramid Texts* document the mortuary beliefs of the Egyptians during a period of political decline. The young vigorous culture of what is known as the Old Kingdom had reached its zenith during the reigns of the kings of the Fourth Dynasty, the Great Pyramid of Khufu (*c.* 2600 BC) being the abiding memorial of the royal power that could then concentrate the resources of the land on the immense task of raising such a stupendous structure as a royal tomb.[30] Since this pyramid, and those of the other Fourth Dynasty monarchs, contains no funerary inscriptions, we do not know whether the mortuary faith and practice evidenced by the later *Pyramid Texts* was current then. However, even if the work of the Heliopolitan priests represented a new departure made for the benefit of the Fifth and Sixth Dynasty kings, it is likely that the material they utilized came from popular usage and dated back at least to the Fourth Dynasty.[31] Accordingly, we may be justified in assuming that, even in the stable society of this time, the idea that a man's deeds might be called in question after death was already current. It is important to notice this probability, because our earliest definite evidence, which is of a particularly striking character, concerning belief in a *post-mortem* judgment, comes from a period of social disturbance consequent on a break-down of a strong central government. The question naturally arises whether this evidence, which we must proceed to examine, is to be interpreted as indicating a new outlook due to unstable social conditions,[32] or as a development of an already existent idea.

It is the tombs of private persons, not of kings, which, from the Fifth Dynasty onwards through the First Intermediate Period (2200–2050 BC), next provide, in their furnishings and inscriptions, our main source of information about the Egyptian view of human destiny and the judgment of the dead. These are obviously the tombs of persons of high social standing and of considerable economic resources.[32a] The fact that they adorned the walls of their tombs with realistic scenes from everyday life not only reveals the state of life to which they were accustomed, but indicates also their conception of their *post-mortem* state of being.[33]

These scenes were evidently designed to provide an enduring record of the completeness of life which the deceased had achieved. According to contemporary Egyptian mortuary belief, the tomb was the 'house of the *ka*', which dwelt therein.[34] This mysterious entity, the *ka*, was a kind of double of the living person, conserving his vital being, which, after death, lived on in the tomb, requiring regular food offerings and the satisfaction of other needs.[35] The *ka* was imagined as indwelling the *ka*-statue, which was a very exact portrait of the living person,[36] while his embalmed body lay in the sepulchral chamber below, being visited from time to time by the *ba*, another mysterious concept of Egyptian anthropology, represented in art as a human-headed bird.[37]

Buried in this manner, after the due performance of all the necessary funerary ritual, the dead man believed that he had achieved the status of an *akh*, which may be approximately translated as 'glorified being'.[38] An expression, frequently used in tomb inscriptions at this period, clearly conveys the idea of completeness of attainment: the deceased claims that he is an '*akh*, effectively equipped with all that is necessary'.[39] This emphasis upon the achievement of a state of perfect completeness eloquently reflects the Egyptian idea of the *summum bonum* of human destiny, and it implies the existence of a stable enduring order of things; for change would involve the alteration of a perfect state.[40] This well balanced and enduring order constituted *maāt*, as we have seen. Its maintenance here on earth, for the Egyptian, was bound up with the power and authority of the pharaonic government, and any violation of it was effectively punished.

According to the Egyptian philosophy of life, therefore, the wise man, who respected and maintained *maāt* in this life, and, at death enjoyed the benefits of a proper funeral, could expect to achieve a state of eternal beatitude as an *akh*, with all his mortuary needs provided for by his own foresight and the continuous maintenance of this provision being ensued by the proper ordering of society in Egypt. But, as the royal control gradually broke down towards the end of the Old Kingdom, the social order correspondingly weakened and offences went unpunished. Among the crimes that began to multiply was the violation of tombs: they were either robbed of their rich contents or they were taken over by others, the body of its owner being cast out.[41] Such actions constituted the direst of misfortunes from the Egyptian's point of view; for his eternal future was thereby ruined. To guard against this new danger, resort had to be made to other means than appeal to the guardians of the civil law. Inscriptions now begin to appear in tombs, which by a mixture of threat and cajolery sought either to prevent the violation of the tomb or to supply the lack of mortuary offerings, if the arrangements made by deceased were no longer respected.

Two such inscriptions may be quoted from among several examples. The first, dating from the Fifth Dynasty (c. 2480 BC), is inscribed on the tomb of Hotephiryakhet, who was a priest of Neferirkere and of the sun-temple of King Nuserre at Abusir. It reads:

Judge, attached to Nekten, Hotephiryakhet; he saith, 'I have made this tomb as a just possession, and never have I taken a thing belonging to any person. Whosoever shall make offering to me therein, I will do (it) for them; I will commend them to the god for it very greatly; I will do this for them, for bread, for beer, for clothing, for ointment, and for grain, in great quantity. Never have I done aught of violence toward any person. As the god loves a true matter, I was in honour with the king.' Judge, eldest of the hall, Hotephiryakhet; he saith: 'I have made this my tomb upon the western arm in a pure place. There is no tomb of any person therein, in order that the possessions of him, who has gone to his *ka*, might be protected. As for any people who shall enter into this tomb as their mortuary property or shall do an evil thing to it, judgment shall be had with them for it, by the Great God. I have made this tomb as my shelter; I was honoured by the king, who brought for me a sarcophagus.'[42]

The most notable points for our attention in this inscription are, first, that the dead man, Hotephiryakhet, seeks to persuade whoever might read the inscription to make a mortuary offering to him, promising that in return he will earnestly commend them to the god. He evidently assumes that in the after-life he will be able to do this, implying thereby that the god would take favourable notice of such commendation. He does not name the god; but there can be little doubt that it is Rē, the sun-god, to whom reference is made.[42a] A reminiscence of the concern expressed in the *Pyramid Texts* about the possibility of complaint being made against one after death appears also here in Hotephiryakhet's declarations that he had come honestly by his tomb, and that he had done no act of violence. In the second part of the inscription, the dead man endeavours to protect his tomb by threatening any would-be violator of it with the judgment of the Great God. It is not clear whether this judgment would be visited upon such a person during his lifetime or after death. In another inscription such punishment is clearly described as happening to the guilty in this life.[42b] No indication is given of the process of this judgment; the implication is that the 'Great God' would act upon the complaint of the deceased. As to the identity of the 'Great God', it would again seem reasonable to think that the sun-god is meant.[43]

The other inscription of the two mentioned above has an even greater significance for our subject. It dates from the Sixth Dynasty (*c.* 2350–2200 BC), and is inscribed on the tomb of Herkhuf, an Assuan noble, who had undertaken some long journeys of exploration into Nubia and elsewhere on the orders of King Mernere and King Pepi II. It is a long inscription; the part that concerns us appears at the entrance to the tomb and reads as follows:

I came today from my city, I descended from my nome, I built a house, I set up the doors. I dug a lake, and I planted trees. The king praised me. My father made a will for me, (for) I was excellent – [one beloved] of his father, praised of his mother, whom all his brothers loved. I gave bread to the hungry, clothing to the naked, I ferried him who had no boat. O ye living, who are upon earth, [who shall pass by this tomb whether] going down-stream or going up-stream, who shall say: 'A thousand loaves, a thousand jars of beer for the owner of this tomb'; I will [–] for their sakes in the nether world. I am an excellent equipped spirit, a ritual priest, whose mouth knows. As for any man who shall enter into [this] tomb [as his mortuary possession, I will seize] him like a wild fowl; he shall be judged for it by the Great God. I was one saying good things and repeating what was loved. Never did I say aught evil, to a powerful one against any people, (for) I desired that it might be well with me in the Great God's presence. Never did I [judge two brothers] in such a way that a son was deprived of his paternal possession.'[44]

This inscription on the tomb of Herkhuf, although many of its passages can be paralleled in other inscriptions, constitutes one of the most significant documents both in the history of ethics and in the evolution of the idea of a *post-mortem* judgment. Like the former inscription, it is concerned to persuade those who visited the tomb to utter the magical formula designed to conjure up the prodigious quantities of food and drink for the deceased, and it contains a similar, if a more graphically expressed, threat against any intending robber of the tomb. But it also contains a positive affirmation of the *post-mortem* value of a virtuous life. The public parade of his virtues by this Egyptian nobleman of about the twenty-four century BC may sound egotistical and complacent to us; but it attests the important fact that in Egypt at this time there was a recognized standard of moral behaviour, which was positive and remarkably high.[45] It extended beyond family affection and professional obligations to 'good neighbourly' service – feeding the hungry and clothing the naked, and providing transport for the traveller; speaking benevolently and eschewing opportunities of damning another's reputation with a powerful person. The fact that Herkhuf rehearses many of his virtuous acts apparently to win the sympathy of visitors to his tomb, so that they might recite the formula for the magical supply of food, does not detract from the significance of the recitation. For it attests that such virtuous behaviour was generally appreciated, and it was calculated to evoke a sympathetic response in those who heard of it. But that is not all. Herkhuf also believed that such behaviour would count in his favour with the 'Great God'. The fact means that not only did Herkhuf threaten the would-be violator of his tomb with divine judgment; he also recognized that he, too, would be subject to this judgment. For this only can be the meaning of his statement: 'I desired that it might be well with me in the Great God's presence'.[46]

The conception of a *post-mortem* judgment in Herkhuf's inscription appears to mark an advance on what seems generally to have been envisaged in the *Pyramid Texts*. Instead of the rather negative concern lest damaging complaints might be preferred against one after death, Herkhuf aims at recommending himself to the 'Great God' by a record of good deeds done to his fellow men, particularly to the poor and needy. This more positive approach recalls the suggestion of that isolated statement which we duly noted in the *Pyramid Texts*: 'He desires that he may be justified (*maā kheru*) through that which he has done'.[46a] The justification sought there would seem to imply moral qualification; if this were so, Herkhuf's inscription might represent a detailed statement of moral virtues implied in the acts which would merit the designation *maā kheru*. This implication would in fact confirm what seems to be indicated by other considerations, namely, that already, at an earlier period of the Old Kingdom, a moral ideal was recognized as not only commendable in this life, but as having significance in the life beyond.

A distinguished German Egyptologist has seen in these tomb inscriptions an *Idealbiographie*, which, he thinks, really represented a kind of ideal righteous man, so that the inscriptions are not truly records of the acts of individual men. To have confessed to any departure from this ideal would, in his opinion, have been tantamount to revolt against the established social order.[47] However, even if a definitive pattern can be clearly discerned in the extant inscriptions, the fact does not distract from the ethical and religious significance of the Egyptian achievement at this early period. For the very existence of an *Idealbiographie* implies a strong moral tradition capable of producing such an approved standard of moral behaviour. And, even if this *Idealbiographie* were assumed by the dead or ascribed to them according to social convention, an impetus of some moral kind must surely have existed to cause the individual Egyptian to profess a high ideal which had a significance extending beyond this life. Moreover, there is the practical consideration that, for a man to declare on his tomb that he had 'fed the hungry and clothed the naked', in the hope that it would commend him to the 'Great God', when he knew that he himself had done none of these things, would be highly dangerous, for the 'Great God' would surely have detected and punished the deceit.

That such an ideal way of life was thus recognized, and that it was related to the 'Great God', is a fact of supreme moral and religious importance. The anonymous deity here described as the 'Great God' is undoubtedly Rē, the sun-god. As we have seen, Rē was essentially associated with *maāt*, the fundamental order of the universe. When Hotephiryakhet and Herkhuf, therefore, threaten would-be violators of their tombs with the judgment of the 'Great God', it is assumed that the sun-god, the supreme deity of the Egyptian pantheon, concerned himself about such acts of violence. The logic behind the assumption can be readily discerned. Such acts impaired the social order, *maāt*, on which the well-being of the Egyptian state was built. Normally the pharaoh would have seen to the punishment of such subversive action; for, as the son of Rē and his representative on earth, it was his task to maintain the *maāt* of the state. But, with the break-down of pharaonic government towards the end of the Old Kingdom, the punishment of such offences was no longer assured. Consequently, men had to look beyond the king for security and redress, namely, to Rē himself. They evidently felt that they could do this with confidence, and so they warned any who might rob their tomb that Rē would exact retribution for the crime, in addition to what they would themselves inflict on the intruder. But, not only did they thus invoke the supreme deity as the guardian of that social order which should guarantee to them the eternal security of their tombs, they also recognized Rē as rewarding the good deeds of men after death. —

It would appear, therefore, that, so far as our records go, by the middle of the third millennium BC in Egypt divine sanction was invoked for the social order, which embodied the moral values of the Egyptians. The practice or violation of these values had consequences which extended into the after-life, so that a man's conduct in this life decisively affected his destiny after death. The Egyptians have the distinction of being the first of mankind to reach this conception. It is, accordingly, important for the history of ethics to discover why this was so; for, as we shall see, their neighbours in Mesopotamia, who had attained a comparable degree of cultural development, did not hold a similar view. Two causes suggest themselves by way of explanation. The first is that, whereas the Mesopotamian view of death permitted no hope of a happy after-life,[47a] the Egyptians believed that they possessed the means of securing a state of eternal well-being after death. This belief involved the existence of a stable form of society, for one's provision for the after-life depended on respect for the property of the dead as well as for that of the living. During the middle period of the Old Kingdom such conditions were afforded through the strong government of such pharaohs as Khufu and Khafra; but the weakening of the royal power later destroyed this assurance/ Faced then with the lack of redress of injustice in this world, the Egyptians looked for it from the supreme deity who embodied *maāt*, the fundamental principle of order and justice. Hence, the moral values became endowed with divine authority; if the king and his ministers of state failed to maintain them, they did not lose their validity and their final vindication was assured. Thus the Egyptians, early in their history, solved the problem of finding an ultimate sanction for their moral code by positing it in the nature of supreme deity, and they avoided the problem of innocent suffering in this life by believing in a *post-mortem* adjustment of the inequalities of justice here.

It is to be noted, for future reference, that in these inscriptions, although a judgment of the dead is assumed as an established belief, nothing is said of its process. A tribunal of the 'Great God' or Rē is mentioned, but no indication is given of how it operated. The evidence of the *Pyramid Texts* envisaged some *post-mortem* court, similar to those of magistrates in contemporary Egypt, at which complaints might be made against the deceased. The tomb inscriptions, however, provide no clue as to how Rē would cause it to 'be well' with the man who had striven to do good deeds while on earth.[48]

From this early period we are fortunate in having two writings of the *genre* known as Wisdom Literature, for which Egypt became famous. They, each, provide information that illuminates and supplements the evidence of the *Pyramid Texts* and the tomb inscriptions which we have been studying. The earlier document purports to be instructions about social conduct given by Ptah-hotep, the vizier of King Izezi, a pharaoh of the Fifth Dynasty.[49] The following passage affords an interesting commentary upon the conception of *maāt*. Ptah-hotep is represented as addressing his son:

> Justice (*maāt*) is great, and its appropriateness is lasting; it has not been disturbed since the time of him who made it, (whereas) there is punishment for him who passes over its laws. It is the (right) path before him who knows nothing. Wrongdoing has never brought its undertaking to port. (It may be that) it is fraud that gains riches, (but) the strength of justice is that it lasts, and a man may say: 'It is the property of my father'.[50]

The other writing, known generally as the *Instruction for King Meri-ka-rē*, takes the form of advice given by one of the kings of the Tenth Dynasty (*c.* 2150–2060 BC) to his son: many of its sayings indicate that it was composed at a time of great social upheaval.[51] The document contains one passage of very great importance for understanding the development of the idea of a *post-mortem* judgment; but, before considering it, it is instructive to look at another passage which describes the outlook that inspired those tomb inscriptions that we have been examining:

> (so) also the soul goes to the place which it knows, and deviates not from its way of yesterday. Enrich thy house of the West; embellish thy place of the necropolis, as an upright man and as one who executes the justice upon which (men's) hearts rely. More acceptable is the character of one upright of heart than the ox of the evildoer. Act for the god, that he may act similarly for thee, with oblations which make the offering-table flourish and with a carved inscription – that is what bears witness to thy name. The god is aware of him who acts for him.[52]

Clearly a philosophy of life had been established which was not limited to this world, but contemplated human destiny as extending beyond death. Man's life was under divine surveillance, and the wise man would live in constant awareness of the fact, making moral preparation, as well as practical provision, for his demise. However, this admonition to remember one's mortality and what lay beyond was not accompanied by an ascetical or this world-denying attitude; life here was to be enjoyed, but with the consciousness that conduct here had a *post-mortem* significance.[52a]

In the other passage, the old king warns his son about the judgment after death, after having advised him in detail on his way of life. This advice is particularly interesting, because it indicates that a high standard of moral conduct was expected of the pharaoh himself:

> Quiet the weeper; do not oppress the widow; supplant no man in the property of his father . . . Be on thy guard against punishing wrongfully. Do not slaughter; it is not of advantage to thee. (But) thou shouldest punish with beatings and with arrests; this land will be (firmly) grounded thereby – except (for) the rebel, when his plans are discovered, for the god knows the treacherous of heart, and the god condemns his sins in blood. . . .[53]

There is next a curious reference to a book which seems to have some *post-mortem* significance: 'He who reads in the *sipu*-book . . . god, free-moving of foot in difficult places, (his) soul comes to the place which it knows. It does not miss the ways of yesterday. No magic can oppose it, (but) it reaches those who give it water.'[54] It is unfortunate that a break occurs in the text just after the mention of the '*sipu*-book'. It is tempting in the light of later evidence to wonder whether this book contained some record of one's life; however, the context seems rather to suggest that it was a book containing knowledge that would help towards attaining eternal well-being after death.

From this exhortation to a life of righteous action the old king passes on to warn his son of the coming judgment:

> The council which judges the deficient, thou knowest that they are not lenient on that day of judging the miserable, the hour of doing (their) duty. It is woe when the accuser is one of knowledge. Do not trust in length of years, for they regard a lifetime as (but) an hour. A man remains after death, and his deeds are placed beside him in heaps. However, existence yonder is for eternity, and he who *complains of* it is a fool. (But) as for him who reaches it without wrong-doing, he shall exist yonder like a god, stepping out freely like the lords of eternity.[55]

To the witness of this passage we may add that of a statement near the end of the writing. The old king finally exhorts his son: '*Open* thy face, that thou mayest be raised as a man. Thou shalt reach me, without having an accuser.'[56]

This passage reveals that the belief in a *post-mortem* judgment, which the earlier evidence had indicated under a varying and imprecise imagery, had now assumed a more developed pattern. A tribunal is conceived, having a number of judges, severe of character. The accuser is evidently a supernatural being, possessed of omniscience, so that no faults might remain hidden – possibly the reference here is to Thoth, the god of wisdom, who played the rôle of the divine recorder in later conceptions of the judgment of the dead, as we shall see.[57] The process of judgment seems to be imagined as having two stages. First, the deceased is confronted by a divine prosecutor, who knows the whole record of his life. The implication here probably is that, when an indictment is made, the dead man is then called upon to justify himself. After hearing his defence, the next stage is suggested by the statement that a man's 'deeds are placed beside him in heaps'. In this manner, it was, perhaps, thought that concrete evidence would be produced, by which the truth of the dead man's defence of himself, against the charges made by the divine recorder, would be demonstrated. The idea of making heaps of a man's deeds, presumably one heap of the good and another of the bad, is picturesque, and it was probably inspired by trading practice. The conception thereby implied of a deed is also interesting. For a deed seems to be thought of as something that endured in a concrete fashion after its enactment, and so could be produced after death, having in some way been previously stored in the next world.[58]

It is to be noted that nothing is said of the nature of the punishment incurred by an adverse verdict, although punishment is clearly threatened. The reward of virtue, however, is described in terms suggesting some form of *post-mortem* divinization.

The mortuary beliefs of the Egyptians during the Middle Kingdom (*c.* 2160–1580 BC) are attested by the great corpus of the so-called *Coffin Texts*, by inscriptions on funerary stelae, and by certain literary documents. The *Coffin Texts* in particular witness to a gradual democratization of the royal mortuary ritual.[59] What, according to the evidence of the *Pyramid Texts*, appeared to be the exclusive privileges of the pharaohs after death are now assumed by non-royal persons of social standing and affluence; although it must be remembered that some of the material used in the *Pyramid Texts* was probably drawn from the funerary practice and beliefs of private persons, so that the degree of this democratizing process may not have been quite so great as it has sometimes been thought. However that may be, what is of special concern to us is that these *Coffin Texts* indicate both that the influence of the Osirian ritual was increasing and that the idea of the *post-mortem* judgment was beginning to acquire the form which was to characterize it in the New Kingdom period and after.

The ritual assimilation of the deceased with Osiris now becomes a basic concept of the mortuary faith, and with it the Osirian title of *maā kheru* is automatically adopted. The following formula, from the *Coffin*

Texts, illustrates this vicarious justification and triumph which the dead thus acquired by magical identification or assimilation with Osiris:

> O Thoth, justify Osiris against his enemies! Justify Osiris N against his enemies, in the great tribunal which is in Heliopolis, on this night of combat when this enemy is overthrown; in the great tribunal which is at Busiris, on this night when the *djed*-column is raised; in the great tribunal which is at Letopolis, in this night of the nocturnal meal; in the great tribunal which is at Buto, on the night when the right of Horus over the patrimony of his father is established. . . .[60]

This passage, with its esoteric references to a number of tribunals and nocturnal happenings, is evidently inspired not only by the Osiris legend, but by knowledge of mystery-dramas, connected with the cult of Osiris, enacted at various Osirian cult-centres.[61] The mention of Thoth is significant; for we have already noticed a probable allusion to his rôle in the *post-mortem* judgment in the *Instruction for King Meri-ka-rē*, and we shall presently see how great that rôle becomes in the later conception of the judgment.

The emphasis in this passage is on justification as triumph against one's enemies, rather than on ethical justification. The *motifs* concerned are not unrelated to each other, and, since the reference is to the Osirian legend, the idea involved is that of the vindication of a just man against the evil adversary, who has both murdered him and then falsely accused him. The idea, as it is applied here in this mortuary context, recalls what seems to have been the earliest conception of a *post-mortem* judgment, namely, that the deceased might find himself accused of misdeeds in the next world.[62]

Justification acquired thus by ritual means, whether the emphasis be on the triumphant refutation of one's enemies or one's moral worth, may rightly be viewed as an undesirable concept. Indeed, a number of scholars have interpreted the increasing Osirianization of the mortuary faith as a declension from a higher moral conception.[63] According to them, the prospect of a judgment after death lost its deterrent effect when men came to believe that by magical means, i.e. by ritual assimilation with Osiris, they could acquire vicarious justification, irrespective of the moral quality of their lives. Their view is intelligible, and the evidence of resort to magic in the mortuary faith and practice of the Egyptians is abundant and impressive. But there is also strong reason for thinking that this threat to the moral significance of the *post-mortem* judgment, which the use of ritual magic constituted, was more apparent than real. Indeed, the very fact that belief in such a judgment grew more elaborate, and achieved the graphic presentation which we are to study, contradicts the supposition. For such a concentration of concern on an issue that could so easily be solved by magic would be very difficult to explain. Apart from this general consideration, however, there is evidence indicating that the Egyptians about this time came to conceive of the *post-mortem* judgment in a manner that precluded a magical solution.

Already, namely, in the *Instruction for King Meri-ka-rē*, the idea had appeared that a man's eternal destiny would not depend only upon the absence of complaints made against him, or, if complaints were made, his ability to refute them. Instead, a man was to be judged on the concrete evidence of his own moral achievement: his deeds, good and ill, would be laid in heaps before him. This suggestion of an objective and automatic demonstration of the moral quality of a person's life after death is developed in a significant way. The *Coffin Texts* contain abundant reference to weighing in a balance to assess merit or demerit, and thus to determine a man's fate. The following quotations clearly illustrate the notion involved: 'O Osiris N, this is the balance of Rē, in which he weighs *Maāt*';[64] 'The offence of which thou art accused is eliminated, thy fault is wiped out, by the weighing on the balance, in the day of the evaluation of qualities';[65] 'Thou causest the weighing to be made as Thoth'.[66]

In another *Coffin Text*, which takes the form of an invocation of the sun-god, and is reproduced later in the *Book of the Dead*, the balance is actually hypostatized as an awful deity, thereby witnessing to the dread in which it was held:

> Thou canst protect me from this god of mysterious form, whose two eyebrows are the two arms of the balance, who casts his lasso over the wicked (to hale them to) his block, who annihilates the souls, in that day when evil is assessed, in the presence of the Master of all! – Who is this god, whose two eyebrows are the two arms of the balance? It is Horus who presides at Letopolis. Others say: it is Thoth, it is Nefertem, the son of Sekhmet, this one who raises his arm.[67]

Leaving aside for the moment the many questions of detail which this conception raises, we may consider the general significance of this idea of a *post-mortem* weighing. The process of weighing appears to be more than a metaphor for making an assessment. The instrument used is realistically envisaged; it is obviously conceived in terms of scales or balances in actual use in Egypt.[67a] But the essence of the concept lies in the fact that such a means of assessment is impersonal and automatic. Unless its movement is interfered with, a balance will inevitably indicate the comparative weights of what is set in each of its scale-pans. That it could be personified, as the last passage shows, and imaged as a fearsome god, does not contradict this aspect of its function; indeed, far to the contrary, the notion attests the reality of the fear with which this ordeal after death was contemplated. Accordingly, we are justified in concluding that, however potent may have been the tendency to magic, the Egyptians had come to conceive of the *post-mortem* judgment as a transaction that was inevitable and automatic in its operation, and from which there could be no appeal or escape.

From these references and allusions in the *Coffin Texts* no clear picture emerges of what was to be weighed on this ominous balance, what the position of the scale-pans indicated, who supervised the weighing, or what were the consequences of the respective verdicts. The reference to 'the balance of Rē, in which he weighs *Maāt*' is certainly explicit; but it raises difficulties. For, whereas Rē's part in such an act of assessment, and his connection with *Maāt*, are intelligible in the light of previous evidence, the weighing of *Maāt* is obscure in this context. According to the *Instruction for King Meri-ka-rē*, we should expect that the weighing would have been of a man's good and evil deeds. On the other hand, as we shall see, in the later representations of this *post-mortem* weighing, namely, in the *Book of the Dead*, it is the heart of the deceased that is balanced against *Maāt*. The passages cited also reveal a variety of opinion concerning the identity of the god responsible for the weighing. Rē, Thoth, Horus and Nefertem are mentioned. All, except the last, have known rôles in the judgment of the dead;[68] but what is said of them in these *Texts* suggests that, although the conception of the judgment has now come to include this notable feature of the weighing, the imagery is still imprecise and the identities of the deities connected with it not exactly determined. Nevertheless, a definite step forward has been taken. Instead of the primitive view, closely modelled upon secular practice, according to which the dead were concerned to avoid accusations and to ingratiate themselves, by good conduct, with the 'Great God', it was now believed that they had to undergo this impersonal assessment, symbolized by the forbidding balance which gave its verdict unmoved by threat, prayer or cajolery.

That the prospect of such a trial after death, to which the *Coffin Texts* make numerous but enigmatic reference, had become a really effective belief by this time is attested by two Middle Kingdom literary texts. *The Complaints of the Peasant* purports to be an account of the efforts made by a peasant to obtain redress for injustice which he had suffered; the incidents are supposed to have happened during the reign of Neb-kau-Rē Khety III (*c.* 2100 BC).[69] The peasant is presented as a man of surpassing eloquence, as the Egyptians reckoned it, and, because of his eloquent statements of his cause, the magistrate concerned protracts the case, in order to enjoy listening to his arguments. In two passages the peasant is represented as seeking to persuade the magistrate to give him justice by drawing comparisons between a good magistrate and the function of a balance; the comparison appears to have eschatological overtones:

Desire to live long, as it is said: 'Doing justice is the (very) breath of the nose'. Carry out punishment against him who should be punished, and none shall equal thy scrupulousness. Does the hand-scales err? Does the stand-balance incline to the side? Is even Thoth indulgent? . . . Thy tongue is the plummet (of the balance), thy heart is the weight, and thy two lips its arms . . . Do justice for the sake of the Lord of Justice, the justice of whose justice exists! Thou reed-pen, papyrus and palette of Thoth, keep apart from doing evil! It is good if thou art good – good indeed. Now justice lasts unto eternity; it goes down in the necropolis with him who does it. When he is buried and interred, his name is not wiped out upon earth, (but) he is remembered for goodness. That is a principle of the word of god. It is the hand-scales – (then) it does not tilt. It is the stand-balance – (then) it does not incline to the side. . . .[70]

It is significant that the peasant, wearying at last in his eloquence, after his ninth pleading of his case, threatens the dilatory magistrate that he will complain of him in the next world: 'Behold, I have been appealing to thee, (but) thou didst not hear it. I shall go that I may appeal about thee to Anubis.'[71]

The other writing takes the curious form of a dialogue between a man, who is tired of life, and his soul.[72] Oppressed by his sufferings, the man contemplates suicide; his soul opposes his intention. In the following passage the would-be suicide looks forward to the judgment after death as vindication after the injustices of this life: 'Make the West pleasant for me! Is that (so) bad? Life is a circumscribed period: (even) the trees must fall. Trample down wrongs – (yet) my wretchedness endures. Let Thoth, who propitiates the gods, judge me. Let Khonshu, the scribe in truth, defend me. Let Rē, who *pilots* the sun barque, hear my speech.'[73]

The evidence surveyed, coming from various sources, reveals that at this time in Egypt concern with the *post-mortem* destiny of man was not concentrated so much on the question of making sure that one would survive death; for the funerary ritual ensured this. Instead, what was tending to become a more engrossing issue was the assessment of one's moral achievement. Although a reticence seems to have been observed about the consequences of an adverse verdict, the possibility of failing the test invested the symbol of the balance with dread. But this belief in a *post-mortem* judgment clearly affected the Egyptian *Weltanschauung* in a positive as well as in a negative sense. Not only did the thought of judgment evoke fear, it also sanctioned the view that in the next life the inequalities of this would be adjusted. For the social ethic this belief was especially important in times of social upheaval such as the First Intermediate Period, when established values could not be maintained. If *maāt* did not prevail here, Rē and the other gods would see that it prevailed in the next world. Thus belief in a *post-mortem* judgment had a very necessary rôle in preserving common faith in the social order and the values it sponsored. However, it is also important to notice that this faith was not shared by all, and that there were people who were sceptical of the traditional evaluation of man's life. The so-called *Song of the Harper*, of which several versions have been found inscribed on tombs of the New Kingdom period and which was reputed to derive from a poem originally inscribed on the tomb of Antef, a king of the Eleventh Dynasty (*c.* 2160–2000 BC), eloquently expresses this view.[74] After noting the fact that so many earlier tombs were ruined, thus frustrating the hopes of their owners, there comes the bitter comment, which has so often been echoed in the literatures of later peoples:

> There is none who comes back from (over) there,
> That he may tell their state,
> That he may tell their needs,
> That he may still our hearts,
> Until we (too) may travel to the place where they have gone.[75]

The poet goes on to recommend a *carpe diem* philosophy of life, without one reference to the traditional belief in a judgment after death, concluding with the refrain:

> Make holiday, and weary not therein!
> Behold, it is not given to a man to take his property with him.
> Behold, there is not one who departs who comes back again![76]

Such cynicism doubtless represented the views of a minority, although the fact that the poem continued to be used in the Eighteenth and Nineteenth Dynasties indicates that such an attitude had become an established tradition.[77] However, the fact that the mortuary faith and practice continued to command the allegiance of the Egyptians proves that this scepticism remained very limited in its effect. That it did exist at all is significant; for it shows that the Egyptians could be critical in their thinking about traditional religious conceptions.[78] Consequently, the idea of a *post-mortem* judgment did not establish itself wholly unopposed. Its acceptance and elaboration must reflect a deeply rooted conviction, felt by the majority of the Egyptians, that a man's moral conduct had an enduring significance and that a definitive assessment of it would be made after death, with eternal consequences of good or ill.

The threat, made in final desperation by the Eloquent Peasant, that he would take his complaint to Anubis, which we noted as being a reference to the earlier conception of the judgment after death, was not a reminiscence only of an outmoded idea. The *Coffin Texts* witness to the fact that the new *motif* of weighing by means of a balance had not superseded the former notion, based on current legal practice, that the dead might have to face charges of wrongdoing. As the following passage from the *Coffin Texts* shows, the idea of a trial before a divine tribunal was still an effective part of eschatological belief: 'O Osiris N, there is no god who presents a case against thee; there is no goddess who presents a case against thee, on the day of the assessment of qualities before the Great One, the Lord of the West'.[79] In another example, the deceased is represented as enlisting the aid of the divine tribunal against a malicious accuser (a reminiscence here doubtless of the accusation against Osiris brought by Set): 'Hail to ye, Lords of *Maāt*, members of the tribunal which is behind Osiris, who cause the iniquitous to be slaughtered, who attend Hetepeskues. I have presented myself to you, so that you may exterminate the evil one who accuses me . . .'[80]

The continuance of this idea of the *post-mortem* judgment, namely, as a process of denial or refutation by the deceased of accusations brought against him, explains the curious dualism of procedure that finds expression in the *Book of the Dead*, where belief in the judgment after death attains its fully developed form. For, as we shall now have occasion to see, the retention of the older view after the introduction of the concept of the balance, made the trial into a two-fold process, involving two different *motifs* which cannot easily be related to each other.

The eschatological beliefs of the Egyptians during the New Kingdom period (*c.* 1580–1090 BC) find abundant and confusing expression in the so-called *Book of the Dead*.[81] Written on rolls of papyrus and placed in the tombs in close proximity to the dead, the texts concerned were designed to facilitate the journey to the next world. The *Book of the Dead* does in fact represent a continuation of the mortuary faith of the Old Kingdom, but in a democratized and Osirianized form. Much material from the *Pyramid Texts* and the *Coffin Texts* has been incorporated into it, and it equals these earlier collections in its fantastic imagery and its use of magic. However, like its predecessors, the *Book of the Dead* reveals beneath its bizarre and often repulsive concepts, insights and aspirations of great significance for the history of religions. Further, because some of the superior versions are illustrated with vignettes depicting scenes of the mortuary ritual or the next life, the *Book of the Dead* affords invaluable evidence, of a very graphic kind, about the manner in which the Egyptians conceived of man's destiny after death. And on no topic is this evidence more graphic than on the judgment of the dead.

Two chapters of the *Book of the Dead* are especially concerned with the *post-mortem* judgment, namely, Chapters 30 and 125, and they are sometimes accompanied by representations of the assessment by weighing.[82] Since these chapters and the illustration of the transaction involved raise many intricate problems, a detailed examination of the pictorial presentation of the judgment scene will first best serve the purpose of our study. Of the many existing depictions of the scene, the version given in the *Papyrus of Ani* is undoubtedly the finest and most complete. This *Papyrus* was made for a scribe named Ani, who held important ecclesiastical offices at Thebes and Abydos; it dates from the beginning of the Nineteenth Dynasty (*c.* 1320 BC).[83] The scene, which is beautifully drawn and coloured, is charged with dramatic tension.[84] Ani and his wife, dressed in festal attire, are seen on the left, watching, in attitudes of humility and apprehension, the transaction that is taking place in the middle of the scene. By the postures of the dead man and his wife the artist has eloquently suggested that, whatever may have been a person's status and achievement before death, when he enters the Hall of the Two Truths (*Maāti*) for judgment, he can only abide in fear and trepidation the assessment that will then be made of his life.

The impersonal nature and the ominous solemnity of this assessment is vividly conveyed by the great black balance that dominates the centre of the scene. From its beam are suspended the two scales: one contains the hieroglyphic sign of the *ib* or heart; the other a feather, the symbol of *Maāt*.[85] The heart of Ani is being weighed against Truth (*Maāt*). Kneeling close by, the jackal-headed mortuary god Anubis adjusts the plummet of the balance, to ensure absolute exactitude. To his right stands the ibis-headed Thoth, the god of wisdom and the divine scribe. Holding his scribe's palette and reed-pen, he records the fateful verdict of the scales. Behind him crouches a fearsome hybrid monster, made up of the parts of a crocodile, a lion, and a hippopotamus. It is named Am-mut, the 'eater of the dead'; its function is obvious.[86]

To emphasize still further the fateful character of this dramatic scene, the artist has added a number of secondary figures of symbolic significance. Close to the shaft of the balance stands Shai, the personification of destiny.[87] Behind him are depicted the figures of Meskenit and Renenit, goddesses who presided respectively over childbirth and the nursing and rearing of the infant.[87a] The human-headed bird, perched on the portal of a tomb, just above the goddesses, is the *ba* or soul of Ani.[88] The curious rectangular object, with a human head, shown immediately below the left side of the beam of the balance, may depict the chest in which the umbilical cord of the child was preserved after birth.[89] Thus, in these subsidiary figures, the artist has assembled intimate reminders of various aspects of Ani's life, from his birth to his death, concentrating their witness on this fateful moment when his eternal destiny is irrevocably decided.

The figures in the upper register are intended, in terms of the perspective of the scene, to be witnessing the weighing of Ani's heart. They are twelve in number, including seven members of the traditional Ennead of Heliopolis and other related deities.[90] Their presence recalls both the ancient theology of Heliopolis and the legend of Osiris's trial. Their task, as we shall see, was to confirm the verdict recorded by Thoth.

The three groups of hieroglyphic text in the picture play an important part in the exegesis of the scene. The text, written before and above the figure of Ani, is that of Chapter 30 of the *Book of the Dead*, in which the deceased implores his heart not to witness against him on this awful occasion. We shall examine the significance of this text later.[91] The text above the right-hand beam of the balance and before Thoth represents Thoth's announcement of the verdict of the weighing:

Words spoken by Thoth, who transmits *Maāt* to the Grand Ennead, which is in the presence of Osiris: 'Hear this statement, in conformity with *Maāt*! I have judged the heart of Osiris (Ani). His soul (*ba*) has stood in witness thereof.[91a] His case is exact on the Great Balance. No crime has been found in what he has done. He has not diminished the food offerings in the temples, he has not disturbed the performance of the rites. He has done no evil act; he has not caused to issue from his mouth evil words whilst he was on earth.'

The divine tribunal, to whom this report is made, is represented as replying in the text inscribed before them:

Words spoken by the Grand Ennead to Thoth-who-is-in-Hermopolis: 'Confirmed is that which comes forth from your mouth. Just (*maā*) and righteous is Osiris (namely) the scribe Ani. He is vindicated (*maā kheru*). He has not sinned, nor done evil before us. Am-mut shall not have power over him. Food offerings shall be given to him. Entrance into the presence of Osiris shall be granted to him; he shall abide in the Field of Offerings (i.e. the realm of Osiris) as the sons of Horus.'

A brief inscription above Anubis exhorts him to be careful in his attendance to the balance.

Before analysing this pregnant scene, we must notice its sequel; for the ancient artist clearly intended to show what happened to Ani after he had successfully emerged from this awful ordeal. The next scene on the papyrus scroll is actually designed to depict two successive moments in Ani's experience consequent on his justification.[92] Led by the hand by Horus, the son of Osiris, Ani is introduced to Osiris, who sits enthroned on a canopied dais, attended by the goddesses, Isis and Nephthys. It is not clear whether the artist has intended to suggest that Osiris had from this position witnessed the weighing of Ani's heart, or whether he is enthroned in another room separate from the Judgment Hall.[93] However that may be, the purpose of the scene is made clear by two hieroglyphic texts. In the first, explaining the first episode of the scene, Horus addresses Osiris:

Words spoken by Horus, the son of Isis: 'I come to you, O Un-nefer, bringing Osiris Ani. His heart is just, coming forth from the balance. He has not sinned against any god or goddess. Thoth has put the judgment in writing.[94] This is the sentence of the Ennead: righteous and very true! Let there be given to him the bread and beer which passes before Osiris; let him be as the followers of Horus for ever.'

In the next part of the scene, the justified Ani is depicted kneeling before Osiris; he raises one hand in adoration and in the other he holds the *kherp* sceptre, symbolizing his high rank on earth. Around him, heaped in great abundance, are food offerings of various kinds. Ani addresses Osiris, the great ruler of the dead:

> Behold, I am before thee, Lord of the West. There is no iniquity in my body. I have not consciously spoken a lie; neither have I been double-hearted. Grant that I may be like the favoured ones who are in thy following, and that I may be an Osiris, greatly favoured of the Good God (*ntr nfr*), beloved of the Lord of the Two Lands (i.e. the Pharaoh). A true royal scribe, one beloved, am I, Ani, *maā kheru*, before (thee), Osiris.

Thus the scribe Ani achieved his desire: subsequent vignettes in his copy of the *Book of the Dead* show him, and his wife, enjoying their life in the other world of the blessed dead.[95] What was here drawn to illustrate the *post-mortem* experiences of Ani can be paralleled in many other manuscripts, and it represents what the Egyptians at this period imagined they would encounter and undergo after death. It is reasonable to wonder why such scenes were illustrated in these mortuary documents. It could be that these depictions were intended to instruct the deceased about what to expect after death, thus making the *Book of the Dead* a kind of illustrated guide-book to the after-life. However, in view of the magical intent of much primitive art, it is legitimate to think that such representations were intended to help the achievement of what was so fervently desired – that the representation of the deceased successfully passing the awful test of the weighing of his heart would serve as a propitious anticipation of a favourable verdict.[96]

The drama of the weighing of the heart, thus so graphically portrayed, constitutes in itself an intelligible trial of the rectitude of the dead. We have yet to evaluate the full significance of this weighing of the heart against *Maāt*; but, before we can profitably do that, we must take account of another aspect of the judgment of the dead, as it finds expression in the *Book of the Dead*, which it is difficult to relate to this dramatic action of moral assessment.

Chapter 125, which is one of the longest chapters of the *Book of the Dead*, comprises what is described in a number of manuscripts as 'Words spoken when one enters the Hall of the Two Truths. To separate N from his sins, and to see the face of all the gods.'[97] The text that follows has three sections: two 'Negative Confessions', as they have often been misleadingly described but which are really Declarations of Innocence, to be recited by the deceased; these two items are followed by some concluding addresses and other formulae. The idea implicit in these Declarations of Innocence seems logically to contradict the purpose of the weighing of the heart. That transaction, as we have seen, envisaged an assessment of the individual's moral worth which was objective and impersonal. Various deities took part in the process, but only as divine agents fulfilling rôles ancillary to the action of the balance, which was crucial. That the deceased should also have had to declare his innocence concerning a long list of offences, as we shall see, seems to introduce a very different conception of the *post-mortem* judgment. That both conceptions are given place in the *Book of the Dead* suggests that the Egyptians did not find them too obviously incompatible, and that they probably related them in some way. In order to appreciate the nature of the problem better, we must first examine the contents of Chapter 125.

The first of the Declarations of Innocence, which is made to Osiris, appears to take place before the Hall of Two Truths; the second, within the Hall, is made to forty-two deities or demonic beings. In the first Declaration the deceased recites:

Hail to thee, Great God, Lord of the Two *Maāti*! I come to thee, O my Lord, having been led. I contemplate thy perfection. I know thee, and I know the names of the forty-two gods who are with thee in this Hall of the Two *Maāti*, namely, those who live to watch over sinners and drink their blood on this day of the evaluation of qualities, in the presence of Un-Nefer. Behold, 'Sati-mertifi, Lord of the two *Maāti*', is thy name. I have come to thee. I have brought *Maāt*. I have repressed iniquity for thee.

I have not committed iniquity against men.
I have not ill-treated animals.
I have not done wrong in the Place of *Maāt*.
I have not (sought to) know that which was not yet.
I have not tolerated the sight of evil.
I have not been . . .
My name has not reached the Commander of the Barque.
I have not blasphemed (a) god.
I have not impoverished a poor man.
I have not done that which is abominated by the gods.
I have not discredited a servant with his superior.
I have not used poison.
I have not caused weeping.
I have not killed.
I have not given the order to a killer.
I have not caused pain to anyone.
I have not diminished the food offerings in the temples.

I have not spoiled the bread of the gods.
I have not stolen the loaves of the glorified (dead).
I have not had sexual relations with a boy.
I have not committed a sexual act in the sanctuary of the god of my town.
I have not added to, nor diminished the corn-measure.
I have not altered the *aroura* (a measurement of land).
I have not falsified a half-*aroura*.
I have not added to the weights of the balance.
I have not warped the index of the scales.
I have not taken the milk from the mouths of babes.
I have not deprived the small cattle of their pasture.
I have not captured the birds of the gods.
I have not fished in their ponds . . .
I have not deflected water in its season.
I have not made a dike to (deflect) flowing water.
I have not extinguished a fire by force.
I have not neglected the days appointed for the meat-offerings.
I have not stopped the cattle . . .
I have not stopped the procession of a god.[98]

I am pure. I am pure. I am pure. I am pure. My purity is the purity of the great Phoenix which is in Herakleopolis, because I am the nose of the Master of Breath, who causes all in Egypt to live, on the day of the filling out the Eye (of Horus) in Heliopolis, which is in the second month of the second season, the final day, before the Lord of this land. I am one who has seen this filling out of the Eye in Heliopolis. No evil will come to me in this land, in the Hall of the Two *Maāti*, because I know the names of the gods who are of thy company.[99]

The second Declaration of Innocence, which is addressed to the forty-two gods, follows. In the *Papyrus of Ani* these deities are depicted seated, in a long line, in the Hall of the Two *Maāti*.[100] The deceased is represented as addressing each in turn:

O Wide-of-Stride, who cometh from Heliopolis, I have not committed inquity.
O Embracer-of-the-flame, who comes forth from Kher-Aha, I have not robbed.
O Great-of-Nose, who comes from Hermopolis, I have not been covetous.
O Eater-of-shades, who comes from the Cavern, I have not stolen.
O Terrible-of-Face, who comes from Ro-stau, I have not killed any man.
O Double-Lion, who comes from heaven, I have not diminished the corn-measure.[101]

It would be tedious, and it is unnecessary, to go through the whole list of protestations addressed to these forty-two fantastic beings. The offences, of which the deceased declares himself to be innocent, comprise a similar range of moral and ritual transgressions as that in the First Declaration made to Osiris. Some of the second list of offences are very obscure, and those that are identifiable, and are not in the former list, do not notably extend the range of Egyptian morality beyond that already indicated in the earlier evidence which we have surveyed.

After protesting his innocence to these forty-two deities or demons, the deceased is directed by this 125th Chapter of the *Book of the Dead* to conclude his attestations with the following formula, which really constitutes a mingled threat and command to these deities:

Hail to you, O gods of this place! I know you, I know your names. I shall not fall under your blows. You will not report that I am evil to this god in whose retinue you are. My case shall not come through you. You shall say that *Maāt* returns me, in the presence of the Universal Lord; for I have practised *Maāt* in Egypt. I have not offended the god. My case shall not be *reported as evil.* . . .

Hail to you, O gods who are in this Hall of the Two *Maāti*, who have no deceit in your bodies and who live of *Maāt* in Heliopolis, who nourish yourselves of your substance in the presence of Horus-who-is-in-his-solar-disc. Save me from Baba, who feeds on the entrails of the great, in this day of the great reckoning. Behold, I come to you, without evil, having committed no deceit, without iniquity within me, without an hostile witness against me. I have done nothing . . . I live on *Maāt*, I feed on *Maāt*.[102]

The deceased then proceeds to set forth his own good deeds in a manner reminiscent of those 'ideal biographies' which were inscribed on tombs in the later period of the Old Kingdom, as we have seen; these statements of good neighbourliness had doubtless established an approved tradition. He announces, still addressing, it would seem, the forty-two deities:

I did that of which men speak, that in which the gods rejoice. I have contented the god by that which he desires. I have given bread to the hungry, water to the thirsty, clothing to the naked, a boat to him that had none. I have made provision for divine offerings and for the offerings to the blessed dead. Save me, therefore, and protect me! Make no report against me in the presence of the Great God.[102a]

Then follows a further affirmation of purity, concluding with a reference to knowledge of some curious myth:

I am pure of mouth and pure of hands. I am one to whom it is said: 'Come in peace' by those who see him. For I have heard the great words which the Ass said to the Cat in the house of *ḥzpd.rz* . . .

After this claim to esoteric knowledge, the dead man then makes the only overt reference to trial by weighing in this chapter. He declares that he has come 'to testify to *Maāt*, and to set up the balance'.[103]

The deceased next addresses Osiris:

O thou god who holds thyself high on thy throne, Master of the *Atef*-crown, whose name has been made 'Master of Breath', thou canst protect me against these messengers who sow unhappiness and stir up distaste . . .; for I have practised *Maāt* for the Master of *Maāt*. I am pure. My breast is pure, my after-part is clean, my middle is in the well of *Maāt*.[104]

There follows an interrogation of the deceased, which contained a number of esoteric references. At the end of it, which also concludes the series of formulae which have made up this Chapter 125, the following rubrics give directions concerning its use:

To be done on entry to the Hall of the Two *Maāti*. A person should recite this formula, being pure, purified, clothed in garments of fine linen, shod with white sandals, (the eyes) painted with stibium, and (the body) anointed with ointment of myrrh. Let him offer for himself a young bull, birds, incense, bread, beer and vegetables. Then thou shalt put this ritual design in writing on pure ground, with red earth, strew with soil which has not been fouled by pigs or goats. As for him, for whom this book is made, he shall prosper, his children shall prosper. He shall be in the good graces of the king and his courtiers. There shall be given to him loaves, jars, bread . . . and meat that has been set forth on the altar of the great god. He shall not be turned back from any gate of the West. He shall be brought in with the kings of Upper and Lower Egypt. He will be in the retinue of Osiris. A formula proved a million times.[105]

The long Declarations of Innocence and the formulae, with their esoteric references, and the concluding rubrics, which constitute this 125th Chapter, ill accord with the noble idea that finds expression in the weighing of the heart of the deceased against the symbol of *Maāt*. Except for its one brief and unilluminating reference to the balance, which we noted, this chapter suggests a conception of the *post-mortem* judgment that is fundamentally different from that of the weighing on the balance. Since both ideas were held together in the Egyptian mortuary faith at this period, it would seem that some synthesis between them had been achieved. We must, accordingly, endeavour to explain the origin of these contrary traditions and understand how the Egyptians reconciled them, as they apparently did.

It would seem that two inferences can be safely made about Chapter 125 of the *Book of the Dead*. The first is that the chapter is obviously of a composite nature; for the Second Declaration of Innocence constitutes a veritable anticlimax to the First, since the First, by virtue of its being addressed to Osiris, renders any further attestation logically superfluous, if not contradictory. The other inference is that the idea which inspires these Declarations appears to be older than that behind the weighing of the heart – indeed, it seems to stem from that conception of the *post-mortem* judgment which finds expression in the *Pyramid Texts*, whereby the deceased fears that he will be accused of misdeeds after death.

It is possible that the First Declaration may have been composed originally for royal use, since it contains no mention of the committing of an offence against the king, as does the Second.[106] In its present setting in the *Book of the Dead*, this First Declaration is clearly addressed to Osiris; but there is ground for doubting whether this was the deity to whom it was addressed in its original form. The opening salutation ('Hail to thee, Great God, Lord of the Two *Maāti*') could well be directed to the Sun-god; for the two boats used by Rē, respectively, for his unceasing journey through the day and the night sky were described as the two *Maāti*, probably from the idea that the diurnal journey of the Sun-god was both an essential part of the cosmic order and the means by which the deity observed all that happened on earth.[107] The Hall of the Two *Maāti*, before which this Declaration is made, might also derive from the solar cult, it being a designation of the tribunal of Rē, the Sun-god.[108]

If these inferences are sound, the First Declaration may well, therefore, represent a later Osirianized version of an affirmation of innocence used originally in the royal mortuary ritual, which conceived of the dead king as having to justify himself before the tribunal of Rē. As such, it would probably date from the Herakleopolitan period (*c.* 2242–2060 BC). The formula would doubtless have been produced in response to the Heliopolitan tradition which had located the royal hereafter in the sky, with Rē as the lord of *Maāt*.[109]

The Second Declaration of Innocence presents an altogether different problem. It has often been, understandably but wrongly, supposed that the forty-two deities, to whom in turn the deceased addressed himself, were representatives of the forty-two nomes or districts into which Egypt was divided, so that complete cognisance was taken of misdeeds done anywhere throughout the land.[110] The forty-two were also not judges or legal assessors, as has sometimes been asserted; they were in fact demonic beings who executed the wicked, as the titles of many of them clearly indicate.[111] It seems likely that they were in origin local demons, evoked to punish the wicked. Since they were mainly connected with Lower Egypt, they were possibly brought into a mortuary formula for the use of nobles, and so designed to provide a kind of universal cover against complaints coming, after death, from any area in which the deceased might have operated.[112] In the *Book of the Dead*, these forty-two local demons, originally feared as executioners, are represented in a kind of executive rôle in the company of the Great God, a designation which there seems to apply to Osiris, but which may originally have meant Rē, the Sun-god.

The redactors of this 125th Chapter appear also to have adapted the earlier 'ideal biography' for use in this context, as we noted in passing. Such material seems to have represented the solar tradition which finds expression, for example, in the tomb-inscription of Herkhuf, although the high moral significance manifest there seems rather obscured at this place in the *Book of the Dead*. The premium set upon knowledge of esoteric myths, and the magical import of the concluding rubrics, create an unfortunate impression and provide evidence for those scholars who think that the high moral insight implicit in the Old Kingdom conception of the judgment of the dead suffered declension later, owing to the invocation of magic in the mortuary cultus.

This interpretation brings us back to the problem of relating the conception of the *post-mortem* judgment, which underlies Chapter 125, with that which inspires the representations of the weighing of the heart. Basic to the discussion of this problem is a proper understanding of the significance of the heart in ancient Egyptian thought, and of Chapter 30 of the *Book of the Dead*.

To the Egyptians the heart was not only a vital organ of the body, it was also the conscience – in fact, it was actually hypostatized as 'the god which is in man'.[113] As such, it was regarded as both capable of, and disposed to, acting as an independent witness against its owner at his trial after death. This belief was so firmly established that a special prayer, addressed to the heart, was inscribed on a scarab-shaped amulet and laid on the place of the heart during the ritual of embalmment.[114] This prayer forms Chapter 30 of the *Book of the Dead*, and, as we have already seen, it was to be uttered by the deceased at the fateful moment of the weighing of his heart against *Maāt*. It reads in the version given in the *Papyrus of Ani*:

Heart of my mother, heart of my mother, my breast, the heart of my transformations! Rise not up as a witness against me, turn not against me before the tribunal. Act not as an enemy against me in the matter concerning the balance. For thou art my *ka*, which is in my body, thou art the Khnum who fashions my members that they may be well. Mayest thou go forth to that place desired. Cause not my name to smell evil in the nose of the tribunal. Speak no lie against me before the good gods. Let thy hearing be good.[115]

The transference of ideas, which lies behind this prayer relative to the process of weighing the heart against *Maāt*, is obscure. For the deceased addresses his heart as an entity capable of willing and taking action in the rôle of a witness before the divine tribunal; yet the pictorial representation of the weighing indicates the heart as a passive entity, whose weight is compared with that of *Maāt*. The former idea has been seized upon by those scholars who have thought that the *post-mortem* judgment in the *Book of the Dead* represents a declension from the higher moral conception of the earlier period. Accordingly, they interpret Chapter 30 not as a petition by the deceased to his heart, but as a magical spell by which he seeks to control it on this fateful occasion.[116] But even if this interpretation could be proved on grammatical grounds, the crucial fact is overlooked that the Egyptians conceived of the decisive test as an automatic and impersonal weighing of the heart against truth (*Maāt*). How the discrepancy between the idea of the heart as an independent witness and that of its passive rôle in the weighing is to be explained is not clear. Perhaps the issue should not be pressed in evaluating the existential significance of the transaction in the *Book of the Dead*, for both ideas are, on the last analysis, symbolical. What is more important is the fact that the Egyptians came to think of the judgment after death as a weighing of the heart, which represented a man's conscience, against truth, personified as *Maāt*. So far as the illustrations of the transaction afford an indication of the decisive position of the scales, it would seem that moral probity was signified by the exact balancing of the heart and *Maāt*.[117]

It is possible that the conception which lies behind Chapter 30, namely, of a *post-mortem* trial, at which a man's heart (conscience) might assume the rôle of witness for the prosecution, derives from a different tradition from that implicit in the idea of the weighing of the (passive) heart. A sarcophagus, found at El-Bersheh and dating from the beginning of the Middle Kingdom, seems to provide evidence of this. It bears a text, which appears to be a kind of rubric, reading: 'To cause that the heart of a man does not oppose him in the next world'.[118] The Egyptians were apparently very apprehensive about their heart after death: they feared both that it might be taken away from them[119] and that it might act as a witness against them. Although the sarcophagus just mentioned does not bear the text of what became Chapter 30 of the *Book of the Dead*, the rubric certainly indicates that the fear that the heart might give damning testimony was already current and inspired measures for coping with the contingency. According to the directions given at the end of the more common version of Chapter 30, for engraving the text on a scarab-shaped amulet, the text itself dates back to the Old Kingdom and was of divine origin: 'This formula was found at Hermopolis, at the foot of the majesty of this august god (i.e. Thoth), on a tablet of stone of the South, being a writing of the god himself, during the time of Men-kau-rē, by the royal son Djedefhor. He found it while making an inventory in the temples...'[120]

It would seem, therefore, that this concern about the rôle of the heart after death was ancient, extending back probably into the First Intermediate Period. It is possible that, in origin, it represented a refinement of the primitive belief that accusations might be brought against the deceased at a *post-mortem* tribunal, by making the accuser the individual's own heart or conscience, instead of men or deities. In turn, the notion of weighing, as a means of assessment, may have stemmed naturally from the imagery used in the *Instruction for King Meri-ka-rē* of a man's deeds being set in heaps before him.

Whatever the origins of the two traditions which find joint expression in such representations of the weighing of the heart as that in the *Papyrus of Ani*, there can be no doubt that the attention was focused on the verdict of the balance. And that verdict was conceived by the Egyptians as being placed beyond the interference of gods or men, whatever their magical powers. If this had not been so, and it was believed that the verdict could be manipulated, the great and continuing concern about the *post-mortem* judgment, evidenced in the Egyptian mortuary documents, would be wholly inexplicable.[120a]

But now we must, at last, face the problem of relating this high moral notion of the weighing of the heart against *Maāt* with the doubtful morality of Chapter 125. As we have seen, the two conceptions concerned represent two different traditions about the nature of the *post-mortem* judgment. Their presence in the *Book of the Dead* could be explained simply as due to the innate conservatism of the Egyptian mind: that nothing hallowed by religious use was ever abandoned, despite the most obvious illogicalities that resulted. However, a more satisfying explanation does suggest itself, which also has the merit of being reasonable in terms of what we know of Egyptian thought and practice.

Starting from the reasonable assumption that, because these two different conceptions were incorporated into the *Book of the Dead*, a relation was seen between the weighing of the heart and the Declarations of Innocence, we may look for some sequential order. Although the actual chapters of the *Book of the Dead*, so far as their contents are concerned, show no such order, it is perhaps significant that in the *Papyrus of Ani* the weighing of the soul is the first *post-mortem* incident illustrated, and the weighing is illustrated again in Chapter 125.[121] These facts suggest both the priority of significance accorded to the weighing and a close relationship between the weighing and the Declarations of Innocence. Moreover, it is to be noted that the vignette of the weighing appears, from its juxtaposition to the text of Chapter 125, to indicate that the action is subsequent to the recitation of the two Declarations of Innocence.[122] If we are right in attaching importance to these details, it would seem that not only a sequential, but also a consequential, nexus was intended between the Declarations and the weighing.

What such a nexus could have been is not hard to seek. After the deceased has asserted that he had not committed the offences particularized in Chapter 125, his heart is then weighed against *Maāt*, to test its truthfulness. The fact that in the illustration of the weighing in the *Papyrus of Ani* the deceased, after the favourable verdict, is pronounced 'true of voice' (*maā kheru*) is likewise significant; for, although the title *maā kheru* became a stereotyped epithet, it was singularly appropriate in this context, with its implied reference to the vindication of Osiris.

This interpretation, accordingly, not only explains the apparent incongruity of the fact that two different conceptions of the *post-mortem* judgment are incorporated into the *Book of the Dead*, but it enables us to appreciate the full significance of the emphasis clearly given to the weighing of the heart in Egyptian eschatology. Although respect for tradition ensured the preservation of a more primitive view of the judgment after death, a deepening moral sensitivity conceived of a mode of personal evaluation that was objective and impartial. This newer and nobler view was, therefore, related to the earlier view in such a way that a venerable ethical tradition was preserved and integrated with a more developed insight.

In the light of these considerations, it may justly be claimed that, despite its bizarre imagery, the conception of the *post-mortem* judgment, as it finds its most complete expression in the *Book of the Dead*, represents a most significant achievement in both the history of religions and of ethics. The intimations, already found in the Old Kingdom, that a happy after-life was not to be obtained only by the practice of ritual magic, but that it must be deserved by the moral quality of one's life on earth, reached this maturity of expression in the New Kingdom. No other people were to achieve a comparable view of the eternal significance of a morally good life until many long centuries had passed, as we shall see.

That the ancient Egyptian mortuary faith was permeated by magical notions and practices there can be no denying; the evidence of it is too obvious and abundant. As the many illustrations of the judgment scene in the funerary papyri show, the hope was doubtless strong that a pictorial representation of one's successful emergence from the grim test of the balance might have some magical potency in influencing the actual decision:[123] a like motive is perhaps to be seen in mediaeval Christian paintings where the artist has depicted the patron in the company of the saints. But, however that may be, the prospect of a *post-mortem* assessment of his moral conduct was surely a disturbing reality for the Egyptian, and evidence of the vigour of the belief can be traced down the centuries into the Christian era. As the following examples show, the belief was not limited to any particular class or rank in Egyptian society.

In an inscription, which Rameses IV (1164–1157 BC) caused to be set up at Abydos in honour of Osiris, incidental reference is made to the *post-mortem* judgment in commemorating Osiris's rôle as the judge who commissions Thoth to reward or punish the dead, according to their deserts: 'I found thy majesty as the *King of the Underworld*, even as here in Egypt. (For) thou art he who sends forth him (i.e. Thoth) who does good to the righteous and evil to those who act contrariwise, in the other world.'[124] Then, from a royal testimony to that of a private man. In the text inscribed upon his funerary stele, an Eighteenth Dynasty (1570–1305 BC) official named Baki declares:

I was truly a just man, free from sin, who had set God in his heart, being very conscious of his power. I am come to this city (i.e. the necropolis), which is in eternity, having done good on earth: I did no evil deed and there is no fault of which I may be reproached. My name has not to be pronounced in connection with any bad action or with any sin. I have rejoiced in speaking truth (*Maāt*), for I know that it is profitable for a man to practice *Maāt* on earth from his beginning to his end, because it is a perfect defence to him who has so done on that day when he arrives before the tribunal which discerns intentions, judges conduct, punishes the sinner and cuts off his soul (*ba*). While I lived, I was not condemned; no accusation was laid against me. No fault was imputed to me before them (i.e. the members of the *post-mortem* tribunal). I went forth justified (*maā kheru*), and I was numbered among the blessed, whose *ka*'s are transformed.[125]

The following extracts from an inscription on a grave at Memphis, dating from the Eighteenth or Nineteenth Dynasty, contains picturesque references both to the ancient solar hereafter and to the balance:

If one is glorified for piety, then shall I be the pilot of the 'Ship of the Million'; I shall be reckoned from boat to boat among the followers of Rē, when he journeys through the heaven. If one is glorified for integrity, then shall my soul be the Master of the Balance before the Great God, the Lord of the West.[126]

Of special interest are the passages concerning the judgment after death in the tomb-inscription of Petosiris, a priest of Hermopolis, who lived about 300 BC. They reveal that some eight or nine centuries after the belief in a *post-mortem* judgment had achieved its fullest development, namely, in the *Book of the Dead*, it was still an effective factor in the Egyptian *Weltanschauung*. Petosiris thus attests his own faith, and warns those who read his inscription of what they must ultimately face:

The West (*Amentît*) is the port of him who is without sin. Happy is the man who arrives there. None reaches it except he whose heart has been exact in the practice of *Maāt*. There is no distinction there between the poor and the rich (*n dnw šw*(ꜣ) *r bwꜣw*); favour is shown only to him who is found to be without sin, when the balance and the weight are placed in the presence of the Master of Eternity. None escapes the verdict when Thoth as the Baboon, from the height of his throne, is concerned to assess each according to that which he has done upon earth.[127]

An echo of the warnings given to would-be violators of their tomb in the inscriptions of nobles of the Old Kingdom occurs here in the inscription of Petosiris:

Thoth is here to deal with him who acts (wrongly). He rests not until he has judged the affairs, whether they are good or ill, he accords to every act that which it deserves. He who does evil on earth and is not punished for it, he will be punished in the other world in the presence of the lords of *Maāt*; for it is an abomination unto them that a man should act unjustly and that he should assault the dead.[128]

The impartiality of the *post-mortem* judgment renders irrelevant, according to Petosiris, the social distinctions of this life. This theme finds dramatic expression in a popular story which has been preserved to us in a manuscript dating from the second century AD, but which clearly derives from an older source. The story belongs to a cycle of tales concerning the supernatural wisdom of a young boy, Senosiris. The child is actually the reincarnation of an ancient sage; he is born to a prince named Satmi, in response to the earnest prayer of his wife who had hitherto been barren. The story is employed as a kind of parable concerning the change of fortune that might result from the assessment of a man's life after death.[129]

One day, in Memphis, Satmi observes from the roof of his house the funeral procession of a rich man, who was being carried to the necropolis with all the pomp and lamentation customary for those who could pay for such obsequies. Immediately after this spectacle he noticed the squalid disposal of a poor man, who was carried out of the city, rolled only in a mat, and with none to lament him. Struck by the contrast, Satmi uttered the wish that his end would be like that of the rich man. He is profoundly shocked, therefore, when he hears his son exclaim: 'May there be done to thee in Amentît that which is done for that poor man in Amentît, and may that not be done to thee in Amentît what is done to that rich man in Amentît'.[130] To enlighten his father on his mysterious utterance, the *Wunderkind* Senosiris takes him into the underworld, after the manner in which Virgil was to lead Dante to see the Inferno. The underworld is pictured as having seven immense halls. As the awe-struck father and his prescient son pass into the fifth hall, they observe that the pivot of the door turns in the single right eye of one of the damned, who cries out in agony. In the sixth hall, they see the door-keepers of Amentît calling those whose cases are to be tried in the seventh hall. There they behold Osiris, enthroned, with Anubis on his left and Thoth on his right, and about them the members of the divine tribunal. In the midst is the great balance, on which the misdeeds of a man are weighed against his good deeds. Thoth has his accustomed rôle of scribe, and Anubis supervises the transaction. Those whose misdeeds outweigh their good deeds are delivered to 'Amaît, the bitch belonging to the lord of Amentît', so that their bodies and souls are utterly destroyed. Those who pass the awful test are conducted to heaven. The man, whose good and bad deeds equally balance, is placed among the dead 'furnished with amulets who serve Sokarosiris'.[131]

Then comes the final revelation that forms the *raison d'être* of the story:

While Satmi marvelled at that which he saw in Amentît, Senosiris, standing before him, said: 'Satmi, my father, seest thou that exalted personage, clothed in garments of fine linen, who is close by where Osiris sits? That poor man, whom you saw carried out from Memphis, with none to follow him, and rolled in a mat, the same is he! He was brought to the underworld, his misdeeds were weighed against the merits which he had on earth, and his merits were found to outweigh his misdeeds. Since at the time of life, inscribed to his account by Thoth, there was not a sum of happiness adequate to his time on earth, it was ordered, on behalf of Osiris, that the funerary equipment of that rich man, whom you saw borne out of Memphis with full honours, should be transferred to the poor man. Further, it was decreed that he should be assigned a place among the venerable souls, the followers of Sokarosiris, close to the seat of Osiris. That rich man, whom you saw, he was brought to the underworld, his misdeeds were weighed against his merits, and the former outweighed the latter which he had while on earth. It was decreed that he should be punished in Amentît, and it was he, whom you saw, with the pivot of the door of Amentît planted in his right eye and rotating on this eye whenever the door is closed or opened, whilst his mouth utters great cries. By the life of Osiris, the Great God, if I said to thee on earth: "May it thus be done to thee as it is done to the poor man, and may it not be done to thee as it is done to the rich man!", it was because I knew what would happen to him.'

The story shows a few variations in detail from the presentation of the judgment in the New Kingdom copies of the *Book of the Dead*; but these variations are not significant, and they do, in fact, prove that the tradition was too vital to become stereotyped and unchanging. Thus the weighing of a man's merits against his demerits seems to indicate a more practical way of dealing with the mixture of good and bad in human nature than the idealistic assessment of the heart against the abstract concept of *Maāt*. But of greater significance is the presentation of the *post-mortem* judgment as exclusively a balancing of a man's good and evil achievements; there is no mention of the deceased's attesting his own innocence. Consequently, despite the many fantastic elements in the story, the judgment of the dead is conceived as the decisive evaluation of the individual's moral worth, without any suggestion that resort might be made to magic to gain a favourable verdict.

This account of the visit of Satmi and Senosiris to the underworld is clearly a popular tale, and, so, we may reasonably infer that the picture it gives of the *post-mortem* judgment was widely known and accepted.

The concern shown therein about social inequality in this world and its reversal in the next is remarkable. It suggests that the doctrine of the judgment of the dead had now assumed, in addition to its personal meaning, a social significance. How this fact is to be interpreted in terms of social background or history is uncertain, since the origin of the cycle of stories to which this one belongs is obscure. The belief in the reversal of fortune hereafter could, with equal reason, be seen here as the pious hope of the poor or as an officially propagated anodyne to quieten social discontent.[132] The striking parallel which this story constitutes to the parable of Dives and Lazarus in the *Gospel of Luke* rightly excites curiosity. We shall have later to examine the parable as evidence of a primitive Christian belief in a judgment immediately following death. So far as the question of its relationship to the Egyptian story is relevant, it must suffice to note that the evidence points to the latter's priority in origin.[133]

Belief in a judgment after death, symbolized by the balance or scales, can be traced on into the Roman period of Egyptian religion,[134] and, as the curious *History of Joseph the Carpenter* shows, it passed in turn into Coptic Christianity.[135] The idea of weighing the deeds of men had already been adopted into Jewish apocryphal literature,[136] and the variant concept of the weighing of souls had entered into Greek thought, as we shall see.[137] Ultimately the idea found expression in mediaeval Christian art, with the archangel Michael assuming the rôle of 'Master of the Balance' which Thoth had held in ancient Egypt.[138]

Of the fate of those who were condemned at the *post-mortem* judgment there is no clear information in the Egyptian documents. The monster Am-mut, the 'eater of the dead', which is depicted as waiting expectantly by the great balance, would seem to constitute a very obvious witness to the fate of those who were not pronounced *maā kheru*. However, if this monster did devour the unjust dead, did this imply complete extinction? The word 'dead' (*mwt*) is ambiguous, owing to the complex nature of the Egyptian conception of man.[139] According to this anthropology, the body, the *ka*, the *ba*, and the heart were all vital and essential factors of the living person: hence provision is made for all of these in the mortuary cultus. Did Am-mut devour all these entities in the case of condemnation? The story of Satmi and Senosiris, as we have just seen, provides an explicit statement that the condemned were devoured body and soul.[140] Yet, in the sequel, the rich man, who had been condemned, was undergoing the strange torment that is so graphically described.

The confusion concerning the fate of the unjust, which is thus manifest in this tale, is found in other sources. Frequent reference is made in the funerary literature to 'enemies' (*ḫftiw*), of Osiris or Rē in

Fig. 3   Ancient Egyptian conception of Hell: the damned are being tormented in pits of fire.

the next world, who are punished in various ways.[141] In the *Amduat*, which purports to describe the underworld, these 'enemies', represented either in human form or by hieroglyphs denoting 'shadows' or 'souls' (*b3w*), are shown in pits of fire.[142] With these indications of the perpetual torment of the damned must also be set the idea of 'second death', about which concern is shown in the *Book of the Dead*.[143] From this conflict of eschatological imagery we can, accordingly, only safely deduce that the Egyptians believed that some awful fate awaited those whose hearts were found to be not right with *Maāt* in the judgment after death.[144]

In any history of the eschatological beliefs of mankind, the ancient Egyptian conception of the judgment of the dead rightly demands priority of attention. But, not only did the idea first emerge in Egyptian religious thought, it also achieved its greatest elaboration there. The idea, as we shall see, has played an important part in many other faiths;

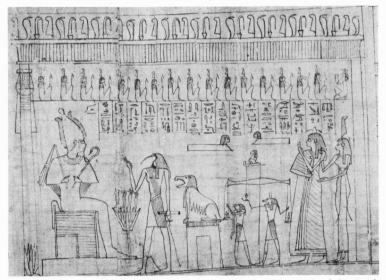

Fig. 4   The weighing of the heart, from a late copy of the *Book of the Dead* (2nd–1st cent. BC). The deceased is shown holding the symbol of *Maāt* and being attended by the goddess Maāt herself (Ryl. Hieroglyphic Pap. No. 3).

in some, as for example in Christianity, that part has been essential. In Egypt, however, the concept cannot be said to have been essential to the logic of the religion current there. In essence, the Egyptian mortuary cultus was a magic technique for the acquisition of immortality or resurrection from death. Moral considerations were essentially irrelevant to the successful operation of this technique.[145] Nor was belief in a *post-mortem* judgment essentially required by the Egyptian concept of deity. Egyptian religion was singularly unconcerned to relate human destiny to divine purpose.[146] As we have seen, the idea of a judgment after death had originally a two-fold practical origin, namely, fear that one's *post-mortem* well-being might be harmed by complaints made about one's moral conduct in this world; and the desire to secure one's tomb from violation by appeal to *Maāt*, the universal order which Rē, the Sun-god, embodied and maintained. But it must also be recognized, in all fairness to the ancient Egyptians, that this conception of Rē as the embodiment of *Maāt* could have a more positive effect. Herkhuf's statement, that he desired that it might be well with him in the Great God's presence, shows that the thought of Rē's association with *Maāt* could prompt a man to live as a good neighbour to his fellows, particularly to the poor.[147]

Because belief in *post-mortem* retribution thus emerged so early, it would appear that Egyptian religious faith never experienced that disturbing problem, felt by many other religions, of reconciling the inequalities of human life here with the idea of a just God. We shall meet this conflict in our later studies. However, the noting of these differences should not diminish our respect for the moral achievement of the ancient Egyptians in conceiving, so early and so vividly, of a judgment after death. That they did not concern themselves with the problem of innocent suffering and divine omnipotence was largely due to their faith in Osiris; for the legend of his death, resurrection and justification, not only provided the *rationale* of the mortuary cultus, but it afforded the divine pattern in terms of which each individual saw his own personal destiny.[148]

2

ANCIENT MESOPOTAMIA:
'who is now an evildoer . . .?'

Mesopotamia shares with Egypt the distinction of being the birthplace of one of the earliest literate societies. By the middle of the fourth millennium BC a flourishing city-state civilization existed in the area to the north of the Persian Gulf, which was characterized by distinctive religious beliefs and practices, attested both by written documents and archaeological data.[1] At this early period burial customs suggest that a view of the after-life was held such as is found in most primitive cultures, namely, that the dead still have the needs which they had in this life and require the ministrations of the living.[2] From the point of view of our particular subject, the so-called 'royal graves', found by Sir Leonard Woolley at Ur, are especially significant. Their evidence indicates that a royal personage was accompanied in death by a retinue of attendants and servants, who were put to death at the time of burial, complete with the equipment and ornaments of their offices.[3] The purpose of such a mass inhumation seems obvious: the dead prince expected to enjoy in the after-life the same social and economic advantages which he had possessed in this world – even to the very persons of his court or household. Such a conception of the *post-mortem* existence is crude to the extreme, and it was clearly based on the assumption that one's destiny here could be exactly reproduced or continued in the other world. Such a view necessarily constitutes the very antithesis to the idea of a *post-mortem* judgment whereby the individual's eternal destiny is determined by the moral quality of his life in this world.

These 'royal burials' at Ur constitute a problem; for their apparent testimony runs counter to what we otherwise know of the Mesopotamian view of human destiny from the later written sources.[4] This view finds its most eloquent expression in the words of Siduri, one of the *dramatis personae* in that supreme masterpiece of Mesopotamian literary achievement, the *Epic of Gilgamesh*. Designed apparently as a commentary on human life, the composition tells of the futility of man's quest for immortality in terms of the career of an ancient hero, Gilgamesh.[5] Shocked by immediate contact with death when his friend Enkidu dies, Gilgamesh sees in the event a presage of his own demise and he is appalled.[6] Rejecting the common fate of mankind for himself, Gilgamesh sets out to learn the secret of immortality from the only human in Mesopotamian legend reputed to have obtained it, namely, Uta-napishtim, the hero of the Flood.[7] During his hard and hazardous journey to the place, at the world's extremity, where Uta-napishtim dwelt, Gilgamesh encounters Siduri, the wine-maiden, who is evidently intended to personify an hedonistic view of life.[8] However, as the speech of Siduri shows, it is not just sheer hedonism of which she is the protagonist, but of a *carpe diem* philosophy, which was firmly based on the Mesopotamian evaluation of man. Having learned the nature of Gilgamesh's quest, Siduri replies:

> Gilgamesh, whither rovest thou?
> The life thou pursuest thou shalt not find.
> When the gods created mankind,
> Death for mankind they set aside,
> Life in their own hands retaining.
> Thou, Gilgamesh, let full be thy belly,
> Make thou merry by day and by night.
> Of each day make thou a feast of rejoicing,
> Day and night dance thou and play![9]

The belief, which finds expression here, that the gods, being themselves immortal, withheld immortality from men whom they had created, stems from the Mesopotamian conception of the *raison d'être* of mankind. In both Sumerian and Akkadian cosmogonic texts the view is set forth that mankind was created to serve the gods, by building temples for them and offering sacrifices for their sustenance.[10] With this view of the purpose of man's being went a corresponding estimate of human destiny. So long as the gods wanted his services, the individual lived, and, if he were zealous and careful in their service, his divine masters would reward him with prosperity. This was his destiny, namely, to participate in the divine ordering of things in this world. Once the gods ceased to need him, his *raison d'être* ended, and he died.[11]

The logic of this simple explanation of the purpose of human life was, however, frustrated by the inability of the ancient Mesopotamians to free themselves from the instinctive belief, present among all primitive peoples, in some form of *post-mortem* survival. Unable to accept the logical conclusion of their conception of man, namely, that death was personal extinction, they tormented themselves with a grim eschatology. Death, for them, involved an awful transformation whereby the deceased person became an *edim* or *etimmu*, a grisly being, and departed to an underworld, which was, significantly, named *kur-nu-gi-a*, 'the land of no-return'.[12] This place of the dead was imagined as a city, enclosed by seven walls and gates, shrouded in darkness and inhabited by awful monsters: there the dead existed miserably, 'their sustenance earth, and clay their food'.[13]

To dwell there in 'the land of no-return' was the common lot of all. Rich and poor, king and slave, all were in a like state of wretchedness. This *post-mortem* equality seems to be symbolized in the myth of the *Descent of Ishtar into the Underworld*.[13a] The narrative describes how the great celestial goddess, for some unspecified purpose, chose to visit the realm of the dead.[14] At each of its seven gates Ishtar is required to surrender some ornament or article of her clothing, until, completely naked, she comes into the presence of the dread Erishkigal, the Queen of the underworld, where she is struck by sixty diseases and expires.[15] On her delivery by the intervention of the other gods, and her return to the upper world, she receives back at each gate in turn what she had been forced to surrender. This stripping of the bright goddess of love and fertility, as she descends to the land of the dead, would appear to be an allegory of the common fate of all in death – all the attributes of a living person, together with all appurtenances of rank or wealth, must then be shed, so that all the dead are become equal in status and being, and share a common misery.[16] The belief is vividly expressed in the *Epic of Gilgamesh*. The hero's friend, Enkidu, is forewarned of his coming death by dreaming that he had descended to *kur-nu-gi-a*. On waking he tells Gilgamesh of his awful experience, and what he saw there:

> In the h[ouse of dus]t, which I entered,
> I loo[ked at the kings (?)], and (behold!) the crowns had been deposited.
> I beh[eld the potentates], those who (used to wear) the crowns,
> Who from the days of old had ruled the land,
> In the house of dust, which I entered,
> Dwell high priest and acolyte;
> There dwell incantation priest and ecstatic;
> There dwell the attendants of the lovers of the great gods.[17]

Thus, in the 'house of dust', neither the trappings of royalty nor high ecclesiastical status counted for anything. Nothing, significantly, is said of the evaluation of moral worth; good or bad, no distinction was observed between them. The only distinction that seems to have been imagined to exist among the dead was determined apparently by either the manner of their deaths or the mortuary service of their surviving relatives. The evidence for this belief is of an inferential nature, and it is provided by the Twelfth Tablet of the *Epic of Gilgamesh* and by a number of divinatory tablets. The Tablet concerned is inscribed with the text of an episode quite unrelated to the theme of the narrative contained on the other Tablets of the *Epic*.[18] It tells how Enkidu descended into the underworld in search of two mysterious objects which Gilgamesh had lost. Through not observing certain tabus, which would have given him safe passage, Enkidu is held in the underworld. At the petition of Gilgamesh, the shade of Enkidu is permitted to re-visit the world of the living.[19] On meeting, Gilgamesh inquires of his dead friend about the underworld. At first Enkidu refuses to tell him, because the truth is too awful to hear.[20] Eventually he discloses what he knows; the text unfortunately is in a very damaged condition, so that its meaning is uncertain. The general implication is that the condition of the dead is somewhat ameliorated by mortuary offerings made for them by their relatives, and that to perish in some unknown place was the worst of fates, for it prevented the unfortunate one from descending to the place of the dead and forced him to feed on scraps and offal left in the streets.[21] This view of the condition of the unburied and uncared-for dead inspired the widespread belief, attested by a multitude of tablets, that the shades of such became vengeful and plagued the living – disease and misfortune were attributed to the attacks of the restless ghosts of the unknown and neglected dead.[22]

The logic of the accepted eschatology would seem, therefore, to have rendered any idea of a *post-mortem* judgment inconceivable for the Mesopotamians. And this conclusion is supported negatively by the extant evidence. Although references do occur in texts to judges in the nether-world, no clearly established belief concerning a judgment after death is attested as it is in Egypt. In a text describing the arrival in the underworld of Ur-Nammu, prince of Ur, who ruled at the end of the third millennium BC, these judges appear rather as the authorities who assigned to the dead, or perhaps to the more notable among them, their places in the realm of the dead.[23] It is likely that the idea involved here derived from that view of the after-life which inspired the royal burials at Ur, which we noted. The judges who are invoked in this text are the Anunnaki, demonic beings who were probably in origin ancient chthonian gods of the Sumerians.[24] They are invoked in a somewhat similar rôle in some other texts relating to Tammuz, who appears to have been a fertility god of the dying-rising type;[25] but in all these references to decisions that might be made concerning the dead in the underworld there is never any suggestion of an evaluation of the moral quality of their previous life on earth.[26]

In seeking to find some hint of a Mesopotamian belief in a *post-mortem* judgment, reference has sometimes been made to certain texts found in tombs at Susa, in Elam, which date from about the sixth or seventh century BC.[27] The very fact that they have to be laid under contribution for this purpose is significant; because, not only do they come from an area outside the main centres of Mesopotamian culture, but their witness is most problematical. The following texts appear to contain the most likely references to such a judgment, or rather, to a *post-mortem* assessor. In the first the deceased seems to be invoking the aid and comfort of his own protecting deity on the journey which will bring him before a dread tribunal:

> Come and I will come, O my god, my master,
> To face the Anunnaki.
> I will traverse the *gigunu*.[28]
> I will take thy hand before the gods supreme,
> Hearing my sentence, I will seize thy feet.
> Illuminating the house of darkness, O my god,
> Thou shalt cause me to cross
> The marshes of weakness and of pain.
> In this place of difficulty
> Thou wilt watch over me.
> Thou wilt give me water to drink and oil
> In this place of thirst.[29]

The other text appears to describe the journey of the dead to the next world:

> They take the route, they proceed on their path.
> The gods Ishnikarab and Lagumal go before.
> Shugurnak[30] in the pit pronounces a word.
> He is there; he speaks to the *muskekil*:[31]

Professor Ebeling, who has cited these tablets as evidence of a *post-mortem* judgment, translates the word *muskekil* as 'weighter' or 'assessor';[32] but this interpretation has been contested, and, even if it could be substantiated, its testimony would be very meagre and enigmatic.[33] We may notice also, in this context, that a scene which

appears on several seal-stones has also been identified as a representation
of the judgment of the dead. It depicts a strange half-human, half-bird
figure, chained and held before a deity, who seems to be delivering a
judgment on him.[34] Since there is evidence that the Mesopotamians
conceived of the dead as being clothed like birds with 'garments of
wings', the figure has been interpreted as a dead human being.[35] Unfortunately the scene has no accompanying text which explains it; and
it has also been interpreted with equal reason as a representation of the
Zu-bird, a mythical figure that has no connection with a *post-mortem*
judgment.[36]

Against these very doubtful indications of some idea of a judgment
after death the logic of the Mesopotamian estimate of human nature
and destiny is overwhelming. It is, moreover, confirmed by a remarkable document which takes the form of a dialogue between a master
and his servant, in which the cynicism bred of the Mesopotamian view
of life finds eloquent expression:

'Servant, obey me.' Yes, my lord, yes. 'I will do something helpful for my
country.' Do (it), my lord, do (it). The man who does something helpful for
his country, – his helpful deed is placed in the bowl of Marduk. 'No, servant,
I will not do something helpful for my country.' Do it not, my lord, do it not.
Climb the mounds of ancient ruins and walk about: look at the skulls of late
and early (men); who (among them) is an evildoer, who a public benefactor?[37]

The difference between the Mesopotamian and Egyptian evaluations
of human destiny is so striking that many attempts have been made to
account for it. Difference of geographical environment has sometimes
been invoked to explain the grimmer outlook of the Mesopotamians.[38]
Such environmental differences have tended perhaps to be rather exaggerated in this connection, and, even if they did exist to such a
degree, it would be difficult to see how they alone caused the Egyptians
to believe that they had the means of achieving a happy destiny after
death, while their Mesopotamian neighbours were wholly pessimistic.
However, when the two outlooks are compared, it is the Egyptian
which must be adjudged the more extraordinary of the two. The
Mesopotamian view of death was a more realistic appreciation of the
evidence of man's demise than the Egyptian belief that by means of
a magical technique, centred on Osiris, the fact of death could be
reversed, or its disintegrating process stayed, and a state of everlasting
felicity achieved. Where the Mesopotamian evaluation failed to be
completely realistic was in overcoming the deeply rooted conviction,

common to all early peoples, that the individual in some way survived death. But even here their apparent predisposition to realism prevailed, to preclude their imagining that the *post-mortem* state could be anything but grim, miserable and hopeless. Consequently, since none were exempt from this fate, no ground existed for supposing that the individual's condition after death could be improved or worsened by his conduct in this life. It would seem, therefore, that, if we seek to make a comparative evaluation, the ancient Egyptians came to believe in a *post-mortem* judgment through fear that their well-being after death might be adversely affected by complaints then brought against them,[39] the Mesopotamians, on the other hand, convinced of the inevitable wretchedness of the after-life, were consequently unconcerned about the *post-mortem* significance of their conduct in this life.[40] The conclusion, to be drawn from this comparison, would seem to be that belief in a moral assessment after death can only arise where there is hope of eternal beatitude.

3

HEBREW RELIGION:
Judgment as Divine Vindication

The religion of ancient Mesopotamia, from its beginning to its end, was essentially polytheistic. Although the national gods of Babylon and Assyria acquired great prestige when their respective states won political hegemony, no deity of the Mesopotamian pantheon ever came near to being accepted universally as the supreme god. Very different was the situation in Israel; for there, despite the existence of an eschatology remarkably similar to that current in Mesopotamia, Yahweh, an ancient desert god, came to be regarded not only as the national god, but also as the one and only God of the universe.[1] This movement to monotheism profoundly affected the traditional eschatology and finally led to a grandiose conception of a Last Judgment. Another factor in this process was the gradual exaltation of Yahweh as a just and righteous God. The association of deity with the maintenance of the moral law was known in Egypt, as we have seen, and several of the Mesopotamian gods were closely concerned with justice; but the attribution of moral qualities to Yahweh caused a peculiar spiritual tension which we must study, for it led ultimately to belief in a *post-mortem* judgment. Yahwism was in origin and essence an ethnic religion. Its *raison d'être* was the relationship between Yahweh and his Chosen People, Israel; in this relationship the individual Israelite had significance only as a member of the holy nation, whose conduct could affect the nation for good or ill.[2] Phenomenologically it was not a natural religion, in the sense that it had gradually emerged among the Israelite people as an expression of their attempt to understand human nature and destiny and to mould them according to their aspirations and fears. Instead, it was a faith that had been consciously adopted at a particular time and for a specific purpose. This statement is admittedly an over-simplification of a very complex situation; but it is a legitimate inference from a basic proposition of Hebrew religion, namely, that once, on a momentous occasion, Yahweh had entered into a formal covenant with Israel, making the nation his Elect People, who in turn pledged themselves to serve him and no other god.[3] Behind the Sinai-Covenant tradition, which records this occasion, lies a long and complicated process. The protagonists of the cult of Yahweh only gradually succeeded in getting their deity accepted as the national god by the various Semite tribes which, during the second half of the second millennium BC, were also gradually welded together as a single people under the name of Israel.[4]

In struggling to establish the supremacy of their god, the devotees of Yahweh had to oppose and suppress those elements in the traditional religious beliefs and practices of their people which seemed to them to be dangerous to that supremacy. Among the objects of their attack were the mortuary cults, of a primitive character, which presupposed a significant after-life for the dead. Because the beliefs that inspired these cults were associated with other deities, the Yahwists denounced the practice of them as disloyalty to Yahweh.[5] Moreover, they also sought to present a doctrine of human nature and destiny that negated the very basis of such mortuary cults. In the story of the creation and fall of Adam, the progenitor of mankind, the fate of the individual is pronounced in the words of Yahweh, uttered in condemnation of Adam's original sin: 'Dust thou art, and unto the dust shalt thou return'.[6]

However, despite the logical implication of this declaration, the Yahwist thinkers no more than the Mesopotamians could envisage complete personal extinction. They believed that at death the psycho-physical organism that constituted the living individual was irreparably shattered, and that what survived, which is never defined, descended beneath the earth to She'ol.[7] This place of the dead was conceived variously as an awful pit or a walled city, covered with dust and enshrouded in darkness. As it is graphically described by the tormented Job, it seems to be a Hebrew version of the Mesopotamian *kur-nu-gi-a*, the 'land of no-return':

> Before I go whence I shall not return,
> Even to the land of darkness and of the shadow of death;
> A land of thick darkness, as darkness itself;
> A land of the shadow of death, without any order,
> And where the light is as darkness.[8]

The Hebrew conception of She'ol seems, however, to have differed, in its original form, from the Mesopotamian underworld by its not having a divine ruler such as Nergal[9] – Yahwist monotheism doubtless precluded the idea that another deity existed even in the infernal regions, and the dualism implied in the conception of Satan had not yet developed, as we shall see.[10] However that may be, except for a few problematic references, it would seem that She'ol and its denizens were considered to be outside the interest and care of Yahweh.[11] Thus in *Psalms* lxxxviii. 12 (13 in Hebrew) the question is asked, clearly implying a negative answer: 'Shall thy wonders be known in the dark? And thy righteousness in the land of forgetfulness?' And in *Isaiah* xxxviii. 18, 19 the negation of *post-mortem* existence is significantly contrasted with the positive character of life in this world:

> For Sheol cannot thank thee,
> death cannot praise thee;
> those who go down to the pit cannot hope for thy faithfulness.
> The living, the living, he thanks thee,
> as I do this day.[11a]

The logic of Yahwist eschatology meant that a common fate awaited all: good and bad, rich and poor, master and slave, all descended to She'ol and existed there in a state of equal wretchedness. This basic equation in the underworld is eloquently presented in the books of *Isaiah* and *Ezekiel*, although with certain variations of significant origin. In passages curiously reminiscent of that quoted above from the *Epic of Gilgamesh*,[12] but with a very different animus, the descent into She'ol of notorious enemies of Israel and their condition there are mockingly described. Thus in *Isaiah* the king of Babylon is taunted about the reception he will meet on entering She'ol after death:

> Sheol beneath is stirred up
> to meet you when you come,
> it raises the shades to greet you,
> all who were leaders of the earth;
> it raises from their thrones
> all who were kings of the nations.
> All of them speak
> and say to you:
> 'You too have become as weak as we!
> You have become like us!'
> Your pomp is brought down to Sheol,
> the sound of your harps;

maggots are the bed beneath you,
and worms are your covering.

.   .   .   .   .

All the kings of the nations lie in glory,
each in his own tomb;
but you are cast out, away from your sepulchre.[13]

.   .   .   .   .

In *Ezekiel* the fate of Israel's enemies in She'ol is commemorated,
beginning with the Egyptians:

The mighty chiefs shall speak of them, with their helpers, out of the midst of
Sheol: 'They have come down, they lie still, the uncircumcised, slain by the
sword'.

Assyria is there, and all her company, their graves are set in the uttermost
parts of the Pit...

Elam is there, and all her multitude about her grave; all of them slain, fallen
by the sword, who went down uncircumcised into the nether world, ... and
they bear their shame with those who go down to the Pit.

Meschech and Tubal are there, and all their multitude, their graves round
about them, all of them uncircumcised, slain by the sword; for they spread
terror in the land of the living. And they do not lie with the fallen mighty men
of old who went down to Sheol with their weapons of war, whose swords were
aid under their heads, and whose shields are upon their bones; ...[14]

There follow briefer descriptions of the fate of the Edomites, the
'princes of the north', and the Sidonians.

It would seem that two different factors have operated to produce
this imagery, which, while presenting the traditional view, suggests
that differences could exist in the condition of the dead in She'ol,
notorious evildoers being in more wretched situations of various
kinds. One of these factors probably stemmed from the primitive practice of burying warriors, equipped with their weapons, which was
deemed an honourable form of disposal, and which, the prophet proclaims, would be denied to Israel's enemies. The other factor was
hatred for those enemies, at whose hands Israel had suffered so much.
Consequently, although existence in She'ol is clearly assumed as the
common *post-mortem* fate of all, it was hoped that in this gloomy realm
the Gentile oppressors of Israel would suffer more than the common
lot; in other words, hatred of foreign oppressors had given the impetus

to imagining She'ol as a place of retribution for the wicked. But, it must be noted, nothing is said of a judgment, and punishment falls on national armies, for national iniquity, not on individuals for personal sin.

The date of these passages in *Isaiah* and *Ezekiel* is significant. They appear to relate to the mid-sixth century BC, when the state of Judah had been overthrown and its people, or the more important part of them, were in exile in Babylonia.[15] The disasters that had befallen Israel during this period had inevitable repercussions for Yahwism. Many Jews began to question either the power or the justice of Yahweh. If Yahweh had the power to save his chosen people, why had he allowed them to be overthrown and suffer in this way? The traditional answer of the Yahwist prophets was no longer accepted, namely, that Yahweh was punishing his people for their disloyalty.[16] The question began to be asked: 'Wherefore hath Yahweh pronounced all this great evil against us? Or what is our sin that we have committed against Yahweh our God.'[17] And the complaint was heard: 'The way of Yahweh is not equal'.[18] Faced with this growing criticism, and the disillusionment and scepticism it implied, the prophets sought an answer in two directions. In the place of the old concept of communal responsibility expressed in the adage: 'the fathers have eaten sour grapes, and the children's teeth are set on edge', emphasis began to be laid upon personal retribution for personal failure: 'every man shall die for his own iniquity: every man that eateth the sour grapes, his teeth shall be set on edge'.[19]

This move away from the old Yahwist concept of communal responsibility, with its concomitant stress upon the moral responsibility of the individual, had the effect, however, of exposing one of the fundamental weaknesses of Yahwism. If the sufferings of the individual were no longer to be explained as due to the 'sins of the fathers', how were they to be accounted for when the person concerned obviously did not deserve the misfortunes which befell him? In other words, the problem of the innocent sufferer now began to be felt as a problem of theodicy. And it was made more acute by the Yahwist doctrine of man. For, if the significance of the individual's life was limited to this world, and, after death he descended to the gloomy realm of She'ol, where there was no distinction between good and bad, how could undeserved suffering here be justified? The problem inevitably involved the character of Yahweh. The prophets had presented him as both a just and an omnipotent God.[20] But, if Yahweh was responsible for whatever misfortunes afflicted the righteous, how could he be regarded as a just God? The dilemma, moreover, could not be solved by positing some form of *post-mortem* redress, because the traditional eschatology precluded such a solution.

The problem was not academic; it was deeply felt, and how deeply is attested by one of the noblest products of ancient Hebrew literature, namely, the *Book of Job*. In this writing the case of the righteous sufferer *vis-à-vis* the justice of an omnipotent deity is poignantly debated.[21] Job is set forth as a just and upright man, who is afflicted with loss of fortune and personal pain, almost beyond endurance. He knows that his torment comes from God, and he knows also that he has done nothing to deserve it.[22] He repudiates the explanation of his so-called 'comforters', that he must have sinned secretly;[23] but he agonises over the conflict between his experience and his faith in Yahweh as a just God. At the heart of his problem lies his acceptance of the orthodox view of man's end in She'ol:

> For there is hope for a tree,
> if it be cut down, that it will sprout again,
> and that its shoots will not cease.
> Though its root grow old in the earth,
> and its stump die in the ground,
> yet at the scent of water it will bud
> and put forth branches like a young plant.
> But man dies, and is laid low;
> man breathes his last, and where is he?
> As waters fail from a lake,
> and a river wastes away and dries up,
> so man lies down and raises not again;
> till the heavens are no more he will not awake,
> or be roused out of his sleep.[24]

The logic of this faith was felt in all its poignancy by Job. He foresees that he will die unvindicated, and descend into She'ol, beyond the concern of Yahweh, whom he has loyally served and trusted as just and righteous. If Yahwism had taught that there would be a judgment after death, at which the injustices of this life would be righted, Job's problem would have been solved, or, rather, never have arisen. But there was no sanction for such a solution. At one point Job seems almost to have won through to such a faith, in his desire to trust Yahweh. Thus he is depicted, in a well-known passage, as confident that Yahweh could not finally desert him:

> For I know that my Vindicator lives,
> and at the last he will stand upon the earth;

and after my skin has been thus destroyed,
then from my flesh I shall see God,
whom I shall see on my side,
and my eyes shall behold, and not another.[25]

Unfortunately the confused state of the extant Hebrew text makes it impossible to be sure of the original meaning of the passage, and the sequel indicates that, whatever the meaning, Job did not thus achieve the solution of his problem.[26] For, shortly after, he is represented as commenting bitterly:

One dies in full prosperity,
being wholly at ease and secure,
his body full of fat
and the marrow of his bones moist.
Another dies in bitterness of soul,
never having tasted of good.
They lie down alike in the dust,
and the worms cover them.[27]

The solution that is offered in the *Book of Job* to the problem of innocent suffering is not eschatological. Job is not ultimately vindicated at a *post-mortem* judgment; instead, the concluding chapters of the poetical part of the work seeks to solve the problem by dwarfing it into insignificance by displaying the immensity of God's cosmic activity,[28] while the prose epilogue rights the wrongs of Job's case by a 'happy-ever-after' ending, according to which God rewards Job with greater prosperity than that which he had formerly enjoyed.[29]

In the history of Hebrew religious thought the significance of the *Book of Job* lies in its witness to the inadequacy of Yahwist eschatology to provide an answer to the obvious conflict between the facts of experience, and in the attribution to Yahweh of both omnipotence and moral power. By limiting the significance of the individual's life to this world, Yahweh's justice had to be demonstrated in the fortunes of men: that the righteous should be rewarded by prosperity, and the wicked punished by misfortune. But the evidence of experience too often showed that this ideal situation did not obtain, and that the reverse did almost as frequently occur.[30]

The tension in Hebrew religion, which the *Book of Job* thus reveals, is significant for our study of the idea of a *post-mortem* judgment. Yahwism, which was in origin and essence an ethnic faith, by insisting on the moral character of its deity, created a problem for its own eschatology. Its simple-minded assumption that the individual would be content with the assurance that Yahweh rewards the pious with long life and prosperity in this world, and punishes the wicked with a short life and misfortune during it, was so obviously contradicted by the facts of experience that the justice of Yahweh was challenged thereby. Moreover, little comfort was derived by the individual Israelite from the thought that the nation would continue in its service to Yahweh, when he had descended into the dark anonymity of She'ol.[30a] In other words, the concept of a just and omnipotent God demanded an eschatology which promised that the justice of his dealing with individual men and women would be vindicated after death, since too often it was not demonstrated in this life.

It was characteristic of Yahwism, however, that when a more adequate eschatology did eventually emerge, it arose out of the national situation. An indication of fresh thinking in this connection is provided in *Ezekiel*. The need to maintain the nation's faith in the adversity of the Babylonian exile caused the prophet to proclaim that Yahweh would resurrect the seemingly dead nation. In his vision, Ezekiel sees a valley full of dry disarticulated bones, and Yahweh bids him to pronounce words to turn them into human bodies and animate them:

So I prophesied as I was commanded; and as I prophesied, there was a noise, and behold, a rattling; and the bones came together, bone to its bone. And as I looked, there were sinews on them, and flesh had come upon them, and skin had covered them; but there was no breath in them. Then he said to me, 'Prophesy to the breath, prophesy, son of man, and say to the breath, Thus says the Lord God: Come from the four winds, O breath, and breathe upon these slain, that they may live'. So I prophesied as he commanded me, and the breath came into them, and they lived, and stood upon their feet, an exceedingly great host.[31]

The purpose of this strange and macabre vision was to assure the dispirited Jewish exiles that Yahweh would resurrect the apparently defunct nation:

Son of man, these bones are the whole house of Israel. Behold, they say, 'Our bones are dried up, and our hope is lost; we are clean cut off'. Therefore prophesy, and say to them, Thus says the Lord God: Behold, I will open your graves, and raise you from your graves, O my people; and I will bring you home into the land of Israel. And you shall know that I am the Lord, when I open your graves, and raise you from your graves, O my people. And I will put my Spirit within you, and you shall live, and I will place you in your own land; then you shall know that I, the Lord, have spoken, and I have done it, says the Lord.[32]

This prophecy of the resuscitation of the broken nation, and its restoration to its holy land, is consistent with the traditional Yahwist outlook, namely, of Yahweh's concern for his Chosen People, Israel. It is, in effect, an assertion by Ezekiel that Yahweh would demonstrate his power and providence, which the Exile seemed to contradict, by re-establishing a revived Israel in the land of his ancient promise. However, the vivid imagery of the resurrection and re-animation of the dead bodies is significant; for it indicates that the idea of a divine *post-mortem* vindication could now be envisaged, and also the manner in which it would be achieved. The physical re-constitution of the dead, and their re-animation, were demanded by the Hebrew conception of man as essential pre-conditions for such an act of vindication. For a living person was essentially a psycho-physical organism, and, if after death, life was to be renewed, both the physical body and its animating spirit had to be restored and re-integrated into the living individual.

Although the concept of a *post-mortem* resurrection of the dead was thus perhaps adumbrated in the fifth century BC, it is not until some three centuries later that documentary evidence occurs of its establishment as part of the accepted faith of the Jews.[33a] What caused the idea to emerge then as an established belief is not clear; but the fact that the first historical reference is made in connection with an episode of the Maccabaean War is surely significant.[34] When burying a number of Jewish warriors who had fallen in battle against the Seleucid forces, it was discovered that they had each in his possession 'consecrated tokens of the idols of Jamnia'.[35] This evidence of their infringement of the sacred Law was taken as the cause of their deaths. 'All, therefore, blessing the *works* of the Lord, the righteous Judge, who maketh manifest the things that are hid, betook themselves to supplication, beseeching that the sin be wholly blotted out.'[36] Judas Maccabaeus, the Jewish leader, faced with this contingency, collected a large sum of money, which he sent to Jerusalem, 'to offer a sacrifice for sin, doing therein right well and honourably, in that he took thought for a resurrection. For if he were not expecting that they that had fallen would rise again, it were superfluous and idle to pray for the dead ... Wherefore he made the propitiation for them that had died, that they might be released from their sin.'[37]

The incident dates from the middle of the second century BC, and it would appear that the record of it in II *Maccabees* was composed not long after its occurrence.[38] The record contains a number of significant points. The first is the assumption that the deaths of these soldiers in battle was divine punishment for their sin of idolatry. The reaction of their comrades, when the offence was discovered, appears to have been inspired by the old sense of communal solidarity; for they seek to avert further evil consequences that might derive from the offence by supplicating Yahweh. Thirdly, the action of Judas, which is clearly commended, presupposes that belief in a resurrection of the dead was well known, and it seems to imply that those resurrected would be condemned as guilty of the sin of idolatry, unless they were released by the propitiatory sacrifice made by their friends.

The development of Jewish eschatology implied in this account is immense; for it involves the related ideas of a *post-mortem* resurrection and judgment. How this change had come about is unknown, beyond the suggestion contained in the *Ezekiel* passage that the idea of a resurrection or resuscitation of the dead was at least known as an allegorical image of the restoration of the defunct nation of Israel. Fortunately this witness of II *Maccabees* to so great a change in Jewish eschatological belief does not stand alone: it is supported by other documentary evidence of the same period. The most notable, in terms of our subject, is provided by the *Book of Daniel*. In the concluding oracles of this strange writing, which so eloquently expresses the spirit of apocalyptic revelation that now begins to characterize Jewish religion, Daniel is told that his people will be delivered from a 'time of trouble', of unprecedented severity, 'every one whose name shall be found written in the book. And many of those who sleep in the dust of the earth shall awake, some to everlasting life, and some to shame and everlasting contempt.'[39]

The passage reveals the combining of a number of existent, but disparate, ideas into a new and dramatic eschatology. The concept of a book in which God records the names of His elect was an ancient one, but its terms of reference applied essentially to this world and to the faithful of Israel living therein. Thus, in *Exodus* xxxii. 33, Yahweh is represented as saying to Moses: 'Whosoever hath sinned against me, him will I blot out of my book', and in *Psalms* lxix. 28, reference is made to the 'book of the living'.[40] Such a concept does indeed imply an act of divine judgment; but it concerned qualification for a theocratic community, and was in no way comparable to the recording of the individual's *post-mortem* destiny in the Osirian judgment, which we have noticed.[41] However, in *Daniel* the concept has clearly taken on an eschatological significance. An ultimate act of divine deliverance is envisaged, involving both living and dead Israelites. The language used is admittedly obscure; it would seem that those of the living who will share in this salvation have been judged worthy of inclusion in 'the book', but nothing is said of the fate of those whose names are not in the divine record. If the words: 'And many (*rabim*) of those who sleep in the dust of the earth shall awake . . .' are to be taken literally, not all the dead would be resurrected.[42] The reason for this limitation is not evident; for the sequel shows that resurrection was not imagined as the privilege of the righteous only, thus implying that renewal of life depended on moral qualification. However that may be, the succeeding statement clearly indicates belief in a *post-mortem* judgment, namely, that the resurrected dead shall awake: 'some to everlasting life, and some to shame and everlasting contempt'.

Of the nature of this *post-mortem* judgment and the identity of the judge this passage in *Daniel* is tantalizingly vague. Likewise also is its description of the respective fates of the righteous and the wicked. The 'shame and everlasting contempt', which the latter will experience, would seem to imply some form of eternal punishment, though no indication is given of its specific form beyond its psychological nature, nor of the place where those so condemned would suffer their penalty.[43] Of the fate of the justified the following verse gives what appears to be a poetic account, although it may derive from a belief that the dead were transformed into stars: 'And those who are wise shall shine like the brightness of the firmament; and those who turn many to righteousness, like the stars for ever and ever'.[44]

Vague though this passage in *Daniel* is in its description of an ultimate act of divine salvation, involving a resurrection and judgment of the dead, and obscure as may be the ideas and imagery employed, it constitutes a landmark in the development of Hebrew religious thought, and, in turn, as we shall see, for Christian eschatology. It means that the prophetic doctrine of Yahweh as the one true God, who had selected Israel to be his own peculiar people, had been re-adapted to meet the realities of Israel's political situation. Since Israel's sovereignty in the land of Yahweh's ancient promise was either lost or in jeopardy, Yahweh's status and power could only be vindicated by supposing that he would ultimately intervene in the course of world affairs to restore his people to their rightful position. Such an intervention would necessarily involve the overthrow of Israel's oppressors, and hence constitute a judgment upon them. But the promise of such a future rehabilitation of Israel was not enough to maintain the faith of those Jews suffering at the hands of foreign oppressors; something more than a vicarious identification with a remote posterity, which would enjoy such redemption, was necessary. Hence, as we have seen, the promise was made that when Yahweh finally intervened in world-affairs to save his people, this salvation would not be enjoyed only by those Israelites then living, but that past generations would be raised from the dead to participate in it. However, consciousness of the fact that all would not deserve such beatitude meant that belief in this final resurrection of the dead involved the concomitant belief in a final judgment.

The essentially apocalyptic character of the *Book of Daniel* invests the chronology of the events described with a mystic symbolism that makes it uncertain whether the final resurrection and judgment are regarded as happening in the present world-order, or whether they implicate the catastrophic end of this order and its supersession by another.[45] Such imprecision or obscurity characterizes both Jewish and Christian apocalyptic, as we shall see, and in the nature of things it is under-standable; for the apocalyptists were concerned to stimulate faith, not to give precise information about future events. But of another aspect of this Danielic eschatology there is no uncertainty, namely, that it is true to the Yahwist tradition in being primarily concerned with the destiny of the nation, and not of the individuals who comprise it. Correspondingly its terms of reference are essentially nationalistic: it is not concerned with the fate of mankind, but with that of Israel. The dead who are revivified and judged are Jews: nothing is said of the Gentiles in this context. This myopic outlook naturally stems from the Jewish conviction that Yahweh was primarily interested in Israel, his chosen people, and that he shaped world-history for the achievement of Israel's destiny; so far as the fate of other nations was considered, it was generally in terms of their ultimate overthrow for their oppression of Israel.[46] This view finds dramatic expression in the great judgment scene in Chapter vii. in which the four beasts symbolize the kingdoms that afflicted Israel: 'I beheld till thrones were placed, and one that was ancient of days did sit: his raiment was white as snow, and the hair of his head like pure wool; his throne was fiery flames, and the wheels thereof burning fire. A fiery stream issued and came forth before him: a thousand thousands ministered unto him, and ten thousand times ten thousand stood before him: the judgment was set, and the books were opened . . .'[47] The awful imagery of the divine judge here was destined, as we shall see, to inspire the Christian conception of a final judgment delivered on all mankind; but in *Daniel*, in its original form, it is essentially the judgment which the God of Israel passes on the nations that had oppressed his people.

From the second century BC Jewish eschatology grows more complex in its imagery, owing probably both to a natural tendency to speculate about human destiny and to foreign influences. The so-called *Book of Enoch*, in its older section, contains a remarkable account of a series of journeys that Enoch is supposed to have made, whereby he learned of the fates of both angels and men.[48] After visiting a fiery abyss in which the fallen angels are imprisoned forever, thus implying the existence of some myth of God's punishment of angelic beings who had transgressed His law,[49] Enoch comes to She'ol, which is represented as a great mountain containing four hollow places, and the purpose of these is explained to him:

> Then Raphael answered, one of the holy angels who was with me, and said unto me: 'These hollow places have been created for this very purpose, that the spirits of the souls of the dead[50] should assemble therein, yea that all the souls of the children of men should assemble here. And these places have been made to receive them till the day of their judgment and till the appointed period [till the period appointed], till the great judgment (comes) upon them.'[51]

This description of She'ol constitutes a most notable departure from the traditional conception which we have noticed. Instead of being the place to which all the dead descended and remained for ever, She'ol is here conceived as a kind of waiting place where the dead assembled until their fate is decided at a judgment that is to be made at some pre-ordained time in the future. This remarkable revision of the traditional eschatology is followed by an even more remarkable innovation in the further explanation that is given of the four hollow places.

In answer to Enoch's inquiry why the hollow places were separated from each other, Raphael replies:

> These three have been made that the spirits of the dead might be separated. And such a division has been made for the spirits of the righteous, in which there is the bright spring of water. And such has been made for sinners when they die and are buried in the earth and judgment has not been executed upon them in their lifetime. Here their spirits shall be set apart in this great pain till the great day of judgment and punishment and torment of those who curse for ever, and retribution for their spirits. There He shall bind them for ever. And

such a division has been made for the spirits of those who make their suit, who make disclosures concerning their destruction, when they were slain in the days of the sinners. Such has been made for the spirits of men who were not righteous but sinners, who were complete in transgression, and of the transgressors they shall be companions: but their spirits shall not be slain in the day of judgment nor shall they be raised from thence. Then I blessed the Lord of glory and said: 'Blessed be my Lord, the Lord of righteousness, who ruleth for ever'.[52]

The account of these compartments of She'ol and of those who inhabit them contains many obscurities, but generally it seems to indicate a belief that after death the souls of the dead were separated out according to their moral character. Of the process of judgment implied here nothing is said.[52a] The righteous are assigned to a place of refreshment – the 'bright spring of water' mentioned here is of considerable significance, for it suggests the influence of Egyptian ideas of the afterlife, of which there are other indications in *Enoch*, as we shall see.[53] The dead who are assigned to the other 'hollow places' appear to be divided out according to the nature of their transgressions. The criteria used in differentiating them is obscure, but it is clear that they are all suffering for their misdeeds. Consequently it would seem that two judgments were envisaged: one followed immediately after the death of each individual, the other, the 'great judgment' which all would undergo, at some preordained date in the future – we may note that in what is said of the first category of sinners a *pre-mortem* judgment also appears to be contemplated.[53a] It is impossible to relate these various judgments in a logical sequence, because the retribution suffered by the wicked is described as continuing for ever, thus eliminating the *raison d'être* of a final judgment.

The apparent illogicality of this eschatology in *Enoch* may perhaps be explained by the possibility that the author of this section of the work has endeavoured to synthesize two different traditions concerning human destiny after death. We have already suggested that the *refrigerium* theme, which appears in the account of the after-life of the righteous, derives from Egyptian eschatology. From the same source might well have come the idea that the wicked were punished eternally in 'hollow places', for the notion is frequently depicted in the vignettes of Egyptian mortuary literature and on the walls of tombs.[54]

Except for one brief enigmatic reference at the end of Raphael's explanation, the passage makes no mention of a resurrection. The absence of such a concept would also be consistent with an Egyptian derivation of this description of the fate of the dead in *Enoch* because the Egyptian mortuary faith, as we have seen, did not contemplate a resurrection after the manner in which it came to be conceived in Judaism.[55] The idea of a final judgment was, however, so firmly established in Jewish thought that the author of this part of *Enoch* incorporated it into his picture of the fate of the dead, although it was logically negated by the definitive nature of the judgment which had been pronounced on the dead immediately after death. The dislocation or contradiction of theme, which the concepts of an immediate *post-mortem* and a final judgment cause here, has an additional interest for the comparative aspect of our study. As we shall see, a similar contradiction occurs in Christian eschatology; however, the cause there was different, since it did not arise from the adoption of a different eschatological tradition as it seems to have done in *Enoch*.[56] Nonetheless, both Christian eschatology and that of *Enoch* attest the inherent difficulty of adjusting an eschatology concerning the destiny of individual men and women to that of an eschatology that conceives of a final judgment at the end of the present world-order. As we shall also see in our study of the eschatologies of Islam and Iran, a problem must inevitably arise about the condition of the dead between the time of death and that of a final judgment, when individual destinies will be eternally determined.

Although the passage which we have been considering makes no explicit reference to a resurrection coincident with the final judgment, we may note that in another part of *Enoch*, probably of different authorship,[57] the two events are foretold:

> And in those days shall the earth also give back that
> which has been entrusted to it,
> And Sheol also shall give back that which it has received,
> And hell shall give back that which it owes.

> For in those days the Elect One shall arise,
> And he shall choose the righteous and the holy from among them:
> For the day has drawn nigh that they should be saved.[58]

The expectation of a final universal judgment became an established constituent of the Jewish *Weltanschauung* from the second century BC. Stemming from the old prophetic belief in the 'Day of Yahweh', when the god of Israel would save his people and punish their enemies,[59] the concept had steadily widened in scope and acquired a more transcendental form, so that this final vindication of divine sovereignty became associated with both the notion of the resurrection of the dead and the catastrophic end of the existing world-order; in turn it was connected with the Messianic hope as the last quotation from the *Book of Enoch* showed.[60] The universality of this last judgment is graphically presented in the *Book of Jubilees*, which also dates from the second century BC:

> The judgment of all is fixed; it is written on heavenly tablets, according to right, even the judgment of all those who turn themselves from the path prescribed for their passage. If they do not follow it, judgment is accordingly ordained for every creature and every species. Nothing which is in heaven and on earth, in the light or in the darkness, in She'ol or in the depths, or in any obscure place, can escape it; all their judgments are fixed, written down and engraved.[61]

In so far as the *Book of Enoch* may rightly be regarded as being in the main tradition of Jewish apocalyptic, the passage concerning the *post-mortem* judgment passed on individuals, which we have examined, gives it a unique distinction. For it is the collective aspect of divine judgment that predominates in Jewish thought; the essential theme being that Yahweh's ultimate vindication of his sovereignty over those who have opposed him and the retribution which he enacts for their pride and enmity.[62] It is significant that this theme prevails also in the writings of the Qumrân community,[63] and it surely inspired the Zealots in their resistance to Rome.[64] In other words, even after the traditional Yahwist doctrine of man had been adjusted to the individual's demand for significance, the ethnic factor in Yahwism remained fundamental, so that the eschatology continued to concentrate on the providence of the national deity for his elect people, *vis-à-vis* the nations of the world.

The literature of Hellenized Judaism contains little that is significant concerning belief in a *post-mortem* judgment. The most notable treatment of the subject occurs in the *Wisdom of Solomon*, which dates from the first century BC.[65] In a passage describing the fate of the righteous man, a kind of type-figure, who is persecuted and killed by the wicked, the victim curiously becomes the judge in the judgment after death:

> They (the wicked) shall come, when their sins are reckoned up, with coward fear; and their lawless deeds shall convict them to their face. Then shall the righteous man stand in great boldness before the face of them that afflicted him, and them that made his labours of no account. When they see *it*, they shall be troubled with terrible fear, and shall be amazed at the marvel of *God's* salvation.[66]

In a subsequent passage warning is given of coming judgment; but it is not clear whether it is to take place in this world or the next:

> Awfully and swiftly shall he come upon you; because a stern judgment befalleth them that be in high place: for the man of low estate may be pardoned

in mercy, but mighty men shall be searched out mightily. For the Sovereign Lord of all will not refrain himself for any *man's* person, neither will he reverence greatness: because he has made *both* small and great, and alike he taketh thought for all; but strict is the scrutiny that cometh upon the powerful.[67]

We may usefully note here what Josephus records of the beliefs of the Pharisees in this connection. This Jewish historian of the first century AD was actually a native of Judaea and brought up there; his books, however, were written in Greek for Gentile readers.[68]. According to him, the Pharisees believed that 'souls have power to survive death and that there are rewards and punishments under the earth for those who have led lives of virtue or vice: eternal imprisonment is the lot of evil souls, while the good souls receive an easy passage to a new life'.[69] This account of Pharisaic eschatology is undoubtedly presented in terms that Josephus thought would be intelligible to his non-Jewish readers; however, there is no reason for rejecting it as untrue in substance. The New Testament writings confirm that the Pharisees believed in the resurrection of the dead, which implied, as we have seen, a *post-mortem* judgment.[70] Whether they believed in 'rewards and punishments under the earth', as Josephus puts it, is, however, more questionable since he seems to be equating their belief with Greek eschatology, which we shall study later;[71] his statement can, nevertheless, be regarded as a fair interpretation of Pharisaic eschatology for Gentile readers, especially in view of what we have seen in the *Book of Enoch* and other evidence which we have now to consider.[72]

It is in the last expression of Jewish apocalyptic faith, dating from the tragic years immediately following the extinction of the Jewish national state in AD 70, that the most complete statement concerning the *post-mortem* state and the last judgment is found. In the so-called *Salathiel Apocalypse*, which forms part of the apocalyptic writing known as II(IV) *Esdras*,[73] the fate of the dead, immediately after death, is described:

For concerning death the teaching is: When the determinate sentence hath gone forth from the Most High that a man should die, as the spirit leaveth the body to return to him who gave it, it adoreth the glory of the Most High first of all. And if it be one of those that have been scorners and have not kept the way of the Most High, and that have despised his law, and that hate them that fear God, these spirits shall not enter into habitations, but shall wander and be in torments forthwith, ever grieving and sad, in seven ways.[74]

The seven ways in which these transgressors are condemned to be tormented are then described.[75] An account follows of the seven ways in which the righteous are rewarded for their faithfulness.[76] These descriptions of the respective fates of the wicked and righteous, consequent on their deaths, imply an immediate *post-mortem* judgment such as the *Book of Enoch* envisages; but, like that earlier writing, the *Salathiel Apocalypse* also contemplates a final judgment.[76a] Thus the seer Esdras is represented as asking God whether it will be possible to intercede for the ungodly on the day of judgment, and he is informed: 'The day of judgment is a day of decision, and displayeth unto all the seal of truth ... so never shall any one pray for another in that day, neither shall one lay a burden on another, for then shall all bear every one his own righteousness or unrighteousness'.[77]

Of the final judgment itself II(IV) *Esdras* gives a most impressive account, and it constitutes a remarkable parallel to the majestic presentation in the Christian apocalypse known as the *Revelation of St John the Divine*.[78] It is preceded by a description of the resurrection of the dead:

> And the earth shall restore those that are asleep in her, and so shall the dust those that dwell in silence, and the secret places shall deliver those souls that were committed unto them. And the Most High shall be revealed upon the seat of judgment, and compassion shall pass away, and longsuffering shall be withdrawn: but judgment only shall remain, truth shall stand, and faith shall wax strong: and the work shall follow, and the reward shall be shewed, and good deeds shall awake, and wicked deeds shall not sleep. And the pit of torment shall appear, and over against it shall be the place of rest: and the furnace of hell shall be shewed, and over against it the paradise of delight. And then shall the Most High say to the nations that are raised from the dead, see and understand whom ye have denied, or whom ye have not served, or whose commandment ye have despised. Look on this side and that: here is delight and rest, and there fire and torments. Thus shall he speak unto them in the day of judgment.[79]

Although great attention is thus given to the *post-mortem* destinies of individuals, these passages from the *Salathiel Apocalypse* and the *Ezra Apocalypse* attest the continuing strength of the old Yahwist tradition. It causes the judgment which the individual faces after death to be a kind of anticlimax; because the assessment then made has only a temporary significance and will be superseded by the verdict pronounced at the final judgment. It also creates the illogicality which we have already noticed in Jewish eschatology, namely, that the final judgment can only confirm the verdict of the immediate judgment, thereby reducing its drama and significance; for there appears to be no suggestion that the penalties decreed at the immediate judgment have a purgatorial effect, thus preparing the wicked for ultimate salvation at the final judgment, as is the scheme of mediaeval Christian eschatology.[80] The truth would seem to be that so firmly established was the idea of Yahweh's ultimate assertion of his sovereignty that it prevented the development of a really effective concept of a personal judgment after death. The final judgment was in origin and essence part of Yahwism, which was basically and always an ethnic, not a personal, religion. This fact is clearly evident in the *Ezra Apocalypse*; for it is the nations, not individual persons, that are arraigned before the divine tribunal for judgment.

It is, accordingly, significant that, after the shattering of the national hope in the catastrophe of AD 70, the judgment after death comes to be viewed more in terms of personal involvement.[80a] Thus it is recorded of the famous rabbi Johanan ben Zakkai that, on his death-bed, he was profoundly moved by the prospect of personally encountering God as his judge:

Now I am about to be brought before the King of Kings, before the Holy One (blessed be He!), who lives and dwells for (a century and centuries upon centuries), who if He is displeased with me, is displeased with an eternal displeasure, and, if He binds me, binds with eternal bonds, and, if He puts me to death, inflicts on me an eternal death. He is one whom I can appease neither by words nor by money. Since two ways lie before me, the one to the garden of delight, and the other to Gehenna, and I know not along which I shall be taken, should I not weep?[81]

And, in the *Pirke Aboth*, R. Eleazar ha-Kappar is recorded as presenting the destiny of men very succinctly in terms of divine judgment:

They that have been born [are destined] to die, and they that are dead [are destined] to be made alive, and they that live [after death are destined] to be judged, that men may know and make known and understand that he is God, he is the Maker, he is the Creator, he is the Discerner, he is the Judge, he is the Witness, he is the Complainant, and it is he that shall judge, blessed is he, in whose presence is neither guile nor forgetfulness nor respect of persons nor taking of bribes; for all is his. And know that everything is done according to the reckoning.[82]

This statement, even while concentrating on the personal aspect, nonetheless aptly expresses the quintessence of the Hebrew conception of the judgment of the dead. Whereas the Egyptian anticipation of judgment after death stemmed from fear that complaints might be made hereafter against one's conduct in this life,[83] for the Hebrew *post-mortem* judgment meant God's ultimate assertion of his sovereignty over his creatures. And so the Talmudic conception really continues, in a *post-mortem* and a personal context, the belief enshrined in the Fourth Commandment: 'I Yahweh your God am a jealous God, visiting the iniquity of the fathers upon the children to the third and the fourth generation of those who hate me, but showing steadfast love to thousands of those who love me and keep my commandments'.[84]

4

GRAECO-ROMAN CULTURE:
the Problem of a Non-Theistic Judgment of the Dead

Guided by a sound instinct, we turn back always to ancient Greek culture in seeking to understand the basic ideas of our Western society. We know that the *Weltanschauung* of mediaeval Europe derived from a fusion of Jewish religious insight and Greek metaphysical thought, the catalytic factor being the movement that stemmed from Jesus of Nazareth. Having already traced the evolution of the idea of a *post-mortem* judgment in Jewish eschatology, we naturally turn now to see whether or in what manner the idea found expression in Greek religion. The need to do so, however, is not only part of a necessary preparation for our subsequent study of the Christian doctrine of the judgment of the dead; to know how so brilliant a people as the Greeks dealt with the question whether man has to answer in another life for his conduct in this, has its own intrinsic interest. This interest is, moreover, enhanced by the fact that the Romans also were profoundly affected by the Greek culture which they adopted.

Our quest has to start far back in the Aegean culture that preceded the invasion of what was to be Hellas or Greece by Indo-European peoples about the middle of the second millennium BC.[1] This culture, which had its centre in Crete, though ruined by the invaders, was not completely eliminated, and many of its religious traditions evidently survived and were incorporated into the complex structure of Greek religious faith and practice.[2] It is unfortunate that so far the decipherment of records written in the so-called Linear B script have thrown but meagre light upon religion in Crete or the Greek mainland during the period which they document (*c.* 1400–1200 BC).[3] Much may possibly be learned, if the tablets inscribed with the Linear A script are ever deciphered;[4] in the meantime our knowledge of ancient Cretan religion comes almost wholly from archaeological data, and, consequently, lacks the confirmation and illumination that written sources would provide.

What may be deduced, relevant to our subject, from archaeological remains, is very puzzling. The general indication of the evidence of burial practice is that the Cretans believed that the dead continued to live on in some way in their tombs or in some subterranean realm, where they still needed food and drink.[5] In this other world they were still apparently in the care of the Great Goddess, whom they had served in the world above.[6] Such a primitive conception of the state of the dead is intelligible, and it can be paralleled by the funerary practices of other ancient peoples.[7] There is, however, some apparent indication of the existence of a different belief. In what appears to be a funerary scene painted on a sarcophagus found at Haghia Triada an object looking like a boat is depicted as being presented to the dead man or carried to his tomb.[8] If it is a boat, its presence at once suggests that the deceased is to make a journey by sea, presumably to the land of the dead. Such a notion at once recalls a tradition preserved by Hesiod (*fl.* 730 BC), that some of the ancient heroes had been transported at death to the islands of the blessed (ἐν μακάρων νήσοισι), where they lived untouched by sorrow.[9] In this delectable land, Hesiod says, they were ruled by Kronos.[10] This statement could be very significant for us, because Kronos was remembered as the ancient god, connected with Crete, whose rule had been supplanted by Zeus, the chief god of the invading Indo-Europeans.[11] If Hesiod does, accordingly, preserve the memory of a pre-Hellenic belief, which, as we shall see, differed from Hellenic belief, that some heroic personages were transported at their deaths to a transmarine paradise, the Haghia Triada sarcophagus assumes a new significance. From its size and ornate character it was undoubtedly made for some important person, and the fact is further indicated by the elaborate mortuary rites which are depicted as being performed on his behalf.[12] We may, therefore, have in this sarcophagus concrete evidence of the belief, of which Hesiod preserves the memory. The man concerned, because of his eminence, was believed to have a special *post-mortem* destiny. Instead of joining the company of the ordinary dead beneath the earth, he would journey to the islands of the blessed, perhaps in the boat which was placed in his tomb.[13]

On what grounds such a differentiation of *post-mortem* destiny was made we have no knowledge. It would seem likely that the owner of the Haghia Triada sarcophagus was accorded such a blessed after-life because of his wealth or social importance. No moral factor need have been involved in the achievement of this better lot after death. Hesiod gives no reason why some only of the heroes were transported to the isles of the blessed;[14] in the *Odyssey*, however, the hero Menelaus is excepted from the common fate, as we shall see, in being promised everlasting felicity in Elysium because he had married Helen and thus was related to Zeus.[15] It would, accordingly, seem likely, if the Greek poets were drawing upon pre-Hellenic tradition here, that the ancient Cretans and Mycenaeans believed in a form of *post-mortem* judgment or distinction, based on social status, possibly involving a claim to divine descent.[16]

The passage from the *Odyssey*, to which reference has just been made, has a further interest for us. Menelaus is promised that he would not die, but that he would be conveyed to 'the Elysian plain . . . where dwells fair-haired Rhadamanthys, and where life is easiest for men'.[17] Now, not only does the fate promised to Menelaus contradict that decreed for all other men according to Homeric theology,[18] but both the names 'Elysion' ('Ηλύσιον) and 'Rhadamanthys' are not of Greek derivation and thus indicate that the poet was here drawing upon an alien tradition.[19] But this is not all: the mysterious Rhadamanthys, who is described as dwelling in Elysion, is represented in Greek legend as the brother of Minos, the king of Crete, and also as being, with Minos, one of the judges in Hades.[20]

The confusion of legendary lore manifest in this passage can only safely be interpreted as preserving, in a very garbled form, some memory of ancient Cretan eschatology which accorded special destinies after death to certain eminent personages. It would seem that a kind of paradise called Elysion was imagined as the eternal dwelling-place of this elect company, which may have included the priest-kings of Crete, if 'Minos' was the dynastic title as some evidence suggests.[21] The famous painted sarcophagus, found at Haghia Triada, could thus be our sole surviving record of the mortuary ritual performed to achieve the transportation of a Cretan magnate to this paradise which Hesiod describes as situated 'along the shore of deep swirling Okeanos'.[22]

There is another curious scrap of possible evidence concerning the existence of some concept of a *post-mortem* judgment in pre-Hellenic religion. In certain Mycenaean tombs miniature scales or balances, with figures of butterflies, have been found.[23] Since the butterfly could symbolize the soul in later Greek thought,[24] and since the balances are too fragile for practical use, it has been thought by some scholars that belief in *psychostasia* or the weighing of the soul is thereby indicated.[25] That some eschatological symbolism was involved would seem to be certain, but its exact significance is difficult to determine. Balances could symbolize the apportioning of fates to living men: thus in the *Iliad* Zeus is represented as weighing in golden balances the fates of Achilles and Hector at their fatal encounter.[26] On the other hand, the

Fig. 5 The *Kērostasia*, from a Greek vase-painting. Hermes holds the scales on which the fates of two heroes are balanced. Zeus watches the assessment.

fact that the Mycenaean balances have been found in tombs suggests that they had some mortuary significance. It is in matters like this that our lack of written evidence is most keenly felt. We can only speculate on the meaning that such objects could have in the mortuary ritual of the Mycenaeans. In such speculation we may also wonder whether the Egyptian belief in the weighing of the heart of the deceased had any influence here; for Egyptian influence can be traced in many other aspects of Cretan and Mycenaean culture.[27]

There remains one more puzzling fact which we must consider in seeking for evidence of some concept of *post-mortem* judgment in pre-Hellenic religion. At Eleusis, a little town close to Athens, there were celebrated annually mystery rites which were believed to confer upon those initiated into the mystery a happy lot after death. Unfortunately, despite the devoted research of many scholars, the origin and nature of this Eleusinian mystery-cult still remain obscure, owing to the lack of truly informative evidence.[28] However, certain factors are clear, and they have a special significance for us. First, it is evident that the rites were of very ancient origin and undoubtedly predate the coming of the Hellenes. They were linked with the cult of two goddesses, Demeter and Persephone. The former was a corn-goddess, whose cult seems to have been introduced at Eleusis, from some unknown place, about the second half of the fifteenth century BC.[29] Persephone or Kore, the daughter of Demeter, was known to the Greeks, and the fact is very significant for us, as the goddess of the underworld and the wife of Hades or Pluto.[30] Next, we are fortunate in possessing a brief statement at the end of the so-called *Homeric Hymn to Demeter* describing the privilege conferred by initiation into the Eleusinian mysteries: 'Happy is he among men upon earth who has seen these mysteries; but he who is uninitiate and who has no part in them, never has a lot of like good things (οὔκοθ᾽ ὁμοίων αἶσαν ἔχει) once he is dead, down in the darkness and gloom (Φθίμενος περ᾽ὑπὸ ζόφῳ ἠερόεντι)'.[31] The apposition of the fates of the initiated and the uninitiated here, although the exact nature of the *post-mortem* situation of the former is not described, indicates that initiation into the mysteries celebrated at Eleusis was the decisive factor in determining a person's destiny at death. So far as our knowledge goes, it was essentially the fact of initiation which secured this *post-mortem* beatitude, not moral character or achievement. There was indeed one moral condition requisite for initiation, namely, that one should not have committed murder; but this prohibition was probably intended to prevent the pollution of the rites and the sanctuary in which they were performed.[32]

The fact of the great antiquity of the Eleusinian mysteries, and that of their connection with goddesses of the corn and the underworld, go to reinforce the other evidence we possess concerning the eschatology of the Aegean peoples before the incursion of the Greeks. From our study of this sparse and disparate material there is reason for concluding that there was some belief in a form of *post-mortem* judgment or discrimination, in the sense that all of the dead did not share in the same fate, as, for example, was the view current in Mesopotamian and early Hebrew religion. However, this differentiation was not made on grounds of moral character and achievement. Kings and nobles, perhaps by virtue of their claims to divine descent, expected to be transported to some remote paradise, where they would enjoy everlasting felicity. The Eleusinian mysteries suggest that for ordinary folk also there probably existed cults, connected with chthonian deities, which promised a happy lot after death to those who underwent a ritual of initiation. Again, no moral criteria seem to have been involved, and we have, accordingly, to conclude that these Aegean tests to determine a person's *post-mortem* destiny compare very unfavourably, in terms of ethical insight, with the Egyptian belief in the judgment of the dead.

It has been necessary to assess pre-Hellenic belief in this connection, because such an assessment will help to illuminate the puzzling situation which we encounter when we examine Greek ideas about judgment after death. This situation finds its earliest literary expression in the Homeric epics, the *Iliad* and the *Odyssey*. In these writings a very distinctive evaluation of human nature and destiny is set forth, which evidently represented the view of the poet and his public.[33] Man is regarded as a living organism compounded of three parts: his body, his *thymos* (θυμός), and his *psyche*. The *thymos* was the conscious self, and the *psyche* something akin to the life-principle.[34] To the Homeric Greeks a human being was only truly a human being when body, *thymos* and *psyche* were all functioning properly together as an inter-related whole. Death shattered this living whole: with the dissolution of the body, the *thymos* was merged with the air, and the *psyche*, transformed into a shadowy replica of the living person and known as the *eidōlon*, descended into Hades, which was conceived as an immense cavern or cavity below ground.[35] There, with the wraiths of all the other dead, bereft of self-consciousness and capable only of chirping sounds, the *eidōlon* lived on in dismal gloom.[36] Such a state is remarkably like that of the Mesopotamian dead in *kur-nu-gi-a*, or that of the departed in the Hebrew She'ol, as we have seen.[37] Since this transformation and descent into Hades was the common fate of all, Homeric eschatology no more found place for a *post-mortem* judgment than did the eschatologies of Mesopotamia or early Israel. Good or bad, rich or poor, king or peasant, all alike shared this shadowy consciousless existence in the realm of the dead, over which ruled Pluto and his queen Persephone.[38]

The eleventh book of the *Odyssey* contains a graphic description of the dead in Hades.[38a] It occurs incidentally in the account of Odysseus' descent into Hades, whither he went to consult the dead seer Teiresias concerning the succession of misfortunes that prevented his return

home to Ithaca after the Trojan War.[39] The idea of a living man
descending into the realm of the dead had already found expression in
Mesopotamian literature; there it seems to have been used as a means
of describing the awful nature of the underworld and its baleful rulers
and ministrants.[40] Such does not appear to have been the primary purpose of the Homeric poet in sending his hero down into Hades; for,
apart from developing his theme of Odysseus' wanderings as due to
the spite of the god Poseidon, the poet seems intent on using the visit
of Odysseus to Hades to describe the fortunes of other actors in the
Trojan drama. He does this through the reports given to the hero by
the shades of those with whom he had been involved in former times,
and who had subsequently died and descended to Hades.[41] It is in the
course of his encounters with these ghosts that the concept of the state
of the dead incidentally emerges. The grim pathos of their condition
informs the description of Odysseus' first meeting with them: 'Then
there gathered from out of Erebus the spirits of those that are dead,
brides, and unwedded youths, and toil-worn old men, and tender
maidens with hearts yet new to sorrow, and many, too, that had been
wounded with bronze-tipped spears, men slain in fight, wearing their
blood-stained armour'.[42] Although Odysseus recognizes many whom
he knew among these shades, no communication with them is possible
until they drink of the blood of an animal which he had sacrificed. The
fact is significant of the poet's view of the dead: these *eidōla* or shades
of former living persons have no memory until a fleeting restoration of
consciousness is effected by imbibing blood, the substance of life.[43]

That death was thought to reduce what survived of the dead to a
common state of dismal wretchedness is stated by the poet in a most
remarkable manner. While in Hades, Odysseus meets the shade of
Achilles, the most renowned of all Greek heroes who had fought at
Troy. Odysseus is represented as saluting the dead Achilles and con-
gratulating him on the great reputation he had won. In concluding, he
seeks to reconcile Achilles to his fate: 'Wherefore grieve not at all that
thou art dead, Achilles'.[44] Achilles' reply is devastating in the contrast
it makes between life here and hereafter: 'Nay, seek not to speak sooth-
ingly to me of death, glorious Odysseus. I should choose, so I might
live on earth, to serve as the hireling of another, of some portionless
man whose livelihood was but small, rather than to be lord over all the
dead that have perished.'[45] The grim negation that death imposed on
all social values and distinctions is here stated in all its stark reality. For
the military aristocracy, described in the Homeric epics, martial glory

82

and renown were the most highly prized of all values. Yet the poet, mindful of the accepted eschatology, had the insight to perceive that even the greatest hero of all would be in no better state in Hades than the meanest of men.[45a]

The logic of the Homeric doctrine of human nature and destiny was obvious: the shadowy unconscious *eidōla* of the dead, because they were unconscious and insubstantial, existed in a state so neutral and apathetic that the idea of a *post-mortem* judgment, and of reward or punishment consequent upon it, was simply irrelevant and meaningless. It is surprising, therefore, that, shortly after this meeting with the ghost of Achilles, Odysseus has another series of encounters which implicate a wholly different situation, namely, that the dead are judged in Hades and certain evildoers are terribly punished. The first of these encounters is described as follows: 'There then I saw Minos, the glorious son of Zeus, golden sceptre in hand, giving judgment to the dead from his seat, while they sat and stood about the king through the wide-gated house of Hades, and asked him for judgment'.[46] The discrepancy which this passage constitutes in relation to what had gone before is obvious, but it is difficult to assess it accurately. Minos is depicted rather as a legislating (θεμιστεύοντα) and judicating king, and this portrait, as we have seen, may well derive from some pre-Hellenic memory of the sovereignty of the Cretan king. But why Minos, who is described as the son of Zeus, should be making or administering laws for the dead in Hades is unknown to us. It is possible that he was relegated there in Greek legend rather after the manner in which the ancient Aegean god Kronos, who was superseded by the Hellenic high-god Zeus, was assigned some lesser rôle.[47] In other words, Minos, the great law-giver of an earlier and now obsolescent order of things, was transferred to Hades, where he legislated for those 'dead and gone', as Homer describes them.[48] The nature of the judgment given by Minos is also puzzling. The dead are not described as being judged by him, but as asking for judgment, or rather perhaps justice (οἱ δέ μιν ἀμφὶ δίκας εἴροντο ἄνακτα).[49] The impression conveyed by the passage as a whole is that of a royal court, at which the king makes laws and receives pleas from those who believe that injustice has been done them by others. This conception is reminiscent of a certain aspect of the Egyptian idea of the *post-mortem* judgment, and, like the Egyptian idea, it was doubtless conceived in terms of current practice in royal courts in the Aegean area.[50]

How far this passage in the *Odyssey* is to be interpreted as evidence of belief in a judgment of the dead is difficult to assess. In the first place, in view of the condition of the dead, namely, as unconscious wraiths, which is attested to throughout the Homeric epics,[51] and which, as we shall see, formed the accepted evaluation in Greek thought on into the Graeco-Roman period, and because that condition was the common lot, in which all shared, whether good or bad, the idea of a *post-mortem* judgment was essentially irrelevant and illogical. Then, the judgment which Minos is depicted as administering to those who petition him is not recorded as issuing in any form of retributive punishment of the guilty or reward of the righteous. There were indeed, as we shall presently see, certain notorious individuals who were punished in Hades, but their cases are not connected with the judgment given by Minos. The juridical activity of Minos, as described here, could perhaps be interpreted as implying that he legislated for the dead in Hades, in the sense that he gave to them laws to obey as denizens of the under-world.[52] But such an interpretation would mean that the transaction could not be properly regarded as a judgment of the dead. The simplest solution to the problem which the passage raises, therefore, seems to be that already suggested, namely, that the memory of the great power once wielded by the kings of Crete had led to the transference of Minos to Hades, where he was imagined as continuing to legislate and judge in that shadowy realm for those who were 'dead and gone'.

The problem which Minos and his tribunal constitute is paralleled by that contained in what follows in the *Odyssey*. Odysseus relates how 'I saw Tityos ... lying on a levelled ground, ... and vultures twain beset him one on either side, and gnawed at his liver ... For he had dealt violently with Leto, the famous bedfellow of Zeus, as she went up to Pytho through the fair lawns of Panopeus'.[53]

The account of the next sufferer whom Odysseus meets has provided the classic instance of perpetual torment and supplied a corresponding word to the languages of many peoples:

Moreover I beheld Tantalus in grievous torment, standing in a mere and the water came nigh unto his chin. And he stood straining as one athirst, but he might not attain to the water to drink of it. For often as that old man stooped down in his eagerness to drink, so often the water was swallowed up and it vanished away, and the black earth still showed at his feet, for some god parched it evermore. And tall trees flowering shed their fruit overhead, pears and pomegranates and apple trees with bright fruit, and sweet figs and olives in their bloom, whereat when that old man reached out his hands to clutch them, the wind would toss them to the shadowy clouds.[54]

No reason is given for these strange torments which are inflicted upon Tantalus. The Homeric poet doubtless drew on a tradition known to his readers, and it may fairly be assumed that the nature of Tantalus's offence was well known. Later writers indicate that he had in some signal manner intruded upon the divine prerogative.[55] No cause also is given for the ceaseless labour and torment that afflicts the third sufferer seen by Odysseus. This is Sisyphus, who toils to push a huge stone up a hill, the weight of which sends it rolling back each time the summit is reached.[56]

Since the torture suffered by Tityus is definitely stated to be punishment for his having outraged the supreme god, Zeus, it is reasonable to suppose that the torments of Tantalus and Sisyphus are also retributive, most probably for some heinous offence against Zeus. In view of the nature of their sufferings, it would also appear that these three notorious sinners had to be excepted from the common destiny, in that in Hades they still retained their physical bodies and their consciousness; for presumably they knew that they were being punished and the reason for it.[56a]

Why the Homeric poet chose to include these three examples of *post-mortem* retribution, thus contradicting the general theme of his eschatology, is unknown. It would seem improbable that both the sinners and their fates were invented by him; more likely would it be that they were so well known in current folklore that the poet felt it necessary to record that his hero had seen them during his visit to Hades. It is perhaps significant that Odysseus is not described as having held converse with them as he had with the shades of those he knew. Tityus, Tantalus and Sisyphus just appear in his narrative as type-figures, well established as minatory examples of the fate that awaited any human who trespassed upon the privileges of deity.

Whatever may have been the motive of the poet in presenting Minos as the judge of the dead or describing the punishment of the three sinners, there can be no doubt, in view of the key importance of the Homeric epics in the scheme of Greek education, that the picture given therein of the underworld exercised an immense influence on people's ideas of human destiny. This picture, as we have just noted, was not a consistent presentation, and its two diverse views of human destiny, though first finding literary expression in the *Iliad* and *Odyssey*, must surely have reflected an existing divergence of popular opinion among the Greeks. However, the epics had the effect both of giving the two views a dramatic concretion, and of ensuring their propagation.

In so far as there was an established doctrine of human nature and destiny among the Greeks throughout both the classical and Hellenistic periods, it found expression in the Homeric phrase: 'the strengthless heads of the dead' (νεκύων ἀμενηνὰ κάρηνα).[57] Life in this world was the only full and proper life for men and women; what survived death was but a negative shadowy replica of the living person. This evaluation is reflected in literature[58] and art,[59] and in funerary epitaphs. An official inscription commemorating the Athenian dead who fell in the battle of Potidaea in 432 BC can say no more of the dead warriors than that, 'The air has received their souls (ψυχὰς), the earth their bodies. By the gates of Potidaea were they slain.'[60] And private persons proclaimed their belief that life had no ultimate significance in epitaphs such as this:

I was not, I became; I was, I am not – just this!
And if any man asserts the contrary, he will lie; I shall not be.[61]

Such an estimate of man and his destiny clearly afforded no ground for belief in a judgment after death. Even though that primitive inability to envisage complete personal extinction caused the majority of the Greeks, as it caused the Mesopotamians and Hebrews, to think that something of the individual did survive death, that something, since it was a consciousless wraith, could not be regarded as the responsible representative of the living person, to be punished or rewarded for the deeds of that person. However, the thought of some form of *post-mortem* survival was a potent source of fear, and, as we shall see, it tormented many and inspired a terrifying eschatology.[61a] Some philosophers were concerned about its depressing effect upon men's lives, and they sought by the exercise of reason to deliver their fellow-men from the terror of death and the hereafter. Most notable among those who sought to do this service was Lucretius, the Roman disciple of Epicurus,[62] and in the third book of his *De Rerum Natura* he employed his considerable talents in logic and literary expression to show that the disintegration of the human person wrought by death was so complete, that nothing survived.[63] Because of this total extinction, he argued, there could be no suffering after death: 'For if by chance anyone is to have misery and pain in the future, he must needs himself also exist then in that time (*in eo tum tempore*) to be miserable. Since death takes away this possibility, . . . we may be sure that there is nothing to be feared after death, that he who is not cannot be miserable (*nec miserum fieri qui not est posse*).'[64]

The effort made by Lucretius in this connection is significant of the enduring influence of the idea, so graphically presented in Homer, of retributive punishment after death. Lucretius endeavoured to re-interpret this ancient fear in terms of life in this present world, thus notably anticipating a mode of rationalizing away primitive beliefs that is often practised today. 'There is no wretched Tantalus,' he argues, 'as the story goes ("*ut famast*"), fearing the great rock that hangs over him in the air and frozen with vain terror; rather it is in this life that the fear of gods oppresses mortals without cause, and the fall they fear is any that chance may bring.'[65] The sufferings of Tityus are explained as the torment of the passions.[66] Sisyphus and his unceasing but futile struggle with his rock symbolizes the griefs of the over-ambitious in this world.[67] He also re-interprets a punishment unmentioned by Homer: young girls, in the flower of their beauty (*aevo florente*), who toil uselessly in seeking to fill with water a leaking urn, represent the torment of discontent. Developing his theme, he maintains that the terrors of the underworld are really the fear of punishment experienced in this world by the evildoers and the guilty conscience. He concludes that, 'the fool's life becomes a hell on earth'.[69]

This attempt by Lucretius to re-interpret the traditional view of Hades as a place of retribution, and the earlier attempt of the comedian Aristophanes seemingly to ridicule such belief,[70] attest to the fact that, despite the accepted evaluation of human nature and destiny, there was a significant body of opinion which affirmed that after death men would be judged on their conduct here. This belief was authorized by the poetry of Homer, which was truly the 'Bible of the Greeks';[71] but it gradually assumed a more elaborate form under the impetus of other forces. We have just noticed that Lucretius deals with an example of *post-mortem* punishment not mentioned by Homer; it will be our task now to trace out the development of this other side of Greek eschato-logical belief, and to assess its significance for our study.

What is perhaps the most eloquent testimony to a basic human factor which operated among the majority of ancient Greeks, as it has done among men of other nations, to make them fear the possibility of a *post-mortem* judgment is uttered by an aged man named Cephalus in the course of the dialogue of Plato's *Republic*:

But you know, Socrates, when a man faces the thought that he must die, there come upon him fear and foreboding about things that had not troubled him before. Once he laughed at the tales (μῦθοι) about those in Hades, of pun-ishment to be suffered there by him who here has done injustice. But now his soul is tormented by the thought that these may be true, and whether from the bodily weakness of old age, or because he is now nearer that other world, he himself sees those things more clearly. He comes full of fear and suspicion. He begins to reckon up and consider if he has done any injustice to any man. And finding in his life many such acts, often, like a child, he awakes out of sleep in terror, and lives in expectation of evil. But with him that is conscious of no injustice in him, kindly hope, the nurse of age, as Pindar calls it, is always present, . . .[72]

Plato also provides a valuable clue to identifying those who then propagated an eschatology concerned with rewards and punishments in the after-life. In the *Republic* he represents one of his characters, Adeimantus, in discussing the nature of justice, as referring to those who taught that virtue would be rewarded and vice punished in the next world:

Musaeus and his son (Eumolpus) endow the just with gifts from heaven of an even more spirited sort. They take the righteous to another world and provide them with a banquet of the saints, where they sit for all time drinking with garlands on their heads, as if virtue could not be more nobly rewarded than by an eternity of intoxication . . . When they have sung the praises of justice in that strain, with more to the same effect, they proceed to plunge the sinners and unrighteous men into a sort of mud-pool (εἰς πηλόν τινα) in the other world, and they set them to carry water in a sieve (κοσκίνῳ).[73]

This description was obviously intended to ridicule the teaching of Musaeus and Eumolpus, who were the legendary teachers of Orphism,[74] the other Greek mystery-cult which clearly exercised a great influence on Greek religious thought, although our knowledge of its origins and doctrines is very imperfect and problematic. That Orphism must have been distinguished by its emphasis upon *post-mortem* retribution, and that its eschatology included a more elaborate imagery than that of Homer, are evident from a variety of sources. Aristophanes refers to immersion in mud as a punishment for evildoers in Hades; it would seem that he had those uninitiated into the mysteries in mind, since in his continuing account of Hades he describes, by way of contrast, the blessed state of those who were initiated.[75] Plato refers to judges in the underworld, Minos, Rhadamanthys, Aiakos and Triptolemus, the latter being an Orphic figure.[76] And in the *Gorgias* he represents Socrates as referring to the teaching of the Pythagorean sage Philolaus about the fate of the uninitiated: 'these uninitiate will be the most miserable of all, and will carry water into their leaky jar in a sieve equally full of holes'.[77] Further evidence of this belief, that it was the

uninitiated rather than evildoers who were punished in Hades, is provided by what Pausanias tells of a famous picture of Hades, painted at
Delphi in the fifth century BC by Polygnotos,[78] and by similar scenes
on certain vases, found in southern Italy and dating from the fourth
and third centuries BC.[79]

Orpheo-Pythagorean doctrine, so far as it can be determined from
the very fragmentary and disparate data available, did not apparently
envisage the *post-mortem* destiny of the individual as definitively fixed
by a judgment pronounced after death. According to what can be made
out from the extant sources, human destiny could be understood only
in terms of the origin of human nature. The key to this seems to have
been provided by the myth of the murder of Dionysos-Zagreus, the
son of Zeus, by the wicked Titans. These monsters, having eaten the
divine child, were blasted by Zeus and from their ashes mankind arose.
This myth was evidently intended to explain the dual nature of man,
namely, that his soul is ethereal and immortal, having derived from the
divine child, but it is imprisoned in a material body of Titan-origin.[80]
There were probably other allegorical interpretations of the dual nature
of man: Plato explains human nature and destiny in terms of the inability
of souls to maintain their ethereal position and their consequent
descent and cohabitation with matter.[81]

The conception of human nature denoted here obviously implies a
departure from that expounded in the Homeric poems. Instead of the
distinction between the conscious self (*thymos*) and the *psyche* as the
unconscious principle of life, by the sixth century BC the *psyche* had
evidently come to be regarded as the pre-existent conscious self that
survived the death of the body.[82] Together with this conception went
belief in the transmigration of the soul. Empedocles, who seems to
have been connected with Pythagoreans, believed that he remembered
earlier lives not only in human feminine form, but also in the forms of
a fish, a bird, and even a bush.[83]

This process of metempsychosis was regarded as the penalty suffered
by the soul for some original fault, and its continuance resulted from
the soul's ignorance of its true nature and its willing involvement with
matter. The poet Pindar, who seems to have been influenced by Orphic
ideas, writes cryptically of 'those from whom Persephone shall exact
the penalty of the primal woe, in the ninth year she gives up again their
souls to the sunlight of the world above'.[84] Empedocles speaks, equally
obscurely, of 'an oracle of Necessity (*'Ανάγκης χρῆμα*)', which decrees
that those demi-gods (*δαίμονες*) who sin in various specified ways,

shall wander far from the blessed for three thousand seasons 'in the forms of all manner of mortal things and changing one baleful path of life for another'.[85] In the *Phaedrus* Plato, who, despite the caustic reference to Orphic eschatology which we earlier noticed, seems to reflect Orphic thought, outlines a carefully articulated scheme of metempsychosis. Those souls who fall from their primal state of beatitude and involve themselves with matter, and the evil inherent in it, have to pass through a series of incarnations, some of them in bestial form for ten thousand years before regaining their former state. Certain enlightened souls, however, can reduce this awful burden of births and deaths, and all the concommitant misery, by living as philosophers during three successive incarnations during the third millennium of the 'sorrowful weary wheel' of mortal existence.[86]

According to this Orphic interpretation of human destiny, it would appear that after each incarnation, the soul, having experienced the death of its body, went to Hades for judgment. If Plato is following the Orphic scheme in the *Phaedrus*, his account is very illuminating. The fallen souls, having become incarnated, are

on the termination of their first life, brought to trial; and, according to their sentence, some go to the prison-houses beneath the earth, to suffer for their sins, while others, by virtue of their trial, are borne lightly upwards to some celestial spot, where they pass their days in a manner worthy of the life they have lived in their mortal form. But in the thousandth year both divisions come back again to share and choose their second life, and they select that which they severally please. And then it is that a human soul passes into the life of a beast, and from a beast who was once a man the soul comes back into a man again. For the soul which has never seen the truth at all can never enter into the human form; it being a necessary condition of a man that he should apprehend according to that which is called the generic form, which, proceeding from a variety of perceptions, is by reflection combined into unity. And this is nothing more or less than a recollection of those things which in time past our soul beheld when it travelled in the company of the gods, and, looking high over what we now call real, lifted up its head into the region of eternal essence.[87]

In view of the earlier evidence, which we noted, that initiation was regarded by the Orphics as the decisive factor in determining one's *post-mortem* state, the relation of this view to the process of metempsychosis, as it is, for example, presented by Plato, is difficult to discern. The apparent discrepancy may, however, be due to the nature of Plato's presentation. It is essentially philosophical; therefore, while it undoubtedly reflects Orphic view, it is probably a far more sophisticated interpretation than that held by the ordinary Orphic teachers and initiates.[87a] While these accepted the principle of metempsychosis, accounting thereby for the nature and situation of man, they surely attached primary importance to initiation as the factor which made them spiritually superior to their fellow-men. A truer reflection of what an Orphic initiate believed is probably to be found in the formulae inscribed on thin sheets of gold and placed in the graves of the faithful, for their use in the next world.[88] The following example shows that, although cognizant of the doctrine of metempsychosis ('the sorrowful weary Wheel'), the initiate was taught to believe that he could now attain to a state of divine beatitude:

> Out of the Pure I come, Pure Queen of Them Below,
> And Eukles and Eubouleus, and other Gods and Daemons:
> For I also avow me that I am of your blessed race.
> And I have paid the penalty for deeds unrighteous,
> Whether it be that Fate ($M\tilde{o}\rho\alpha$) laid me low or the Gods Immortal
>
> . . . . . .
>
> I have flown out of the sorrowful weary Wheel;
> I have passed with eager feet to the Circle desired;
> I have sunk beneath the bosom of Despoina, Queen of the Underworld;
>
> . . . . . .
>
> And now I come a suppliant to Holy Phersephoneia
> That of her grace she receive me to the seats of the Hallowed –
> Happy and Blessèd One, thou shalt be God instead of Mortal.[89]

The Orpheo-Pythagorean doctrine of metempsychosis, like that in Hinduism and Buddhism, undoubtedly helped to explain the inequality of fortune experienced in this life.[90] Theoretically the situation of each individual was of his own making in this or in former lives. However, the fear that naturally follows from belief in *post-mortem* survival, namely, that there may be punishment for former misdeeds, was evidently felt, so that for the Orphics each life was not immediately followed by a new incarnation; instead there was an intervening period of either reward or punishment, which some infernal judge or judges decreed. Such a belief already had the authority of Homer; but it is evident the situation of the dead in Hades was a fruitful theme for speculation, as it has been in other religions, and imagination, prompted by fear, greatly elaborated the original Homeric picture.

Because neither Greek nor Roman religion were controlled by powerful priesthoods which were concerned to maintain and promote orthodoxy, eschatological belief was never formally defined. In Graeco-Roman society variety of interpretation of the traditional Homeric concept of Hades continued to characterize religious faith and practice. It even produced, as Cicero shows, the strange idea, which Dante was later to elaborate, that the damned were punished not in a subterranean Hades but in the turbulent air that surrounded the globe.[91]

Among the more notable of these ideas of *post-mortem* judgment we may notice what seems to have been the belief of the neo-Pythagorean sect that built the underground basilica, near the Porta Magiore, at Rome.[92] The members of this community, which flourished during the first century AD, conceived of salvation as the ascent of the soul into the Aether, its true and original home. Condemnation to Hades, which was the lot of the uninitiated, meant the endless transmigration of the soul, and the sufferings attendant in the experience of so many incarnations.[93]

The way in which the traditional picture of Hades, with the torment of the damned, could be combined with an esoteric doctrine of metempsychosis is to be seen, dramatically presented, in Virgil's *Aeneid*. Following the precedent of Odysseus' visit to Hades, the Latin poet conducts his hero through the underworld, which task provides him with excellent opportunities both to develop his theme of Rome's imperial destiny and to comment upon many other matters.[94] He depicts Aeneas as wondering at a host of shades (*animae*) gathered on the banks of a river. He is informed by the shade of his father, Anchises, that the river is that of Lethe, from the drinking of which the dead lose all memory of their former life. They gather on its banks, because they have now to be incarnated again in the world above.[95] To Aeneas's further inquiry his father explains at length the process of human destiny. After death, the souls of men expiate their former misdeeds:

Some are being stretched out to the empty winds; from some the stain of guilt is washed away under swirling floods or burned out in fire. Each of us suffers his own spirit; then through wide Elysium are we sent, a few of us to abide in the joyous fields; till lapse of days, when time's cycle is complete, takes out the inbred taint and leaves unsoiled the ethereal sense and pure flame of spirit. All these, when they have rolled time's wheel through a thousand years, the god (*deus*) summons in vast throng to the river of Lethe, in sooth that, reft of memory, they may revisit the vault above and conceive desire to return again to the body.[96]

Behind such esoteric teachings there surely lay a deeply rooted fear of what might be experienced beyond death, particularly by way of retribution. The penal aspect of Hades clearly loomed large in many minds. Apart from the type-figures of tormented sinners such as Tityus, Tantalus and Sisyphus, man's imagination soon conceived other forms of torment, designed as punishment to fit social, rather than religious, crimes. Plato, in his curious myth of Er in the *Republic*, had described in detail the *post-mortem* punishment of Ardiaeus and other tyrants and notorious sinners:

fierce men, like coals of fire to look upon, came forward, and some they took in their arms and dragged away, but Ardiaeus and others they bound hand and foot and head, threw them down, and flayed them. They dragged them out of the way to a place apart, and there carded them on thorns, saying to all that passed that they were being taken away to be plunged into Tartarus, and explaining why this was done to them.[97]

Virgil, as we have briefly noted, continued, in his generation, this tradition of Hades as place of retributive punishment. In the under-world, Aeneas comes to a parting of the ways: one leads to Elysium, the other to the place where the wicked are punished.[98] An horrific description follows of this place which has the form of an immense fortress, encircled by a river of fire. From within come groans and the sound of flogging and the clank of iron chains.[99] Aeneas is informed that here Rhadamanthys 'hold his iron sway; he chastises, and hears the tale of guilt, exacting confession of crimes, whenever in the world above any man, rejoicing in vain deceit, has put off atonement for sin until death's late hour'.[100] Awful demons, with writhing snakes, tor-ment these sinners. Elsewhere others, guilty of specified crimes, suffer, some rolling a huge stone, some hanging outstretched on the spokes of wheels.[101]

The cynical Lucian, writing during the second century AD,[102] describes the underworld scene in a way that must reflect popular belief, even though an undercurrent of mockery runs through his description. In his tractate *Menippus* he depicts Minos as judging the dead, who stand naked and downcast before him. The place of punish-ment has all the engines of torture and execution of the world above – the lash, the stake, the rack, the gibbet and the wheel. All classes of men are punished, repenting of their sins there: kings and slaves, governors and paupers, the rich and beggars. The classical victims are also there – Ixion, Sisyphus, Tantalus and Tityus. But, curiously, the mass of dead mankind is not involved in this torment; instead they are seen as skeletons, lying in confused heaps, except for those, chiefly Egyptians, whose corpses have been embalmed.[103] In another tractate he makes his Cynic philosopher Menippus caustically to observe that 'Hades is a democracy', since the dead are not only stripped of their former wealth and rank, but physical beauty and distinction have disappeared with the flesh, leaving only a common skeletal form.[104]

So far as our evidence permits us to know, there seems to have been a growing tendency both to increase the horrific nature of Hades, and to make it the place where retributive punishment of an ever more revolting character was meted out to specified categories of sinners. Indeed from the Homeric picture of the dismal abode of the unconscious ghosts of the dead, where only three notorious sinners for ever paid the penalty of their crimes, the conception of the underworld gradually evolves, as we have noted, until it inspired the terrible picture in the *Apocalypse of Peter*, an early Christian writing that undoubtedly drew upon an earlier tradition.[105] Two eminent scholars have disputed the origin of this tradition, the one maintaining that it derived from Orphic sources[106] and the other arguing that its shocking imagery was of eastern derivation.[107] The question, though interesting, does not closely concern us. What is evident, as we have seen, is that later Greek and Latin writers attest to the existence of a well established belief in a *post-mortem* judgment and to either a temporary or an everlasting expiation suffered by the guilty for their past misdeeds. The imagery, in which this belief finds expression, is a traditional one, and Homer provides our earliest evidence of it. However, despite its vivid presentation and established authority, the ultimate sanction of the belief remained obscure. In the original Homeric version, the connection of Zeus, the supreme deity, with Hades and its purpose is vague; only three sinners appear to suffer there on his condemnation. Moreover, since Zeus was never regarded as the creator of the universe, Hades or Tartarus had not been brought into being as part of his design or providence.[108]

This theological uncertainty, which stems from the fundamental lack of an authoritative theology in Greek religion, left Greek eschatology deficient at the most vital points. The fact is particularly evident in the matter of the judgment of the dead. In the first place, no clearly defined divine judge emerges. As we have seen, the memory of the legislative power of the Cretan king seems to have led to the placing of Minos in Hades as a judge who legislated and heard pleas. But his status and judiciary powers remain essentially vague; indeed it is not even certain that he did judge the dead on the quality of their former lives. In later accounts of Hades, other judges are associated with Minos or are mentioned alone; but they are all shadowy figures. Similarly, in notable contradistinction to the Egyptian conception, Greek and Roman literature witness to no firmly established tradition as to the way in which the dead were judged.[109] Indeed, the whole process of judgment after death and the consequent punishment of sinners, as it finds expression in the various sources, appears only to reflect a deeply rooted fear or intuition that evil done in this world must be expiated in the next. Apart from the Pythagorean and Orphic sects who had certain distinctive ideas about human destiny, the eschatological beliefs of most people seem thus to stem from the basic fears and uneasiness concerning death and the hereafter common to all mankind, and they were clothed in a traditional imagery which reflected the confusion and imprecision of Greek polytheism.[110]

That the fear of death was the primary factor which inspired the eschatology of both Greek and Graeco-Roman society is revealed, with a remarkable consistency of feeling, in funerary sculpture and painting throughout some seven centuries. In this art attention was clearly concentrated upon death as a snatching or calling away from what an English poet so eloquently described as 'the warm precincts of the cheerful day'. Generally classical Greek art concentrated on the pathos of death – the deceased is shown in some quiet domestic scene, which is profoundly touching for its restrained suggestion that this gentle happiness has for ever ended.[111] In later representations the horror of the summons finds more vivid expression, sometimes in mythological imagery of the ravishing of the daughters of Leucippus or the carrying off of Ganymede.[112] Most significant of all is perhaps the depiction of the dread event in Etruscan art.[113] In tomb paintings of the later period, the deceased often appears menaced, though unconcerned, by horrific demons; most notably by Charun, whose hammer deals the death-blow or Tuchulcha, entwined with writhing snakes.[114] The terror of death is clearly manifest in these gruesome monsters. The fact that their victim seems to be quite unconscious of their terrible presence is surely significant: thus is symbolized the awful beyond that ever awaits the living, and to which they are suddenly summoned. For us the fact that the Etruscan artist, as indeed in a minor key did also the artists of Greece and Rome, was content to leave the matter there has a further significance. It means that they refrained from depicting the torments of Hades. Although the reason for this apparent reticence could have been fear of the magical potency that such a baleful depiction might have in a tomb, it seems more likely that it was the onset of death which was the emotional focus: judgment and expiation were the subsequent consequences of that dread and definitive event.[115]

Unsystematized and uninspired by an authoritative theology though it was, the significance of Graeco-Roman eschatology must not be underestimated. Apart from its very obvious interest as a constitutive part of the *Weltanschauung* of one of the greatest civilizations of mankind, its legacy to Christianity was important. Virgil's writings were doubtless prized not only for their seeming prophecy of the coming of Christ, but also for their eschatological imagery; and it is surely significant that Dante, the author of great mediaeval vision of the after-life, had Virgil for his guide through the awesome scenes of the Inferno.[116] The imagery of Christian eschatology will be our next subject of study; but before passing on to that, and to some degree in preparation for it, we must briefly notice one further aspect of the Graeco-Roman view of human destiny after death. Although the Greek conception of the temporal process was cyclical, the destiny of man, according to the traditional view that derived from Homer, was extended linearly, and it was definitively divided by death.[117] The *eidōlon* or shadowy relic of the individual person apparently continued to exist for ever, without change, in Hades. Under Pythagorean and Orphic influence, this conception was transformed, so that the destiny of the uninitiated soul conformed to a cyclic pattern in time. Metempsychosis meant an endless process of birth and death, interspersed with periods of reward or punishment. Initiated souls learned how to break out of this ever recurring cycle of existence in time, and return to a state of eternal bliss. The temporal process was, accordingly, conceived as unceasing, and thus differed radically from the conceptions current in the Judaeo-Christian religions, in Islam and Zoroastrianism; for these faiths envisaged a definitive end to the temporal process, and this end would be coincident with a Final Judgment, conducted by God or His representative.[118]

Additional Note on the *Psychostasia*

Reference has been made above (p. 79) to the action of Zeus in deciding the fates of Achilles and Hector, as described in the *Iliad* XX. 209–11. This action is often referred to as a *psychostasia* or weighing of souls. But, as Miss Jane Harrison pointed out long ago in her *Prolegomena*, p. 183, it is better described as a *kērostasia*, since it was the 'kēres of death' that Zeus weighed in his golden scales (cf. E. Wüst in *P.W.*,

XXIII. 2 (1957), 1442–4; L. Kretzenbacher, *Die Seelenwaage* (1958), pp. 29–36). According to Plutarch, Aeschylus wrote a play entitled the *Psychostasia*, which dealt with the determining of the fates of Achilles and Memnon. The subject is depicted in varying ways in vase-paintings and sculpture. Such presentations of a so-called *psychostasia* clearly concern the assessing of the fates of two rival heroes, and, thus, are not to be regarded as instances of a Greek conception of a *post-mortem* weighing of the souls of the dead (cf. Kretzenbacher, 30–6). There is, however, the possibility that Orphic eschatology may have included some idea of a *post-mortem psychostasia*, for in the *Katabasis* preserved in fragmentary form on *Papiro Bolognese* 3 the words χειρὶ τάλαντα appear. According to R. Turcan, in his interesting study of this *Katabasis*, 'Peut-être le poète évoquait-il ici la figure de Dikè' (*R.H.R.*, 150, p. 170).

The few sculptured representations of Kairos with a pair of scales, which now exist, seem to symbolize the determining of the right *kairos* or moment of a person's death, and are thus similar in concept to the depictions of the *kērostasia* (cf. Kretzenbacher, *op. cit.*, pp. 41–4). The conception of Nemesis is puzzling in this context. From being a personification concerned with both right and justice, and good and bad luck, in human affairs, Nemesis came progressively to be regarded as the divine Avenger of specific crimes. However, there is evidence of a popular cult of Nemesis, which seems to have equated her with Dikē ('justice'), and endowed her with a certain eschatological significance, so that the symbol of the scales was sometimes attributed to her. In Roman culture 'Aequitas' acquired something of the significance of this popular conception of Nemesis or Dikē: consequently the *libra* or scales appears as a symbol on some Roman gravestones (cf. Kretzenbacher, pp. 45–8). The fluidity of these concepts, however, serve as further evidence of the general imprecision of Greek and Roman eschatology.

5

CHRISTIANITY:
the Problem of relating a Saviour God to a Jewish Eschatology

In the Christian religion belief in the judgment of the dead has ever been basic and integral to its theology, and it has profoundly affected the Christian *Weltanschauung*, especially in the earlier ages of its history. Yet this belief, from the beginnings of the faith, has constituted a fundamental discrepancy relative to the doctrine of salvation through the death of Christ. This discrepancy is evident in the credal statements of the Church which are regularly recited by the faithful at divine worship. Thus, in the so-called Nicene Creed, which forms a traditional part of the Liturgy, the declaration is made:

> I believe ... in one Lord Jesus Christ, ... Who for us men, and for our salvation, came down from heaven, ... and was crucified for us under Pontius Pilate ... the third day he arose again according to the Scriptures, and ascended into heaven, and sitteth on the right hand of the Father. And he shall come again with glory to judge both the quick and the dead.[1]

A more detailed statement is made in the *Quicunque vult* or so-called 'Creed of Saint Athanasius':

> (Christ) suffered for our salvation: descended into hell, rose again the third day from the dead. He ascended into heaven, he sitteth on the right hand of the Father, God Almighty: from whence he shall come to judge the quick and the dead. At whose coming all men shall rise again with their bodies: and shall give account for their own works. And they that have done good shall go into life everlasting: and they that have done evil into everlasting fire.[2]

In these statements Christ appears in two different, and logically contradictory rôles, namely, as the Saviour and the Judge of mankind. Theologians have, of course, laboured to relate these rôles, as we shall presently see; but their efforts inevitably have the character of a *tour de force*, made to reconcile two radically different traditions that stem from the peculiar complex of factors out of which Christianity arose during the last decades of the first century. To understand the Christian belief in the judgment of the dead, and the curious form it has assumed in the scheme of Christian eschatology, we must examine the original situation which produced these two different conceptions of Christ.

The origins of Christianity, considered as a historical phenomenon, are inherently obscure owing to the nature of the relevant evidence, and the problem they consistitute has been bedevilled even from the first century by theological interests. The earliest documents of the faith, namely, the Epistles of Paul, present the problem in a peculiarly acute form. These Epistles are of primary importance of understanding Christianity as it existed within two decades of the crucifixion of Jesus; but on grounds of internal evidence they reveal that Paul's interpretation of the faith was then being opposed by another, which undoubtedly represented the teaching of the original community of the disciples of Jesus, located at Jerusalem.[3] That such a conflict should have occurred naturally raises many questions of basic import. To the actual teaching of Jesus itself we have, unfortunately, no direct access. The Gospels, which purport to be accounts of his life and teaching, were all written some four decades after the Crucifixion, and, although they evidently incorporate original Palestinian tradition, they represent the interpretations about Jesus current at that later period in Greek-speaking churches, outside Palestine.[4] Consequently, to trace out the earliest form of any Christian belief involves the investigation of a very complicated situation, and this is certainly so with regard to belief in the judgment of the dead.

So far as a primitive tradition concerning the message of Jesus can be discerned, it would seem to be preserved in the following verse from the earliest of the Gospels, namely, the *Gospel of Mark*: 'Jesus came into Galilee, preaching the gospel of God, and saying "The time is fulfilled, and the kingdom of God is at hand; repent, . . ."'[5] The brevity of the statement and its essentially Jewish character have the ring of an authentic memory. The message of Jesus, as here presented, is fully within the tradition of contemporary Jewish apocalyptic, and it accords well with one who was associated with the prophetic figure of John the Baptiser.[6] It proclaims an eschatological situation. The imminent advent of the kingdom of God meant, for Jews, the near approach of the catastrophic end of the existing world-order, which in turn implied the divine vindication of Israel before the nations of the world and the punishment of those nations for their oppression of the chosen people of Yahweh.[7] In other words, Jesus announced to his fellow-Jews that the Final Judgment of God was about to happen, and he urged them to prepare themselves for it by repentance. In terms of current Jewish thought, this meant repenting of past infringements of the sacred Law and complete fulfilment in the present of its requirements.[7a] By implication each Jew could by his own volition and consequent action render himself ready for membership of God's kingdom when it appeared. Although no mention is made here of a resurrection of the dead, this eschatological event was doubtless implied; for elsewhere in the Markan Gospel Jesus is represented as affirming belief in the resurrection of the dead when questioned about it by members of the sect of the Sadduceans.[8]

That the original Jewish disciples connected Jesus with the establishment of the Kingdom of God, and doubtless with all which that eschatological event implied, is clearly attested by the question which the disciples are depicted as asking the Risen Jesus just before his ascension from the Mount of Olives: 'Lord, wilt thou at this time restore the kingdom to Israel?'[9] The passage is, moreover, of further interest from our point of view, because it reveals that the disciples associated Jesus with this eschatological event. The reason for this association is, of course, well known: they identified Jesus with the promised Messiah, who would effect the salvation of Israel and judge the Gentiles according to current apocalyptic belief.[10] This identification finds its most dramatic expression in the *Gospel of Matthew*: 'But when the Son of man shall come in his glory, and all the angels with him, then shall he sit on the throne of his glory: and before him shall be gathered all the nations'.[11] This awesome scene of the Final Assize is set forth in terms of traditional Jewish apocalyptic, and we have already noticed a similar scene in the Jewish apocryphal writing known as IV *Esdras*.[12] However, in *Matthew*, after thus setting the scene of the Last Judgment in typical Jewish imagery, the whole nature of the transaction suddenly changes and becomes invested with a distinctively Christian ethos and imagery. For the verse that links the two conceptions starts with the situation envisaged by Jewish apocalyptic, but it quickly changes to a simile which has no nationalistic connotation:

Before him will be gathered all the nations, and he will separate them one from another as a shepherd separates the sheep from the goats, and he will place the sheep at his right hand, but the goats at the left. Then the King will say to those at his right hand, 'Come, O blessed of my Father, inherit the kingdom prepared for you from the foundation of the world; . . .'[13]

In the account that follows it is no longer nations that are being judged, but groups of individuals, and they are rewarded or punished according to their attitude towards the followers of Jesus. Thus, when the King rewards those on his right hand for the various acts of mercy and succour which they had done to him, and they ask in surprise how they had so ministered to him, he replies: 'Truly, I say to you, as you did it to one of the least of these my brethren, you did it to me'.[14] Similarly, when he dismisses those on his left hand 'into the eternal fire prepared for the devil and his angels', because they had done no acts of mercy to him, and they protest, he explains: 'Truly, I say to you, as you did it not to one of the least of these, you did it not to me'.[15] The narrative concludes by affirming that at this Last Judgment the eternal destinies of mankind are decreed: 'And they will go away into eternal punishment, but the righteous into eternal life'.[16]

This conception of the Last Judgment was evidently current in the Greek-speaking Jewish Christian community for which the *Gospel of Matthew* was written somewhere about AD 80. As such, it has all the appearance of being a piece of traditional Jewish apocalyptic adapted to the views of Jewish Christians. Thus, it is significant that the criterion by which individuals are adjudged worthy or not of the divine kingdom is the performance of good works for the benefit of Christ's disciples. In other words, eternal beatitude is merited by a person's moral achievements, or, conversely, damnation incurred. It is to be noted for future reference that nothing is said about the death of Christ as effecting salvation.

The Gospels give many other incidental indications of a view of human destiny which envisaged a *post-mortem* judgment where the verdict would be decided by the individual's own action or inherent nature. For example, Jesus is described as giving the drastic advice: 'If your right eye causes you to sin, pluck it out and throw it away; it is better that you lose one of your members than that your whole body be thrown into hell'.[17] The explanation attached to the Parable of the Tares is especially notable in that it provides a definite eschatological interpretation to the Parable's conclusion that the tares would be sorted out from the wheat at harvest time.[18] The tares or weeds are interpreted as the 'sons of the evil one', while the good seed means the 'sons of the kingdom'. In other words, an element of predestination is implied; for the good seed, being such by nature, is sown by the Son of man, and the weeds, likewise being naturally such, are sown by the Devil. At the harvest, which is 'the close of the age', just as weeds are collected and burned, 'the Son of man will send his angels, and they will gather out of his kingdom all causes of sin and all evildoers, and throw them into the furnace of fire; there men will weep and gnash their teeth. Then the righteous will shine like the sun in the kingdom of their Father.'[19]

The conception of the Last Judgment, which underlies all these passages, despite the variations due to Christian adaptation, clearly derives from Jewish apocalyptic tradition. It envisages the Great Assize of Yahweh which will mark the catastrophic end of the present world-order. The theme is essentially that of the final vindication of Israel or of the Elect People of God before the Gentiles, and the signal punishment of the latter for their idolatry and wicked oppression of the Chosen People. These Elect ones are vindicated and rewarded by God in virtue of their being, by birth, members of the Holy Nation; doubtless faithfulness to their Lord and obedience to His commands were also expected as the natural consequences of their unique status.[19a] Salvation or the reward of eternal beatitude was, accordingly, merited by birth and a devout life. At the Last Judgment the Messiah would preside. His rôle was primarily that of the judge of the Gentiles; he was the saviour of the righteous Elect only in the sense that his coming delivered them from the oppression of the heathen.[20]

The same conception informs the awful imagery of the *Apocalypse* or *Revelation to John*, which so profoundly influenced Christian eschatology as mediaeval art graphically attests. Thus, in the vision of the opening of the fifth seal, the prophet John interprets the divine judgment to come as the vindication and avenging of the martyrs, who long for the punishment of their oppressors: 'I saw under altar the souls of those who had been slain for the word of God ... they cried with a loud voice, "O Sovereign Lord, holy and true, how long before thou wilt judge and avenge our blood on those who dwell upon the earth?"'[21] After a cosmic cataclysm which virtually destroyed the universe, the servants of God are sealed on their foreheads, and they are significantly described as coming, to the number of one hundred and forty-four thousand, from the twelve tribes of Israel.[22] Then the prophet sees 'a great multitude which no man could number, from every nation, from all tribes and peoples and tongues, standing before the throne and before the Lamb, clothed in white robes, with palm branches in their hands'.[23] The relation of this multitude to that of those sealed out the tribes of Israel is not clear. The multitude of the white-robed is identified to John as those 'who have come out of the great tribulation; they have washed their robes and made them white in the blood of the Lamb'.[24] Their reward is to stand before the throne of God, 'and serve him day and night within his temple ... They shall hunger no more, neither thirst any more; the sun shall not strike them, nor any scorching heat. For the Lamb in the midst of the throne will be their shepherd, and he will guide them to springs of living water; and God will wipe away every tear from their eyes.'[25]

Although the symbolic figure of the Lamb is Christian, the general ethos of the vision is Jewish.[25a] At the catastrophic end of the world, the Elect of God, who had suffered for their witness to His truth, are separated out from the rest of mankind and given their reward of eternal beatitude. There is no mention of their being judged; the fact of their martyrdom, together apparently with that of their divine election, secured their everlasting bliss.

The judgment of the dead comes late in the course of the narrative of *Revelation* in its extant form.[25b] After a millennial reign of Christ, with the resurrected saints, which is followed by a period of universal strife until the Devil is thrown into a lake of fire and brimstone,[26] the general resurrection takes place, preparatory to the Final Judgment:

Then I saw a great white throne and him who sat upon it; from his presence earth and sky fled away, and no place was found for them. And I saw the dead, great and small, standing before the throne, and books were opened. Also another book was opened, which is the book of life. And the dead were judged by what was written in the books, by what they had done. And the sea gave up the dead in it, Death and Hades gave up the dead in them, and all were judged by what they had done. Then Death and Hades were thrown into the lake of fire. This is the second death, the lake of fire; and if any one's name was not found written in the book of life, he was thrown into the lake of fire.[27]

A list of the sinners who would be condemned to this ultimate torment is then given, after describing the new heaven and earth, which would succeed the former, and the new Jerusalem: 'as for the cowardly (δειλοῖς), the faithless, the polluted, as for murderers, fornicators, sorcerers, idolaters, and all liars, their lot shall be in the lake that burns with fire and brimstone, which is the second death'.[28]

The strange mixture of mythological and apocalyptic imagery, with the surprising hypostatization of Death and Hades,[29] in this narrative creates a very confused picture of the precise order and nature of the eschatological events envisaged. However, from the point of view of our special interest, it is evident that again the fundamental pattern of Jewish apocalyptic expectation is present. The end of the present world order is primarily conceived in terms of the vindication and reward of God's elect servants after a period of great tribulation. This vindication will involve the signal overthrow and punishment of the forces, both demonic and human, which had persecuted them. To this clearly defined drama there appears to be attached, without any obvious *raison d'être*, a brief statement about the destiny of the undistinguished mass of mankind. They are to be judged in the presence, apparently, of God, out of a written record of their lives. The nature of this record is obscure, and it is made doubly so by the mention of another book called the 'book of life'. So far as the nature of this latter book may be discerned from the sequel, it would appear that it was a record of those already deemed worthy of acquital, and, therefore, doubtless meriting reward. As such, the implication would be that the individual fates of men and women had previously been determined, and that the Last Judgment was in fact the publication of these already existing verdicts.[30] However that may be, what is particularly significant is that it is explicitly stated that the rest of mankind, apart from the Elect, are judged on the quality of their deeds, which means that their salvation or damnation depends entirely on their own merits or demerits. It is notable that no mention is made of salvation through the vicarious death of a divine saviour. In the *Apocalypse of John* Christ is portrayed primarily as the terrible Avenger of the Elect who have suffered in his name.

The eschatological tradition which we have been studying clearly stems from the teaching of Jesus, and it was basically patterned upon current Jewish apocalyptic belief that God would eventually vindicate Israel and punish their heathen oppressors. Jesus proclaimed this signal event to be imminent and sought to prepare his fellow-Jews for its coming. His followers, believing after his unexpected death that he was still the Messiah, thought that he would shortly return, with supernatural power and glory, to fulfil his Messianic rôle, which would include his presiding as Judge at the Great Assize of the nations, and would condemn the oppressors of his servants to eternal torment and reward those who had faithfully served him with everlasting bliss, the form of which was variously conceived.[31]

But there was also, as we have briefly noted, another interpretation of Jesus, and with it went another eschatology. Of this interpretation Paul was the protagonist. He believed that he had been specially commissioned by God to present Jesus to the Gentiles in a form that would be intelligible to them.[32] Like other Jewish Christians, Paul recognized Jesus as the Messiah of Israel, but, unlike those who formed the Mother Church of Jerusalem, he did not emphasize this aspect of Jesus to his Gentile converts. Instead, and owing doubtless to his own peculiar antecedents and psychological make-up, he saw in the death of Jesus not an unfortunate event that had unexpectedly and problematically interrupted his Messianic career, as did the Jerusalem Christians, but a divinely planned event. God, he believed, desiring to rescue mankind from their enslavement to the demonic powers which ruled the world, had sent a pre-existing divine being, whom Paul calls the 'Lord of glory', into the world to be incarnated in the person of Jesus. He did this to deceive the demonic powers. The plan was successful; for the *archontes*, to use Paul's terminology, not recognizing the true nature of their victim, crucified him, and thereby forfeited their control over men.[33] This interpretation of the Crucifixion was essentially mythological, and it was fundamentally different from the teaching of the original Christian community at Jerusalem, which included the disciples and apostles of the historical Jesus. It was an interpretation, however, that could be understood and appreciated by Gentiles, whereas the presentation of Jesus as the Jewish Messiah was both alien and offensive to them. Paul's interpretation, which he claimed had been specially revealed to him, meant in effect the presentation of Jesus as a saviour-god, who saved his devotees by his own sacrificial death.[34]

This interpretation of the death of Jesus was the key-factor in a soteriological system of a very esoteric kind. Paul saw the whole of mankind in a state of spiritual perdition, due to some original sin committed by its progenitors and the continual sinning of subsequent generations. He conceived of this perdition either in terms of mankind's enslavement to demonic powers, as we have seen, or of their being subject to the wrath of God.[35] From this dire situation men could not save themselves by their own efforts, namely, by good works. They needed a saviour to deliver them from their otherwise hopeless condition.[36] We have noticed one way in which Paul thought that this deliverance had been achieved; elsewhere in his writings he uses ideas drawn from the Jewish sacrificial cultus to describe the death of Jesus, thereby suggesting that his death had been a vicarious act of atonement, or the payment of a penalty or a ransom.[37] But, whatever the similes and metaphors used, it is clear that Paul taught that through the death of Christ alone could men and women be saved from eternal damnation, and not by their own moral effort. Moreover, he also taught that by accepting Christ as Lord and Saviour and being baptized the convert was spiritually reborn and incorporated into the Risen Christ. In his *Epistle to the Romans* Paul describes at some length, and in a most remarkable fashion, the transformation which he believed baptism effected:

> Do you not know that all of us who have been baptized into Christ Jesus were baptized into his death? We were buried therefore with him by baptism into death, so that as Christ was raised from the dead by the glory of the Father, we too might walk in newness of life. For if we have been united with him in a death like his, we shall certainly be united with him in a resurrection like his. We know that our old self was crucified with him so that the sinful body might be destroyed, and we might no longer be enslaved to sin. For he who has died is freed from sin. But if we have died with Christ, we believe that we shall also live with him. For we know that Christ being raised from the dead will never die again; death no longer has dominion over him. The death he died he died to sin, once for all, but the life he lives he lives to God. So you also must consider yourselves dead and alive to God in Christ Jesus (ζῶντας δὲ τῷ Θεῷ ἐν Χριστῷ Ἰησοῦ).[38]

The effect of the rite of baptism, according to this passage, was to initiate the neophyte into a new form of life 'in Christ Jesus'. In other words, baptism, as Paul presents it here, consists of a ritual dying and rebirth to a state of incorporated being in the divine saviour. The rite was a ritual re-enactment of the death, burial and resurrection of Christ.[39] That it was thus understood by the early Christians is evident both from the fact that the neophyte was baptized completely naked and by the submersion of the body, thereby symbolizing a complete divestment of one's former self and the acquisition of a wholly new state of being.[40]

To Paul, accordingly, the baptized Christian, by being thus regenerated and incorporated into Christ, was saved and had entered into eternal life. In other words, his ritual death had anticipated his physical death, and he had already commenced an existence of immortal beatitude while still living in his material body.[41] Such a conception inevitably caused many obvious problems, chief among which was that of post-baptismal sin. Ideally the baptized Christian, having become a new creature and incorporated into Christ, should have been immune to sin. As Paul's letters only too painfully show, this was not so. However, the problem did not then become too acute, because Christians lived in daily expectation of the return of Christ and the end of the world. Paul himself eloquently witnesses to this belief. He writes to reassure his converts in Thessalonica who were troubled by the fact that some of their number had died before Christ's Second Coming:

> For this we declare to you by the word of the Lord, that we who are alive, who are left until the coming of the Lord, shall not precede those who have fallen asleep. For the Lord himself will descend from heaven with a cry of command, with the archangel's call, and with the sound of the trumpet of God. And the dead in Christ will arise first; then we who are alive, who are left, shall be caught up together with them in the clouds to meet the Lord in the air; and so we shall always be with the Lord. Therefore, comfort one another with these words.[42]

Paul's soteriology thus, in effect, rendered the idea of a *post-mortem* judgment unnecessary, at least so far as baptized Christians were concerned; and it is difficult to see what significance it could have had relative to the rest of mankind, since they were already doomed to a state of perdition. It is true that in the course of his writings Paul makes many incidental references to the judgment of God after death, but they only indicate that, like most of his contemporaries, he generally accepted the notion of a *post-mortem* judgment and did not notice the implicit contradiction that such references constituted to the logic of his view that the baptized Christian was *in Christo*.[43] Similarly Paul had much to say about moral conduct, and he is found warning his Corinthian converts:

> Do you not know that the unrighteous will not inherit the kingdom of God? Do not be deceived; neither the immoral, nor idolaters, nor adulterers, nor homosexuals, nor thieves, nor the greedy, nor drunkards, nor revilers, nor robbers, will inherit the kingdom of God. And such were some of you. But you were washed, you were sanctified, you were justified in the name of the Lord Jesus Christ and in the Spirit of our God.[44]

Paul reasonably concluded that the Christian, by virtue of his having accepted Christ as his saviour, would live a virtuous life and manifest what he calls the fruits of the Spirit.[45] But he is urgent and uncompromising that salvation can only be won by faith in Christ, and not by the performance of good works, for sin had rendered every man guilty before God: 'since all have sinned and fall short of the glory of God, they are justified by his grace as a gift, through the redemption which is in Christ Jesus, whom God put forward as an expiation by his blood, to be received by faith'.[46]

Owing to the disappearance of the Mother Church of Jerusalem in the overthrow of the Jewish national state by the Romans in AD 70, Paul's version of Christianity became the established form of the faith.[47] Catholic Christianity, as it emerged at the beginning of the second century, was, accordingly, a salvation-religion centred on a saviour-god. This meant that eternal salvation was guaranteed to its devotees by the saving or redeeming efficacy of the sacrificial death of the saviour. This state of grace was acquired by ritual identification with Christ through baptism, which implied faith in his character and authority and acceptance of what was believed to be his teaching. However, although this Pauline evaluation of Christ thus became orthodoxy, the original Jewish Christian eschatology was also accepted and coloured the outlook of Christians. As we have seen from the evidence of both the Matthaean Gospel and the *Apocalypse of John*, it was firmly believed that Christ would shortly return with supernatural power to bring the existing world-order to a catastrophic end and to judge those who oppressed his Elect, whom he would reward for their faithfulness with everlasting felicity. These eschatological expectations were greatly excited by the Roman destruction of Jerusalem and its famous Temple in AD 70, and in the apocryphal discourse in the *Gospel of Mark* there is preserved the memory of the conviction that the Last Day was imminent. Jesus is represented as assuring his disciples that men 'will see the Son of man coming in clouds with great power and glory', and that 'he will send out his angels, and gather his elect from the four winds, from the ends of the earth to the ends of heaven'.[48] And he is depicted as further confirming this assurance: 'Truly, I say to you, this generation will not pass away before all these things take place. Heaven and earth will pass away, but my words will not pass away.'[49]

The continuing delay of the Second Coming of Christ, however, meant that the Church had gradually to adapt itself to living in a world that persisted, contrary to expectation, in existing. Already in the Lukan and Johannine Gospels there is evidence of eschatological re-interpretation. *Luke* represents Jesus, on being asked when the kingdom of God would come, as replying: 'The kingdom of God cometh not with observation: neither shall they say, lo here! or, there! for, lo, the kingdom of God is within you'.[50] According to the *Gospel of John*, which dates from the end of the first century, the advent of God's kingdom is presented in a completely spiritualized form as the giving of the Holy Spirit to the faithful.[51] This process of de-eschatologizing the primitive form of Christianity profoundly affected the whole structure and outlook of the faith, and its repercussions for the idea of the judgment of the dead were immense.[52]

First, we may briefly notice that a new conception of Christ was gradually introduced. From that of the essentially eschatological figure who was about to intervene catastrophically in the cosmic process, and gather to their eternal reward his Elect, they being already incorporated into him, Christ now began to be imagined as dwelling in heaven as the mediator between God and men. The author of the *Epistle to the Hebrews* sets forth this new conception in terms of an analogy between the intercessory office of Christ and that of the Jewish high priest; it is significant also that Christ is depicted as continuously employed in this office, and not in the rôle of the eschatological Judge:

Since then we have a great high priest who has passed through the heavens, Jesus, the Son of God, let us hold fast our confession. For we have not a high priest who is unable to sympathize with our weaknesses, but one who in every respect has been tempted as we are, yet without sinning. Let us then with confidence draw near to the throne of grace, that we may receive mercy and find grace to help in time of need . . . he holds his priesthood permanently, because he continues for ever. Consequently he is able for all time to save those who draw near to God through him, since he always lives to make intercession for them.[53]

These passages are illuminating, because they reveal that Christians were now faced with a different situation from that which Paul and other Christians of the first generation envisaged. They had to make provision for the now too evident fact that, instead of being suddenly caught up to heaven in a state of baptismal purity, successive generations of Christians would have to continue living on in the world, after their baptism, until they died. Consequently, they would be continuously subjected to temptation of various kinds, to which many would unfortunately succumb, thereby staining themselves with sin, even if only of a venial nature, after being baptized. This situation meant that the Church could no longer regard itself as the company of the Elect, awaiting the imminent coming of their Lord to take them to their eternal reward; rather it had to see itself as a divinely founded institution having the pastoral care of the faithful from their birth or baptism on to their death. Living in the midst of a pagan society and prone to temptation and sin, the faithful needed constant guidance and spiritual support. To meet such needs the Church gradually developed a sacred hierarchy and a sacramental system, as well as a discipline of penance and absolution.[54] The *Epistle to the Hebrews* incidentally reveals how far these new provisions for faith and practice had already developed:

> Therefore let us leave the elementary doctrines of Christ and go on to maturity, not laying again a foundation of repentance from dead works and of faith toward God, with instruction about ablutions, the laying on of hands, the resurrection of the dead, and eternal judgment.[55]

However, despite these adjustments and developments designed to cope with the needs of the faithful on a lifetime basis, the Church still retained the primitive eschatology, derived from Jewish apocalyptic, of a Last Day, involving the catastrophic end of the world, and the resurrection and judgment of the dead. Although the old emphasis upon the immediacy of these things was no longer made, the *Weltanschauung* of Christianity remained essentially teleological, in that it was informed by a profound sense that the whole cosmic process was the manifestation of the purpose of God, which was moving irresistibly to its *telos* or final end. Indeed, the Christian outlook grew steadily more teleological, as the Church's scholars sought to relate the career of Jesus and the founding of the Church to God's purpose as it was discerned in the Hebrew scriptures.[56]

But this retention of belief in a general resurrection of the dead and a Final Judgment inevitably involved many problems relative to the new conception of the Church's mission. One obvious problem was that of where and in what condition were the dead until the day of resurrection and judgment? For, if they had thus to wait with their eternal destiny undecided, awkward questions had to be faced: were their souls still indwelling their disintegrating bodies?; if they were not, where were they accommodated? Further, were the souls of the dead conscious or unconscious?

The situation was still further complicated because there was some scriptural evidence to support the idea of an immediate judgment after death. The *Gospel of Luke* provides two notable instances in which Jesus seems to have implied that a man's fate was decided immediately after death. Thus, at the Crucifixion the penitent thief is promised by Jesus: 'Truly, I say to you, today you will be with me in Paradise'.[57] More notable perhaps, because of its vivid imagery, is the so-called parable of Dives and Lazarus. The reversal of the fortunes of the rich man and the poor man after death clearly meant that their respective destinies were decided as soon as they died. Thus is the reward of Lazarus described, with the use of a typical Jewish metaphor: 'The poor man died and was carried by the angels to Abraham's bosom'. Similarly definitive is the fate of Dives: 'The rich man also died and was buried; and, in Hades, being in torment, . . .'[58] Their respective situations are also clearly outlined in Abraham's reply to Dives' request that Lazarus should be sent to cool his tongue as he suffered in the flame: 'Son, remember that you in your lifetime received your good things, and Lazarus in like manner evil things; but now he is comforted here, and you are in anguish. And besides all this, between us and you a great chasm has been fixed, in order that those who would pass from here to you may not be able, and none may cross from there to us.'[59] The parable is a strange one, and, despite its Jewish ethos, no parallel to it is known in Rabbinic sources.[60] Its most obvious parallel is afforded by the Egyptian story of Satmi and Senosiris, which we have noticed at some length.[61] *Luke*, it would seem, had derived it from some Jewish source; and it is, of course, not improbable that the idea of a reversal of fortune after death might have occurred independently to a Jew as it had once done to an Egyptian.

However that may be, the *Gospel of Luke* did provide scriptural warranty for belief in an immediate *post-mortem* judgment. Such a concept was obviously more natural and logical than that of a Last Judgment, for which all the dead must wait until the world came to an end. But, since the latter concept was so firmly established in Christian tradition, the acceptance of the idea that the individual would immediately be judged after death inevitably created a problem of relating such an assessment of a person's fate to the verdict that would be given at the Last Judgment.

There were, however, many factors at work which caused an effective compromise to be evolved, so that the idea of an immediate or particular judgment after death might become an article of orthodox belief without obviously contradicting the established faith in a Last Judgment of all mankind. For, apart from the need to account for the condition of the dead, from the time of each individual's demise until the day of Final Judgment, there was the natural feeling that only the saints were in a state of spiritual preparedness to go straight to heaven. The great majority of ordinary Christians, while not deserving of immediate damnation as were certain notorious sinners, were nevertheless stained by their sins and needed purification. Moreover, there was also a ready recognition that such purification should be painful, for expiation ought to be made for having sinned, even if one had subsequently repented and been forgiven. Accordingly, the belief gradually developed that, at the judgment immediately after death, there was imposed upon the dead man or woman purgatorial punishment appropriate to his or her failures. This penalty had to be borne, if needs be, to the day of Final Judgment, when the purified soul would be allowed to pass on to the Beatific Vision.[62]

The doctrine of the Immediate or Particular Judgment received Papal endorsement in the bull *Benedictus Deus* in 1336, but the conception of Purgatory had been greatly elaborated before that time.[63] The idea that fire would be the purifying element was probably suggested by I *Corinthians* iii. 13–16; whether it would be material or symbolic fire seems to have been at first uncertain; but the human mind, always prone to think in a concrete imagery, soon produced a thoroughly materialistic picture of Purgatory and the situation of those suffering there.[64] Great ingenuity was devoted to devising what were deemed to be suitable punishments for the various categories of sinners. Mediaeval literature contains many accounts of visions of the other world, in which Purgatory appears as a veritable Hell. For example, Hincmar, Archbishop of Rheims (806–82), records the visit of one Bernoldus to Purgatory, where he saw forty-one bishops, fettered and filthy, suffering alternately from cold and heat, while the king Charles the Bald, who had died in 877, was steeped in mud and eaten by worms, and others were driven by demons through flames into an awful pit of black water or immured in stone.[65] In that superb monument of mediaeval eschatology, the *Divina Commedia* of Dante, the topography of Purgatory is carefully described; it is comparted to accommodate specific groups of sinners who suffer the appropriate torments prescribed for their sins: those guilty of pride are weighed down by enormous stones; the envious, clad in sackcloth, have their eyes sewn up with iron thread; the lustful expiate their vice in fire.[66]

It would appear that the fear of Purgatory came to equal, and perhaps even to dominate, that of Hell. This was doubtless due to its more immediate prospect and to the fact that its torments really paralleled those of Hell; moreover, the Church, through its penitentiary system, which included the possibility of obtaining remission or alleviation of the pains of Purgatory, tended to emphasize this aspect of its doctrine.[67] It is significant also that the prospect of immediate judgment seems to have become so closely associated with the natural fear of death that attention became concentrated on the final moment of dying as the most fateful moment of a person's destiny. In what is probably the earliest extant Christian account of a death-bed scene this notion finds dramatic expression. The curious Coptic writing, dating from about the end of the fourth century, known as the *History of Joseph the Carpenter*, purports to be a description of the death of Joseph told by Jesus to his disciples, and it became, in its Latin translation, very popular, since it represented the ideal death-bed in terms of Christian piety: both Jesus and Mary attended the dying Joseph.[68] As the moment of death approaches, Jesus tells how he saw a troop of demons coming to the house where Joseph lay; among them was Death, Amenti (the personification of the ancient Egyptian underworld), and the Devil. They are described as being full of wrath against 'each soul, which goes forth from the body, and especially against sinners, in whom they seek the little soul belonging to them'.[69] Jesus puts this gruesome band to flight; then he implores God to send angels to accompany the soul of Joseph on its awful way until He receives it.[70] In explaining his action to his disciples, Jesus is represented as stressing a man's need in the hour of death, of divine mercy for his passage to 'the dreadful judgment-seat and the account he must render there'.[71] When the last moment had come, Jesus summons Death to do his office of separating Joseph's soul from his body. The soul is received by the archangels Michael and Gabriel in a silken cloth and conveyed to God the Father.[72]

The belief in the fateful nature of the moment of death, which is thus so graphically presented in this early writing, finds abundant expression in later literature and art.[73] Many are the depictions in mediaeval paintings of the soul, as a little naked figure, leaving the body at its last breath, beset by angels and devils who contend for its possession. Most impressive among such representations is the great fresco of Francesco Traini in the Campo Santo, Pisa, designed to portray the Triumph of Death.[74] Its significance for us lies particularly in the fact that the painting evidently had a didactic purpose, and was thus concerned to present in pictorial form an established and approved tradition. Consequently, the depiction of souls being dragged forth from the mouths of corpses by demons or angels may reasonably be interpreted as expressive of a belief that at the moment of death a person's eternal fate was already sealed.[75]

That such variety of belief could be held seems strange. But it must be remembered that in the matter of eschatological doctrine the

Church, while affirming belief in the resurrection and judgment of the dead, never attempted to define its teaching about them in the same meticulous manner in which it dealt with the dogma of the Trinity or the Nature of Christ. Consequently, as we have just seen, varieties of belief could be held which, on analysis, are found to be contradictory. However, despite such discrepancies, these beliefs powerfully affected the opinions and outlook of Christian society, and to those that we have already noted, we may add yet another.

In both the Apostles' and the Athanasian Creeds belief is affirmed that Christ 'descended into Hell'.[76] This statement does not seem to have been originally intended as an attestation of the reality of Christ's Death; it appears rather to refer to a passage in I *Peter* iii. 19ff., which states that Christ, having died, 'went and preached to the spirits in prison (τοῖς ἐν φυλακῇ πνεύμασιν), who formerly did not obey, when God's patience waited in the days of Noah, during the building of the ark, in which a few, that is, eight persons, were saved through water'. This cryptic utterance seems to imply that those who perished in the Flood and had descended into the underworld were given the benefit of hearing the gospel of Christ.[77] The reason why this privilege should have been limited to that one particular generation of all those multitudes who had died before the time of Christ is not stated, nor is it in any way apparent. However, obscure though the passage was, it seems to have caught the imagination of subsequent generations of Christians and it prompted much speculation. The line this speculation took was a natural one. Christians, taught to venerate the great figures of the Old Testament, were understandably concerned about the fate of these ancient servants of God who had lived and died long before the coming of Christ, and who had been deprived thereby of hearing his saving word. Were they to be regarded as for ever doomed to dwell in Hades because they had missed, through no fault of their own, the opportunity of everlasting beatitude? The answer was soon found by supposing that Christ, during the three days from his death to his resurrection, descended into Hades to save those saints of ancient Israel.[78] The idea of such a descent into the underworld also inspired many to speculate on what the descent of the Son of God into Hades might further mean. Doubtless mindful of the pagan legend of Herakles' rescue of Alkestis from Thanatos (Death),[79] Christian thinkers claimed that Christ overcame and fettered the ruler or rulers of Hades, variously conceived as Death or Satan.[80] In the apocryphal *Acts of Pilate*, dating perhaps from the fifth century, this victory is graphically described.

Then follows an account of the deliverance of the Old Testament heroes:

> And when they had thus said, the Saviour blessed Adam upon his forehead with the sign of the cross, and so did he also unto all the patriarchs and prophets and martyrs and forefathers. And he took them and leaped up out of hell. And as he went the holy fathers sang praises, following him and saying: Blessed is he that cometh in the name of the Lord. Unto him be the glory of all the saints.[81]

What element of judgment was involved in this transaction is not clear. The implication seems to have been that the great figures of the Old Testament deserved to be rescued from the fate that automatically befell all who had not accepted Christ. That Adam, who had committed the original sin, was reckoned among them is somewhat surprising. However, the early Christians seem to have been much concerned about the fate of Adam, as the progenitor of mankind. It was believed, according to an appropriate symbolic pattern, that the place where Adam was buried was the centre of the earth, and at this spot the cross of Christ had been set up, so that the sacrificial blood of the Saviour, percolating down through the ground, had washed the bones of Adam, thus redeeming the first of mankind.[82]

This redemption by Christ of the Old Testament heroes was really required by the Christian philosophy of history; for the happenings recorded in ancient Hebrew literature were regarded as constituting a veritable *Praeparatio Evangelica*.[83] It was, accordingly, fitting that those who had prepared the way for his incarnation should be specially enabled to enjoy the fruits of the Saviour's coming which they had foretold. But the logic of Christian soteriology, namely, that none could be saved unless he accepted Christ and was baptized, meant that all the great poets and philosophers of Greece and Rome, whose works were highly prized by Christian scholars, were doomed to everlasting torment in Hell. Since this notion was found to be intolerable, a solution was achieved by inventing a special compartment of Hell, called Limbo, to accommodate those who in ancient times had lived virtuous lives but had not known Christ. They suffered no torment, only a wistful melancholy over the unfortunate fact that the date of their birth precluded their hearing the saving truth of the Gospel and being baptized. Dante, led by Virgil who shared in this fate, met in Limbo, according to the *Divina Commedia*, all the famed figures of classical culture, such as Homer and Heraclitus, Socrates and Plato.[84] Another eschatological problem, for which special provision had to be made, was caused by the absolute emphasis laid upon baptism as an essential prerequisite of salvation. What was the fate of infants who died before baptism, for they inherited original sin, although they had committed no actual sin? While some rigorist theologians uncompromisingly assigned such unfortunates to Hell, a more tolerable solution was found by inventing a *limbus infantium*, were unbaptized children would for ever remain, deprived of the Beatific Vision but not in torment.[85]

These instances of special *post-mortem* treatment arise, as we have seen, out of conflicts between the logic of the Church's theology and feelings of justice and humanity. The adjustments which were made might have had repercussions for the doctrine of the judgment of the dead, either in its immediate or final aspect, if the issue had been pressed. However, basic though the doctrine was to the structure of Christian belief, the fact that it had never been precisely formulated meant that it continued to have a certain fluidity in content and imagery, which enabled such adjustments to be made. This factor seems to have operated also with regard to the relation between the imagery of Hell and Purgatory. As we have noticed, the torments of Purgatory came to be depicted so vividly and in such materialistic terms that they appear to differ little, except that they were temporal and not eternal, from the everlasting punishment of the damned, which they would suffer in their resurrected bodies.[86] With what apparent avidity Christians could contemplate the torments of Hell, and how ingenious and detailed they could be in imagining what were deemed appropriate tortures find remarkable expression in the so-called *Apocalypse of Peter*, which ranked next in popularity to the canonical *Apocalypse* or *Revelation of John*.

This writing, of which we unfortunately do not possess the complete text, dates from the early second century, and was already being quoted as an authoritative witness by Clement of Alexandria (*c.* 150–215).[87] It will suffice to give a few specimen passages illustrating the kind of horrors that were conceived for the damned:

And I (the Apostle Peter is speaking) saw also another place over against that one, very squalid; and it was a place of punishment, and they that were punished and the angels that punished them had their raiment dark, according to the air of the place. And some there were there hanging by their tongues; and these were they that blasphemed the way of righteousness, and under them was laid fire flaming and tormenting them . . . And there were also others, women, hanged by their hair above that mire which boiled up; and these were they that adorned themselves for adultery . . . And in another place were gravel-stones sharper than swords or any spit, heated with fire, and men and women clad in filthy rags rolled upon them in torment. And these were they that were rich and trusted in their riches, and had no pity upon orphans and widows but neglected the commandments of God ... *And* other men and women being cast down from a great rock (precipice) fell (came) to the bottom, and again were driven by them that were set over them, to go up upon the rock, and thence were cast down to the bottom and had no rest from this torment. And these were they that did defile their bodies, behaving as women: and the women that were with them were they that lay with one another as a man with a woman.[88]

Other men and women shall stand above them, naked; and their children stand over against them in a place of delight, and sigh and cry unto God because of their parents, saying: These are they that have despised and cursed and transgressed thy commandments and delivered us unto death: they have cursed the angel that formed us, and have hanged us up, and withheld from us (*or,* begrudged us) the light which thou hast given unto all creatures. And the milk of their mothers flowing from their breasts shall congeal, and from it shall come beasts devouring flesh, which shall come forth and turn and torment them for ever with their husbands, because they forsook the commandments of God and slew their children[89] ... they that slew them shall be tormented eternally, for God willeth it so ... Beside them *shall be* girls clad in darkness for a garment, and they shall be sore chastised and their flesh shall be torn in pieces. These are they that kept not their virginity until they were given in marriage, and with these torments shall they be punished, and shall feel them.[90]

And so it continues: all kinds of wickedness are catalogued, and the punishments of those who have practised them are carefully described. The torments are clearly conceived in terms of what would cause terrible and degrading suffering in living persons. That the dead could suffer thus was, of course, provided for by the doctrine of a physical resurrection at the Last Day. The eschatological importance of this doctrine was fully realized by Christian thinkers, as the following passage from the *De Testimonio Animae* of the apologist Tertullian (*c.* 160–220) shows:

we affirm that thou continuest after the consummation of life, and that thou waitest for a day of judgment, and that thou art doomed according to thy deservings either to be tormented or to be comforted, in either case eternally. For the receiving of which things we say that thy former substance must of necessity return unto thee, and the material part, and the memory of the self-same human being, both because thou canst feel nothing either evil or good without the faculties of the sensible flesh, and because there is no mode of judgment without the presentation of the actual person, who hath deserved to suffer judgment.[91]

It should be noted that there were Christians who did not share in this crudely materialistic eschatology. The great Alexandrian scholar Origen (c. 185–254) is the most notable example of them. He maintained not only that the 'resurrection of the flesh' was not to be understood as a resuscitation of the physical body, with all its sensuous faculties, but also that the fire of Hell must be thought in a figurative sense as a purifying element, and that the experience of it would be temporary. According to his doctrine of *apokatastasis*, in the end all souls, and even the demons, would be purified and reunited with God.[92] Although Origen's views greatly influenced many Eastern Christians, his eschatology, with its universalism, was rejected as unorthodox.[93] Christians generally found it easier, and, it would seem, more congenial, to believe in both a Purgatory and a Hell where sinners would suffer physically the most horrible and revolting tortures that a morbid imagination could devise.

The awful nature of the Second Coming of Christ and the Last Judgment was emphatically and continuously kept before the mind of the faithful by the Church in the West, despite the development of the doctrine of Purgatory, during the Middle Ages. Ecclesiastical art, both in sculpture and painting, have left some very impressive and eloquent monuments of this aspect of mediaeval Christianity.

Christian art in its primitive period, namely, during the fourth and fifth centuries, seems rarely to have attempted to represent the judgment of the dead. The surviving examples show a restraint of imagery and concern only for the Particular or Immediate Judgment of the soul.[94] What appears to be the earliest depiction of the Last Judgment is in the Church of St Apollinare Nuovo, Ravenna, and dates from about the beginning of the sixth century. It is, significantly, an essentially symbolical presentation. It shows, in mosaic, the seated figure of a beardless Christ, attended by two angels, separating the sheep from the goats, according to *Matthew* xxv. 31ff.[95] It has been maintained that Byzantine art preferred to direct the minds of the faithful to the Last Judgment by the symbolism of orientation: worshippers faced the east, whence Christ would come in glory, and they contemplated either an immense cross or a representation of Christ in majesty on the roof of the apse. This preference for symbolism was expressive of a reaction against Manichaeism, which vividly portrayed its eschatological beliefs, including a Last Judgment.[96]

The most notable Byzantine exception to this attitude is the great mosaic Last Judgment in the basilical Church at Torcello, near Venice. The work dates from about the twelfth century, and is partly narrative and partly symbolical in its presentation. The wall, upon which it is set, is divided into five registers of scenes. The top register shows the Descent of Christ into Hades and the rescue of the souls of the righteous who had lived before his first coming. In the next scene Christ is depicted, seated in a mandorla, attended by the Virgin Mary and John the Baptist and the Twelve Apostles. The scene next below represents the resurrection of the dead. The presence of Christ is symbolized by an empty throne, upon which are placed the Cross and the Book. Two figures, perhaps of Adam and Eve, kneel before this throne in attitudes of supplication. In the next register are shown the saved and the damned, the latter being thrust by angels into Hell, which appears in the last and bottom register complete with the naked figures or heads of the damned in the midst of flames. On the other side of the bottom register, Paradise is seen in terms of 'Abraham's bosom', into which the redeemed pass, while the figures of the Virgin, John the Baptist, and St Peter with his keys, commemorate the intercession which has assisted their passage past the divinely appointed keeper of Heaven. One other significant episode is to be noted: the company of the saved is separated from the damned by the figure of the archangel Michael, who holds a pair of scales, the balance of which two demons try to upset.[97]

The scene is clearly designed to constitute, through its several parts, a related whole of realistic and symbolic imagery, expressive of Christian eschatological belief. Although it has no known prototype in Byzantine art, it is difficult to suppose that this Torcello 'Last Judgment' is a creation *de novo*, because its constituent scenes imply a sophistication of conception that surely indicates the product of a long tradition of thought and artistic expression. Whether the assemblage of these scenes into an articulated whole was being done here for the first time, and, if so, whose was the genius responsible, cannot be answered. The problem is, moreover, made more complicated by the fact that about the same time in France, namely, the twelfth century, sculptured representations of the Last Judgment, showing a remarkable analogy, were being created at Autun, Saint-Denis, Beaulieu (Corrèze) and Conques.[98] Since that on the tympanum over the main entrance of the cathedral of Saint Lazare at Autun is one of the earliest, as well as one of the most interesting, of the many 'Dooms' (as they are conveniently called) that adorned the churches and cathedrals of mediaeval Europe, we shall examine it in some detail as representative of what might fitly be called the official conception of the Last Judgment; for the cathedral sculptors worked under ecclesiastical direction and according to an approved theological pattern.[99] Our commentary on the Autun 'Doom' will include comparative references to notable features in other examples.

The central part of the Autun tympanum is dominated by the seated figure of Christ, enclosed in a mandorla, symbolic of light and glory, and attended by angels. The gesture of his hands seems to direct the attention of the observer to the two different scenes that are being enacted on either side of him. The gesture could, however, be interpreted as one designed to reveal the wound-prints of the nails, since this is a well-established feature of other Dooms.[100] The Autun version seems to differ from the majority in not emphasizing the redeeming sufferings of Christ. It does not show the Cross and other instruments of the Passion which appear in other Dooms as the 'signs of the Son of Man' to be revealed at his Second Coming.[101] On the other hand, the dominating size of the Christ-figure, enshrined in the mandorla, creates an awe-inspiring impression of the advent of the divine Judge of mankind. The impression is further confirmed by the Latin inscription around the edge of the mandorla:

Omnia dispono solus meritos (que) corono
Quos scelus exercet me judice poena coercet.[102]

That Christ is appearing at his Second Coming is also indicated by four angels, one at each cardinal point, who sound large horns, announcing the Last Day.

The middle register of the Autun tympanum is of greater width than the other two, thus evidently to signify that the scenes depicted therein should command the attention. The figure of Christ separates these scenes, but they are clearly interrelated as a series of consequential events. The first event, which causes the others, takes place immediately to the left-hand of Christ. This event, which Gislebertus, the sculptor of the Autun tympanum, locates here, is usually placed in the central foreground of other Dooms, thus indicating its crucial character.[103] The event or happening concerned is the *psychostasia* or weighing of souls. Although necessarily depicted here as a single transaction, it was obviously intended to represent an ordeal that every human soul would have to undergo. The weighing is done by Michael the archangel, and its depiction in mediaeval representations of the Last Judgment constitutes a most remarkable and novel feature that demands special investigation, especially since it appears as the crucial transaction that decides the eternal destinies of the dead.[104]

That the idea of the weighing of souls should suddenly have become accepted into Christian eschatology, and that the supervision of so decisive a transaction should have been committed to the archangel Michael, clearly constitute a two-fold problem of considerable importance. The appearance of the idea in Christian art certainly seems to be sudden, but the way had already been prepared in literature.[104a] St

Fig. 6 Sculptured scene of the Weighing of the Soul on the Cross of Muiredach Monasterboice. See p. 231, n. 104a.

Augustine of Hippo had written that 'Good and evil actions shall be as if hanging in the scales, and if the evil preponderate the guilty shall be dragged away to hell'.[105] St John Chrysostom had used even more explicit imagery: 'In that day our actions, our words, and our thoughts will be placed in the scales, and the dip of the balance on either side will carry with it the irrevocable sentence'.[106] But the idea did not originate with these great scholars of the fourth and fifth centuries, and it is probable that it was already well established in popular Christian thought long before their time. The idea itself could have been suggested by certain passages in the Old Testament, as, for example, *Job* xxxi. 6, where Job is represented as saying: 'Let me be weighed in a just balance, and let God know my integrity!'[107] However, there appears to be a more likely line of tradition that leads back to Egypt, where the idea of the *post-mortem* weighing of the heart or the deeds of the deceased found its earliest and most graphic expression, as we have seen.

In an apocryphal work, known as the *Testament of Abraham*, which seems to have been composed in Egypt by a Jewish Christian during the second century, not only does the idea of the weighing of souls appear, but it is performed by an archangel.[108] The book takes the form of a conducted tour of the next world, arranged by the archangel Michael for the patriarch Abraham, in order to alleviate his fears about dying. In the first of the two passages which particularly concern us, Abraham sees an angel resplendent in light before a crystal table, 'who held the balances, (and) weighed (ἐζυγίαζεν) the souls; and the fiery angel, who had the fire, proved (ἐδοκίμαζεν) the souls'. To Abraham's request for an explanation Michael replies: 'These things which you see, holy Abraham, is the judgment (*krisis*) and the retribution (*antapodosis*)'.[109] The account continues: 'And behold the angel who held the soul in his hand, brought it before the Judge. And the Judge said to one of the angels who ministered to him: "Open for me that book and find for me the sins of this soul". And, having, opened the book, he found the assessment of its sins and righteous acts, and he delivered it neither to the tormentors nor to the saved, but set it in the middle (τὸ μέσον).'[110] In the other passage the angel holding the balances is identified as 'Dokiel, the archangel, the just weigher (ζυγοστάτης), and he weighs the just deeds and the sins according (ἐν) to the justice of God'.[111]

Since the judgment described in this writing is clearly conceived as a judgment of individual souls and not the Great Assize of the nations according to Jewish apocalyptic tradition, and since the archangel who supervises is particularly denominated the *dikaios zugostatēs*, thus recall-ing Anubis and his office in the Osirian judgment scene, an Egyptian derivation of this *psychostasia* appears most probable.[112] The probability is further confirmed by the fact that the *Testament of Abraham* seems to have been written in Egypt, and it is significant also that the so-called *History of Joseph the Carpenter*, an Egyptian Christian writing which we have already noticed, refers to the 'just balances' as a *post-mortem* concept requiring no explanation.[113]

In view of the familiarity of the Egyptian Christians with repre-sentations of the weighing of the heart or deeds of the dead, which were to be seen on many ancient mortuary objects, there can be little doubt that from such sources the idea was easily accepted into their eschatological imagery. The two documents with which we have been concerned, because of their evident popularity,[114] must have been in-strumental in spreading the idea among Christians outside of Egypt. And since it was an idea that could be readily grasped and graphically presented, its success was assured. Although it never seems to have been officially promulgated, the introduction of the *psychostasia* into painted and sculptured depictions of the Last Judgment on the tympana or walls of cathedrals and churches, from the twelfth century, constituted a veritable endorsement by ecclesiastical authority, despite the fact, as we shall see, that it could encourage some unorthodox ideas among the faithful.[115]

The decisive rôle accorded to the archangel Michael as the supervisor of the weighing of souls in the mediaeval Dooms is surprising, since there is no scriptural warranty for Michael's exercise of such an office. However, it is possible to trace out something of the way in which the archangel came to acquire his vital part in determining the destinies of men. Already in the *Revelation of John* Michael had acquired great eschatological status as the leader of the heavenly host that overthrows the Devil and his angels.[116] The *Epistle of Jude* also shows that Christians were familiar with the legend, recorded in the Jewish apocryphal writ-ing known as the *Assumption of Moses*, that Michael had contended with Satan for the soul of the dying Moses.[117] This suggestion thus sanctioned the belief that Michael might defend men at the awful moment of death from the attack of the Devil and his minions. It is not surprising, therefore, to find in the second century, as the so-called *History of Joseph the Carpenter* graphically shows, that Michael was imagined as receiving the soul of Joseph when it left the body, in order to convey it safely to God.[118] In the *Testament of Abraham*, as we have just noted, Michael is the guide of the patriarch in the next world; however, the archangel who does the weighing of souls is Dokiel, not Michael. How Michael came to acquire the office is not clear. What would seem to be the most likely cause was the reputation which Michael had as the champion of mankind against the Devil. Since, as we have seen, the human soul was in greatest peril from demonic seizure at the moment of death, the need of Michael's succour was greatest then.[119] But the weighing of the soul, which seems originally to have been associated with the Immediate Judgment, also constituted a terrible ordeal which was closely linked with the moment of death, and fear was evidently felt that the Devil might interfere at this critical juncture. This fear finds dramatic expression in many of the mediaeval Dooms. Thus in the Autun Doom, which has been our basic example, a fearsome demon, supported by another, attempts to pull down the beam of the scales in which a human soul is being weighed. Michael counters his action, and keeps the balance favourably inclined. This contest between the archangel and demons is featured in many representations of the weighing of the soul.[120] In other words, it would appear that the *post-mortem* weighing of the soul came to be regarded not primarily as an unequivocal assessment of the individual's moral worth, but rather as a contest between Michael and the Devil for possession of the soul – indeed, a kind of extension of the struggle that had been waged at the moment of death.

Michael thus appears not as the impartial 'weighter of souls' as was Anubis in the Osirian judgment, but as the champion of man against the Devil. In the Autun Doom Michael is depicted as a gentle figure tenderly, but effectively, caring for the soul whose fate is in jeopardy, while two other little human souls cling about his knees for protection. In later representations of the Last Judgment Michael often appears as a martial figure, in armour, who threatens the interfering demons with his lance.[121]

The *psychostasia*, which thus appears as the central transaction in many Dooms, is a truly remarkable development of mediaeval eschatology. For it seems to imply that the eternal destiny of men and women will be decided in this way at the Last Judgment, thus apparently ignoring the whole purpose of the doctrine of the Immediate or Particular Judgment and of Purgatory. This anomaly resulted perhaps from the transference of the weighing of the soul from the Immediate Judgment, to which it originally seems to have belonged according to the *Testament of Abraham*, to the Last Judgment. That the idea of such an ordeal,

Fig. 7 The Ladder of Salvation (early 12th cent.). Mural painting in the Church of Saints Peter and Paul, Chaldon, Surrey. The Ladder is an allegory of human life. In the top-left section, St Michael weighs souls; to the right Christ rescues Old Testament souls from Hell. The two lower scenes depict the torments of the damned.

though firmly established in tradition, had never been precisely formulated is evident also in the confusion manifest about the nature of the transaction itself. In most depictions a little nude figure, representing the soul, is shown in one scale-pan, while, balanced against it in the other scale-pan appears some hideous object, sometimes a demon or demonic mask.[122] In the sculptured scenes at Bourges and Amiens, instead of the soul, a chalice and the *Agnus Dei* are respectively depicted.[123] In other versions, rather illogically, a soul appears in each scale-pan.[124] Such confusion of imagery is curious; it may possibly be due to the inability of the mediaeval artists to find some easily recognizable symbol for good and evil deeds, since in the *Testament of Abraham* it is these deeds of the individual that are balanced against each other.

The position accorded to Michael in the mediaeval *psychostasia* is also strange. The archangel appears to be the arbiter of man's eternal destiny, not Christ. Such an impression was obviously not intended; but the fact that it is conveyed attests to the dangers that attend the combination of *motifs* of diverse origin and inspiration and their translation into pictorial form as a series of interrelated actions. That the idea of the weighing of the soul and of St Michael as man's champion against the Devil and his hosts appealed to the popular mind is proved by the fact that the *psychostasia* was often depicted as an independent event in ecclesiastical art,[125] and it forms the theme of a poem entitled the *Pelerinage de l'âme*, which was very widely read in mediaeval France.[126] However, despite this popularity, the notion never seems seriously to have threatened orthodox belief, and the fact that the *psychostasia* is absent from some important representations of the Last Judgment suggests that it was not everywhere regarded as an essential transaction.[127]

Returning to our analysis of the Autun Doom, we have next to note the two scenes which are intended to portray the consequences of the *psychostasia*. The souls that have passed that test depart, to the right of Christ, to their reward in Heaven. St Peter appears, key in hand, supervising the ascent of the saved into Heaven, which is represented as a large building with 'many mansions'. An angel is, delightfully, portrayed as pushing one of the redeemed up through a window of Heaven. This Romanesque 'Last Judgment' at Autun, despite its quaintly primitive presentation, is in some ways more realistic than later versions. It attempts to show Heaven as a city, probably the 'Heavenly Jerusalem', capable of accommodating the elect as an earthly city would its inhabitants.[128] In such notable Dooms as those at Bourges and Reims, which date from the thirteenth century, Heaven is represented symbolically as 'Abraham's bosom', according to the metaphor used in the *Gospel of Luke* (xvi. 22, 23). Accordingly, Abraham is depicted as a venerable seated figure, holding a number of souls in the bosom of his robe, while angels carry other souls to be deposited there.[129]

Both the mediaeval artist and writer found it more difficult to depict the joys of Heaven than the torments of Hell. This is not surprising, since spiritual beatitude is harder to conceive than the physical sufferings of the damned. Hence in all the Dooms the fate of those who pass, to the left of Christ, into Hell arrests the attention by its more lively depiction. In the Autun tympanum the placing of the *psychostasia* immediately to the left of Christ allowed little space for showing the fate of the damned. However, what is shown is sufficiently graphic. A demon, leaning out of the mouth of Hell, represented as the awful monster Leviathan, seizes two souls to drag them to torment, while another demon thrusts other unfortunates into what appears to be a back entrance to Hell.[130] In the Dooms sculptured on the walls of other cathedrals the damned are usually shown as marshalled by demons in a line and led away to Hell, within the awful depths of which others are already suffering.[131] In the many paintings of the Last Judgment the terror and torments of the damned are shown in realistic detail, the artist obviously being intent to emphasize the horror and pain of the tortures practised by demons on those who had merited the condemnation of their Maker. It was apparently believed, contrary to the view expressed by Paul and in the *Revelation of John* that Satan and his hosts would be finally overthrown and destroyed, that Hell would be manned by a brood of demonic monsters who would take a truly fiendish delight in torturing the damned.[132]

In the bottom register of the Autun tympanum the resurrection of the dead is portrayed. According to the Latin inscription above the scene, it is evident that the sculptor thought that at their resurrection the dead already knew their fates; for over the figures of the resurrected, who are portrayed immediately below the scene of the reward of the just, the inscription reads: '*Quisque resurget ita quem non trahit impia vita et lucebit ei sine fine lucerna diei*'.[133] Above those resurrected to damnation the minatory words appear: '*Terreat hic terror quos terreus allegat error, Nam fore sic verum notat hic horror specierum*'.[134] The resurrected are shown as divided into two groups by an armed angel, doubtless reminiscent of the cherubim, with flaming sword, which kept Adam and Eve from the Garden of Eden.[135]

This division between the saved and the damned as they rise from their graves is not typical of the Dooms, although it does occur in a number of paintings of the Last Judgment.[136] Such a division then would, of course, render the *psychostasia* meaningless. The fact that two such different notions of the way in which the fate of individuals would be decided at the Last Day were current further illustrates the fluidity of imagery which still prevailed in Christian eschatology, despite the great concern of the Church to keep the faithful ever mindful of their latter end. It is also interesting to note in this context that the idea, so impressively presented in the *Revelation of John*, that the dead would be judged according to written records of their lives, is not represented in these mediaeval Dooms. It occurs in the famous hymn *Dies Irae*, as we shall see;[137] its absence in sculptured and painted conceptions of the Last Day may possibly be due to the technical difficulty of presenting such a transaction.

The dead are generally represented as rising naked from their tombs. The matter was debated, and the ruling made that 'it will seem that they will be naked, for the reason that we shall be in the same shape as Adam was before his sin, and even in fairer shape ... there will be neither deformity nor infirmity'.[138] This conclusion is significant, and it finds expression in all the representations of the Last Day. Men and women are depicted in their physical prime, with the attributes of their sex;[139] no aged person or child appears among them.[139a] Sometimes rank is indicated: kings by wearing crowns, bishops by mitres, clerics by the tonsure, and pilgrims by scrips adorned by cross or scallop shell.[140] In some Dooms the saved are clothed, while the damned remain nude.[141]

Among various attendant figures, the Autun tympanum shows the Virgin Mary seated on the right of Christ, with John the Baptist standing below. Their postures have no obvious significance. In representing them thus, Gislebertus, the Autun sculptor, did not reproduce a notable feature that occurs in most other mediaeval representations of the Last Judgment. In these the Virgin and John the Baptist or St John the Divine appear standing or kneeling on either side of Christ in attitudes of intercession.[142] The idea, portrayed thereby, is known as the *Deisis* or Intercession, and it constituted an important feature in the pattern of *motifs* that made up the conception of the Last Judgment.[143] These two holy persons were believed to intercede with Christ, conceived as the stern Judge, for erring humanity. Owing to the great exaltation of the Virgin Mary in mediaeval Christian thought and devotion, she became the intercessor *par excellence*, on whom the hopes of sinners were set.

Regarding her as more approachable and tender than her divine Son, it was thought that Mary might soften his righteous wrath towards sinners. She is sometimes represented as baring her breasts to invoke his compassion.[144] In a French poem of the fourteenth century entitled *L'Advocacie Nostre-Dame* her plea is made to Christ:

> Beau fils regarde les mamelles
> De quoy aleitier te souloie
> Et ces mains dont bien te savoie
> Souef remuer et berchier!
> Ainsi la douce Virge sainte
> Fesoit à son Filz sa complainte,
> Comm'mère qui enfant doctrine
> En demonstrant li sa poytrine.[145]

Many were the Dooms, in either sculptured or painted form, in many lands of mediaeval Christendom. Those that survive vary greatly in size and artistic quality, from the superb sculptured versions which adorn the great French cathedrals to the crudely executed paintings found in village churches of England.[146] But the same purpose and spirit inspires them all, namely, to keep Christians ever mindful of the awful Judgment of God which they must inevitably face some day – that terrible Last Day which God would finally determine. The same note of sombre foreboding was struck in the verses of the *Dies Irae*, the thirteenth-century hymn which the Church ordered to be recited at Masses for the dead and on All Souls Day.[147] Although much of the austerity of the original Latin is lost in translation, the rendering of W. J. Irons, which is still used in Anglican worship, conveys something of the atmosphere of the original:

> Day of wrath and doom impending,
> David's word with Sibyl's blending!
> Heaven and earth in ashes ending!
> O, what fear man's bosom rendeth,
> When from heaven the Judge descendeth,
> On whose sentence all dependeth!
>
> Wondrous sound the trumpet flingeth,
> Through earth's sepulchres it ringeth,
> All before the throne it bringeth.
> Death is struck, and nature quaking,
> All creation is awaking,
> To its Judge an answer making.

Lo! the book exactly worded,
Wherein all hath been recorded;
Thence shall judgment be awarded.
When the Judge his seat attaineth,
And each hidden deed arraigneth,
Nothing unavenged remaineth.
What shall I, frail man, be pleading?
Who for me by interceding,
When the just are mercy needing?

This sense of impending doom was not a sentiment that the Church alone was concerned to instill in the faithful. It was firmly established in the popular mind and constantly stimulated by folk-drama as the mediaeval miracle plays dramatically show. In England the cycles of plays staged annually by the city guilds of Chester, York and Wakefield each included one devoted to the Last Judgment.[148] The York version comprised a dialogue in which the *personae dramatis* were God, Jesus, two Apostles, three Angels, two Good Souls, two Bad Souls, and three Devils. In the final scene, before the judgment seat of Christ, the vindication of the just and the condemnation of the wicked follow the pattern of the Last Judgment in *Matthew* xxv. 31ff., where the criterion, as we previously saw, was service to Christ in the persons of his poor and helpless.[149]

Most poignant of all this popular dramatizing of·man's ultimate obligation to face divine judgment was the presentation in the famous morality play known as the *Summoning of Everyman*. Death, sent by God to summon Everyman, comes upon him suddenly as he is immersed in the business of life and forgetful of his end. He pronounces his awful summons:

On thee thou must take a long journey;
Therefore thy book of count with thee thou bring,
For turn again thou cannot by no way.
And look thou be sure of thy reckoning,
For before God thou shalt answer, and show
Thy many bad deeds, and good but a few;
How thou hast spent thy life, and in what wise,
Before the chief Lord of paradise.[150]

The play ends with its moral made urgently clear:

For after death amends may no man make,
For then mercy and pity doth him forsake.

1 (*above*) The weighing of the heart of the scribe Ani, from the *Papyrus of Ani* (see pp. 28–30).

2 (*below*) The justified Ani is led by Horus into the presence of Osiris, whom he then worships. From the *Papyrus of Ani* (see pp. 30–1).

3 The Last Judgment. A mosaic representation on the west wall of the
Cathedral of S. Maria Assunta, Torcello, dating from 12th cent.
(see pp. 118–19).

4 The Last Judgment, sculptured over the western portal of the Cathedral of St Lazarus, Autun (Bourgogne), in the 12th cent. by Gislebertus (see pp. 119ff.). The head of the Christ has subsequently been restored.

5 The Last Judgment (13th cent.), on the tympanum of the central portal of the Cathedral of Bourges. The *psychostasia* is depicted in the central register, and the Resurrection in the bottom register (see pp. 126ff., 232, n.121).

6 The Last Judgment on the Mappa Mundi (*c.* AD 1300), in Hereford Cathedral. The scene has unique interest because the *Deisis* depicts the Virgin Mary exposing her breasts in a gesture of supplication to Christ the Judge (see pp. 128–9). The Resurrection and those saved are shown to the right of Christ, and the damned to his left. The placing of the Last Judgment over this map of the world is significant of the mediaeval *Weltanschauung*.

7 The gathering of the damned into hell, from the *Commentary of St Beatus of Liebana of the Apocalypse* (Spain: 12th cent.). Rylands Latin MS. 8, fol. 196.

8 The Archangel Michael weighing souls, which are depicted here as two
identical figures weighed against each other (see p. 126). Other dead rise out
of the ground: above Michael, Christ appears with saints. From the
polyptych of Van der Weyden (15th cent.) in the Hospice de Beaune
(Bourgogne).

9 The damned are led off to the cauldron of Hell. This is one of the few Dooms in which the damned are clothed (see pp. 127, 128). Cathedral of Reims (13th cent.).

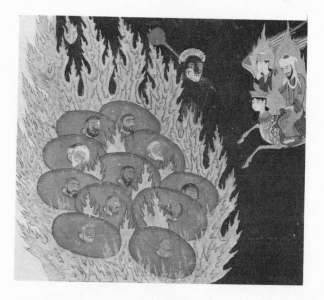

10 Islamic view of the fate of the damned (see pp. 142ff). The torment of those who had not given alms is shown here. Mediaeval Turkish manuscript (Bib. Nat. suppl. turc. 190).

11 Tibetan Buddhist depiction of the Judgment of the Dead. Before the tribunal of Yama the wicked are punished (see p. 177).

12 The Judgment of the Dead in Japanese Buddhist imagery. Emma-Ô presides at his tribunal, and the damned pass to their punishment (see p. 191).

If his reckoning be not clear when he doth come,
God will say: '*Ite, maledicti, in ignem eternum*'.
And he that hath his account whole and sound,
High in heaven he shall be crowned;
Unto which place God bring us all thither,
That we may live body and soul together.[151]

Before leaving the subject of the mediaeval portrayal of the Last Judgment, we must briefly notice what may fairly be considered as both its most stupendous and culminating achievement, although it also heralded the dawning of a new age. It is the great Last Judgment which Michelangelo painted on the end wall of the Sistine Chapel, Rome, in 1536-41. This tremendous presentation of the theme, which dominates the whole Chapel, at first sight seems far removed from the mediaeval Dooms with its writhing mass of nude figures of heroic proportions.[152] Yet the main symbolism is still there: the instruments of Christ's Passion, the Virgin (though she does not intercede), and the dominant figure of Christ, returning in power and glory as the awful Judge. The dead are also depicted rising from their graves, with a realism equal to that of some mediaeval artists,[153] and the angels sound their trumpets. But there are other features reflecting the ethos of Renaissance humanism. The damned are ferried to their doom by Charon, the boatman who carried the souls of the dead across the river Styx to the Hades of classical literature.[154] At the entrance to Hell stands Minos, the judge of the Greek underworld, entwined by snakes, awaiting the damned with a sardonic grin.[155] The angels are not winged, and the saved rise to Heaven by some inner motive force. The nude bodies of both the saved and the damned are expressive of Michelangelo's preoccupation with man in all his physical energy and strength. This mighty painting doubtless marks an epoch in the spiritual life of its creator, and it would seem he strove out of an amalgam of mediaeval faith and classical humanism to fashion an interpretation of mankind and its destiny according to the insights of his own peculiar genius. The nude Christ, despite the wounds of the Passion, is rather an Apollo, terrible in his strength and beauty, and wholly alien to the hieratic Christ of mediaeval eschatology.[156]

The Reformation profoundly affected the structure of Christian eschatology. This was caused by the Reformers' repudiation of the doctrine of Purgatory, which had become associated with the worse abuses of the mediaeval system of Indulgences – indeed it was the appearance of the papal commissioner Tetzel in the neigbourhood of Wittenberg, hawking Indulgences that stirred Martin Luther to his original act of public protest against the authority of the Pope.[157] However, despite their rejection of belief in Purgatory, the Reformers were as convinced and as zealous as the Catholics about the prospect of divine judgment, and the reality of Heaven and Hell. But, by abandoning the idea of Purgatory, they landed themselves in the very difficulties that Purgatory had been invented to solve.[158] Primarily, they were faced with the problem of accounting for the fate of soul from the moment of death to the Last Judgment. John Calvin in his first theological work, the *Psychopannychia*, sought to refute the teaching of certain Anabaptists who held that men's souls slept from the moment of death until they were resurrected in their bodies for the Final Judgment. Calvin maintained that 'The souls of the faithful, after completing their term of combat and travail, are gathered into rest, where they await with joy the fruition of their promised glory; and thus all things remain in suspense until Jesus Christ appears as the Redeemer'.[159] Since the faithful, though resting in death, were conscious and in a state of serene promise, their fates were virtually decided immediately after death; they had only to wait until the Last Judgment to enter into final glory. The wicked likewise already knew their eternal doom after death: 'they are chained up like malefactors until the time when they are dragged to the punishment that is appointed for them'.[160] Of the ultimate fate of the damned Calvin writes: 'Since no description could adequately express the horror of the vengeance of God upon the unbelievers, the torments they have to endure are symbolized to us by corporal things: namely, by darkness, weeping, gnashing of teeth, everlasting fire and worms incessantly gnawing at their hearts ...'[161]

Owing to the centrifugal tendency inherent to it, Protestantism produced varieties of eschatological belief as it did in treating other topics of doctrine. It is interesting, for example, to note the teaching of the seventeenth century German Philadelphian Johann Wilhelm Petersen, because he and his followers seem to have recognized the need for a kind of purgatory between death and the Final Judgment. They believed that, after a kind of preliminary sorting, the elect were settled in a peaceful abode where they would happily await the millennium. The rest of the dead would be severally assigned to one of three places of remedial torment, where devils would punish them. At the resurrection the non-elect would be judged by Christ and the Elect. Those who had apparently used the interval to reform themselves and whose names were found inscribed in the Book of Life would join the company of the Elect for an eternity of bliss, while those whose names were not contained in the Book were to be cast into the lake of fire and brimstone, together with Satan and his angels.[162] Petersen seems to have taken this form of ultimate torment literally, for he warns sinners of how they would be afflicted:

with sulphur and pitch . . . moths will be your beds and worms your blankets. You will lie, bound as it were hand and foot, in the darkness where there will be weeping and gnashing of teeth.[163]

While all Protestants believed in a Last Judgment and Heaven and Hell, since this belief was so patently endorsed by holy scripture, there was much conflict of opinion, however, on various issues involved in this belief. Some found the high proportion of the damned a problem,[164] others the eternal nature of the sufferings of the damned;[165] 'the worm that dieth not' also provoked much speculation, and so did the question whether hell-fire was to be understood figuratively or realistically.[166]

Since the seventeenth-century belief in the traditional eschatology has gradually declined in the Protestant churches. Humanitarian feelings steadily rendered Christians uncomfortable about the apparent contradiction between the idea of a God of love and a vengeful Judge, who finally condemns the majority of his creatures to eternal torment. It is notable also that already in the seventeenth century there was a seeming reluctance to describe the tortures of the damned in detail as earlier writers had done.[167] In time some theologians sought to ameliorate the idea of eternal damnation by theories of conditional immortality or ultimate universal salvation.[168] Perhaps one of the most significant statements of the perplexity of modern Christian theologians about the traditional eschatology of the Church is to be found in the Report of the Commission on Christian Doctrine, appointed by the Archbishops of Canterbury and York, which was published in 1938. The following extracts from the section of the Report dealing with 'Judgment, Hell, and Heaven' are especially valuable for showing the ameliorating nature and the fluidity and uncertainty of modern eschatological belief:

Christian doctrine insists upon the reality of 'abiding consequences' of every act of moral choice. When such a choice has been made, neither the world at large nor the person choosing can ever again be the same as if the choice had not been made or had been made differently.

According to the traditional scheme, the period of open choices closes with death, after which there remains only submission to the consequences of choices made during earthly life. This is, no doubt, consonant with the stern emphasis laid in the New Testament upon the decisiveness of choices made in the life on earth. On the other hand, it would not be easy to find in the New Testament a basis for definitely and rigorously excluding all hope of further opportunity; indeed, there are passages which taken by themselves are universalist in tendency, and there are some Christians who, partly because of these passages, accept the universalist position, and accordingly believe in further opportunities in the future life; . . .[169]

The Report goes on to point out that such a universalist position cannot be based upon specific scriptural declarations, but is an inference from the doctrine of the Love of God.[170] The Report continues:

But if any freedom of choice is attributed to the human will, this together with the universal facts of moral experience compels man to face the possibility that he may refuse for ever to respond to the call of Divine Love, and this possibility is prominent in the New Testament. Such a refusal must involve exclusion from the fellowship of that love. Some hold that the soul might continue for ever in that state of exclusion; others that at some point the soul which totally rejects the Divine Love must perish out of existence. Between these two we (the members of the Commission) do not feel called to judge. Both may be held compatible with Scripture; both can be supported by ethical arguments. In either case, such a soul is 'lost'.

Whether in fact any soul will suffer final loss in either sense it is not possible for man to pronounce. But if we leave this open, as we must, that must not be allowed to obscure the reality of the final and irreversible 'damnation' of evil. God's judgment upon sin is not provisional, nor His repudiation of it reversible. . . .[171] As the essence of Hell is exclusion from the fellowship of God, so the essence of Heaven is that fellowship . . .[172]

The sincerity and humanity of these statements can be readily admitted and admired; but it must be recognized that the evident reluctance to affirm uncompromisingly the inevitability of eternal damnation for the wicked contrasts notably with the rigorist attitude of the so-called 'ages of faith'. We are naturally shocked at the readiness with which earlier generations of Christians believed that the larger part of mankind would ultimately be doomed to Hell. Their attitude, however, was logical; for Christian soteriology taught that faith in Christ was essential to salvation. At the Final Assize the sheep must necessarily be separated from the goats, and the eternal fates of each must inevitably be different. If salvation could ultimately be achieved by some other means, Christ would not be the unique Saviour of mankind and the essential character of Christianity would be done away. Hence a true instinct inspired the opening declaration of the Athanasian Creed: 'Whosoever will be saved: before all things it is necessary that he hold the Catholick Faith. Which Faith except every one do keep whole and undefiled: without doubt he shall perish everlastingly.' The dilemma of modern Christian theology is that of shedding the mythology of an ancient eschatology and its rigorist exclusiveness which involves contemplating the eternal damnation of most of mankind, while maintaining faith in Christ as the unique Saviour of men.

6

ISLAM:
Judgment or Predestination

Muḥammad, as the Hebrew prophets and Jesus of Nazareth before him, came forth, primarily, to warn men of the imminent judgment of God. Addressing himself to his people, he proclaimed: 'So flee to Allah; lo, I come from Him to you as a warner clear; and set not along with Allah another god; lo I come from Him to you as a warner clear'.[1] He saw himself, the last of a long line of prophets, divinely commissioned to warn the Arabian peoples. So he speaks in the name of Allāh: 'Thus we have sent it down; an Arabic Qur'ān, and we have turned about in it some threatening; mayhap they will show piety, or it will come fresh to them as a reminder'.[2]

Like all the founders of the great religions, Muḥammad did not act *in vacuo*. He had been nurtured in Meccan society as it existed in the seventh century AD, and his message, even when allowing for his own personal genius and inspiration, was expressed in concepts and language intelligible to the people of Mecca at that time.[3] It is unfortunate, therefore, that the evidence we have of pre-Islamic relgious faith and practice in Arabia is so meagre and uncertain that it is difficult to assess the degree of Muḥammad's originality, especially with regard to eschatological belief. What is certain is that the Arabs of this period were both polytheists and fatalists.[4]

The evidence, such as it exists, of pre-Islamic religion is puzzling. On the one side, this evidence attests to a simple-minded belief that deities existed, generally attached to specific localities or tribes, who would bless their devotees, if diligent in their service, with material well-being.[5] There is no clear indication of what was expected in an after-life; but the existence of a mortuary cultus presupposes belief in some form of *post-mortem* survival, probably in the grave, where the dead would need food and drink.[6] This primitive outlook, which the archaeological data indicate, seems to be contradicted by the evidence of early poetry and tradition. According to this testimony, the Arabs, before their conversion to Islam, viewed man's life as subject to the sudden and inexplicable intervention of an impersonal Fate or Destiny. Misfortunes befell individuals without apparent rhyme or reason. The irrational process is aply described in a later saying which undoubtedly comes from the pre-Islamic era: 'What reaches you could not possibly have missed you, and what misses you could not possibly have reached you'.[7] The belief finds more eloquent expression in some lines of the poet Zuhair:

I know what To-day unfolds; what before it was Yesterday, but blind do
I stand before the knowledge To-morrow brings.
I have seen the Dooms trample men as a blind beast at random treads –
whom they smote, he died: whom they missed, he lived on to strengthless eld.[8]

Such an evaluation of human experience obviously did not envisage the fortune or length of a man's life as being determined by his moral conduct, still less did it implicate the idea of a *post-mortem* judgment. How the pre-Islamic Arabs came to conceive of such an impersonal and irrational force as having so definitive a control over mankind, despite their belief in the existence and operation of other personified deities, raises an interesting question of some significance to our subject. Of particular interest is the fact that there is evidence that, before Muḥammad's day, Time was seen by some as the decisive factor in human existence. In the *Qur'ān*, Muhammad is represented as condemning an interpretation of life which is remarkable for its appreciation of the fundamental and decisive rôle of Time: 'They say: "There is nothing but this present life of ours; we die and we live, and it is only Time which destroys us"'.[9] Such a view seems to imply a considerable degree of sophistication, and it would say much for the quality of Arabian thought at this period, if Time was conceived, in this context, as a purely abstract impersonal entity. There is some evidence, however, that Time was personified: a deity named 'Aud, a rare word for Time, was known, and regarded as responsible for the effects of old age,[10] and there is reason for thinking that some knowledge of Zurvān *darēgho-chvadhāta*, an Iranian deity who personified the destructive aspects of Time, may have reached Arabia during the period of Persian dominion.[11] The particular importance of these facts for our study lies in their suggestion that there probably existed in Arabia before the time of Muḥammad the concept of an omnipotent deity who arbitrarily decided the fortune of life for each individual, and who, if he did not cut life short, inexorably destroyed men as all-devouring Time. And the importance of this suggestion is significantly reinforced by the fact that there is some evidence that Allāh, under which name Muḥammad knew the Supreme Deity, was associated with Time.[12]

The conception of a Supreme Deity who determined the nature of the individual's life for good or ill, irrespective of moral merit, clearly could neither have prompted nor sanctioned belief in a *post-mortem* judgment. Muḥammad's essential association of Allāh with a Final Judgment on mankind raises, therefore, a problem of accounting for the origin of so notable a concept. That Muḥammad derived both the name and the idea of a Supreme Deity from existent religious tradition seems to be certain,[13] and, as we shall see, he imagined Allāh as dealing with individual persons in the same arbitrary way as Time was believed to act. His association of such a deity with a signal act of judgment, which would for ever fix the eternal condition of men in accordance with the qualities of their faith and their deeds, would thus appear to stem from some other tradition than that which he inherited from his own people. The fact that he knew something of both Judaism and Christianity, and was influenced in varying ways by each, at once suggests a most likely source of eschatological concept and imagery, and, as we shall presently see, the suggestion is confirmed by the evidence of the *Qur'ān*.[14] There is, however, another possible source of inspiration which we must notice first, since it was provided by the countryside in which Muḥammad lived. Ruins of earlier civilizations were to be seen in various parts of the land, witnessing to the overthrow of human achievements;[15] and popular legend doubtless exaggerated the wealth and grandeur of the peoples concerned, and recounted the causes of their downfall. Pre-eminent among the centres of earlier culture was Ma'rib, the capital of the Sabaean kingdom of Southern Arabia; the bursting of its great dam about AD 450 seems to have ruined the flourishing life and achievement of Saba (or Shebah).[16] Muḥammad was evidently impressed by such evidence of the overthrow of human affairs, and he connected them with Jewish traditions of divine wrath which had fallen upon evildoers, most notably upon the inhabitants of Sodom and Gomorrah who persisted in their wickedness despite the warnings of Lot.[17] Thus he represents Allāh as telling how the Sabaeans had been punished for their ingratitude and unbelief: 'But they turned away, so We sent upon them the flood of the dam and gave them instead of their two gardens, two which produced bitter fruit, and tamarisks and lote-trees a few. Thus did we recompense them for the unbelief which they showed; do We (so) recompense any but the unbelieving?'[18]

Convinced that he was chosen to lead his countrymen from the worship of other gods to the recognition of their obligation to Allāh, the One True God, Muḥammad saw himself, like the Hebrew prophets, of whom he had a strange and curious knowledge, as primarily a warner of an impending doom, greater than any that had gone before, in that it would be both catastrophic and final. The scepticism and opposition which he met probably caused him to accentuate the motif of divine retribution, and he eagerly seized, therefore, upon whatever native tradition could provide by way of illustration of the signal over-throw of the power and pride of earlier generations. In so doing, he was in effect re-interpreting existent Arabian belief in a supernatural power, sometimes personified as Time, which inexorably brought mis-fortune, decay and death to all men. In the place of such an essentially impersonal deity, he presented a supreme personal God, the creator of mankind, who would exact vengeance from His creatures who turned from Him to other gods and did not heed His chosen messenger, Muḥammad.[19]

Although the threat of Final Judgment holds so primary and essential a place in his teaching, Muḥammad was really concerned with the current situation in Mecca or Medina and not with the situation of mankind after death.[20] He threatened his countrymen with both the certainty and the imminence of divine judgment, because he sought to win them to his gospel or reconcile himself to their obduracy. Thus, in what seems to be an early Medinan oracle this apologetical concern finds expression.

The people ask thee about the Hour. Say 'Only Allah knoweth about it. How is one to know? Mayhap the Hour may be near.' Verily Allah hath cursed the unbelievers, and hath prepared for them a Blaze, in which to abide for ever, without finding friend or helper. On the Day when their faces will be turned about in the Fire, they will say: 'Oh would that we had obeyed Allah and had obeyed the messenger!' They say: 'O our Lord, we obeyed our chiefs and our great ones, and they led us astray from the way'.[20a]

In another passage of the *Qur'ān*, apparently of Meccan origin, the sequence of Muḥammad's thought in this connection is further revealed. Faced with the scornful scepticism of those who reject his mission, he takes comfort in the thought of their coming disillusionment:

Nay, thou art astonished, and they make fun,
And when they are reminded, they do not mind,

And when they see a sign, they seek to make fun,
And say: 'This is nothing but magic manifest;
When we die and become dust and bone, are we to be raised up,
And our fathers of olden time as well?'
Say: 'Yes, in abject submission'.
For it is but one scaring shout, and there they are looking (round)
They say: 'Oh, alas for us, this is the Day of Judgment'.
This is the Day of Distinction, which ye used to declare a lie
Round up those who have done wrong, and their spouses, and what they used
to worship
Apart from Allah, and guide them to the path of the Hot Place; . . .[21]

This passage indeed clearly shows how, by proclaiming the threat of the coming of divine judgment, Muḥammad was inevitably involved in a *post-mortem* eschatology. Imminent though he believed the Final Judgment to be, Muḥammad, as other prophets before and since his day, was wary about committing himself to some precise forecast of the time of the final *dénoument* of the present world-order and the hour of the Great Assize. But the realization, that many of his opponents might die before these mighty events occurred, obliged him to allow that for them, as indeed for the majority of mankind, the Judgement of God would be a *post-mortem* experience. Accordingly, he was led to presenting it as the culmination of an eschatological drama, involving a series of interrelated events of *post-mortem* significance.

In the following passage from the *Qur'ān* the conception of the Last Day and Judgment significantly follows the pattern of Judaeo-Christian apocalyptic in envisaging both a cosmic catastrophe and a resurrection of the dead as preparatory to the Judgment:

When the heaven shall be cleft,
And shall give ear to its Lord and become amendable,[22]
When the earth shall be stretched out,
Shall cast up what is in it and become empty,
And shall give ear to its Lord and become amendable,
O man, lo (then), thou art toiling heavily to thy Lord and art about to meet Him.
Then as for him who is given his book in his right hand,
He will be reckoned with easily,
And will turn back to his family well pleased;
But as for him who is given his book behind his back,
He will call for destruction,
And roast in a Blaze.[23]

The separation of the blessed and the damned, as described here by their respective reception of books in their right or left hands, is both curious and distinctive. The transaction implies that a decision has already been made about the fate of each person in terms of a written assessment of his life. The form of this assessment is somewhat obscure. According to one passage in the *Qur'ān*, as well as the distinction made by placing the book in either the right or left hand, it would seem that each person received his verdict in writing, rather after the manner in which Thoth recorded the verdict of the scales in the Osirian judgment in the Egyptian *Book of the Dead*.[24] Other passages, however, suggest that the fateful book contained a record of the individual's life; according to Surah X. 62, the assurance is given: 'Thou are not engaged in any business, nor dost thou recite any qur'ān of it, nor do ye any work, without Our being witnesses of you when you are busy in it, nor does there escape thy Lord even the weight of an atom in the earth or in the heaven, nor less than that nor greater, but it is in a clear book'.[25]

This mode of assessing the eternal state of the individual was, however, only one of several images under which Muḥammad conceived of the Final Judgment. A weighing of the souls of the dead is also visualized: 'We shall place the balances (of) justice on the day of resurrection and no soul shall be wronged, even to the extent of the weight of a grain of mustard-seed. We shall make the assessments. We shall know how to cast the account'[26] ... 'He whose balances shall be heavy will know a happy life. He whose balances shall be light shall be cast into Hell.'[27]

In other passages of the *Qur'ān* the Judgment is described in terms of the great Assize, to which all mankind are brought, in a manner also reminiscent of Judaeo-Christian tradition:

So when the trumpet shall be blown a single blast,
And the earth and the mountains shall be moved, and shattered at a single blow,
Then will happen the thing that is to happen,
The heaven shall be rent asunder, for then it will be weak,
The angels (will be) on its borders, and above them eight shall then bear the throne of thy Lord.
That day ye shall be mustered, not one of you concealed; ...[28]

Although this particular passage goes on to describe the delivery to each man of the record of his life, in the way which we have noted, other passages add further details to the picture of the awful tribunal before which mankind will be brought for judgment. Thus the ministers of the divine court are depicted as waiting in silence before Allāh as He sits in judgment: 'On the day when the spirit[29] and the angels shall stand in ranks they will not speak; except him to whomsoever the Merciful may give permission, and who says what is correct'.[30] The dead are also represented as being brought before the dread tribunal for interrogation: 'A blast is blown on the trumpet: "This is the day of the promise". Each soul comes accompanied by a driver and a witness.'[31] The intercession of others will avail nothing;[32] but this rigorist view was slightly abated later: 'How many an angel is there in the heavens whose intercession availeth nothing; except after Allah giveth permission to whom He pleaseth, and consenteth!'[33]

The consequences of acquital or condemnation are graphically described in many parts of the *Qur'ān*. Thus Muḥammad encourages the faithful with Allāh's promise of future bliss:

But these who have believed and done the works of righteousness – verily We (*scl.* Allāh) do not allow to go lost the reward of any who do well in deed. For these are gardens of Eden, with the rivers flowing beneath them, in which they will be adorned with bracelets of gold, and wear green garments of satin and brocade, reclining therein on couches; a good reward and a good place to lie in![34]

The material delights of the blessed, conceived doubtless in terms of what was imagined by the Meccans to be delectable living, is further described according to masculine taste:

Except the servants of Allah single-hearted. For them is a provision assigned, of fruits; while they are seated in honour, in gardens of Delight, on couches, facing each other, and there is passed round among them a cup of (wine) from a spring, white, a pleasure to those who drink, in which there is no deprivation (of the senses), nor do they therefrom become intoxicated. With them are damsels (i.e. *houris*) restrained in glance, wide-eyed, as if they were eggs (or pearls), well-guarded.[35]

Equally vivid and concrete are the descriptions of the damned in Gehenna:

as for them who have disbelieved, garments of fire have been cut out for them, while from above their heads is poured hot (water), by which what is in their bellies and their skins are melted, and for them are crooks of iron. Every time that for very anguish they wish to get out of it, they are thrust back into it, and (to them it is said): 'Taste the punishment of the Burning'.[36]

So intent does Muḥammad seem to have been to show his hearers that the punishment of the wicked would be unceasing that he even anticipated the objection that such punishment would soon utterly destroy their bodies. Accordingly he represents Allāh giving assurance on this point:

> Verily those who have disbelieved Our signs, We shall roast in fire. Whenever their skins are cooked to a turn, We shall substitute new skins for them, that they may feel the punishment; verily, Allah is sublime, wise.[37]

Muḥammad's eschatology, as we have seen, necessarily presupposed a physical resurrection of the dead. Since there is no evidence of such a belief in pre-Islamic Arabia, Muḥammad undoubtedly derived the notion from either Judaism or Christianity.[37a] It is evident that it was greeted with sceptical mockery by his countrymen. Some verses of the *Qur'ān* recall their scornful rejection:

> They used to say:
> 'When we have died and become dust and bones, are we verily to be raised again?
> And also our fathers of former generations?'
> Say: 'Verily the former generations and the later
> Are surely going to be brought together to the meeting-place of a day appointed.
> Then ye, O ye erring ones who count false,
> Will assuredly eat of a tree of zaqqūm,
> And fill with it your bellies
> And then drink down upon it hot water,
> Drinking as drinks the (camel) crazy with thirst.'
> This will be their reception-feast on the Day of Judgment.[38]

Muḥammad doubtless found himself faced, as Jewish and Christian thinkers have been faced, with the problem of what would be the condition of the dead from the time of their demise until the Day of Judgment. Some hint of Muḥammad's mind on the question seems to be preserved in Surah XX. 102–4. Allāh speaks:

> On the day when the trumpet shall be blown, – and We shall round up the sinners that day blue – [38a]
> They will mutter among themselves: 'Ye have only remained a ten-days'.
> We know best what they will say; the most exemplary of them religiously will say: 'Ye have only remained a day'.[39]

A similar view appears to find expression in the conclusion of the curious story of the Seven Sleepers:

> Thus We raised them up, that they might question among themselves; one of them said: 'How long have ye remained?' they said: 'We have remained a

day, or part of a day'. They said: 'Your Lord knoweth best how long ye have remained; . . .'⁴⁰

The idea which seems implicit in these passages is that, at the Resurrection, the dead will have no knowledge of the time which has elapsed since dying; in fact, they will think that they have just awakened from a deep sleep. It is possible, therefore, that Muḥammad believed that at death the individual lapsed into a state of complete unconsciousness, unaware of the decay of his body, and that from this state he would be suddenly awakened by the trumpet heralding the Last Judgment.⁴¹

In terms of strict logic, Muḥammad's doctrine of God conflicts with the fundamental emphasis which he laid upon the Final Judgment. That each human being would ultimately have to account to God for his conduct, and that his eternal destiny would depend upon God's assessment of that conduct, logically presupposes that each person is essentially free to choose how he or she should behave. In other words, divine judgment implies human free will. However, Muḥammad presented Allāh's power and knowledge as so absolute that each individual is predestinated to salvation or damnation. A catena of Quranic passages can be cited in which Allāh is represented as declaring that He alone determines the destinies of men. Thus, to give but two examples: 'Allah leadeth astray whom He willeth and guideth whom he willeth. So let not thy soul waste itself in sighs because of them; verily Allan knoweth what they do';⁴² 'If We (*scl.* Allāh) willed, We should cause to come to every soul its guidance; but true is the saying of Mine, "Assuredly I shall fill Gehenna, with jinn and men together" '.⁴³

In this matter, Muḥammad, like many other prophets, was surely the victim of his own spiritual experience and aspiration.⁴⁴ His sense of being specially chosen by Allāh to reveal His will to the peoples of Arabia profoundly convinced him of the inscrutable nature of the purpose of Allāh, and this conviction went to reinforce his inherited conception of a supreme deity, whose ways were unpredictable and whose power was absolute, a deity that some of his countrymen may have identified with a personification of Time like the Persian god Zurvān. However that may be, the very *raison d'être* of his mission presupposed that those to whom he was sent had the freedom of will to respond to or reject his message, thus determining what their fates would be at the Last Judgment. But disappointment, and a natural resentment caused by the rejection of his message, probably led Muḥammad to seek an explanation that would both justify the omniscience of Allāh and encourage himself. He found it in the doctrine of man's predestination to either eternal bliss or eternal punishment by Allāh. It was a solution already employed by the Hebrew prophets and early Christians to account for the obduracy of those who rejected the divine truth which they preached to them.[45]

Despite this radical discrepancy in the logic of his teaching, Muḥammad, by virtue of his own sense of mission and his own undoubted genius, made Islam into a living faith not only for his own countrymen, but also for the peoples of the many lands which were later subjugated by the armies of the Crescent. And basic to that faith has ever been the belief that Allāh would finally judge all men, and decree their eternal destinies for good or ill. The essential criterion of that judgment was, and still is, belief in Allāh and acceptance of His prophet.[46] The very name of the faith, i.e. Islam, connotes two ideas fundamental to belief in a Final Judgment, namely, that the individual should submit himself to God and that he has the freedom of will to make such submission.[47]

Because of its basic significance and its emotive power, belief in divine judgment after death prompted much speculation and produced some strange mortuary practices during the subsequent history of Islam. It was natural that, faced with an experience so terrifying in the hereafter, men should seek for some means of escape from it, or at least for succour in passing through the dread ordeal. Since the *Qur'ān* seemed to hint that Allāh's compassion might, on a rare occasion, cause Him to listen to an intercessor,[48] attention was given increasingly to the possibility of obtaining mercy by such means. This concern finds expression in a celebrated *hadīth* (tradition):

On the day of Resurrection, the believers, disquieted at the prospect of being held imprisoned, will say: 'Let us beseech some one to intercede for us with the Lord, so that He may let us go forth from here'. They will seek Adam and say to him: 'Thou, Adam, art the father of mankind. God made thee with His hands, he placed thee in paradise, He caused the angels to prostrate themselves before thee, and He taught thee the names of all things. Intercede, then, for us with thy Lord that He may let us go forth from here.' Adam replies: 'I am not he whom you need'. And he recalls the sin he had committed in eating of the fruit of the forbidden tree. 'Go to Noah, the first prophet whom God sent to the peoples of the earth.' They find Noah, who answers them: 'I am not the one you need', and he reminds them of the fault he committed in asking God for that he knew not. 'Seek Abraham, the Friend of God.' They find Abraham, who answers them: 'I am not he whom ye need', and he recalls the three lies which he had told. 'Find Moses, to whom God gave the Law, and with whom

He spoke face to face.' They find Moses, who replies: 'I am not he whom ye need', and he recalls the sin he committed in killing a man. 'Go to Jesus ('Isâ), the Servant of God, and His Messenger, His Spirit and His Word.' They find Jesus, who answers them: 'I am not he whom ye need. Go to Muḥammad, the man whose sins, passed and future, God has forgiven.' 'They will find me,' says Muḥammad, 'and I will ask audience of God in His dwelling-place. Audience will be given to me, and, when I see Him, I shall prostrate myself. I shall await His pleasure and He will say: "Arise, Muḥammad; speak, thou shalt be heard; intercede, it shall be granted; ask, thou shalt obtain".'[49]

This exaltation of Muḥammad as the unique intercessor between God and men was greatly elaborated in process of time, and he was even pictured as reviving the faithful with vivifying water from a mystic basin (Hawdh) that stood near to the fateful balances, on which their souls were weighed, and close also to the awful Sirât, which they had to cross.[50] This Sirât or Bridge constituted a further ordeal which faced men after death. The Qur'ân mentions a 'way of Hell' and 'a right path' for believers;[51] but the idea of a bridge that the dead must cross probably derived from Iranian eschatology, as we shall see.[52] The passage of this Bridge was itself a form of judgment. Thus, according to an early hadîth: 'The believer will pass over it, swift as sight, or as lightning, or as wind, or as the race-horse. Such will escape, safe and sound; others will be torn (by hooks), others will fall fainting into the fire of Hell, and it will continue until the last passes or is carried away.'[53] Such a proliferation of tests, as evidenced here by the weighing of souls and the crossing of the Sirât, detracts from the solemnity and the significance of a Final Assize, at which God is the Judge. However, the tendency to pile up post-mortem tests and ordeals is a natural one, being expressive of human fear when confronted with the dreadful unknown, and it occurs in the eschatologies of other religions.[54]

The traditional eschatology, and its later elaborations, did not go uncriticized among the Muslims. During the ninth century (Christian era), the rationalist movement of the Mu'tazilites criticized the anthropomorphism implicit in the traditional conception of Allâh and His operations, and the imagery of the Last Judgment was deemed to have no relation to reality.[55] However, orthodox reaction, which successfully combated such scepticism, vigorously affirmed the reality of both the Last Judgment and the various episodes connected with it, such as the delivery of the fateful books, the weighing of souls, and the crossing of the Sirât. According to Ibn Batta (d. 997), it was even necessary to believe in the trumpet of the Last Judgment.[56]

What was surely the strangest and most notable development of
Muslim faith and practice concerning judgment after death was the
belief in the so-called 'Chastisement in the Tomb'. The idea probably
derived from a verse of the *Qur'ān* (xlvii. 29): 'How then when the
angels take them away (i.e. at death), beating them before and
behind?'[57] Whether the idea represented the teaching of Muḥammad
or not,[58] it certainly presupposes a view of the condition of the dead
which differed from that which Muḥammad appears to have held, as
we have seen. Thus it was believed that a dead man retained or recov-
ered consciousness, and, after he was laid in the tomb, he was visited by
two angels, named, Munkar and Nakīr.[59] The encounter that followed
is graphically described in a writing entitled *The Pearl precious for un-
veiling knowledge of the world to come*, which is attributed to the famous
scholar Ghazāli, and seems to date from about the twelfth century:[60]

Then the two interrogators of the tomb come to the deceased, two angels,
black, who tear the earth with their teeth; they have long flowing hair which
trails the ground; their voice is like the deepest thunder, their eyes are like
lightning-flashes, their breath like violent wind. Each holds in his hand a bar of
iron such that many men together could not lift. These two angels could
demolish the greatest mountain by a single blow of that bar.

When the soul perceives the two angels, it trembles, and turns to flee and
enter into the nostrils of the corpse, which retakes the appearance which it had
during the agony of death. It is unable to move, but it both sees and hears. Then
they question him with violence and reprimand him severely. At this moment
the earth becomes for him as water; he can move himself easily, as he wishes,
and encounters no obstacles.

Then they say to him: 'Who is thy Lord? what is thy religion? what is thy
prophet? what is thy *qibla*?'[61]

The man whom God has succoured and strengthened 'by His Sure Word'
(*Qur'ān* XIV. 32), answers them: 'Who has given you authority over me? who
has sent you to me?' This is the reply made by the wise and virtuous. Then one
of the angels will say to his companion: 'He is right. Behold, we have afflicted
him enough.' Then they extend the tomb above him, giving it the form of an
immense vault, and they open for him, on his right side, a door which leads to
Paradise. Then they give him garments of silk and perfumes of Paradise, and
they cause a sweet breeze to blow on him and the repose of Paradise to enfold
him. His life's actions (personified) comes to him, in beauteous form, for converse and communion, and the tomb is filled with light.[62] The deceased thus will
continue to rejoice and enjoy himself so long as the terrestrial world endures,
until the hour of judgment comes. He knows the moment when the hour of
judgment will come, and nothing will delight him more than to see it arrive.[63]

The fate of the impious is wholly different; he is tormented in the tomb until the end of the world and the Final Judgment.

This strange belief became responsible for some macabre funerary practices. The *shahāda*, or confession of faith, was recited in the ear of the dead, who was believed to be still capable of hearing, so that he might be ready to recite it when interrogated by the two baleful angels.[64] Or, immediately after burial, a *fiqi* was employed to act as a *mulaqqin*, or tutor of the dead, and it was his duty to sit before the tomb and instruct its inmate in the right answers in preparation for the awful examination on that 'Night of Desolation'.[65]

The prospect of judgment after death has powerfully affected the thought and practice of the Muslim peoples down the ages. Besides the customs we have just noted, it has prompted many others, some reminiscent of the Christian mortuary cultus, such as invoking the intercession of saints on behalf of the dead, the *ziyāra* or visit to cemeteries, or tomb inscriptions asking for the mercy of God on the deceased.[66]

The emphasis upon faith rather than upon moral character or action, which finds expression in the *Qur'ān*, has also continued to be made. Hence Islam, perhaps even more than Christianity, and in contradistraction to ancient Egyptian religion, has made a proper faith in God, rather than moral virtue, the supreme criterion for salvation at the Last Judgment. This balance of emphasis surely stemmed from Muḥammad's original concern to win his countrymen to an exclusive acceptance of Allāh as the one true God. Moral virtue has, of course, been, and still is, highly valued, and it has naturally been regarded as a necessary concomitant of a proper faith in Allāh; but, as in Christianity the state of being *in Christo* has been regarded as essential for salvation, so in Islam a personal relationship with Allāh, which includes a proper recognition of His Prophet, has been deemed the *sine qua non* of salvation at the Final Judgment.[67]

7

IRAN:
Man's Moral Involvement in a Cosmic Struggle

In ancient Iran there emerged a religion characterized by a dualistic view of the universe, and of man's destiny within it. It conceived of life, at every level, as being a conflict between two opposing forces: good and evil, light and darkness, truth and lie. These contending principles were hypostatized as two deities, and designated by various names, some of which we shall presently notice.

This Iranian religion of dualism has become known generally as Zoroastrianism, from the name of Zarathustra or Zoroaster, its traditional founder.[1] The chronology of Zoroaster's life has been a subject of much debate among specialists in Iranian studies: the balance of opinion seems to indicate that his career is to be dated about 628–551 BC.[2] But not only is his chronology uncertain, everything connected with Zoroaster, whether it be his origin, status, career or teaching, is also invested with problems of great complexity. The fundamental cause of this situation is that the earliest Iranian writings preserved to us are some hymns known as the *Gāthās*, which purport to be compositions of Zoroaster, embodying his doctrine.[3] Now, these hymns are not only written in an archaic form of the Iranian language which is very difficult to interpret, but their contents indicate that Zoroaster was a kind of reforming prophet.[4] This means that he was reforming an earlier Iranian religious tradition, of which he is our earliest witness. In other words, we cannot be certain when studying the *Gāthās* how far the ideas expressed in them are innovations of Zoroaster or have been taken over unchanged by him. Another cause of puzzlement is that Zoroaster's teaching evidently had a profound influence upon subsequent Iranian religion, but to what extent is unknown. Consequently, when later writings present Zoroaster as proclaiming doctrines which find no expression in the *Gāthās*, it is not easy to estimate whether they derive from him or come from an earlier tradition.[5] This uncertainty, as we shall see, also extends to the idea of a *post-mortem* judgment, which assumes some rather curious forms in Iranian religion.

Having thus briefly noticed the inherent complexity of our subject, which is only too obviously reflected in the conflict of opinion evident in specialist studies of Iranian religion, our safest course, in the interests of our subject, will be to look first at what Zoroaster is recorded to have said about a *post-mortem* judgment.

Since the *Gāthās* are hymns, doubtless designed for liturgical use,[5a] deities are invoked in them and ideas are expressed without explanation. This factor, added to those already mentioned, make the meaning of any passage very puzzling at first sight, as we shall see in the following passage which is of fundamental significance for our subject:

(2) I will speak of the spirits twain at the first beginning of the world, of whom the holier thus spake to the enemy: 'Neither thought nor teachings nor wills nor beliefs nor words nor deeds nor selves nor souls of us twain agree'. (3) I will speak of that which Mazdah Ahura, the all-knowing, revealed to me first in this (earthly) life. Those of you that put not in practice this word as I think and utter it, to them shall be woe at the end of life. (4) I will speak of what is best for this life. Through Right does Mazdah know it, who created the same as father of the active Good Thought, and the daughter thereof is Piety of goodly action. Not to be deceived is the all-seeing Ahura. (5) I will speak of that which the Holiest declared to me as the word that is best for mortals to obey: he, Mazdah Ahura (said), 'they who at my bidding render him obedience, shall all attain unto Welfare and Immortality by the actions of the good Spirit'. (6) . . . By his wisdom let him teach me what is best, (7) even he whose two awards, whereof he ordains, men shall attain, whoso are living or have been or shall be. In immortality shall the soul of the righteous be joyful, in perpetuity shall be the torments of the Liars. All this doth Mazdah Ahura appoint by his Dominion.[6]

On analysis, the following situation seems to be implied in this passage. First, Zoroaster envisages the existence of two primal spirits, the one being holy or good, the other hostile or evil. In everything these spirits are essentially opposed to each other, and have been so since the beginning of the world. Next, reference is so made to Mazdah Ahura as to suggest that Zoroaster evidently regarded this being as an omniscient deity, who had created other entities described as 'Right' (*Arta* or *Aša*), 'Good Thought (*Vohu Manah*), and 'Piety' (*Ārmaiti*).[7] Mazdah Ahura is a title (it is usually given as Ahura Mazdah), meaning the 'Wise Lord', and Zoroaster implies that he had received a revelation directly from this supreme deity.[8] Thirdly, Zoroaster proclaims that those who do not conform to this revelation will be punished at the end of life, whereas those who obey will be rewarded with 'Welfare' (*Haurvatāt*) and 'Immortality' (*Ameretāt*).[9] This reward they would obtain through the actions of the 'Good Spirit' (*Spenista Mainyu*), which was apparently the better of the two primal spirits, the other being the *Angra Mainyu* or 'Evil Spirit'.[10]

An obviously complex theological situation is implied here, and the question is how far was it the invention of Zoroaster? The general opinion of specialists in Iranian studies is that Zoroaster had attempted to reform an existing Iranian religion.[11] The ancient Iranians were an Aryan or Indo-European people who had settled in the country that came to be known as Iran during the latter part of the second millennium BC.[12] Since there is reason for believing that their religious traditions were originally closely akin to those of the Aryan tribes that invaded north-western India about the same period, scholars have felt justified in using the evidence of the Vedic literature of the Aryan settlers in India to illuminate early Iranian religion, which is so obscurely documented from native sources, as we have seen.[13] Accordingly, because no deity is known under the title of Ahura Mazdah in the early records of the Indo-Iranian peoples before the references made to him in the *Gāthās*, it has been thought that Zoroaster's omniscient god is to be identified with Varuna, a deity of similar attributes who figures prominently in the *Rig-Veda*.[14] Now, this Varuna was a sky-god of ambivalent aspect, in that he had two sides to his nature, connoting light and darkness, creation and destruction. He was also closely associated with Mithra; indeed the equation Varuna-Mithra may represent this ambivalence of divine attributes.[15]

This conception of a high-god of ambivalent nature doubtless stemmed from an Aryan propensity to trace opposing aspects of natural phenomena to a single divine source. Hence the alternating rhythm, evident in the universe, of life and death, creation and destruction, light and darkness, good and evil was seen as the manifestation of the activity of one supreme deity.[16] The moral repercussions of such a conception would be obvious. Good and evil, in whatever forms of manifestations, would represent the essential pattern of reality, being equal in origin and existential status, and as such reality would have to be accepted by mankind. Moral values would thus have no ultimate supreme validity. The most that a man could hope for in a primitive society, in holding such a view, would be the possibility of obtaining for himself some measure of better fortune by the practice of magic or by winning the favour of some potent deity.[17]

So far as the achievement of Zoroaster can be evaluated, it would seem that he endeavoured to make the supreme deity, whom he named Ahura Mazdah, the author of good only. Faced with the consequent problem of accounting for the separate existence of evil, he sought a solution by positing two primal principles of good and evil, which were unceasingly in mutual conflict. How these opposing entities were related to Ahura Mazdah, seeing that they had existed from the beginning of things, is not clear.[18] It would appear that with this exaltation of Ahura Mazdah, which was in effect an attempt to establish a monotheistic creed, Zoroaster also relegated many Iranian deities to the status of *daevas* or demons,[19] while six others, doubtless of greater moral potentiality, he converted into the *Amesha Spentas*, which were impersonal spiritual entities, some of which appear in the above quoted passage of the *Gāthās*, namely, Right, Good Thought, Piety, Welfare, and Immortality.[20]

Although the relationship between Ahura Mazdah and the two primal spirits is not made clear, Zoroaster left no doubt that men were faced with the personal decision of aligning themselves on one side or the other of these contending cosmic forces. This choice was implied in the passage quoted, and it is clearly enunciated in the following verses from another Gathic oracle:

(2) Hear with your ears the best things; look upon them with clear-seeing thought, for decision between two beliefs, each man for himself before the Great Consummation, bethinking you that it be accomplished to our pleasure. (3) Now the two primal spirits, who revealed themselves in vision as Twins, are the Better and the Bad in thought and word and action. And between these two the wise once chose aright, the foolish not so. (4) And when these twain spirits came together in the beginning, they established Life and Notlife, and that at the last the Worst Existence shall be to the followers of the Lie, but the Best Thought to him that follows Right. (5) Of these twain spirits he that followed the Lie chose doing the worse things; the holiest spirit chose Right, he that clothes him with the massy heavens as a garment. So likewise they that are fain to please Ahura Mazdah by dutiful actions.[21]

Although he thus regarded life in this world as involving each person in the struggle between the forces of good and evil, Zoroaster was by no means ascetical or this world-denying in his outlook. However, it is evident that he was sufficiently realistic to acknowledge that devoted service to Ahura Mazdah did not necessarily earn its reward here, nor were the followers of the Lie demonstrably punished in this life.[22] Accordingly, he proclaims that retribution will come after death. This retribution is set forth in a curious form, and the fact that it is so odd and yet is not explained suggests that the concept was already known to Zoroaster's audience. The following passages make this plain:

> Whoso, man or woman, doeth what thou, Mazdah Ahura, knowest as best in life, as destiny for what is Right (give him) the Dominion through good Thought. And those whom I impel to your adoration, with all these will I cross the Bridge of the Separator. (11) By their dominion the Karapans and Kavis accustomed mankind to evil actions, so as to destroy Life. Their own soul and their own self shall torment them when they come where the Bridge of the Separator is, to all time dwellers in the House of the Lie.[23]

> The minion of the sorcerer prince, at the Bridge of the Winter,
> Offended Zarathustra Spitama by refusing him shelter,
> Him and his beasts of burden who came to him shivering with cold.
> Thus does the evil one's conscience forfeit the assurance of the straight (path);
> His Soul (?) stripped naked (?) shall be afraid at the Bridge of the Separator,
> Having strayed from the path of Righteousness
> By its deeds and those of his tongue.[24]

The second passage appears to record some incident in Zoroaster's career, involving the transit of a bridge, which evokes the thought of a mysterious 'Bridge of the Separator', as constituting a future form of retribution for the uncharitable attitude shown to the prophet at the moment of his need.[24a] The preceding passage reveals that this 'Bridge of the Separator' had also to be crossed at some time by worshippers of Ahura Mazdah, as well as, presumably, by those who had not served the Wise Lord and who had associated themselves with the Evil Spirit or Lie.

This Bridge of the Separator, the *Činvato paratu*, obviously had an eschatological significance, in that it presents an ordeal which men and women will experience after death. As we shall presently see, it figures as such in later Avestan literature, becoming a veritable 'Brig o' Dread'.[25] The two passages quoted reveal nothing about the identity of the 'Separator'. This fortunately is indicated elsewhere by implication. Zoroaster assures a friend: 'Where in Paradise, O Jamaspa Hvogva, I will recount your wrongs ... before him who shall separate (*vicinaot*) the wise and the unwise through Right, his prudent counsellor, even Mazdah Ahura'.[26] It would follow, therefore, that Ahura Mazdah was the 'Separator' at this ominous Bridge, and we may note that according to a later writing known as the *Vedevdât* the Bridge had been made by this supreme deity.[27]

As we have already noticed, Zoroaster speaks of the Bridge of the Separator as something well known to his audience. Accordingly, it would seem that in the religious tradition, which Zoroaster inherited and sought to reform, the notion already existed of a *post-mortem* ordeal connected with the crossing of a bridge. This ordeal had the effect of separating the dead in some unspecified way. From the various remarks and references of Zoroaster, in the passages concerned, somewhat contradictory inferences can be drawn about the form or nature of this process of separation. For example, by saying that he, Zoroaster, would accompany the devotees of Ahura Mazdah across the Bridge, the suggestion is given that the crossing without his presence would be fraught with peril even for the righteous. What this peril would be is not indicated, and nothing is said of what the Bridge spanned – the obvious inference is that the dead were in danger, during their transit, of falling off into whatever lay below.[28] In the light of these inferences, what is said about the experience of those whom Zoroaster obviously regards as opponents to his teaching is puzzling. At the Bridge, not apparently in the crossing of it, they would be tormented by their 'own soul and their own self'. In addition to these conflicting notions, Zoroaster's apparent identification of Ahura Mazdah as the 'Separator' constitutes a further difficulty; for the identification suggests that it is a divine Judge or 'Requiter' who deals with the dead on this fateful occasion, and that the Bridge derives its significance from him and not any specific function of its own.

We are, consequently, faced with the question of what form this idea of a *post-mortem* ordeal connected with a bridge might have had before the time of Zoroaster, and, further, was it originally associated with Ahura Mazdah in such a manner that it constituted a moral test? Some clue to its earlier form is perhaps to be found in a suggestion of Professor R. C. Zaehner. He points out that the only definite identification of the *Činvant*, i.e. the 'Separator' or 'Avenger', apparently to be found in Persian literature occurs in the Pahlavi *Rivāyats*, and that it is a deity called Rashnu who is so identified.[29] Now, as we shall see presently, Rashnu is presented in later documents as the just judge who weighs the souls of the dead, and he is, moreover, associated with the deities of Mithra and Sraosha.[30] By virtue of Rashnu's being the 'Separator' or or 'Avenger', Professor Zaehner thinks that in the pre-Zoroastrian religion Rashnu was 'the "sinister" aspect of Mithra', just as Sraosha was 'the "dexter" or propitious'.[31] The point of this recondite conclusion for us is that before Zoroaster apparently identified Ahura

Mazdah with the 'Separator', another deity, who was really an aspect of Mithra, had this office. In this connection we may also note that there is a complete absence of reference in the *Gāthās* to Mithra, which seems particularly significant when Mithra's peculiar association with Varuna is recalled, together with the possibility that Zoroaster's Ahura Mazdah derives from Varuna.[32]

From the evidence of these complicated factors it would seem reasonable to conclude that, before the time of Zoroaster, the Iranians believed that the dead were faced with the ordeal of crossing a bridge which was controlled by a baleful deity. The idea of such a *post-mortem* ordeal occurs in many religions, and it generally concerns the ritual preparation of the dead for entering the land of the dead. We may instance two examples: in ancient Egypt it was believed that every dead person would encounter perils *en route* for the next world which he could only safely pass, if he knew the correct formula; according to ancient Greek belief, the unburied dead could not cross the river Styx and were left to wander forlorn between the land of the living and that of the dead.[33] The Bridge of the Separator might, accordingly, in its original conception, have constituted a test of ritual preparedness; there is indeed some support for this conclusion in later Persian ritual practice which was designed to secure one's place in the next world.[34] If our inference is sound, it would, therefore, seem that Zoroaster adapted this ancient belief so that the crossing of Chinvat Bridge became a test of a person's allegiance to Ahura Mazdah. The emphasis here, we must note, as in all Zoroaster's utterances, is essentially on correct faith, not on moral conduct.[35] This is not surprising, and, as we have seen, the same stress is laid in many other religions; however, since allegiance to Ahura Mazdah meant placing oneself on the side of the good, Zoroaster's interpretation of this *post-mortem* ordeal made it virtually a moral judgment of the dead.

We may note in passing that Zoroaster's eschatology envisages some form of man's survival of death such that there would be a continuity of consciousness between his *pre-mortem* and *post-mortem* states of being; otherwise the judgment at the Chinvat Bridge would have no real meaning. Since Zoroaster seems to have been rather a prophet, and not a theologian or philosopher, his utterances contain no statements about the metaphysical ideas implied in them. However, he does use two terms, namely, *urvan* and *daēnā*, in connection with the individual's experience after death which attest that he regarded human nature as composite, and that he differentiated the two entities so designated from the *tānū* (body). The *urvan* seems to denote the inner essential self which is usually referred to in English by the word 'soul'.[36] The *daēnā* is much more difficult to define, particularly since its etymology is so obscure. It seems to be used often in the sense of our word 'conscience'.[37] The French Iranian scholar, M. Molé has recently argued at length that *daēnā* is more appropriately translated 'Religion'[38] – the difference implied here between 'conscience' and 'Religion' is perhaps more apparent than real, because 'Religion' in this context connotes a complex of personal response to religious truths and ethical values that might well be designated 'conscience'.

This discussion of Zoroaster's view of the constitution of human nature has also been necessary for considering another aspect of his eschatology. The soul's experience at the Bridge of the Separator is in effect a judgment that occurs immediately after death, and it would normally be understood as determining its fate for all eternity; indeed the eternal significance of the verdict then given seems to be clearly stated in two of Zoroaster's utterances.[39] It is surprising, therefore, to find him talking about another test, by molten metal, which the dead would apparently have to endure some time subsequent to the ordeal of the Chinvat Bridge. As the following two passages indicate, the idea of such a test must also have been familiar to his audience, since he apparently felt that no explanation of such an extraordinary notion was required of him:

> And to him (i.e. man or mankind) came Dominion, Good Thought, and Right; and Piety gave continued life to their bodies and indestructibility, so that by thy retribution (i.e. Ahura Mazdah's) through the (molten) metal he may gain the prize over these things.[40]

> What recompense thou wilt give to the two parties by thy red Fire, by the molten Metal, give us a sign of it in our souls – even the bringing of ruin to the Liar, of blessing to the Righteous.[41]

The fact that these passages presuppose familiarity with some eschatological notion concerning fire and molten metal permits us to assume that Zoroaster envisaged some future cosmic catastrophe involving the destruction of the world by fire, an idea which finds expression in other ancient Near Eastern sources.[42] It allows us also to relate Zoroaster's cryptic utterances to the belief, set forth more explicitly in later Persian writings, that at the end of the world all mankind must pass through an ordeal of molten metal.[43]

It would seem, accordingly, that Zoroaster contemplated two forms of *post-mortem* judgment, the one immediately after death and the other at the end of the world, in a way strikingly similar to the pattern of Christian eschatology which we have studied.[44] Since the final ordeal, namely, that of the molten metal, would seem to imply that the dead suffered physical burning, we have to consider the possibility that Zoroaster also believed in a future physical resurrection of the dead. Such a belief formed part of later Iranian eschatology,[45] so that it would be reasonable to suppose that it had been taught by Zoroaster. It is possible that some evidence of this is contained in the former of the passages quoted above. For the statement that 'Piety gave continued life to their bodies and indestructibility' could be interpreted to mean that the bodies of the dead were in some way preserved in readiness for the ultimate ordeal of the molten metal. How Piety, i.e. *Ārmaiti*, was to effect this preservation is not clear until it is realized that this Zoroastrian abstract entity was probably derived from an earlier concept of the nourishing quality of the earth, personified in terms of the divine Earth Mother.[46] Burial seems to have been the original Iranian means of disposing of the dead before the adoption of the Mazdean custom of exposure.[47] It is possible, therefore, that in this obscure statement Zoroaster was alluding to a folk-belief that the Earth Mother would preserve the dead buried within her until they were reborn or resurrected.[48]

From this obscure and disparate evidence it would seem, accordingly, that Zoroaster attempted to reform the dualistic tradition of Iranian religion, which inspired an amoral magical attitude to life, by exalting Ahura Mazdah as the supreme deity and by calling on his fellow-men to align themselves with the Wise Lord in the struggle against evil, hypostatized in the *Druj* or the *Angra Mainyu*. This identification of the supreme deity with good, and the insistence that men should give whole-hearted allegiance to him, resulted in Zoroaster's reinterpretation of the traditional eschatology in terms of moral judgments or tests of the dead. Consequently, Zoroastrianism became characterized by a *Weltanschauung* that envisaged the world as a battle-ground between the forces of good and evil. In this immense conflict men had to take sides, and their choice would decisively affect their destiny after death; for they would face retribution both immediately after death and at the end of the world.

It is not our task here to attempt to trace out the obscure and complicated development of Iranian religion after Zoroaster's reform down its last phase, before it was virtually extinguished in its homeland by

Islam.[49] It will be sufficient to note that many of the ancient deities, which Zoroaster sought to ignore or suppress, found their way into the later form of Zoroastrianism;[50] moreover, speculation about the relation of Ahura Mazdah or Ohrmazd, as the deity was subsequently called, to the primal spirits of good and evil led to much theological controversy, owing to the various solutions which were offered.[51] Fortunately for our purposes the developments in eschatology appear less complicated, and they produced one very remarkable conception of *post-mortem* judgment.

The most complete, as well as the most vivid, presentation of the judgment of the soul after death is given in the *Dâstân-i Mēnōk-i Krat*, a Pahlavi or Middle Persian writing dating from about the ninth century AD, but obviously embodying an earlier tradition.[52] It is quoted here in full in Professor R. C. Zaehner's translation, because only thereby can the true ethos of the Iranian conception of what awaited the deceased at death be adequately appreciated:

For three days and nights the soul sits beside the head-stone (of the slab on which) the body (is laid). On the fourth day at dawn, accompanied by Sraosha, the blessed, the good Vay, mighty Vahrām (Verethraghna), and opposed by the Loosener of Bones, the evil Vay, and the demons Frēhzisht and Vizisht, and pursued by the malevolence of the evildoer Wrath who bears a bloody spear, (the soul) will come to the Bridge of the Requiter, lofty and dreadful, for thither must saved and damned alike proceed. There does many an enemy lie in wait. (These will it have to face) the malevolence of Wrath who wields the bloody spear and the Loosener of Bones who swallows up all creatures and knows no sating, but Mithra, Sraosha, and Rashnu will mediate (on its behalf); and just Rashnu will weigh (its deeds). He lets his spiritual scales incline to neither side, neither for the saved nor yet for the damned, nor yet for kings and princes. Not for a hair's breadth will he diverge, for he is no respecter (of persons). He deals out impartial justice both to kings and princes and to the meanest of men.

And when the soul of the saved passes over that bridge, the bridge appears to it to be one parasang broad; and the soul of the saved passes on accompanied by the blessed Sraosha. And his own good deeds come to meet him in the form of a maiden more beautiful and fair than any girl on earth. And the soul of the saved says: 'Who art thou? for never did I see on earth a maiden more beautiful and fair than thee'. Then will that form of a maiden make answer and say: 'I am no maiden, but thine own good deeds, young sir, whose thoughts, words, deeds and religion are all good. For when on earth thou didst see one who offered sacrifice to the demons, then didst thou sit (apart) and offer sacrifice to the gods. And when thou didst see a man commit violence, and rapine, afflict good men and treat them with contumely, or hoard up goods wrongfully obtained, then didst thou refrain from visiting creatures with violence and rapine of thine own; (rather) wast thou considerate to good men; thou didst welcome them and offer them hospitality and give them alms, both to him who came from near and to him who came from afar. Thy wealth thou didst store up in accordance with righteousness. And when thou didst see one who passed false judgment, taking bribes and bearing false witness, then didst thou sit down and speak witness right and true. I am thy good thoughts, good words, and good deeds which thou didst think, speak, and do. For though I was venerable (from the first), thou hast made me yet more venerable; and though I was honourable (from the first), thou hast made me yet more honourable; and though I was endowed with dignity (*khwarr*), thou hast confirmed on me yet greater dignity.'

And when (the soul) departs from thence, then is a fragrant breeze wafted towards it, more fragrant than any perfume. Then does the soul of the saved ask Sraosha: 'What breeze is this the like of which in fragrance I never smelt on earth?' Then does blessed Sraosha make answer to the soul of the saved (and say): 'This is a breeze from heaven; hence it is so fragrant'.

Then with its first step it treads (the heaven of) good thoughts, with its second (the heaven of) good words, with its third (the heaven of) good deeds; and with its fourth step it attains to the Endless Light where all is bliss. And all the gods and the Bounteous Immortals come to greet him and ask him how he has fared (saying): 'How was thy passage from those transient, fearful worlds replete with evil to these worlds which do not pass away and in which there is no adversary, young sir, whose thoughts, words, deeds, and religion are good?'

Then Ohrmazd the Lord says: 'Ask him not how he has fared; for he has been separated from his beloved body and travelled on the fearful road'. Then do they serve him with the sweetest of foods, even the butter of early spring, so that the soul may take its ease after three nights of terror at the Bridge which the Loosener of Bones and the other demons brought upon him; and he is sat upon a throne everywhere adorned.

For it is revealed that the sweetest of foods offered by the spiritual gods to a man or a woman after the parting of consciousness and body is the butter of early spring, and that they seat him on a throne everywhere adorned. And for ever and ever will he dwell in a plenitude of bliss together with the spiritual gods.

But when a man who is damned dies, then for three days and nights does his soul hover near his head, weeping (and saying): 'Whither shall I go? and in whom shall I now take refuge?' And during those three days and nights he sees with his eyes all the sins and wickedness that he committed on earth. On the fourth day the demon Vizarsh comes and binds the soul of the damned in most shameful wise, and, despite the opposition of the blessed Sraosha, drags it off to the Bridge of the Requiter. Then Rashnu, the Just, will unmask the soul of the damned as damned indeed.

Then does the demon Vizarsh, eager in his wrath, seize upon the soul of the damned, smite it and despite it without pity. And the soul of the damned cries out with a loud voice, groans, and in supplication makes many a piteous plea; and desperate will be his struggle. When all his strugglings and his lamentations have proved of no avail, no help is offered him by any of the gods nor yet by any of the demons, but the demon Vizarsh drags him off against his will to nethermost hell.

Then a maiden who has yet no resemblance to a maiden comes to meet him. And the soul of the damned says to that ill-favoured wench: 'Who art thou? for never have I seen an ill-favoured wench on earth more ill-favoured and hideous than thee'. And in answer that ill-favoured wench says to him. 'I am no girl, but I am thy deeds – hideous deeds – thy evil thoughts, evil words, evil deeds, and evil religion. For when on earth thou didst see one who offered sacrifice to the gods, then didst thou sit (apart) and offer sacrifice to the demons: demons and lies didst thou worship. And when thou didst see one who welcomed good men and offered them hospitality, and gave alms both to those who came from near and to those who came from afar, then didst thou treat good men with contumely and show them dishonour; nor didst thou give them alms, but shuttest thy door (upon them). And when thou didst see one who passed just judgment, or took no bribes, or bore true witness, or spoke up in righteousness, then didst thou sit down and pass false judgment, bear false witness, and speak unrighteously. I am thy evil thoughts, evil words, and evil deeds which thou didst think and speak and do. For though I was disreputable (at first), thou madest me yet more disreputable; and though I was dishonourable (at first), thou hast made me yet more dishonourable; and though I sat (at first) among the unaware, thou hast made me yet more unaware.'

Then with the first step he goes to (the hell of) evil thoughts, with his second to (the hell of) evil words, and with his third to (the hell of) evil deeds. And with his fourth step he lurches into the presence of the Destructive Spirit and the other demons. And the demons mock at him, and hold him up to scorn (saying): 'What grieved thee in Ohrmazd the Lord, and in the Bounteous Immortals, and in fragrant and delightful heaven, and what complaint hadst thou of them that thou shouldst come to see Ahriman, the demons, and murky hell? For we shall torment thee, nor shall we have any mercy on thee, and for a long time shalt thou suffer torment.'

Then will the Destructive Spirit cry out to the demons (saying): 'Ask not concerning him; for he has been separated from his beloved body and has come through that most evil passage-way. Serve him (rather) with the filthiest and most vile of foods, food produced in hell.'

Then will they bring him poison and venom, snakes and scorpions and other noxious reptiles (which thrive) in hell and give him thereof to eat. And until the Resurrection and the Final Body he must remain in hell suffering much torment and all manner of chastisement. And the food that for the most part he must eat there is rotten, as it were, and like unto blood (2.73–122)[53].

This presentation of the respective fates of the just and the wicked, which bears so striking a resemblance in some of its features to the mediaeval Christian 'Doom' but differs much in others, calls for comment on some details. For example, although the Bridge of the Separator (or Requiter) figures prominently and it is specifically stated that all must cross it, its *raison d'être* is not made clear, and nothing is said of the part it plays in the experience of the damned. It does seem to be implied that Rashnu weighs the deeds of the dead there, and it is possible that the statement that the righteous soul, after this judgment, finds the Bridge one parasang broad, implies that the damned would find it perilously narrow and fall from it. That the damned fall from the Bridge into the hands of Ahriman and thus go to Hell is definitely stated in a mediaeval Parsee writing.[54] The appearance of one's *daēnā* after death certainly constitutes a dramatic episode, and it seems to have been a feature of Zoroaster's eschatology.[55] How such a belief originated is unknown, for, as we have seen, the derivation and meaning of the term *daēnā* is intrinsically obscure. It is also to be noted that, despite the explicit mention of the soul's separation from its body, what is said about the food offered to the saved and the damned, about the faculty of smell, and the torments inflicted by the demons, suggests that the soul was conceived in the very materialistic manner in which it was thought of in the other eschatologies that we have studied.[56] Finally, it is significant that the torments of the damned are not eternal, but would continue until 'the Resurrection and the Final Body'. This later Zoroastrian eschatology, therefore, gives a more precise formulation of the double-phased destiny awaiting men after death which the *Gāthās* seemed to imply. It confirms the suggestion, which we noted, that Zoroaster envisaged an immediate judgment after death and some final ordeal which the dead would experience in their physical bodies. It also means that the torments suffered by the damned after the immediate judgment constituted an expiation preparatory to the final judgment or ordeal.[57]

We see, then, that Zoroastrian eschatology was patterned on a long-term chronology, according to which the fates of individual persons were subsumed in a kind of cosmic scheme which would be terminated by the catastrophic destruction of the world. The indications, which we have noticed, are to be found embodied in a detailed and carefully articulated sacred history or *Heilsgeschichte*, which embraced the whole cosmic process from its creation to its end.[58] A time-scheme or chronology was composed which was made up of a consequential series of four trimillennia, thus giving the whole cosmic process a span of twelve thousand years. The four trimillennia represented different phases or episodes in the struggle between good and evil, personified respectively as Ohrmazd and Ahriman.[58a] After various vicissitudes of fortune, Ohrmazd finally prevails over his adversary and his demonic hordes. This final victory of good over evil brings about the *Frashkart* or ultimate Rehabilitation of all that Ahriman had destroyed or misled.[59] It takes the form of a series of eschatological events, namely, the resurrection of the dead, a final judgment, a further expiation of sins, the ordeal of molten metal, a final ritual act to secure immortality for all, and the reconstitution of the world. Several of these events, although they appear in an apparent consequential series, have no obvious intrinsic connection with each other, and they have probably been assembled from diverse traditions. The classic description of this final phase of the Iranian *Heilsgeschichte* is found in Chapter XXX of the *Bundahishn*, a late Pahlavi writing:[60]

(4) After Sôshyans[61] *comes* they prepare the raising of the dead. . . . (7) First, the bones of Gâyômard[62] are roused up, then those of Mâshya and Mâshyôî (i.e. the first human couple), then those of the rest of mankind; in the fifty-seven years *of* Sôshyans they prepare all the dead, *and* all men stand up; whoever is righteous *and* whoever is wicked, every human creature, they rose up from the spot where its life departs. . . . (10) Then is the assembly of the Saḍ-vâstarân, where all mankind will stand at this time; in that assembly every one sees his own good deeds and his own evil deeds; *and* then, in that assembly, a wicked man becomes as conspicuous as a white sheep among those which are black. . . . (12) Afterwards, they set the righteous *man* apart from the wicked; *and* then the righteous is for heaven (garôdmân), and they cast the wicked back to hell. (13) Three days *and* nights they inflict punishment bodily in hell, *and* then he beholds bodily these three days' happiness in heaven.[63]

The punishment of the wicked during these three days and nights is intense.[64] It is difficult to relate this period of punishment to that which they had already suffered since the first judgment, or to the ordeal that follows. Unless the point of distinction lies in the fact that the damned now suffered, during this interval, in their resurrected bodies, this further period of expiation is indeed inexplicable – possibly the Zoroastrian theologians were contending here with the same difficulty that faced Christian theologians in relating an Immediate Judgment, followed by expiation in Purgatory, with a Final Judgment and condemnation to Hell.[65] However that may be, the Iranian eschatological scheme now passes on to its next episode. Owing to some cosmic disaster, a flood of molten metal streams forth,[66] apparently according to the design of Ohrmazd because it constitutes the last ordeal for mankind:

> Then all men will pass into that melted metal and will become pure; when *one* is righteous, then it seems to him just as though he walks continually in warm milk; *but* when wicked, he walks continually in melted metal.[67]

The only purpose of this ordeal seems to be that of purifying those who are still stained with their sins, even after their being punished for them. As such it prepares mankind for its final restoration:

> All men become of one voice *and* administer loud praise to Aûharmazd and the archangels. (24) Aûharmazd completes *his work* at that time, *and* the creatures become so that it is not necessary to make any further effort about them. (25) Sôshyans, with his assistants, performs a Yazisn *ceremony* in preparing the dead *and* they slaughter the ox Hadhayôs in that Yazisn; from the fat of that ox and the white Hôm they prepare Hûsh, *and* give it to all men, and all men become immortal for ever *and* everlasting. (26) This, too, it says, that whoever has been the size of a man, they restore him then with an age of forty years; they who have been little *when* not dead, they restore them to an age of fifteen years; and they give every one his wife, but there is no begetting of children.[68]

And so, with the defeat and annihilation of the forces of Evil, the world is purified and renewed for all eternity, according to the purpose of Ohrmazd, the Wise Lord and supreme deity of the universe.

In terms of strict logic, Zoroastrianism was not an absolute dualism, because the Good ultimately prevailed and exterminated the Evil. However, it was dualistic in the sense that it saw the world as the battle-ground of the two contending principles which would be equally poised until the fourth trimillennia. In other words, in terms of the span of a man's life, it was a dualism, and it was one which imposed a fateful moral decision on the individual. Consequently, it necessitated a *post-mortem* judgment, since justice was obviously not meted out to men in this world; the criterion was the nature of the choice of alignment, *vis-à-vis* the contending forces, made by each individual. Ohrmazd rewarded those who served him with everlasting bliss in the next life, and he exacted retribution from those who rejected him. This retribution, although it had not to be paid everlastingly, as in some other eschatologies,[69] was sufficiently long and painful to constitute a proper satisfaction and so render the *post-mortem* judgment significant. What seems to have been peculiar to Zoroastrian eschatology was the concept of the *Fraskart*, the ultimate 'making excellent',[70] after expiation, of that part of mankind that chose to ally itself to Ahriman, the personification of Zoroaster's *Druj* or Lie.

8

HINDUISM AND BUDDHISM:
Karma as Judgment

The ideas of a *post-mortem* judgment current in the two great religions that have stemmed from India may be considered together, since in each instance the concept is essentially conditioned by a common conviction. Thus it is believed by both Hindu and Buddhist that the present life of each person is only one of an infinite series of lives, past and to come. The present life, moreover, is determined in its form and character by the individual's conduct in previous lives. We have already met a similar evaluation of human destiny in our study of the Pythagorean-Orphic doctrine of metempsychosis, and have noted its effect upon the idea of judgment after death.[1] This Pythagorean-Orphic doctrine had a considerable influence in the Graeco-Roman world, but that influence was in no way comparable in magnitude to that exercised by the Indian doctrine of the transmigration of the soul. For, not only has the belief fundamentally conditioned the culture of India, it has also, through the diffusion of Buddhism, profoundly affected the *Weltanschauung* of most of the peoples of Asia.[1a]

Although its influence has thus been so deep and so widespread, the doctrine of *saṃsāra*,[2] which means in effect the transmigration of the soul, only appears in Indian literature somewhere about the seventh century BC. Its appearance, and subsequent establishment, wrought a profound change in the Indian view of human nature and destiny from that previously held. The origin of the belief, and the cause of its establishment at this time, are obscure and have led to much discussion among specialists in Indian studies.[3] To appreciate the magnitude of the change, and also to understand something of the apparently inconsistent features of later Hindu and Buddhist eschatology, we must briefly look at the traditional view of the after-life in ancient India before the new belief appeared.

The so-called Vedic literature, which documents this earlier period of Indian history, begins with the *Rig-Veda*. This is a collection of hymns, written in Sanskrit, which were originally used in religious ceremonies by the Aryan peoples who invaded north-western India about the middle of the second millennium BC.[4] These hymns are addressed to various gods, who were mostly personifications of natural phenomena.[5] The view of life that finds expression in them is essentially a vigorous affirmation of the desirability of life in this world. The gods were besought for material blessings: abundance of food and offspring, and a long life. Religion was essentially a transaction: worship and sacrifice in exchange for divine bounty.[5a] There was some consciousness of sin, which took the form of both moral and ritual infringement. In a manner reminiscent of the ancient Egyptian concept of *maāt* or the Iranian *asha*, a cosmic law (*ṛta*), connoting both order and truth, was imagined, and a god called Varuna was regarded as the guardian of *ṛta*. This deity was of an inscrutable nature, and, by sinning against him unwittingly, men were caught in the 'fetters' of Varuna, and had to pray for deliverance.[6] Varuna seems to have confined his concern for the maintenance of law and order to this world, and he does not appear as a judge of the dead.[7]

The eschatological beliefs of this Aryan people, as they find expression in the *Rig-Veda*, are imprecise and in some ways contradictory. A god of the dead, named Yama, the son of Vivasvant, was regarded as 'the first of mortals to die and enter that other world'.[8] From the brief references to him, it would appear that Yama was related to the Iranian Yima, and figured originally in an ancient Aryan myth of a Primordial Man of a Golden Age before death and evil afflicted mankind.[9] The realm of Yama was subterranean, and the *piṭrs* (fathers) dwelt there – its location was doubtless conceived in terms of the grave, as in the mythologies of many other peoples.[10] In one hymn of the *Rig-Veda*, however, it is depicted as a veritable paradise, irradiated by light, where the 'fathers' dwell in company with the gods.[11] Elsewhere in the *Rig-Veda*, and in later Vedic literature, it is pictured as a much more sombre abode.[12] Reference is made to the two dogs of Yama: they each have four eyes, and guard the way to the land of the dead.[13] It is possible that the passage by these formidable guardians constituted a kind of test as to the fitness of the deceased to enter the kingdom of Yama: if not properly buried and equipped with funerary offerings, the unfortunate soul would wander hopelessly between the land of the living and that of the dead.[14]

In the *Rig-Veda* there are a few cryptic references to a division made between the good and the wicked after death. The deceased is invited to heaven, 'with thy good deeds',[15] while the deities Indra and Soma are described as hurling the wicked into an eternally dark prison, from which there is no return.[16] To the same place are also consigned various categories of sinners, including evil-intentioned magicians.[17] No indication, however, is given of how judgment is passed upon them or by whom. Later Vedic literature is a little more specific. Yama is represented as separating those of mankind who speak the truth from those who lie.[18] The familiar concept of weighing also appears: 'In that world they lay (good and bad deeds) on a balance. What of either – whether good or bad – draws (down), the consequences are in accordance therewith. But he who knows, he already ascends the balance in this world, (and) renders unnecessary a weighing in that world. His good works prevail, not his bad works.'[19] In the *Talavakāra-Brāhmana* a detailed account is given of punishments suffered by the wicked in the next world. This hell or purgatory is comparted, like those in other eschatologies, for the punishment of specific crimes. Although nothing is said of a *post-mortem* judgment as such, the penalties suffered are strictly retributive.[20]

It would, accordingly, appear that during the Vedic period of ancient Indian culture there was a tradition of belief concerning *post-mortem* rewards and punishments. The mode of assessment is obscure, as is also the identity of the judge or judges concerned. Deeds deserving of beatitude after death were of both a ritual and moral character, as were also those which merited punishment. It would seem that both this beatitude and damnation were everlasting, and exactly retributive. It is significant, however, in view of the profound change that was to take place in Indian eschatological thought, that the idea of a second death (*punarmṛtyu*) begins to appear in the *Brāhmanas* as a penalty for those who had failed to perform certain necessary sacrifices.[21] In other words, it would seem that some fear had now raised itself about the permanence of *post-mortem* well-being, and that the possibility of having again to experience the grim process of dying was envisaged. The conception of a second death is not unknown in some other religions, and, as we have already seen, the mortuary faith of ancient Egypt provides the earliest example of it.[22] Its appearance in Indian thought at this period, however, is invested with a special interest as being a possible anticipation of the later belief in *saṃsāra*, for the transmigration of the soul implied an unending series of deaths. As a form of *post-mortem* punishment, it interests us also because of its implication of some form of judgment.

However, before we go on to trace out the presentation of the idea of a *post-mortem* judgment in terms of the doctrine of *saṃsāra* and the concomitant doctrine of *karma*, it is important that we properly notice a very significant fact. It is that Vedic literature, which constituted the sacred literature of subsequent Hinduism,[23] contained an eschatology that was essentially different from that authorized by the logic of *saṃsāra*. Thus, the life of the individual in this world was seen as a unique experience which terminated at death and could not be repeated. What survived of the person at death departed to the land of the dead,[24] where it would enjoy endless felicity or suffering according to its merits, which represented both ritual and moral achievement or failure. The other world, accordingly, was imagined as containing both a heaven and hell, the latter being subdivided to provide suitable punishments for various categories of sinners. The punishment was retributive, in some cases exactly so. This eschatology involved the action of a number of gods, although the exact rôle of each is obscure. The idea of a divine judge of the dead occurs in connection with Yama, although it also is imprecise. Yama was certainly regarded as the death-god, who sent his messengers to summon those about to die.[25] According to the legend of Savitri in the *Mahābhārata*, the great epic poem which dates from about the fourth century AD but incorporates much earlier tradition, the length of a man's life was determined by his destiny, though Yama could decide the exact moment of his death.[26] Yama also ruled over the dead, who apparently stayed in his kingdom for ever.[26a]

Such, then, was the tradition of Indian belief concerning human destiny, when the new evaluation appeared somewhere about the seventh or eighth century BC.[27] It is not necessary to our subject that we should try to unravel the complicated problem, already mentioned, of the origins of the Indian doctrine of the transmigration of the soul. It will suffice to quote a passage from the *Bṛhad-āraṇyaka Upaniṣad*, which is one of the earliest documents of the new philosophy of life that now began to be expounded at first, it would seem, in esoteric circles, by a sage to his disciples.[28] As will be seen, the teaching presupposes some curious ideas which probably arose out of speculation connecting the dead with the celestial phenomena, and parallels to it can be found in other primitive religions.[29] The passage concerned is given here in the translation of Dr S. Radhakrishnan:

> Those who know this as such and those too who meditate with faith in the forest on the truth, pass into the light, from the light into the day, from the day into the half-month of the waxing moon, from the half-month of the waxing

moon into the six months during which the sun travels northward, from these months into the world of the gods, from the world of the gods into sun, from the sun into the lightning (fire). Then a person consisting (born) of mind goes to those regions of lightning and leads them to the worlds of Brahmā. In those worlds of Brahmā they live for long periods. Of these there is no return.[30]

Such, then, is the destiny of those enlightened by this esoteric doctrine. After their lengthy journey, they reach a destination where they abide for ever. The significance of the fact that they never return from there is evident by contrast with the fate of those described in the following passage:

But those who by sacrificial offerings, charity and austerity conquer the worlds, they pass into the smoke (of the cremation fire), from the smoke into the night, from the night into the half-month of the waning moon, from the half-month of the waning moon into the six months during which the sun travels southward, from these months into the world of the fathers, from the world of the fathers into the moon. Reaching the moon they become food. There the gods, as they say to king *Soma*, increase, decrease, even so feed upon them there. When that passes away from them, they pass forth into this space, from space into air, from air into rain, from rain into the earth. Reaching the earth they become food. Again, they are offered in the fire of man. Thence they are born in the fire of woman with a view to going to other worlds.[31] Thus do they rotate. But those who do not know these two ways, become insects, moths and whatever there is here that bites.[32]

Behind the strange compound of esoteric speculation and mytho-logical imagery in these passages, it is possible to discern the lineaments of an eschatology combining earlier Vedic concepts with the new idea of metempsychosis. Two 'ways' or 'worlds' for men after death are distinguished which clearly derive from earlier tradition, namely, the *devayāna*, 'the way of the gods' and the *pitryāna*, the 'way of the fathers'.[33] The former is associated with the destiny of the enlightened, which is regarded as the highest form of bliss and which they deserve by virtue of their enlightenment. Those without this redeeming know-ledge, but who have the merit of fulfilling the requirements of the traditional ritual practice, reach the world of the ancestors, and then pass on to experience some curious metamorphosis which begins in the moon. By the process of human generation they are eventually reborn for further incarnated lives. In other words, the lack of enlightenment results in their reincarnation in human form. To these two clearly defined forms of destiny there is added a brief statement, apparently out of context, about a third form of destiny. Those without enlightenment and ignorant of the means of acquiring ritual merit, were reborn in non-human forms, namely, as insects or other noxious animals.[34]

In this primitive form of the doctrine of *saṃsāra* nothing explicit is said about the process of *karma*, which, as we shall presently see, plays such a fundamental rôle in the classic form of the Hindu view of human destiny. Thus no explanation is given why the third group in the passage just quoted should be condemned to be reincarnated in such lowly and disgusting forms of being.

The *Bṛhad-āraṇyaka Upaniṣad* fortunately contains in another section a passage concerning *karma* which indicates that the idea was still a closely guarded secret of the specially initiated. The passage takes the form of a dialogue between a renowned sage, Yājñavalkya, and a disciple who seeks instruction about the disintegration of bodies caused by death. The passage is given also in the translation of Dr Radhakrishnan:

'Yājñavalkya, when the speech (voice) of this dead person enters into fire, the breath into air, the eye into the sun, the mind into the moon, hearing into the quarters, the self into the ether, the hairs of the body into the herbs, the hairs into the trees and the blood and the semen are deposited in water, what then becomes of this person?' (Yājñavalkya replies:) 'Ārtabhāga, my dear, take my hand. We two alone shall know of this, this is not for us two (to speak) in public.' The two went away and deliberated. What they said was karman and what they praised was karman. Verily one becomes good by good action, bad by bad action. Therefore, Ārtabhāga of the line of Garathāra kept silent.[35]

Karman or *karma* means 'deed', 'work', 'action', 'rite'.[36] As the term came to be used in connection with ritual act, it tended to signify not only the action itself but the efficacy of the action. Consequently, the Brahmanic emphasis upon the cosmic potency of ritual sacrifice associated *karma* with the idea of an impersonal force generated *ex opere operato*.[37] The application of this concept to human destiny in connection with that of *saṃsāra* produced a revolution in Indian thinking which is reflected in the passage cited. The rather trite observation that 'one becomes good by good action, bad by bad action' enunciates a principle of fundamental import which finds fuller and more significant expression in the following passage, also from the *Bṛhad-āraṇyaka Upaniṣad*:

According as one acts, according as one behaves, so does he become. The doer of good becomes good, the doer of evil becomes evil. One becomes virtuous by virtuous action, bad by bad action. Others, however, say that a person consists of desires. As is his desire so is his will; as is his will, so is the deed he does, whatever deed he does, that he attains.

On this there is the following verse: 'The object to which the mind is attached, the subtle self goes together with the deed, being attached to it alone. Exhausting the results of whatever works he did in this world he comes again from that world, to this world for (fresh) work. But the man who does not desire, he who is without desire, who is freed from desire, whose desire is satisfied, whose desire is the self; his breaths do not depart. Being *Brahman* he goes to *Brahman*.'[38]

The full proportions of the new evaluation of human nature and destiny are seen in this passage, and its significance for our subject becomes evident. Man is conceived as an immortal being or self (*atman*) indwelling, in this world, a physical body.[39] The life that he is now living here is not the first, but the latest of an infinite series of past lives, and the condition in which he now lives is the result of his conduct (*karma*) in those former lives. At death, the self (*atman*) departs to another world, where it works out the consequences of its *karma*. Later Indian and Buddhist thought, as we shall see, greatly elaborate the conception of these other worlds: some were pleasant places where the consequences of virtuous action would be enjoyed; others were hells where retribution was suffered for evil deeds. When the consequences of its *karma* were worked out, the self was reincarnated in this world. This rebirth resulted from the self's desire or attachment to this phenomenal world, which it took for reality.[40] The form in which the self was reincarnated could include that of non-human species, as we have briefly seen. A fuller statement of this belief occurs in the *Chāndogya Upaniṣad*, which is also one of the earliest documents of this new phase in Indian thought:

Those whose conduct here has been good will quickly attain a good birth (literally womb), the birth of a Brāhmin, the birth of a Kṣatriya or the birth of a Vaiśya. But those whose conduct here has been evil, will quickly attain an evil birth, the birth of a dog, the birth of a hog or the birth of a Caṇḍāla.[41]

In these passages we see, accordingly, an interpretation of human destiny which accounts for the present condition of each living being as due to the operation of *karma*. This principle works as an impersonal force, without reference to any deity, determining the future of each person. It constitutes a veritable *post-mortem* judgment that has a two-fold form of operation. At death, or the termination of an incarnation, the self experiences the consequences of its *karma* during that period: the experience, in joy or pain, corresponds exactly to the nature of its deeds. Having worked out what might be termed the consequences of its immediate *karma*, the self then has to endure the consequences of a kind of entail of *karma* accumulating from all its previous lives, which causes it to desire to exist again in the phenomenal world. The next form of incarnate life in that world is determined also by *karma*, as we have seen: if the form is human, it is varied in social status according to merit; similarly graduated downwards are the non-human forms.

However, according to this Upanishadic doctrine, even the highest mode of existence, namely, as a Brahmin, in this world, is not to be sought as the ultimate goal of endeavour. Beyond that is something wholly different in kind. It finds expression at the end of the last passage of the *Bṛhad-āraṇyaka Upaniṣad* quoted above:

But the man who does not desire, he who is without desire, who is freed from desire, whose desire is satisfied, whose desire is the self; his breaths do not depart. Being *Brahman* he goes to *Brahman*.[42]

Herein is stated the final aim of Indian philosophy and religion; it constitutes *mokṣa*, or 'liberation' from the involvement of the self in the cosmic process, and, thereby, from the entail of *karma*. The conception presupposes an esoteric evaluation both of the nature of the self and of reality. Briefly, the individual self or *atman* is held to be identical with *Brahman*, the principle or ground of true being.[43] The phenomenal world is regarded as not ultimately real; it is the product of *māyā*, illusion.[44] Owing to some primordial misapprehension or ignorance (*avidyā*), the self takes this world for reality and cleaves to existence within it.[45] The consequences of this error are profound. It involves the self in an unceasing cycle of incarnations, which means the repeated experience of birth and death and all the other suffering that stems from living in this world of time and space. It also subjects the self to the consequences of *karma*, the entail of which, as we have seen, is ever conditioning the situation of the self whether during its periods of incarnation here or during its stay in other worlds. This process of *saṃsāra*, and the operation of the law of *karma*, have no end so long as the self remains in this state of primordial error about the nature of reality. In later Hindu, Buddhist and Jain thought an elaborate chronological system of *mahayugas* and *kalpas* was constructed, in order to show through what immense periods of time the unenlightened self, dragging with it the burden of its *karma*, must endure the recurrent experience of birth and death; this chronology was, moreover, cyclic in its pattern, so that there was no hope that suffering would ultimately end.[46]

Salvation from this 'sorrowful, weary wheel' of cosmic existence was to be had only by the self's realization of its identity with *Brahman*, the principle of true reality. The achievement of *mokṣa* had to be earned by a hard discipline of mind and body, calculated to remove completely any desire to continue existence in this world. It was a long and painful process, and it might be extended over several incarnations; for the law of *karma* could operate to elevate the spiritual insight of the self as well as to depress it. The attainment of the ultimate state of grace meant no further rebirth here; for the self would be essentially one with *Brahman*.[47]

We see, then, that in terms of this Indian evaluation of human nature and destiny, judgment was a continuous process. In a sense it did involve a series of immediate *post-mortem* assessments; but, since it was patterned on a cyclical conception of time, there could be no 'Last Judgment' as envisaged in the many other religions which we have surveyed. It is to be noted also that this process of judgment was not ordered by any deity, neither did it involve the idea that the fate of the individual soul was determined by its conduct toward a supreme god, to whom it owed an absolute obedience.[48] It is true that in the various forms of Hinduism, which were subsequently erected upon this Upanishadic doctrine, provision was made for the cults of various gods and the practice of Brahmanic ritual, so that the concept of sin as a religious failure or offence exists. But such forms were essentially practical compromises based upon the Upanishadic view of the determinative operation of *saṃsāra* and *karma* and the fundamental identity of the self with *Brahman*.[49] Even in the *Bhagavadgītā*, the great classic of *bhakti* or devotion to a personal god, it still remains the basic principle, despite the proclamation of the efficacy of such devotion.[50] Thus is the achievement of ultimate deliverance described:

> Abandoning all desires, what
> Man moves free from longing,
> Without self-interest and egotism,
> He goes to peace.
> This is the fixation that is Brahmanic, son of Pṛthā;
> Having attained it he is not (again) confused.
> Abiding in it even at the time of death,
> He goes to Brahman-nirvāṇa.[51]

173

What may perhaps be considered as a classic description of the Indian concept of the ideal path to ultimate bliss, which is essentially that of the individual's achievement of salvation by his own effort, is provided in the following passage from the great epic of the *Mahābhārata*:

> Such (the process of *karma*), O Yuddhishthira, is the fate of all creatures immersed in spiritual ignorance.
>
> Hear now what is the perfect way attained by men of high spiritual perception! By such men as are rich in ascetic ardour and versed in writings, both sacred and secular; those careful in their religious duties, and truthful. Who honour their spiritual guides and their superiors, practising *yoga*, merciful, chaste and pious, men endowed with all virtues.
>
> By mastering their passions, they control their mind, by practising *yoga* they are freed from disease, from fear and vexation.
>
> At their birth, in childhood, in their maturity, and even when still hidden in the womb, whatever their situation, they understand the relation of their soul to the Being Supreme.
>
> By such seers, great of soul, possessed of an intuitive knowledge, who traverse the field of action and return to the celestian abode (i.e. *Brahman*).[52]

Buddhism arose in India during the Upanishadic period, and it incorporated into its doctrine of Man the twin principles of *saṃsāra* and *karma*.[53] It differs, however, from the Upanishadic view, and consequently from that of classical Hinduism, in rejecting the idea that there is a continuing self or *atman* that survives the disintegration of the person at death and is reincarnated.[54] This difference makes Buddhist metaphysics, particularly in the matter of Nirvāṇa, the goal of Buddhist endeavour, a subject of great puzzlement, about which there has always been a considerable divergence of opinion among specialists.[55] Fortunately, for our theme we have only to consider the factor of judgment in Buddhist eschatology, and in this respect the evaluation of it is very similar to that current in Hinduism.

This similarity emerges clearly, for example, in a writing which purports to record the Buddha's answers to a Brahmin student who questioned him about various conditions of fortune which human beings experience in this world. The Buddha replies that the cause is *karma*, and, in answer to the student's further inquiry, he goes on to explain the operation of *karma* by a number of illustrations. The following is a representative example:

> There is the case of a person, a woman or a man, who is given to hurting with hand or clod or stick or knife. . . . He is reborn in hell or, if he attains the state of man, wherever he is reborn he has much ill-health . . .

There is the case of a person, a woman or a man, who is not given to hurting with hand or clod or stick or knife . . . He is reborn in heaven or, if he attains the state of man, he has good health . . .[56]

Thus, in Buddhism, *karma* also acts as a continuous process of judgment both before and after death. Buddhism has likewise shared with Hinduism the belief that many heavens and hells exist, where the dead, before their next incarnation, enjoy or suffer the consequences of their *karma*. One of these, the Paradise of Indra, is borrowed from Hindu mythology, and in its sensuous attractions it equals the joys of heaven promised by Muḥammad to his faithful followers.[57] The ideas of hell also hold their own with anything that Christianity or Islam can produce in the depiction of physical torment. The following extract is a representative example:

To begin with, the wardens of hell subject the sinner to the five-fold trussing. They drive red-hot iron stakes first through one hand, then through the other, and then through his two feet and his chest. After that they carry him along to be trimmed with hatchets. Then, head downwards, they trim him with razors . . .[58]

The Tibetan Book of the Dead is of particular interest to us for its account of a *post-mortem* judgment which clearly derives from Indian sources, although the Tibetan religion is Buddhist in inspiration. The lama is directed to read to a dying person this description of what he would shortly experience:

You are now before Yama, King of the Dead. In vain will you try to lie, and to deny or conceal the evil deeds you have done. The Judge holds up before you the shining mirror of Karma, wherein all your deeds are reflected. But again you have to deal with dream images, which you yourself have made, and which you project outside, without recognizing them as your own work. The mirror in which Yama seems to read your past is your own memory, and also his judgment is your own. It is you yourself who pronounce your own judgment, which in its turn determines your next rebirth. No terrible God pushes you into it; you go there quite on your own. The shapes of frightening monsters who take hold of you, place a rope round your neck and drag you along, are just an illusion which you create from the forces within you. Know that apart from these karmic forces there is no Judge of the Dead, no gods, and no demons. Knowing that, you will be free![59]

As in Hinduism, so the law of *karma* in Buddhism has a two-fold effect. It determines, as we have seen, the fate of the individual after death for the period before his next incarnation, and it also causes that incarnation and conditions its form. The attainment of Nirvāṇa similarly depends on the effort of the individual, who must strive, perhaps through many lives, to eradicate all desire and gain the proper insight by a stern discipline of mind and body.[60]

In process of time the Mahāyāna form of Buddhism developed a kind of soteriology around the idea of the *Bodhisattva*, an enlightened, saintly being, whose compassion led him to seek the salvation of men from the sufferings which their *karma* decreed after death.[61] The most distinguished of these *Bodhisattvas* has been Avalokiteśvara, who is believed to take his devotees to Sukhāvatī, the 'Happy Land' of the Buddha Amitābha.[62] Although the attainment of such felicity by the gracious intervention of a saviour has doubtless represented the goal of many Buddhists, the cult of the *Bodhisattva* does not negate the logic of the Buddhist doctrine of human nature and destiny. The stay of the dead in either a heaven or hell, however prolonged, is not eternal; ultimately they have to be reincarnated and be subject to the process of *saṃsāra* and *karma* until they achieve deliverance and attain Nirvāṇa.[63]

In the history and comparative study of religion, Hinduism and Buddhism represent an evaluation of man and his destiny which differs radically from that common to Judaism, Christianity and Islam, and earlier faiths such as those of Egypt and Iran. In those religions the life of the individual is seen as unique, in the sense that it is not to be repeated again in this world, and its quality definitively determines his eternal *post-mortem* existence. Further, a conception of judgment is implicated as being decreed, and generally executed by a supreme deity on the individual either immediately after death or on some future occasion. Such a view, moreover, is based upon a linear concept of time, which logically negatives any idea of the recurrence of events constituting a human life in this world.

The Hindu-Buddhist evaluation, by being based on a cyclic-patterned *Weltanschauung*, is fundamentally different. For it sees the life of the individual in this world as but one of an infinite series of lives, of which the pattern of some of them could be conceivably repeated. Moreover, this evaluation, although it accommodates belief in the existence of deities, envisages human destiny as determined by an impersonal process that is essentially independent of divine intervention. This process, known as *karma*, does, however, constitute an unceasing judgment operative in the very being of every person. While it may not strictly be described as a 'judgment of the dead', in the sense in which that designation is used in the other religions mentioned, *karma* has this aspect when seen in terms of one period of incarnation only. However, its real significance lies in its unceasing retributive assessment of the individual throughout the millions of lives he may live, if he fails to achieve *mokṣa* or Nirvāṇa. It has thus the unique distinction of accounting exactly for the condition of the individual at every moment of his existence; in such a system there is logically no problem of innocent suffering. The doctrine, accordingly, counsels both resignation to one's present situation and endeavour to change it in the future; it also promises that, when the moment of enlightenment ultimately comes, the individual will be aware of all his past lives and perceive their relation to this moment of consummation.[64]

The Tibetan Conception of the Judgment of the Dead

W. Y. Evans-Wentz reproduces, in his edition of *The Tibetan Book of the Dead*, a photograph of a remarkable painting of the Judgment which was made in Gaugtok, Sikkim, in 1919. He states that it is painted in the monastic tradition. The picture combines Indian, Buddhist and native Bön (Tibetan) eschatological *motifs*. (See plate 11.)

The scene is dominated by Dharma-Rāja, the King of Truth, a form of Yama, the Indian god of the dead. Immediately in front of Yama, who is of terrifying mien, stands Shinje, a monkey-headed being, who is depicted as weighing heaps of white and black pebbles, which respectively represent the good and bad deeds of the dead. A yellow-coloured deity to Yama's right is the advocate for the defence, and a brown-coloured deity to his left is the advocate for the prosecution. Six other deities are assessors; one holds the mirror of *karma*.

Outside the precincts of the tribunal demons punish the damned. Some are immersed in ice, others in flames. A man within a triangle suffers for sorcery; four *lāmas* are crushed by the sacred books they neglected; a murderess is sawn asunder; a prostitute has molten metal poured into her; other evildoers are cooked in a cauldron (*op. cit.*, pp. xxx–xxxiii, 37–9, 166, 240). This scene has much in common with Chinese and Japanese depictions of the *post-mortem* judgment (see below).

9

CHINA:
the Judgment of the Dead
Bureaucratically Organized

The pursuit of our theme through many religions has afforded some curious insights into the variety of ways in which a common notion may find expression. The popular religion of China, as it was known before the Communist revolution, provides a further instance; for it contained a meticulously ordered eschatology which clearly reflected the Chinese disposition for bureaucratic control. It was an eschatology that evidently exercised a potent influence on the Chinese view of life; yet it was in origin a foreign importation, and it appeared comparatively late in the evolution of Chinese religion.

The beginnings of religion in China can be traced back to the Shang Period (c. 1523–1027 BC), and, already then, as the so-called Oracle Bones found at Anyang seem to show, the idea of a soul existed.[1] On these fragments of bone, used for divinatory purposes, a pictogram occurs, representing a man with a large head, which lived on in the Chinese language as *kuei*, a radical denoting 'soul'.[2] There is also some evidence that the ancestor-cult, which has constituted a fundamental and characteristic part of Chinese religion, was already current in some primitive form. Thus, inscribed on the Oracle Bones, besides the character *kuei*, is another from which were derived the characters signifying a 'deceased ancestor' (*tsu*), a protective deity of the soil (*she*), and divine beings (*shen*); the entities so denoted had some phallic significance and were doubtless connected with a primitive fertility cult.[3] There is further significance for us also in the fact that the earliest funerary customs indicate that an effort was made to keep the *kuei* safely inside the body by stopping up its orifices, since the departure of the soul would mean the decomposition of the corpse and the fatal disintegration of the person.[4] The ritual 'calling back of the soul' of the deceased, which finds vivid expression in a poem of the third or fourth century BC, likewise reveals a primitive eschatology: the soul that wanders forth from the body will encounter frightful dangers and inevitably perish.[5]

The Chinese conception of human nature was gradually elaborated, owing particularly to the emergence of the idea of *yin* and *yang* as the two basic alternating principles of all existence operative throughout the universe.[6] Accordingly, during the fourth century BC, the primitive concept of *kuei* came to be interpreted as the *yin*-soul, and was regarded as chthonic in origin and associated with the body from the moment of its conception. It became customary to designate this *yin*-soul during the life of the individual as the *p'o*, and as the *kuei* after death.[7] By contrast to this *yin*-soul, a *yang*-soul was attributed to each person, which was of heavenly origin, in that it was connected with the air or breath; it manifested its presence in the first cry of the infant at birth.[8] Known as the *hun* during life, and as the *shen* at death, this *yang*-soul virtually constituted the personality, in being associated with the mental qualities and the name of the individual concerned.[9] The distinction between these two entities is clearly brought out in a passage of the *Li Chi*, a composition of the Han dynasty which was supposed to record the teaching of Confucius (551–479 BC):

Tsai Wo said, 'I have heard the names of *kuei* and *shen*, but I do not know what they mean'. The Master (i.e. Confucius) said, 'The breath (represents) the abundance of the *shen* (part of a creature), the animal soul represents the *kuei* (part). To be able to make harmony of (the two concepts), *kuei* and *shen*, is the height of philosophy. All creatures inevitably come to die. Dying they inevitably go back to the earth. This is what is meant by *kuei* [? the material soul]. The bones and the flesh moulder below, and, hidden there, make the soil of the land. But the breath soars aloft to become light, (and is found in) the fragrance and the feeling of sorrow at the sacrifice.'[10]

Chinese eschatology, before the establishment of Buddhism during the seventh and eighth centuries AD, is very obscure.[11] That some part of the individual person, whether as the *kuei* alone or the *kuei* and *shen*, was believed to survive the death of the body is certain; but what was thought to be its destiny can only be inferred from the ritual of the ancestor cult. The Chinese, in contrast to many other peoples, did not tend to set mankind over against the rest of the universe as having a special destiny. Instead, they were inclined to integrate man with the rest of nature, and, as we have just noticed, they interpreted human nature as a product of the alternating and completing principles of *yin* and *yang* which operated in every form of being in the universe.[12] According to a distinguished French Sinologist, the primitive Chinese believed that the family stock (*la substance familiale*) was everlasting and conterminous with the earth upon which the family had its habitation and from the products of which its members lived. This *substance familiale* lay buried beneath the ground as *une masse indistincte*, and it was represented above ground, at any given moment, only by the living members of the family, which constituted, as it were, the individualized portion of the family stock. It followed, accordingly, that each birth within the family represented the reincarnation of a portion of the subterranean *substance familiale*, while each death meant in effect the return of a part of the individualized family stock to the *masse indistincte* in the ground below.[13]

From some such conception the ancestor cult stemmed, and it became a basic factor in the integration of Chinese culture and society. Because ancient Chinese society was of a feudal nature, the family of the ruler epitomized the constituent families that made up the state. This situation found concrete expression in the fact that, in the seignorial town, the ancestral temple of the ruler was built adjacent to the altar of the gods of the Soil and of the Harvest, thus signifying the essential nexus between the royal ancestors and the material well-being of their descendants and dependents.[14] In turn, each family had its own ancestor-shrine, where the tablets recording the names of the ancestors were inscribed and venerated. These tablets commemorated the more recently deceased members of a family, and thus conferred upon each a distinct individuality since he was remembered by name. Each subsequent death of a member of the family meant the storing away of the existing oldest tablet. Since this deposition involved the cessation of individually addressed mortuary offerings, the ancestor concerned was regarded as ceasing to exist as a *shen* and entering into the undifferentiated mass of the *kuei*.[15]

This ancestor cult, although punctiliously observed at all levels of society, was linked with the worship of no specific deity. Consequently, belief in *post-mortem* survival does not appear in the pre-Buddhist period of China to have produced any expectation of *post-mortem* judgment.[16] The succession of life and death seems to have been accepted as a natural process, an aspect of the alternating rhythm of *yin* and *yang*, from which there could be no escape. A long life was naturally desired, and in Taoism, which in its original form expressed the fundamental Chinese view that man is essentially a part of nature, the desire for longevity or physical immortality produced some strange ideas and practices.[17] Among the less sophisticated or mystically disposed, the menace of death evoked a profound dread that found expression in the imagined terrors of which the departing soul is so graphically reminded in the poem previously mentioned.[18]

In the philosophical literature of this period little interest is shown in eschatology, and an attitude of agnosticism is generally taken when topics concerning the after-life are raised. Confucius was intent on limiting attention to the affairs of this life, and refused to speculate on supernatural or metaphysical issues. It is recorded of him that, when Chi Lu asked about his duty to the spirits, Confucius replied: 'When still unable to do your duty to men, how can you do your duty to the spirits?' When the disciple ventured to inquire about death, he was told: 'Not yet understanding life, how can you understand death?'[19] Significant also is the view of Hsün Tzŭ (c. 298–238 BC), the so-called Aristotle of China. Commenting upon the traditional mortuary rites connected with the ancestor-cult, he is reported to have said:

The man who observes the rules of proper conduct (*Li*) sedulously cares for life and death. Birth is the beginning of man; death is the end of man. When the end and beginning are both beautiful, the way (*Tao*) of man is complete . . . Funeral rites (*hi*) are the beautification of the dead by the living; they are the sending off the dead very similarly to in their life. Hence we should treat the dead like the living, the absent like the present; their end and their previous life should be alike.[20]

Typical of the philosophical tradition is the recorded reply of Chuang Tzŭ, a Taoist sage of the third century BC, when asked about his apparent indifference to his wife's death:

The form [that was his wife] changed and became alive. And now it has changed again to reach death. In this it has been like the passing of the four seasons, spring, autumn, winter and summer. And while she is thus lying asleep in the Great House (i.e. the Universe), for me to go about weeping and wailing, would be to show myself ignorant of Fate (*ming*). Therefore I refrain.[21]

The effective introduction of the Mahāyāna form of Buddhism into China began in the first century AD, and despite certain opposition, at times extremely sharp, by the T'ang era (AD 618–907) it was firmly established and powerful.[22] Its influence on the religious faith and practice of the Chinese was profound. Taoism, in order to survive, was obliged to take over many Buddhist ideas, and the philosophical tradition was understood and cherished only by the minority of the intelligentsia.[23] Buddhism, however, came to incorporate into its teaching and rituals much that was indigenous to China, and gradually there emerged out of the amalgam of the native tradition, Taoism and Buddhism, a popular religion which constituted the faith of the masses until the Communist revolution.[24] This religion virtually centred around an eschatology which, in effect, supplied the ancient concern of the Chinese for their ancestors with an imaginative ideology which it previously had so singularly lacked.

According to popular belief, derived from Taoism, the universe was ruled by a supreme deity, Yü Ti or the Jade Emperor.[25] As did the emperor of China, Yü Ti governed through an hierarchy of subordinate deities who were each assigned some specific office in this world or the realm of the dead.[26] The realm of the dead comprised ten hells. This number seems to have been a Taoist adaptation of Buddhist teaching, which, as we have already noted, conceived of many hells in which the dead expiated their sins.[27] Over each of these ten hells or prisons (*ti-yü*), a divine being presided. These hells, what happened in them, and their rulers, are graphically described in a number of works, which generally take the form of accounts of the descent into the underworld and the return therefrom of various persons; most notable among these accounts are the legends of the emperor Tsai-tsong and Mu-lien, the latter being a Buddhist monk who descended to rescue his mother from the sufferings of hell and whose legend provides the *rationale* of the popular mortuary ceremony of the *yu-la p'en* or *avalambra*.[28]

From such writings a comprehensive scheme can be traced out of the experiences which the soul underwent from the moment of death until its reincarnation for another period of life in this world. Such a scheme, of course, implied the adoption of the Buddhist doctrines of *saṃsāra* and *karma*, but with the distinction that the Chinese belief assumed a continuity of the soul or self from one incarnation to another.[29] It is also evident that the Chinese differed from the orthodox Buddhist in welcoming a return to this life rather than evaluating all existence in this phenomenal world as evil.[30]

The hour of death was regarded as being carefully fixed and registered by the God of Walls and Moats (Ch'êng-huang), who was the local representative of the Jade Emperor for this purpose in each part of China.[31] At death it was the *hun*-soul that was taken off by the minions of Ch'êng-huang; the *p'o*-soul remained near the body.[32] Brought before Ch'êng-huang, the soul was examined on its conduct, reference being made to registers in which his deeds had been regularly recorded. For his delinquencies he was then punished either by beating or the cangue.[33] This *post-mortem* judgment and punishment constitute a curious anticlimax to the process of judgment and punishment which still lay ahead of the soul; it would seem that such an assessment of a man's life was perhaps originally part of a native eschatology which had later, and illogically, been incorporated into the scheme of Buddhist eschatology.[34] Some evidence of such a transformation is possibly to be discerned in the strange belief that the soul of the deceased was detained in the temple of the God of Walls and Moats, Ch'êng-huang, for forty-nine days after death. During this period various rites were performed on behalf of the dead, concluding on the evening of the forty-ninth day with the ceremonial burning of a paper house, furniture and money, consecrated by the bonzes for the use of the dead man in the underworld.[35]

At the appointed time, after the forty-ninth day, the soul was handed over to specially appointed officials from the underworld, and conducted by them before the first of ten tribunals, over each of which one of the divine rulers of the underworld presided. In illustrations of these infernal courts the rulers are depicted clothed as mandarins, and seated behind a judge's table, attended by officers charged with presenting records from which the soul is judged. The soul, represented in proper human form, kneels, enchained or wearing the cangue, as did the accused before judges seated at their tribunals on earth.[36]

The first tribunal, before which the deceased was brought, was presided over by Ts'in-kuang-wang. This judge assessed the total mass of the good and bad deeds of the dead man. If they were found to balance evenly, he was sent back to be reincarnated in the world, without suffering any further punishment.[37] The souls of suicides were also sent back, to await the completion of the span of life allotted to them; but they were not reincarnated, and they lived on as wretched and malevolent ghosts, intent on causing other living persons to commit the crime of taking their own life.[38] When the properly decreed hour of their death came, these suicides returned to the underworld and were assigned to Wang-sǐ ch'êng, the 'City of the Dead-by-Accident', where they were doomed to abide for ever, being excluded from rebirth on earth.[39] Before they left this first hell, the dead, whose merits and demerits did not equally balance and who had not died by their own hand, underwent a harrowing experience. They were taken to the 'Terrace of the Mirror of the Sinners' (*Sie-king t'ai*), in which they saw the images of

Fig. 8 Torments of the Buddhist Hell. A popular Chinese print depicting the sufferings endured by sinners as they pass through the ten halls *en route* for reincarnation.

all those whom they had caused to suffer.[40] Ts'in-kuang-wang punished none himself, except unfaithful monks, whom he imprisoned until they had recited all their neglected prayers.[41] He was, in effect, the general assessor of all the dead who came before him.

From the tribunal of Ts'in-kuang-wang the dead were sent to the other nine Kings, who was each concerned with the punishment of specific forms of wickedness. The second, Ch'u-kiang wang, dealt with a variety of offenders: dishonest trustees, inefficient doctors, fraudulent marriage-brokers. These culprits were punished by various horrible tortures: some were cut in pieces, some devoured by wild animals, or bound to a red-hot pillar.[42] As in the eschatologies of the other religions which we have studied, so also in that of popular Chinese religion the human mind seems to have used all its ingenuity in inventing the most abominable torments for the damned in hell. Many of these tortures were evidently forms of punishment actually used in the administration of criminal justice in China, as those who suffered in the Christian Hell were taken by artists from contemporary mediaeval practice.[43] Other forms of torment, such as being buried in ice or vermin, or having one's brain replaced by a hedgehog, seem rather to have been the products of a pathological imagination.[44]

It is not necessary to describe all these hells and the punishments inflicted in them. It is, however, of interest to note that the fifth hell was presided over by Yen-lo wang or Yen-wang, whose name was the Chinese form of Yama, the ancient Indian death-god and ruler of the dead.[45] According to Chinese tradition, Yen-wang had formerly been responsible for the first hell; but he was too merciful in his judgments to suit the Jade Emperor, who had demoted him to the fifth hell and replaced him as the ruler of the first hell by Ts'in-kuang-wang, who maintained the necessary standard of impartial severity.[46] There was one unusual feature in the punishments of the fifth hell, controlled by Yen-wang, that deserves mention. The guilty were taken on to a terrace from which they could see their former homes, and so be afflicted by the sight of the misfortunes suffered by their families since their deaths, of which they knew themselves to be the cause.[47]

The tenth hell was the domain of Chuan-lun wang, who was concerned not with the punishment of the dead, but with their preparation for rebirth in the world again. He decreed in what form they should be reincarnated. In one popular illustration of this episode the dead are represented as gazing at a mirror, in which they see the various animals into which their souls will pass for another span of life on earth.[48] Those

Fig. 9 Having completed their punishment, souls behold in a mirror the forms in which they are to be reincarnated, according to their deserts. From a popular Chinese print.

who were about to be reborn were next taken before the Lady Men g whose office it was to prepare the 'broth of oblivion'. Forced to drink it by demons, they forgot completely their experiences in the hells.[49] Thus prepared, they were then brought to *K'u-ch'u-k'iao*, the 'Bridge of Pain', from which they were hurled into a crimson river that carried them to their new birth.[50]

Such, then, was the fate that awaited each soul after death. Even those whose balance of good and evil deeds allowed them to be reborn without suffering in any of the hells, had to wait for twenty-eight months in the underworld before returning to this world. In anticipation of such a verdict, paper mortuary equipment was ritually burnt on the forty-ninth day after death, in the pious hope that it would supply the needs of the soul during this period of waiting.[51] Other rituals were evolved to alleviate the sufferings of the dead, and, if possible, to secure their passage to the paradise of Amitābha.[52] The Mahāyāna doctrine of Bodhisattvas, which the paradise of Amitābha implies, had great vogue in China, and Kuan-yin and Ti-tsang were the two saviours whose aid was mostly invoked to attain to that Happy Land.[53]

This eschatology, with its carefully ordered tribunals and forms of expiation, was essentially a popular faith. Its various episodes were graphically depicted both in large mural paintings in the temples and in popular prints.[54] Thus, in a spirit strikingly reminiscent of that which inspired the presentation of the Christian mediaeval Doom, the religious authorities arranged that the people should be constantly informed of the destiny that awaited them after death. The concept of *post-mortem* judgment involved, since it was linked with the Buddhist doctrine of rebirth, logically envisaged an unceasing recurrence of such judgments. In effect, however, to each person the *post-mortem* judgment doubtless appeared as definitive; for the idea of the 'broth of oblivion', administered to the soul on the eve of its reincarnation, made each span of life virtually a self-contained unit of probation.[55]

The Chinese conception of the judgment of the dead, phenomenologically considered, belongs to the category of those conceptions that regard human life as a natural process of a recurrent kind, unrelated to the control or purpose of a personal God. By virtue of its assumption of the principles of *saṃsāra* and *karma*, the process was essentially a retributive one, whether viewed in terms of one life-span and its *post-mortem* consequences or of its cyclic whole, which was linked to the Buddhist chronological scheme of *kalpas*.[56] Accordingly, it involved no problem of evil or of innocent suffering which require reference to the providence of a supreme personal deity. The Chinese system of *post-mortem* retribution, although it implicated a series of deities, was essentially a bureaucratically organized system modelled on the imperial government of China. As the Emperor was the remote source of all authority in a complex machinery of government, which the peasant knew only in terms of the officials who ordered his life, so the decrees of the remote Jade Emperor would affect him after death through the governors who impassively administered the divisions of the underworld, to which they were appointed. His only hope of succour depended on the intervention of saviours, the Bodhisattvas, who logically had no part in the system.[57]

10

JAPAN:
the Concept of Judgment from an Imported Eschatology

The earliest written records of Japan date from the eighth century AD, and they are essentially mythical accounts of the past, designed mainly to attest the divine origin of the Imperial family.[1] They apparently incorporate earlier material, and, consequently, constitute the chief source of evidence concerning Japanese culture before the establishment and nationalization of Buddhism from the eighth century AD onwards.[2] But, even so, it is doubtful how far these writings preserve a truly native tradition; because Japan had long been open to the influence of the more highly developed civilizations of China and Korea.[3] Despite these qualifications, among the writings concerned there is one that contains a legend of special significance for our subject, and which appears to be of native origin. It is in the *Kojiki*, which was composed during the reign of the Empress Gemmyô (AD 708–14), and provides the cosmogony of Shinto, the national religion of Japan.[4] In its account of the origin of things, the *Kojiki* records the exploits and destinies of two divine beings who form a kind of primordial creative pair, male and female, and as such may probably reflect the influence of the Chinese concept of *yin* and *yang*.[5] The male, Izanagi, 'he who invites', and the female, Izanami, 'she who invites', are the creators of Japan.[6] From the union of these two beings various other deities, personifying cosmic phenomena, were born; the last was the Fire-God, and his birth proved fatal to his mother. Izanami succumbed to the burns she received in delivering the child, and descended into the land of Yomi, the underworld of darkness.[7] Like Orpheus in search of his dead wife Eurydice, Izanagi went down into Yomi to win her back. Although like Persephone in another Greek myth, Izanami had already tasted of food in the underworld, at the behest of her husband she entered the palace of the deities of Yomi to beg for her release. However, she did so on the condition that he did not seek to see her in that dark place. Impatient at her delay, Izanagi ignited his comb and by its light sought for her. He came upon her corpse, lying in a state of horrible putre-faction, and he heard her voice in fierce anger because he had seen her shame.[8] Izanagi fled in terror and disgust from the awful sight, pursued by the terrible denizens of Yomi and by Izanami herself. Regaining the upper world, he blocked the entrance to Yomi with a great rock, and desperately purified himself from its contagion.[9] Izanami stayed in the underworld, to become the 'Great Divinity of Yomi'.[10]

The significance of the myth is great. It reveals a primitive fear of death, inspired particularly by its physical corruption. Izanagi's terrified flight from the horrid spectacle of his dead spouse, and his consequent urge to cleanse himself from death's pollution suggests that Shinto, in its earliest form, had developed no eschatology concerned to speculate in some more sophisticated manner about human destiny after death. Such a primitive reaction to death was not calculated to produce the frame of mind that would envisage the possibility of a *post-mortem* judgment, and this impression is confirmed by the fact that there is no evidence that Shinto taught that retribution would have to be made by men after death.[11] From the witness of myth let us turn to that of archaeology and philology, meagre though it is.

Archaeological evidence witnesses to the existence of belief in some form of *post-mortem* survival from the Neolithic period in Japan, in that funerary equipment of various kinds was buried with the dead.[12] Memory of human sacrifice at princely entombments has been pre-served in written records, suggesting that the custom survived until about the second century of the present era, when it was replaced by the practice of putting earthenware effigies of courtiers and servants in the tomb.[13] Such a custom would suggest a primitive belief, which can be paralleled elsewhere, that the conditions of this life could be repro-duced in the next, so that a prince would arrange for the members of his court to accompany him in death.[14] Evidence of the existence of an ancestor-cult in pre-Buddhist Japan would be pertinent to our inquiry here; but it does not exist in any convincing form.[15] So far as inference can be made from the etymology of the words 'to live' (*iku*), and 'to die' (*shinu*), it would appear that the early Japanese conceived of both life and death as dependent upon breath or breathing.[16] Whether such a view involved the conception of some animating entity, an *anima* or soul, is uncertain. There existed Shinto rites for calling back the soul of the deceased; but the idea involved doubtless came from China.[17]

It is, accordingly, a meagre harvest that can be gleaned from Shinto literature and ritual concerning Japanese belief about human destiny before the establishment of Buddhism. This faith, which was brought from China and Korea, had already developed in its Mahāyāna form, as we have seen, an elaborate eschatology that involved *post-mortem* retribution, and was geared to its doctrine of *saṃsāra*. To the less sophisticated of the Japanese this Buddhist eschatology had a potent appeal. Among the many sects, in which Japanese Buddhism gradually found expression, that of Jôdo-shû, 'the sect of the pure earth', founded by the monk Genkū or Hônen Shônen (1133–1212), became distinguished for its preoccupation with eschatology.[18] Proclaiming that only through the Bodhissattva Amida could salvation be won, this sect, by its promise of attaining the Western Paradise or Pure Land of Amida after death, offered a goal more desirable and intelligible to ordinary folk than the essentially metaphysical concept of Nirvāṇa. The delights of this Heaven were vividly imagined, and so, correspondingly, were the torments of Hell (Jigoku). This place of retribution was divided into eight hot and eight cold divisions, and these in turn were subdivided: over all presided Emma-Ô, who was the Japanese version of the ancient Indian god of the underworld, Yama-rāja.[20]

In popular art Emma-Ô is depicted as seated at his tribunal clothed in the robe of a Chinese judge. Open on the table before him lies a book containing the record of the deeds of the dead who are brought to him for judgment. On either side of his tribunal, mounted on stands, are two human heads. The one on the right is that of a woman; named *Miru-me*, it observes all human sins, even those done in secret. The head to Emma-Ô's left is male; called *Kagu-hana*, it smells out even the smallest offence. Under such scrutiny, the sinner is next dragged by a demon to a large mirror in which he sees reflected all his past misdeeds; then the measure of his guilt is assessed on a huge pair of scales and judgment given.[21]

The naked souls expiate their sins in one of the eight hells, or perhaps in several successively as their sentences require. The process of expiation follows the Buddhist pattern, which we have already noted; the torments suffered by the damned are fiendish in their ingenuity and horror, and in popular art they are depicted with that vivid realism that characterizes Japanese art.[22]

The damned, however, may be saved from their sufferings by the intervention of a compassionate Bodhisattva. Japanese literature contains many tales of such intervention. The salvation is usually achieved by Jizô-bosatsu, a popular figure in Japanese folklore who derives from the Indian Bodhisattva Kshitigarbha. He appears in the tales as a little monk, and often intercedes for a sinner at the tribunal of Emma-Ô.[23] Deliverance generally means return to this world, which is in effect a short-sighted conception of salvation since the person concerned would, logically, have to face judgment again when he died.[24]

In the *kyôgen*, which were farces performed between two *nô* plays, the exploits of Jîzo in saving various persons from *post-mortem* torment take the form of contests between Jîzo and Emma-Ô, in which the latter is outwitted and loses his victim. These *kyôgen* present Emma-Ô not as the dignified though grim judge of the underworld, but as the chief of the devils of Hell, slow-witted and grotesque.[25] In one such farce Emma-Ô is represented as being beaten in a game of chance and having to forfeit his crown, records and famous mirror, besides showing the deceased, who beat him, the road to Paradise.[26]

This degradation of Emma-Ô is reminiscent of a certain aspect of the mediaeval Christian attitude towards the Devil, who, though feared as the Prince of Darkness, was sometimes ridiculed and made a figure of fun.[27] The Japanese reaction, however, was probably inspired by a different kind of motive from that operative in mediaeval Christianity. The proliferation of Buddhist sects in Japan, each promising to its devotees rebirth in some paradise, must inevitably have reduced the fear of being brought before the tribunal of Emm-Ô for judgment.[28] There seems, moreover, to have been in many Japanese a natural tendency to scepticism, which caused them to be unimpressed by the crude imagery of a primitive eschatology, and which led them to find in an austere cult such as Zen a faith more congenial to their own instinctive notions.[29] Thus Daisetz Teitaro Suzuki, the famous exponent of Zen, could ask rhetorically, and for us significantly: 'Who wants to be arrested in the daily manifestations of his life-activity by such meditations as the goodness of a divine being or the everlasting fire of hell?'[30]

EPILOGUE

The belief that man must face judgment after death has stemmed from a variety of presuppositions about human destiny in the religions which we have chosen to study. But this difference of presuppositions has not been matched by a similar difference of imagery. Ideas drawn from current judicial procedure, such as tribunals of judges, accusers and prosecutors, and written records of conduct, have, understandably, been employed in all the religious traditions concerned, in order to visualize this judgment after death. In these conceptions there is, however, one omission from what has been accepted practice in criminal investigation among many peoples: it is the use of torture to secure confession from the accused. Its omission is surely significant, and it is doubtless due to the assumption that the judge of the dead would know the truth without resort to such a method. The notion of weighing the soul, which occurs in many eschatologies and which seems to have originated in ancient Egyptian religion, may perhaps witness to an awareness on the part of many peoples that the administration of justice on earth could too often be frustrated by corrupt officials – hence the idea of an impersonal assessment of merit and demerit by the weighing of the soul or its deeds in the next world.

The execution of the sentence given at this *post-mortem* tribunal, whether it be conceived in terms of an Immediate or a Last Judgment, has also shown a remarkable similarity of expression when translated into either verbal or pictorial imagery. While the representation of the joys of the just has generally tended to be of a rather symbolical kind, the sufferings of the damned have been depicted with such brutal realism that, except for a difference of artistic idiom, a mediaeval Christian picture of Hell might well have portrayed Orphic, Muslim, Tibetan, Chinese or Japanese expectations of the fate of the damned.

It is, however, from the underlying presuppositions of the various eschatologies that the most significant conclusions are to be drawn about the phenomenology of the idea of the Judgment of the Dead. The first of these conclusions is obvious, and it may be briefly stated. Belief in a judgment after death depends essentially on belief in *post-mortem* survival, or to be more exact, on the conception of what part of the human personality may survive death. The religion of Mesopotamia, the early form of Yahwism, and the Homeric tradition in Greek religion, provide relevant examples. The eschatologies of these religions stemmed from conceptions of human nature which regarded death as the irreparable shattering of the psycho-physical organism that constituted the essential person. Consequently, what survived this fatal disintegration could not be the proper subject of a *post-mortem* judgment, and these religions, therefore, did not entertain the notion.

The next conclusion that may be usefully drawn from our study concerns the connection of deity with the judgment of the dead. Among the religions which taught that there would be such a judgment a significant division can be made. It will be more convenient to notice first those which had no strong monotheistic, or even theistic, character. These religions form a group that is also distinguished by belief in metempsychosis or reincarnation, namely, Hinduism, Buddhism and the Orpheo-Gnostic cults. Although deities of various kinds figure in all these faiths, they have no essential rôle in the process of the transmigration of the soul through successive forms of incarnate existence. Such transmigration appears as an automatic and impersonal process, occasioned by some form of primordial ignorance or error about the true nature of reality. The process is retributive so far as each individual is concerned, in that at any given moment the situation of each person, be it good or ill, is the exact consequence of previous conduct, stretching back through innumerable incarnations. The religions concerned, as we have seen, do envisage definite judgments at the end of each period of incarnate life, with consequent rewards or punishments. But such *post-mortem* judgments, with their heavens and hells, are by way of being concessions to the natural tendency to regard death as the definitive end to a life-time, and which evokes fear of supernatural dangers, including retribution for past conduct. But even these short-term assessments do not essentially involve any specific deity, whose purpose or character had to be vindicated against those who, in effect, flouted his sovereignty by their misdeeds. The principle of *karma*, or its equivalent concept in Orphism and Gnosticism, operated without reference to divine sanction or theodicy. It was, moreover, not invoked primarily to maintain a moral code, although it did imply that the individual would inevitably experience the consequences of his actions. The theistic or monotheistic religions have linked belief in a *post-mortem* judgment essentially with the character or purpose of deity. This clearly emerges from the beginning in Egypt. Evil-doing challenged *maāt*, the good order which the Sun-god, Rē, the 'Great God', embodied and maintained. When belief in a Final Judgment became established in Israel, the form it took was essentially that of the ultimate vindication of the sovereignty of Yahweh over those who had opposed his purpose. This conception passed over into Christianity, and, although in process of time two forms of *post-mortem* judgment were envisaged, namely, an Immediate and a Last Judgment, each was essentially a theodicy. Sin was, on the final analysis, rejection of the sovereignty of God, and, in judging and punishing the sinner, God vindicated Himself. The Islamic doctrine of Allah's eventual judgment of mankind is similarly a theodicy, vindicating divine authority, as the Final Judgment in Zoroastrianism was also the ultimate proclamation of the triumph of Ohrmazd over Ahriman, the personification of evil.

In these religions, therefore, belief in the Judgment of the Dead has been a theological necessity. For the only too-evident fact that the wicked in this world continue to flout the divine law and yet prosper, while the godly often go to their graves in misfortune and defame, demands *post-mortem* rectification, if God's providence is to be vindicated. In other words, since the Divine Will clearly does not prevail in this world, faith in its validity can be sustained only by asserting that it will surely prevail in the next.

In the civilizations that have been inspired by theistic religions the moral law has been based upon what has been conceived to be divine law. Accordingly, standards of both public and private conduct have been accepted because they were regarded as having divine sanction. Such codes of behaviour, and the values they express, in all the civilizations concerned have included both ethical and religious precepts. Thus, to take one obvious example, the Ten Commandments combine moral demands such as 'Thou shalt not kill' with ritual requirements like 'Remember the sabbath day, to keep it holy'. Such a combination, in each instance that we may consider, obviously connotes what was regarded as necessary or desirable in the interests of both the social and religious structure of the community or state. As such it was proclaimed as representing the divine will for man, and it was taught that its infringement would be punished both here and hereafter. Where ecclesiastical power has been strong, offences of a religious character have often carried a more rigorous penalty than those that have violated moral values.

The gradual secularization of Western Civilization has had serious consequences for the traditional moral law, which was founded on Christian ethical and religious values, and its repercussions for Christian eschatology merit our concluding comment. The various Western states have progressively distinguished between social and private morality in their penal codes, and they have tended to regard the latter as not being a proper subject for public legislation and control. Consequently, private morality has had to rely increasingly upon the assumption of divine sanction for its validity. Now, since its enforcement has thus steadily lost both the support of the law and of the censure of public opinion, inevitably private morality has needed more the reinforcement of a strongly established eschatology. In other words, because belief in judgment after death, with its eternal consequences of Heaven or Hell, constitute the 'teeth' or ultimate authentication of the Christian ethic, that belief has now become practically even more necessary than it was before.* However, the secularization of Western Society has coincided with a growing uncertainty among Christians, of most denominations, about their traditional eschatology. Although the ancient concepts of Judgment, Heaven and Hell are still current in hymns and prayers, and are enunciated in the reading of the Bible, the imagery in which they were originally presented is now found embarrassing and new forms of interpretation are sought. But attempts at re-presentation in what is deemed to be a more acceptable idiom inevitably rob these ideas of their once urgent reality, and render them but poor shadows of the powerful notions that provided the ultimate sanction of the Christian *Weltanschauung*.

It is not our task to discuss this issue further. The attention, which has been devoted to it here, is justified, since it serves to show the importance of the idea of the Judgment of the Dead in Western Society. Belief in that idea has been a factor of basic significance for the evaluation of man's life in the past; the decline of that belief is having serious consequences in the present. The fact surely demands the attention of both theologian and sociologist.

*Ideally, of course, the Christian moral code should be practised for love of God, and not for the hope of gaining Heaven or escaping Hell. Nevertheless, the validity of that code depends logically upon an ultimate distinction, made by God, between the just and the unjust.

NOTES

Introduction

1 See W. B. Yeats's Poem entitled 'Death':

> A great man in his pride
> Confronting murderous men
> Casts derision upon
> Supersession of breath;
> He knows death to the bone –
> Man has created death.

2 Man's time-consciousness as the source of his religions has been treated at length in the author's book *History, Time and Deity* (1965).

3 Cf. T. Mainage, *Les religions de la Préhistoire: l'age paléolithique*, pp. 165–6; J. Maringer, *Vorgeschichtliche Religion*, pp. 71–88; E. O. James, *Prehistoric Religion*, pp. 21–3; G. Clark, *World Prehistory*, pp. 43–4.

4 Cf. Mainage, pp. 167, 171–2, 188–9; Maringer, pp. 78–9; R. Pittioni, *Die urgeschichtlichen Grundlagen der europäischen Kultur*, pp. 41–4; Clark, pp. 57–8.

5 The inhumation of the dead has suggested a subterranean location for the dwelling-place of the dead, which finds expression in most religions and folklore: cf. A. Bertholet, *Wörterbuch der Religionen*, pp. 183 ('Hel'), 197–8 ('Hölle'); E. B. Tylor, *Primitive Culture*, I, pp. 340ff.

6 On the significance of Palaeolithic 'crouched burials' and the funerary use of a red pigment, cf. Brandon, *Man and his Destiny in the Great Religions*, pp. 9–12.

7 P. Wernert in *H.G.R.*, I, pp. 63, 65. Wernert follows H. Breuil in dating the figures as 'd'âge paléolithique final'. H. Kühn, *Die Felsbilder Europas*, pp. 59–80, would date pictures of this type somewhat later ('sind nicht mehr als eiszeitlich, sondern als nacheiszeitlich zu betrachten', p. 63). Certain schematic figures, without heads, from the same area he describes as 'dämonische Gestalten', and dates them for 2500–2000 BC; cf. *op. cit.*, pp. 96, 101–2. Cf. J. Maringer, *The Gods of Prehistoric Man*, pp. 61–2; J. Hawkes, *Prehistory*, I, p. 214(3). S. Giedion (*The Eternal Present*, pp. 463–8) interprets these headless figures as depictions of shamanistic initiations. See fig. 1. Cf. *R.A.C.*, I, 211–16 ('Akephalos').

8 Cf. Wernert in *H.G.R.*, I, pp. 68–72; H. Breuil and R. Lantier, *Les hommes de la Pierre Ancienne*, pp. 280–5.

9 The evidence seems to be provided by the now well-known picture of a bird-headed being slain by a wounded bison, which was found in a small cave in the cavern-complex at Lascaux. For an illustration and account see H. Breuil, *Quatre Cents Siècles d'Art pariétal*, pp. 131, 134–5, 148, 150–1 (fig.). That it might be our earliest evidence of 'black magic' was first suggested by the author in his *Man and his Destiny*, pp. 20–1, 29–30. For other interpretations see F. Windels, *The Lascaux Cave Paintings*, p. 13; A. Laming, *Lascaux*, pp. 93–6; James, *Prehistoric Religion*, p. 178; Maringer, *Vorgeschichtliche Religion*, pp. 128–32; Giedion, *The Eternal Present*, pp. 507–8.

10 James, *Prehistoric Religion*, pp. 34ff.; J. Hawkes, *Prehistory*, I, pp. 341ff.

11 Cf. J. Mellaart in *I.L.N.*, February 1, 1964, p. 158; *Earliest Civilisations of the Near East*, pp. 81ff.

12 For illustrations see *I.L.N.*, February 8, 1964, figs. 10, 11, 13, 18, 19; Mellaart, *Earliest Civilisations of the Near East*, ill. 62, 65, 86. See fig. 2.

13 Mellaart in *I.L.N.*, February 8, 1964, p. 194; *Earliest Civilisations*, pp. 90, 98.

14 Cf. Mellaart, *Earliest Civilisations*, pp. 96–100.

15 Some figures appear to be standing and others are seated; all have their arms in a position most unlikely for a corpse. According to Mellaart (*Earliest Civilisations*, p. 98), an earlier scene from Level VIII shows 'a man armed with a sling defending a corpse against two black vultures'. Again, one must wonder what relevance such a scene had for the sanctuary. The depiction of vultures devouring the slain is appropriate for the commemoration of a victory as in the famous Sumerian Vulture Stele from Lagash: cf. *C.A.H.*, vol. of plates I, pp. 42–3.

16 Cf. Mellaart in *I.L.N.*, February 8, 1964, p. 194; *Earliest Civilisations*, p. 101.

17 See below, pp. 118ff.

18 Cf. K. M. Kenyon in *Antiquity*, XXVII (1953), pp. 105–7, and plate V; J. Hawkes, *Prehistory*, I, p. 342.

I Ancient Egypt

1 Cf. H. Bonnet, *Reallexikon*, pp. 620b–23a; S. A. B. Mercer, *The Pyramid Texts*, I, pp. 1–7, *Literary Criticism of the Pyramid Texts*, pp. 6ff.; I. E. S. Edwards, *The Pyramids of Egypt*, pp. 151–4; J. Spiegel, in *Orientalia*, XXII (1953), pp. 129–57.

2 Cf. A. Gardiner, *Egypt of the Pharaohs*, pp. 84–7; S. Schott, *Mythe und Mythenbildung in alten Aegypten*, pp. 10–20; S. G. F. Brandon, *Creation Legends of the Ancient Near East*, pp. 20ff.

3 Cf. H. Kees, *Totenglauben und Jenseitsvorstellungen der alten Aegypter*, pp. 132–59; Brandon in *The Saviour God*, pp. 19–27; Bonnet, *Reallexikon*, pp. 568–76.

4 Cf. S. Morenz, *Die Zauberflöte*, p. 74; Bonnet, *Reallexikon*, pp. 570b–571a; Brandon, *ibid*.

5 Cf. Mercer, *Pyramid Texts*, IV, pp. 24–33; Kees in *Pyramid Texts* (ed. Mercer), IV, pp. 123–39.

6 E.g., *Pyr*. 167c–d, 1161b–c (text in K. Sethe, *Die altägyptischen Pyramidentexten*, I, p. 94, II, p. 149).

7 Cf. J. Yoyotte in *S.O.*, IV, pp. 23–4.

8 *Pyr*. 1041–43 (text in Sethe, II, pp. 80–1; trans., Mercer, I, pp. 181–2; L. Speleers, *Les Textes des Pyramides égyptiennes*, I, pp. 71–2). Cf. Yoyotte in *S.O.*, IV, pp. 25–6.

9 *Pyr*. 892: *n šnt* ⸨☐⸩ *tn nsw* (Sethe, I, p. 498). Mercer, II, p. 456, fails to appreciate the significance of the passage when he writes: 'The king probably refers to Rēᶜ'; unless it be taken as a general statement which the deceased applies to himself – he does not commit that particular sin'. Cf. H. Junker, *Pyramidenzeit*, p. 82; Kees, *Totenglauben*, p. 106: 'Das stammt aus der Ideenwelt der Untertanen und passt gar nicht als Konigsspruch'.

10 Cf. Yoyotte, *S.O.*, IV, p. 26.

11 *Pyr*. 386a–b (Sethe, I, p. 201). Cf. Kees, *Totenglauben*, p. 106.

12 See *A.N.E.T.*, pp. 407ff. Cf. J. Spiegel, *Die Idee vom Totengericht in der ägyptischen Religion*, p. 22; R. Anthes in *J.N.E.S.*, XIII (1954), p. 24. n. 20.

12a 'Wo kein Kläger ist, da ist auch kein Richter', Spiegel, *Totengericht*, p. 22. Cf. Bonnet, *Reallexikon*, pp. 334a–35a.

13 *Pyr*. 316d–17a–b (Sethe, I, p. 172). The crucial statement reads *imr.f m3ᶜḥrw.f m.irtn.f* (316d). Sethe translates: 'Er will, dass er gerechtfertigt werde in Bezug auf das, was er (selbst) gethan hat' (*Übersetzung und Kommentar*, I, p. 391). Yoyotte, *S.O.*, IV, p. 25, renders it: '(Le roi N) souhaite d'être justifié par le moyen de ce qu'il a fait'. Cf. Mercer, I, p. 83, II, p. 149; Speleers, I, p. 26; A. Moret, *Le Nil et la civilisation égyptienne*, pp. 216–17.

14 Cf. Brandon, *Creation Legends*, pp. 22–4.

15 Cf. Brandon, *op. cit.*, pp. 22–4, 27–8.

16 See below, pp. 28ff.

17 Cf. Erman-Grapow, *W.B.*, II, sub *m3ᶜ* – *ḥrw*, pp. 15–16: 'die stimme jemds. ist richtig, seine Aussage ist richtig befunden (vor Gericht) = er ist, gerechtfertigt, er triumphirt'.

18 *ᶜbš stš m3ᶜ wsir* (Sethe, I (text), p. 333). Cf. Kees, *Totenglauben*, p. 159. In *Pyr*. 1520a, Osiris is *nb m3ᶜt* (Lord of *maāt*).

19 Cf. Brandon in *The Saviour God*, pp. 19ff.

20 E.g. *Pyr*. 1258c–59b. Cf. G. Thausing, *Der Auferstehungsgedanke in ägyptischen religiösen Texten*, p. 21; H. Frankfort, *Kingship and the Gods*, pp. 111–12; Bonnet, *Reallexikon*, p. 350a.

21 Cf. Spiegel, *Totengericht*, p. 43, *Das Werden der altägyptischen Hochkultur*,

pp. 410–12; Junker, *Pyramidenzeit*, pp. 83–5; Kees, *Totenglauben*, p. 105; Bonnet, *Reallexikon*, pp. 337b–38a; Brandon in *Numen*, V (1957–8), pp. 115ff. In his important article on 'The Original Meaning of *mȝꜥ ḫrw*', in *J.N.E.S.*, XIII (1954), pp. 21–51, R. Anthes interprets the evidence of the *Pyramid Texts* as showing that the expression *mȝꜥ ḫrw* was 'applied to the deceased king when he is transfigured; they who praise him relate in fact that he is acclaimed as right or (in their quality of the celestial counterpart of the court of Heliopolis) repeat this acclamation; this idea is certainly not influenced by a reminiscence of the justified Osiris' (p. 50). He concludes, 'There is, to my knowledge, no primary connection between Osiris and *mȝꜥt, mȝꜥ ḫrw* recognizable, . . .' (p.51); see also in *J.N.E.S.*, XVIII (1959), p. 192. Unfortunately, though he asserts that this statement cannot be refuted by reference to *Pyr.* 1556a (see above), he adduces no evidence in support of his contention. Cf. Yoyotte in *S.O.*, IV, p. 25.

22 Cf. J. H. Breasted, *Development of Religion and Thought in ancient Egypt*, pp. 175–6; Kees, *Totenglauben*, p. 106.

23 In Sethe, II, p. 428.

24 In Sethe, I, p. 144; II, p. 429.

25 Cf. Bonnet, *Reallexikon*, pp. 430a–34a.

26 Cf. A. H. Gardiner, *Egyptian Grammar*, p. 535 (II).

27 Cf. Bonnet, *Reallexikon*, pp. 432b–33b; S. Morenz, *Aegyptische Religion*, pp. 120–3.

28 Cf. S. A. B. Mercer, *Religion of Ancient Egypt*, pp. 207–8.

29 Cf. Frankfort, *Kingship and the Gods*, pp. 51–2, 149; J. A. Wilson, *The Culture of Ancient Egypt*, pp. 47–50.

29a Cf. Brandon, *Man and his Destiny in the Great Religions*, pp. 164, 176, 263–4.

30 Cf. Wilson, *Culture of Ancient Egypt*, pp. 69–73; Gardiner, *Egypt of the Pharaohs*, pp. 79–80.

31 There is clearly much predynastic material incorporated into the *Pyramid Texts*: cf. Mercer, *Literary Criticism of the Pyramid Texts*, pp. 41–54.

32 On the period of decline and disorder cf. Wilson, pp. 104ff.; Gardiner, pp. 107ff.; E. Drioton–J. Vandier, *L'Égypte*, pp. 204–33.

32a Cf. Gardiner, *Egypt of the Pharaohs*, pp. 89ff.

33 Cf. R. Hamann, *Aegyptische Kunst*, pp. 140–55; K. Lange–M. Hirmer, *Egypt*, Abb. 68–77. Cf. Spiegel, *Totengericht*, pp. 7–8.

34 Cf. Bonnet, *Reallexikon*, p. 363 ('Kahaus'); U. Schweitzer, *Das Wesen des Ka im Diesseits und Jenseits der alten Aegypter*, pp. 84–6.

35 Cf. Schweitzer, *Das Wesen des Ka* (*passim*); L. Greven, *Der Ka in Theologie und Königskult der Aegypter des alten Reiches* (*passim*); Brandon, *Man and his Destiny*, pp. 39–42.

36 Cf. E. A. W. Budge, *The Mummy*, pp. 399–400.

37 Cf. *Man and his Destiny*, pp. 42–4 and the references there given.

38 Cf. *op. cit.*, pp. 44–5.

39 *Ꜣḥ ikr ꜥpr:* cf. Spiegel, *Totengericht*, pp. 11–12, 14.

40 Cf. Spiegel, *Totengericht*, pp. 5–8, 25; J. Zandee, *Death as an Enemy*, pp. 66ff.; C. E. Sander-Hansen, *Der Begriff des Todes bei den Aegyptern*, pp. 19–20.

41 Cf. Wilson, *Culture of Ancient Egypt*, p. 109; Gardiner, *Egypt under the Pharaohs*, pp. 162–4, 300–1.

42 *B.A.R.*, I, p. 115; text in K. Sethe, *Urkunden des Alten Reichs*, I, pp. 49–51.

42a The sign *ntr* ('god') is followed by an ideogram representing a bird, apparently of the falcon species, mounted on a standard: this is followed by the adjective *ꜥꜣ* ('great'): Sethe, *op. cit.*, p. 51.

42b In Sethe, *Urkunden*, I, p. 23; cf. Yoyotte in *S.O.*, IV, p. 28 (D).

43 Cf. Junker, *Pyramidenzeit*, p. 88; Kees, *Totenglauben*, p. 105; R. Anthes in *J.N.E.S.*, XVIII (1959), pp. 191–2.

44 *B.A.R.*, I, pp. 151–2: text in Sethe, *Urkunden*, I, pp. 121–3. Cf. Breasted, *Dawn of Conscience*, pp. 125–6.

45 What Spiegel (*Totengericht*, p. 26) calls 'die Idealbiographie' has this ideal status because it was commonly accepted as such at this time, and thereby constituted a moral criterion.

46 The hieroglyphic text as printed in Sethe, *Urkunden*, I, p. 123, line 2, shows some of the signs as damaged: *mr* (sign?) (*n?*) *nfr rn ḥr ntr ꜥꜣ. rn* might properly be translated 'name' as by Bonnet, *Reallexikon*, p. 335a: 'Ich wünschte dass mein Namen schön sei vor dem grossen Gott'. The same formula appears in the tomb inscription of Pepinacht (Sethe, *Urkunden*, I, p. 133, line 1), which Spiegel translates as: '(Denn) ich wünschte, dass es mir gut gehe bei dem grossen Gott'. Kees (*Totenglauben*, p. 105) gives: 'denn ich wünschte, *dass es gut für mich wäre vor dem grossen Gott*'. Cf. Junker, *Pyramidenzeit*, pp. 56–7; Morenz, *Aegyptische Religion*, p. 62.

46a See above, p. 9.

47 Spiegel, *Totengericht*, pp. 25–6. 'Ces petits discours plus ou moins stéréo-types, font de préceiux documents psychologiques: par eux un mort prétend convaincre des vivants!', Yoyotte in *S.O.*, IV, p. 27; J. Sainte Fare Garnot in *H.G.R.*, I, pp. 331–6.

47a Cf. Brandon, *Man and his Destiny*, pp. 74ff.

48 The earliest reference to the 'tribunal of the Great God' dates from the reign of Men-kau-rē (*c.* 2600 BC). The word *ḏꜣ ḏꜣ.t* ('tribunal') was used with reference to both this world and the next: cf. Erman-Grapow, *W.B.*, V, p. 529. It should be noted that in the Memphite cosmogony, a brief and enigmatic reference is made to a divine judgment by Ptah: 'So life is given to the peaceful, and death is given to the transgressor (through this utterance which the Heart conceived and the Tongue

commanded)'; for a discussion of the passage cf. Brandon, *Creation Legends of the Ancient Near East*, pp. 36–8.

49   Cf. J. A. Wilson in *A.N.E.T.*, p. 412a; A. Erman, *Literature of the Ancient Egyptians*, pp. 54–5. Text in K. Sethe, *Aegyptische Lesestücke*, pp. 36–42.

50   88–97 in *A.N.E.T.*, p. 412b (trans. J. A. Wilson).

51   Cf. Wilson in *A.N.E.T.*, p. 414b; Erman, *Literature*, p. 75; Yoyotte in *S.O.*, IV, pp. 34–6; Gardiner, *Egypt of the Pharaohs*, pp. 115–16; S. Donadoni, *La religione dell'antico Egitto*, pp. 157–9; Breasted, *Dawn of Conscience*, pp. 154ff.

52   Trans. Wilson in *op. cit.*, p. 417b; cf. Erman, *Literature*, p. 83. Cf. *Man and his Destiny*, pp. 67–9.

52a See Herodotus, II, 78

53   Trans. Wilson in *A.N.E.T.*, p. 415b; cf. Erman, *Literature*, p. 77; Spiegel, *Totengericht*, pp. 30–1.

54   Trans. Wilson, *ib.*, who suggests (n. 8) that it was 'perhaps an "inventory", helpful in attaining the eternal happiness of the next world'. There seems to have been no idea of a book of life or of sinners in ancient Egypt: cf. Zandee, *Death as an Enemy*, p. 340.

55   Trans. Wilson in *A.N.E.T.*, p. 415b; cf. Erman, *Literature*, pp. 77–8; Yoyotte in *S.O.*, IV, p. 34.

56   Trans. Wilson in *op. cit.*, p. 418a.

57   Pp. 25, 29, 42.

58   The bas-relief at Abydos representing Seti I venerating the cartouches of his predecessors back to the First Dynasty suggests that the Egyptians envisaged the events of the past extended backwards in a linear series; cf. Brandon, *History, Time and Deity*, Plate X. Cf. Spiegel, *Totengericht*, pp. 5–8; Morenz, *Aegyptische Religion*, pp. 78–81.

59   Cf. Bonnet, *Reallexikon*, pp. 669–70 ('Sargtexte'); J. Vandier, *La religion égyptienne*, pp. 86–100.

60   *C.T.* (ed. A. de Buck), IV, spell 338, pp. 335–6.

61   Cf. Yoyotte in *S.O.*, IV, pp. 37–8.

62   Cf. Kees, *Totenglauben*, pp. 102–3. Yoyotte (in *S.O.*, IV, p. 38) emphasizes the significance of the 'guirlande de la justification', which was placed on the mummy, as evidence that the idea of *post-mortem* justification, in this context, stemmed from the legend of Osiris's triumph over Set. Cf. A. H. Gardiner in *E.R.E.*, V, p. 478, n. 1; *Bilderatlas*, 2–4 Lieferung, Abb. 140.

63   Breasted (*Development*, p. 307) recognized that 'The Osirian faith had thus become a great power for righteousness *among the people*', but he thought that this situation was spoilt by the increasing emphasis on magic; *Dawn of Conscience*, pp. 262–5. Cf. Spiegel, *Totengericht*, p. 41; Vandier, *La religion égyptienne*, p. 135; Bonnet, *Reallexikon*, pp. 337b–38b.

64   *C.T.*, V, p. 321c–d (Spell 452). In a dedicatory inscription Ramses III

tells of a balance of electron which he caused to be made for the treasury of the temple of Atum-Rē at Heliopolis; cf. G. Roeder, *Ae.R.T.B.*, I, pp. 144–5.

65 *C.T.*, I, p. 181c–e (Spell 44).

66 *C.T.*, I, p. 209d (Spell 47).

67 *C.T.*, IV (Spell 335), pp. 298–302 (= *Book of the Dead*, chapter 17, 23), in T. G. Allen's ed. and trans., p. 95 (16); (see also A. Piankoff, *The Shrines of Tut-Ankh-Amen*, p. 57). Cf. Spiegel, *Totengericht*, p. 48; Yoyotte in *S.O.*, IV, p. 39; Kees, *Totenglauben*, p. 303. See also *The Papyrus of Ani* (ed. E. A. W. Budge), II, p. 391.

67a Cf. A. Erman and H. Ranke, *Aegypten*, p. 553, Abb. 233; *Dictionary of Egyptian Civilization* (ed. G. Posener), p. 140. See above n. 64.

68 Nefertem was closely related to, or was an aspect of Rē, the Sun-god: in the mortuary faith he had a dual character, benign and grim; cf. Bonnet, *Reallexikon*, pp. 508b–10b.

69 Cf. Wilson in *A.N.E.T.*, p. 407b; Erman, *Literature*, p. 116.

70 Trans. Wilson in *op. cit.*, pp. 409f.; cf. Erman, *op. cit.*, p. 121. Note also the significant statement: 'The balance of men is their tongue. It is the scales which seeks out deficiencies (in weight)', Wilson, *op. cit.*, p. 410a; text in Sethe, *Aegyptische Lesestücke*, p. 24.

71 In *A.N.E.T.*, p. 410a.

72 Cf. Wilson in *A.N.E.T.*, p. 405a; Erman, *Literature*, p. 86.

73 Trans. Wilson, *ib.*; text in Sethe, *Aegyptische Lesetücke*, p. 44.

74 The most complete study of these songs and other related compositions is by M. Lichtheim in *J.N.E.S.*, IV, pp. 191–211; but see also E. F. Werte in *J.N.E.S.*, XXI, pp. 118–28.

75 Trans. Wilson in *A.N.E.T.*, p. 467a; cf. Erman, *Literature*, p. 133.

76 Trans. Wilson in *op. cit.*, p. 467b; cf. Erman, *op. cit.*, p. 134.

77 Cf. Erman, *Literature*, pp. 182–3, 253–4.

78 Cf. Kees, *Totenglauben*, pp. 205–7; Wilson, *Culture of Ancient Egypt*, pp. 113–14; Brandon, *Man and his Destiny*, pp. 59–62; Morenz, *Aegyptische Religion*, pp. 70–1.

79 *C.T.*, I, p. 192e–h (Spell 45).

80 *C.T.*, IV, pp. 253–6 (Spell 255). Hetepeskues appears to have been a protective goddess.

81 Cf. Bonnet, *Reallexikon*, pp. 824a–28a. See also a Moret, 'Le Livre des Morts', in *Au temps des Pharaohs*, pp. 199–243; E. A. W. Budge, *The Book of the Dead*, I, pp. xviiff.

82 For a variety of relevant illustrations see E. A. W. Budge, *Osiris and the Egyptian Resurrection*, I, pp. 329, facing 330, 338, 344; *Book of the Dead*, I, pp. 31–2, II, pp. 149, 150; *Papyrus of Ani*, I, Plates 3, 31, 32, see also pp. 236–7; T. G. Allen, *The Egyptian Book of the Dead*, Plates XXXIV, XXXVI, LXXXI; Yoyotte in *S.O.*, IV, pp. 44–5.

83 Cf. Budge, *Papyrus of Ani*, I, pp. 219–20 (who dated it for 1450–1400 BC); Yoyotte in *S.O.*, IV, p. 44.

84 In *The Book of the Dead: Facsimile of Papyrus of Ani* (ed. E. A. W. Budge), Plate 3; cf. Budge, *Papyrus of Ani*, I, Plate 3. See plate 1.

85 In the *Papyrus of Nebseni* the deceased is represented as being weighed against his heart: cf. Budge, *Book of the Dead*, II, p. 149; see also *Papyrus Cairo 4221*, tomb of Sennutem (XX dyn.). In the *Papyrus of Anhai* (British Museum) the figure of the goddess *Maāt* is shown instead of her feather symbol; cf. Budge, *Osiris and the Egyptian Resurrection*, I, plate facing p. 330; Yoyotte in *S.O.*, IV, p. 44. See fig. 4.

86 Cf. Budge, *Papyrus of Ani*, I, pp. 236–7, II, p. 375; *Osiris and the Egyptian Resurrection*, I, p. 328. See also Spiegel, *Totengericht*, p. 48.

87 On Shai cf. Bonnet, *Reallexikon*, pp. 671a–74a; C. J. Bleeker in *Numen*, II (1955), pp. 28–46; Morenz, *Aegyptische Religion*, pp. 69ff.

87a Cf. Budge, *Osiris and the Egyptian Resurrection*, I, p. 332; Bonnet, *Reallexikon*, pp. 458a–59a, 803a–04b; see also p. 208b.

88 The representation of Ani's *ba* in this position raises an interesting question about the manner in which the artist conceived of the spatial relations of the various entities depicted in the scene. It is also curious that no representation is given of the judgment of Ani's wife, although she appears with him in the vignettes depicting his life in the next world.

89 Cf. Budge, *Osiris and the Egyptian Resurrection*, I, p. 331; Bonnet, *Reallexikon*, p. 459a.

90 Cf. Budge, *Papyrus of Ani*, I, pp. 234–5.

91 Pp. 37ff.

91a *iw bȝ.f ʿḥʿ m mtr r f*, in *op. cit.*, II, p. 372. *r f* could also mean 'to him'. The point is significant: Ani's soul could have been a witness to the truth of the judgment, or a witness on his behalf. Cf. Spiegel, *Totengericht*, pp. 65–6.

92 *Facsimile of Papyrus of Ani*, 4; Budge, *Papyrus of Ani*, I, Plate 4, pp. 239–42. See plate 2.

93 Many scenes of the weighing depict the transaction taking place in the presence of Osiris. See n. 108 below.

94 *wḏˤ św Dḥwty m sšw*, in Budge, *Papyrus of Ani*, II, p. 374. Cf. Spiegel, *Totengericht*, p. 69.

95 See Budge, *Papyrus of Ani*, I, Plates 7, 16, 19. 35.

96 That no scene of the weighing in the various extant versions of the *Book of the Dead* depict an adverse verdict scarcely needs explanation. Yoyotte in *S.O.*, IV, p. 66, thinks it probable that the drama of Chapter 125 was actually performed in certain sanctuaries, 'au profit de particuliers'; he cites, in evidence, the large representation of the weighing of the heart in the small temple at Deir-el-Medîneh. For an account of this temple, which dates from the Ptolemaic period, and the judgment scene, cf. Baedeker's *Egypte* (1902), pp. 295–6; J. Capart, *Thebes*, p. 275, fig. 190;

B. Porter and R. L. B. Moss, *Topographical Bibliography of Ancient Egyptian Hieroglyphic Texts, Reliefs, and Paintings*, II, p. 139 (36).

97 E.g. see *Papyrus of Nu* (British Museum), Chapter 125, in Budge, *Papyrus of Ani*, II, p. 572. Cf. Yoyotte in *S.O.*, IV, p. 51; T. G. Allen, *Book of the Dead*, p. 196.

98 For other trans. see J. A. Wilson in *A.N.E.T.*, p. 34; Ch. Maystre, *Les déclarations d'innocence*, pp. 23–51.

99 Cf. *A.N.E.T.*, pp. 34b–35a; Maystre, pp. 51–5, 122.

100 See Budge, *Papyrus of Ani*, I, Plates 31 and 32.

101 Cf. *A.N.E.T.*, p. 35a. Cf. Allen, *Book of the Dead*, pp. 197–9.

102 Cf. *A.N.E.T.*, pp. 35b–36a; Yoyotte in *S.O.*, IV, pp. 54–5.

102a Cf. *A.N.E.T.*, p. 36a.

103 Cf. Budge, *Papyrus of Ani*, II, p. 588: *r smtr mꜣˁt r rdt iwśw r ˁḥˁw.*

104 Cf. *A.N.E.T.*, p. 36a; Yoyotte in *S.O.*, IV, pp. 55–6.

105 Cf. *A.N.E.T.*, p. 36b; Yoyotte in *S.O.*, IV, p. 57; Spiegel, *Totengericht*, pp. 59–61.

106 In Budge, *Papyrus of Ani*, II, p. 581 (34). Cf. Yoyotte in *S.O.*, IV, p. 64.

107 Cf. Bonnet, *Reallexikon*, pp. 433b–34a; Yoyotte in *S.O.*, IV, pp. 61–3: 'Les Deux Maât correspondent aux deux moments cosmiques de l'action souveraine du dieu universel qui surveille et juge: l'action diurne et l'action nocturne'.

108 Spiegel, *Totengericht*, pp. 51–4, sees in Chapter 125 evidence of Osiris's having supplanted Rē. In one judgment scene Rē is depicted in the place of Osiris: see J. Capart in *C.E.*, XIV (1939), fig. 2.

109 Cf. Yoyotte in *S.O.*, IV, p. 64.

110 E.g. Budge, *Osiris and the Egyptian Resurrection*, I, p. 340; Breasted, *Dawn of Conscience*, p. 257; A. Erman, *Die Religion der Aegypter*, p. 228.

111 E.g. 'O Breaker-of-Bones, who comes forth from Herakleopolis ...'; 'O Swallower-of-Shadows'; 'O Eater-of-Blood, who comes forth from the execution-block ...'.

112 Cf. Yoyotte in *S.O.*, IV, pp. 64–5. See also P. Montet, *Eternal Egypt*, pp. 186–90. The time may be that of Meri-ka-rē.

113 Cf. A. Piankoff, *Le 'Coeur' dans les textes égyptiennes*, pp. 91–3; Bonnet, *Reallexikon*, pp. 227–9; Kees, *Totenglauben*, pp. 54–5; Brandon, *Man and his Destiny*, p. 45.

114 Cf. Bonnet, *Reallexikon*, pp. 297b–98a; Budge, *The Mummy*, pp. 289–98, 311–12.

115 In Budge, *Papyrus of Ani*, II, 439–40. Cf. Yoyotte in *S.O.*, IV, p. 47. Allen (*Book of the Dead*, p. 115) translates from the documents which he uses: 'My heart of my mother, my heart of my mother, my breast that I had on earth, rise not against me as witness, oppose me not in the Council. Weigh not (heavy) against me before the Gods; weigh not heavy against me before the great God the lord of the west. Hail to thee,

thou heart of Osiris presiding over the westerners; hail to thee, viscus. . . .'
Cf. Spiegel, *Totengericht*, pp. 64–5; G. Roeder, *Urkunden zur Religion des alter Aegypten*, p. 254; Piankoff, *Le 'Coeur'*, pp. 81–3.

116 Cf. Breasted, *Development*, pp. 307–9; *Dawn of Conscience*, pp. 262–5; Kees, *Totengericht*, pp. 274–5; J. Černý, *Ancient Egyptian Religion*, pp. 90–1; Budge, *The Mummy*, p. 293; H. Frankfort, *Ancient Egyptian Religion*, p. 118; Yoyotte in *S.O.*, IV, p. 50.

117 Cf. Yoyotte in *S.O.*, IV, p. 47.

118 *C.T.*, II, 130 (Spell 113): *ḥ3f* . . . *r-f*; cf. Kees, *Totenglauben*, p. 274; Yoyotte in *S.O.*, IV, p. 39.

119 Chapter 28 of the *Book of the Dead* in the *Papyrus of Nu* (British Museum) is entitled 'The Chapter of not letting the heart of the overseer of the house of the Seal, NU, triumphant, be carried away from him in the Underworld'. The *Papyrus of Nefer-uben-f* has a vignette to this chapter showing the deceased holding his heart and menaced by an anthropoid monster with a knife: cf. Budge, *Book of the Dead*, II, pp. 141–2; cf. Allen, *Book of the Dead*, p. 113; Yoyotte in *S.O.*, IV, p. 39.

120 In Budge, *Papyrus of Ani*, II, pp. 440–1. Cf. Morenz, *Aegyptische Religion*, p. 231. The oldest known heart-scarab, stamped with an extract from Chapter 30b, is that of the Pharaoh Sebekemsaf of the Seventeenth Dynasty (*c.* 1600 BC); cf. Budge, *The Mummy*, p. 293.

120a Spiegel pertinently observes: 'Wäre dieser Auffassung (achieving *postmortem* justification by magic) aber die ursprüngliche, so hätte sich die Vorstellung von der Waage niemals entwicheln können' (*Totengericht*, p. 63, n. 4).

121 The first two scenes depict Ani and his wife in acts of adoration. The scene of the weighing attached to Chapter 125 appears to be a kind of abbreviation of the first scene: cf. Budge, *Papyrus of Ani*, I, Plates 3 and 32, see also p. 315; *Facsimile*, Plates 31 and 32.

122 The weighing is depicted as taking place at the far end of the Hall of the Two Maāti from the point where the recitation of the Second Declaration of Innocence begins. Cf. Spiegel, *Totengericht*, pp. 68–9; C. Desroches-Noblecourt, in *H.G.R.*, I, pp. 304b–05a; E. Drioton in *Les religions de l'Orient ancien*, pp. 43–4.

123 The employment of the principle of sympathetic magic in art, to effect some desired event, is very ancient, being found in Palaeolithic cave art: cf. Brandon, *History, Time and Deity*, pp. 15–18.

124 In *R-G.L.*, Lief. 10 (H. Kees), p. 16.

125 Cf. *Ae.R.T.B.*, IV, p. 247; *R-G.L.*, Lief. 10, pp. 45–6; Yoyotte in *S.O.*, IV, p. 67. See also A. H. Gardiner in *J.E.A.*, IV, pp. 29–30.

126 Cf. *R-G.L.*, Lief. 10, p. 46.

127 In G. Lefebvre, *Le tombeau de Pétosiris*, I, p. 136, II, p. 54 (inscription 81, ll. 16–22). Cf. E. Suys, *Vie de Petosiris*, p. 135; Bonnet, *Reallexikon*, p. 340;

Erman, *Die Religion der Aegypter*, pp. 339–44; Morenz, *Aegyptische Religion*, pp. 140–1.

128 Lefebvre, *op. cit.*, I, p. 111, II, p. 27 (inscription 55, ll. 2–3). On Thoth's rôle in the mortuary faith cf. P. Boylan, *Thoth, the Hermes of Egypt*, pp. 9, 138–41.

129 Trans. F. L. Griffith, *Stories of the High Priests of Memphis*, pp. 44–50; G. Maspero, *Les contes populaires de l'Égypte ancienne*, pp. 158ff. (E.T., pp. 144–50). Cf. Bonnet, *Reallexikon*, p. 340b.

130 Amentît (*imn.t.t*), i.e. 'the West' was the Osirian realm of the dead: cf. Erman-Grapow, *W.B.*, I, p. 87.

131 Sokarosiris was a Memphite mortuary god, associated with the Memphite district called Sokar, who became identified with Osiris.

132 Cf. P. D. Scott-Moncrieff, *Paganism and Christianity in Egypt*, pp. 46–51; H. I. Bell, *Cults and Creeds in Graeco-Roman Egypt*, pp. 13–14; Griffith, pp. 48–50.

133 Griffith, *op. cit.*, p. 41, dates the demotic papyrus concerned for the close of the first century AD; but the tale is obviously older. See below, pp. 110–11.

134 Cf. S. Morenz, 'Das Werden zu Osiris' (in *Staatliche Museen zu Berlin: Forschungen und Berichte*, I (1957), Abb. I, 2, p. 54).

135 Cf. S. Morenz, *Die Geschichte von Joseph dem Zimmermann*, pp. 2(b), 35, 126.

136 See pp. 214, n. 47; 214, n. 52a.

137 See p. 79.

138 Cf. Boylan, *Thoth*, p. 9: 'the tongue of the balance'; p. 181: 'he of the balance'; *R.A.C.*, V, 250.

139 Cf. Brandon, *Man and his Destiny*, pp. 39ff.

140 Griffith, p. 47, l. 7: 'She (i.e. Ama = Am-mut) does not allow him to breathe ever'.

141 Cf. E. Hornung, 'Die "Verurteilten" des ägyptischen Totengerichtes', in *X. Internationaler Kongress für Religionsgeschichte* (Marburg, 1960), p. 101.

142 Cf. Bonnet, *Reallexikon*, pp. 17b–20a; Erman, *Die Religion der Aegypter*, pp. 233–7; Budge, *From Fetish to God in Ancient Egypt*, pp. 357–68. See fig. 4.

143 See *Book of the Dead*, Chapter 176 (*Papyrus of Nu*), in Budge. *Book of the Dead*, III, p. 600. On the idea of a second death see Zandee, *Death as an Enemy*, pp. 86–8.

144 According to Hornung, *op. cit.*, p. 102: 'Die "Feinde" sind unsterblich, während die "Verklärten" sich allmorgendlich mit dem Sonnengott verjüngen und allnächtlich seinen Tod sterben. Sie bleiben im kosmischen Kreislauf, sie *sind*, während die Feinde "nicht sind".'

145 The properly ordered ritual assimilation of the deceased with Osiris was believed to effect resurrection *ex opere operato*: cf. Brandon in *The Saviour God*, pp. 19–28.

146 Cf. *Man and his Destiny*, pp. 66–9.

147 See above, p. 15.

148 On the sense in which Osiris was 'Everyman' cf. *Man and his Destiny*, pp. 66ff.; see also Morenz, *Aegyptische Religion*, pp. 5, 220.

II   Ancient Mesopotamia

1 Cf. H. Frankfort, *The Birth of Civilization in the Near East*, pp. 49ff.; M. E. L. Mallowan, *Early Mesopotamia and Iran*, pp. 13ff.

2 Cf. A. Parrot, *Archéologie mésopotamienne*, I, pp. 276, 296–7, 318; V. G. Childe, *New Light on the Most Ancient East*, p. 121; C.-F. Jean, *La religion sumérienne*, pp. 144–7; A. Heidel, *The Gilgamesh Epic and Old Testament Parallels*, pp. 150–65.

3 Cf. L. Woolley, *Excavations at Ur*, pp. 52–90; Mallowan, *op. cit.*, pp. 89–98, 99–100.

4 Various other explanations have been advanced. H. Frankfort, *Kingship and the Gods*, p. 400, n. 12, thought that the burials were those of 'substitute' kings and their suites; A. Moortgat, *Tammuz: der Unsterblichkeitsglaube in der altorientalischen Bildkunst*, pp. 54–79, interpreted the burials in terms of a Tammuz ritual. According to Woolley, *op. cit.*, pp. 81–2, 'in the time of the Third Dynasty (*c.* 2100 BC) the burial customs of the people of Ur underwent a profound change, and amongst other things the grave furniture was reduced to a minimum; the graves of the well-to-do folk of that age and of the Larsa age which followed it are beggarly compared with those of our Early Dynastic cemetery'. The change probably reflected a change in religious belief to the pessimistic eschatology documented in the texts examined below. Cf. S. N. Kramer in *A.N.E.T.*, p. 50 ('The Death of Gilgamesh', intro.).

5 Cf. A. Heidel, *The Gilgamesh Epic and Old Testament Parallels*, p. 10; F. M. Th. de Liagre Böhl in *Anthropologie religieuse* (ed. C. J. Bleeker), pp. 37–8; S. G. F. Brandon in *History Today*, XI (1961), pp. 18–27; B. Meissner, *Babylonien und Assyrien*, II, pp. 191–7.

6 Tab. X, col. ii. 1–11; cf. Tab. X, col. iii. 20–5. Since the death of Enkidu is not found in Sumerian texts concerning Gilgamesh, S. N. Kramer thinks, 'The incident ... was invented by the Babylonian authors of the "Epic of Gilgamesh" in order to motivate dramatically Gilgamesh's quest for immortality, which climaxes the poem' (*From the Tablets of Sumer*, p. 221).

7 *Epic of Gilgamesh*, Tab. XI, 189–96. Cf. Ed. Dhorme, *Les religions de Babylonie et d'Assyrie*, pp. 16, 20, 319; Meissner, II, p. 196; F. Jeremias in *L.R.G.*, I, p. 587.

8 On the epithet of Siduri see Dhorme's note, *Choix de textes religieux assyro-babyloniens*, p. 288, col I.-1. Cf. E. A. Speiser in *A.N.E.T.*, p. 189, n. 152.

9 Tab. X, col iii; trans. E. A. Speiser in *A.N.E.T.*, p. 90a. Cf. Heidel, *Gilgamesh Epic*, p. 70; Dhorme, *Les religions de Babylonie et d'Assyrie*, p. 318; T. Jacobsen in *The Intellectual Adventure of Ancient Man*, pp. 210–11; R. C. Thompson in *C.A.H.*, III, pp. 230–1; M. Jastrow, *Some Aspects of Religious Belief and Practice in Babylonia and Assyria*, pp. 373–5; J.-M. Aynard in *S.O.*, IV, p. 100.

10 Cf. Brandon, *Creation Legends of the Ancient Near East*, pp. 76ff., 87–90, 104–8.

11 Cf. M. David, *Les dieux et le destin en Babylonie*, pp. 23, 26, 39–40; Brandon, *Man and his Destiny in the Great Religions*, pp. 100–1; F. R. Kraus in *J.N.E.S.*, IX (1960), pp. 120–1.

12 Cf. Brandon, *Man and his Destiny*, pp. 76–7; on the names of the underworld see Dhorme, *Les religions*, pp. 38–9; Meissner, II, pp. 143–4.

13 See the *Descent of Ishtar into the Underworld* in *A.N.E.T.*, pp. 107a, 108a; *Epic of Gilgamesh*, Tab. VII, col. iv. 33–9. Cf. Heidel, *Gilgamesh Epic*, pp. 170–3.

13a The Semitic version in its most complete form dates from about the middle of the seventh century BC. The text, with translation and commentary, is given by Dhorme, *Choix de textes religieux assyro-babyloniens*, pp. 326–41; for other translations see Speiser in *A.N.E.T.*, pp. 106b–09a; Heidel, *op. cit.*, pp. 121–32; Ungnad, *Die Religion der Babylonier und Assyrer*, pp. 142–8. Fragments of a somewhat different Sumerian version, dating from about 2000 BC have been found: cf. C. N. Kramer, *Sumerian Mythology*, pp. 83–96, also his *From the Tablets of Sumer*, pp. 184–95.

14 In the Sumerian version Inanna (i.e. Ishtar) tells the doorkeeper of the underworld that she desires to attend the funeral rites of her elder sister Ereshkigal (actually the personification of the underworld); cf. Kramer, *Sumerian Mythology*, p. 90; in *A.N.E.T.*, p. 52, n. 1. According to Dhorme (*Les religions*, p. 321), the myth 'renferme une explication de l'invisibilité de la planète Vénus durant une période de sa course'.

15 In *A.N.E.T.*, p. 108a. In the Sumerian version, Inanna (Ishtar) dies and her body is hung on a stake: cf. Kramer, *Sumerian Mythology*, p. 93.

16 Cf. Brandon, *Man and his Destiny*, pp. 80–1; J.-M. Aynard in *S.O.*, IV, p. 84.

17 Tab. VII, col. iv. 40–8; trans Heidel, *Gilgamesh Epic*, p. 61. For other trans. cf. Speiser in *A.N.E.T.*, p. 86a; Ungnad, pp. 86–7; Aynard in *S.O.*, IV, p. 93. In lines 51–4 reference is made to Bêlit-Seri, the 'recorder of the nether world', who keeps account of those due to descend into the nether world on death.

18 Cf. *A.N.E.T.*, p. 97a; Heidel, pp. 93–4; Aynard, p. 96. For a Sumerian prototype see Kramer, pp. 30–7; *Tablets of Sumer*, pp. 222–6.

19 The spirit (*u-tuk-u*) of Enkidu issues from the underworld like a puff of wind (see Dhorme, *Choix de textes*, pp. 322 (28)). Cf. C. J. Gadd, *Ideas of*

The Judgment of the Dead

Divine Rule in the Ancient East, pp. 88–9; R. C. Thompson, *Devils and Evil Spirits of Babylonia*, I, pp. XXIV–XXV.

20 Tab. XII, 89–91: I will not tell thee, my friend, I will not tell thee. (But) if I must tell thee the way(s) of the underworld, which I have seen, Sit down (and) weep (trans. Heidel, *op. cit.*, p. 99). Cf. P. Jensen, *Das Gilgamesh-Epos in der Weltliteratur*, I, p. 53; Ungnad, p. 118; Speiser in *A.N.E.T.*, p. 98b.

21 Tab. XII, 99–153, according to Heidel's restoration of the text (*op. cit.*, pp. 100–1). Cf. Speiser in *A.N.E.T.*, p. 99; Ungnad, p. 118; Aynard in *S.O.*, IV, p. 96. For what seems to have been the Sumerian original of this passage cf. Kramer, *Sumerian Mythology*, pp. 36–7. J. Bottéro, *La religion babylonienne*, pp. 104–5, suggests that in time the Mesopotamian conceptions of the realm of the dead developed, so that distinctions were made between the 'morts glorieux et morts honteux, riches et pauvres, et par conséquent prospères et malhereux, comme ici-bas'. A more probable interpretation of such indications would seem to be that the earlier tradition, which found expression in the royal graves at Ur, was never completely abandoned. Cf. Heidel, *Gilgamesh Epic*, pp. 191–3. It is difficult to see how the Assyrian text telling of the visit of a prince, Kummaya, to the underworld (in *A.N.E.T.*, pp. 109–10) can be interpreted as evidence of a *post-mortem* judgment as Ebeling, *Tod und Leben nach Vorstellungen der Babylonier*, pp. 7–8 and Fish in *B.J.R.L.*, 30, p. 18, suggest.

22 Cf. E. Ebeling, *Tod und Leben*, pp. 84, 122, 132, 138, 145, 147. See also G. Contenau, *Les divinations chez les Assyriens et les Babyloniens*, p. 134; S. Langdon in *E.R.E.*, IV, pp. 444–6; R. C. Thompson in *E.R.E.*, IV, pp. 568–70, *Devils and Evil Spirits of Babylonia*, I, pp. xxiv–xxvi, xxvii–xxxv; Meissner, II, pp. 200, 215–18; H. W. F. Saggs, *The Greatness that was Babylon*, pp. 309–11.

23 Cf. G. Castellino in *Z.A.*, LII (1957), pp. 1f., in *Atti dell'VIII Congresso internazionale di storia delle Religioni* (1955), p. 246–9. Cf. Aynard in *S.O.*, IV, p. 91: 'Ils sont présents bien avant que la terre ne soit organisée et ils sont chargés de la police du monde souterrain'; cf. *op. cit.*, p. 92. Ebeling (*op. cit.*, p. 127) prints a text containing a eulogy of Gilgamesh, in which, *inter alia*, he is saluted as the lord and judge of the underworld; cf. Aynard in *S.O.*, IV, pp. 91–2; Meissner, II, p. 146.

24 In the Sumerian version of the *Descent of Inanna into the Underworld*, the Anunnaki, 'the seven judges, pronounced judgment before her' (i.e. Ereshkigal, the queen of the underworld (in *A.N.E.T.*, p. 55b). According to the *Epic of Gilgamesh*, Tab. X, col. xi. 36–9, the Anunnaki, together with Mammetum, 'the creatress of destiny', allot life and death to mankind (cf. *A.N.E.T.*, p. 93a). On the Anunnaki cf. Jean, *La religion sumérienne*, pp. 78, 122; Kramer in *Mythologies of the Ancient World*, pp. 98, 99, 129; Dhorme, *Les religions*, p. 45; Meissner, II, pp. 41, 146.

25 See Ebeling, p. 54. On the question why Tammuz did not have in Mesopotamian religion a rôle similar to that of Osiris in Egyptian religion cf. Brandon, *Man and his Destiny*, pp. 101–3.

26 In the legend of Adapa, the hero is summoned before Anu, the god of heaven, to answer for his offence in breaking the wings of the south-wind. The story has no bearing on the concept of a *post-mortem* judgment. Cf. *A.N.E.T.*, pp. 101–3; Kramer in *Mythologies of the Ancient World*, pp. 125–6; de Liagre Böhl in *Anthropologie religieuse*, pp. 39–41.

27 Cf. Ebeling, pp. 19–20; Aynard in *S.O.*, IV, p. 97; Meissner, II, pp. 146–7.

28 Ebeling translates (p. 20) *g[e-gu]-na* as 'Grabkammer (?)'. Cf. Aynard in *S.O.*, IV, p. 97, n. 11.

29 In Ebeling, pp. 20–1.

30 'Zwei Götter geleiten ihn, ein guter Engel *gšnikarâb* = *gšnikarâb* = "Er hat das Gebet gehört" und ein böser *Lâgamâl* = "Schonungslos". Der Verstorbene tritt vor *Šugurnak*, der in der Grube, d.i. der Unterwelt, wie es scheint, herrscht', Ebeling, p. 20.

31 In Ebeling, p. 21.

32 '[Er tri]tt zum Wäger und sagt:', Ebeling, *ib.* In text III (*ib.*), Ebeling translates the first line: 'Es stehen, es liegen in der Wagschale (*gabûtu*)'. Cf. Meissner, II, p. 146.

33 Cf. Aynard in *S.O.*, IV, p. 98.

34 See D. J. Wiseman, *Cylinder Seals of Western Asia*, 36.

35 *Epic of Gilgamesh*, Tab. VII, col. iv. 31–2, 38. 'Nous aurions donc là l'image du jugement de l'âme d'un mort, devant le tribunal d'Enki, dieu de l'apsu, c'est-à-dire des eaux souterraines.' A. Parrot, *Le 'Refrigerium' dans l'au-delà*, p. 39. Cf. T. Fish in *B.J.R.L.*, 31 (1948), pp. 1–10.

36 E.g. by Wiseman, *ib.*

37 Trans. R. H. Pfeiffer in *A.N.E.T.*, p. 438 (XI). Cf. S. H. Langdon in *Babyloniaca* (ed. Ch. Virolleaud), VII, p. 207; T. Jacobsen in *Intellectual Adventure of Ancient Man*, pp. 216–17; Kraus in *J.N.E.S.*, XIX, p. 117, n. 5; W. G. Lambert, *Babylonian Wisdom Literature*, pp. 140–9.

38 Cf. *Man and his Destiny*, pp. 70–1.

39 See pp. 7ff.

40 On ancient Mesopotamian respect for law cf. Saggs, *The Greatness that was Babylon*, pp. 196–232. Shamash, the Sun-god, watched over the maintenance of justice during the day, as the Moon-god Sin did at night; cf. Dhorme, *Les religions*, pp. 57, 63–4.

III Hebrew Religion

1 On the origins of the cult of Yahweh see E. Jacob in *Biblisch-historisches Handwörterbuch* (ed. Bo Reicke u. L. Rost), I, 587–8; H. H. Rowley, *From Joseph to Joshua*, pp. 148–63.

2 Cf. Brandon, *Man and his Destiny in the Great Religions*, pp. 109ff.

3 *Exodus* xix. 1ff. Cf. W. Beyerlin, *Herkunft und Geschichte der ältesten Sinaitraditionen*, pp. 10–17; H. Wildberger, *Jahwes Eigentumsvolk*, pp. 9–16.

4 Cf. Brandon, *History, Time and Deity*, Chapter V, where full documentation is given.

5 Cf. A. Lods, *Isräel*, pp. 260, 415, 549–52; W. O. E. Oesterley and T. H. Robinson, *Hebrew Religion*, pp. 326–7; J. Pedersen, *Israel*, IV, pp. 485–6; Brandon, *Man and his Destiny*, pp. 109–20.

6 *Genesis* iii. 19. Cf. Brandon, *Creation Legends of the Ancient Near East*, pp. 123–4, 139; *Man and his Destiny*, pp. 126–7, 129.

7 Cf. A. R. Johnson, *The Vitality of the Individual in the Thought of Ancient Israel*, pp. 9–13, 39–90; G. Pidoux, 'L'homme dans l'Ancien Testament', in *Anthropologie religieuse* (ed. C. J. Bleeker), pp. 157–60, 162–3; Pedersen, *Israel*, I, pp. 179–81; A. T. Nikolainen, *Der Auferstehungsglauben in der Bibel und ihrer Umwelt*, I, pp. 108–12.

8 *Job* x. 21–2.

9 Cf. E. Dhorme, *Les religions de Babylonie et d'Assyrie*, pp. 38–9, 40–4.

10 Pp. 101ff.

11 *Psalms* vi. 5 (Heb. 6); xxviii. 1; xxx. 9 (Heb. 10); lxxxviii. 10–12 (Heb. 11–13); cxv. 17; cxliii. 7; *Isaiah* xxxviii. 11, 18. Cf. Oesterley-Robinson, *Hebrew Religion*, pp. 322–7; R. H. Charles, *A Critical History of the Doctrine of a Future Life*, pp. 35–6; H. Cazelles in *S.O.*, IV, pp. 109–11.

11a Cf. J. Bright in *Peake's Commentary*[2], 446d.

12 Pp. 51–2.

13 *Isaiah* xiv. 9–11, 18. Cf. G. Fohrer, *Das Buch Jesaja*, I, pp. 178–9: 'Nun erheben sich die toten Könige von ihren Thronen, auf denen man sie sitzend glaubt, weil sie in solche Weise begraben oder auf Grabmälern dargestellt sind'.

14 *Ezekiel* xxxii. 21–4, 26–7. Cf. Cazelles in *S.O.*, IV, p. 115: 'Sur tous ces morts Yahvé garde un silence méprisant'.

15 Cf. A. Lods, *Les prophètes d'Israël et les débuts du Judaïsme*, pp. 236ff., 266–7.

16 Cf. Brandon, *Man and his Destiny*, pp. 130–1.

17 *Jeremiah* xvi. 10.

18 *Ezekiel* xviii. 25; xxxiii. 20. Cf. G. A. Cooke, *Ezekiel*, pp. 203–4.

19 *Jeremiah* xxxi. 30.

20 Cf. Lods, *Les Prophètes*, pp. 66–8.

21 Cf. W. O. E. Oesterley and T. H. Robinson, *Introduction to the Old Testament*, pp. 175–8; R. H. Pfeiffer, *Introduction to the Old Testament*, pp. 692–707.

22 *Job* x. 2–9.

23 iv. 7–9, viii. 6ff.

24 xiv. 7–12.

25 xix. 25–7. On the meaning of *go'el* ('Vindicator') cf. W. A. Irwin in

Notes (Hebrew Religion)

Peake's Commentary[2], 345c–d. Cf. Oesterley-Robinson, *Hebrew Religion*, p. 314; A. Heidel, *The Gilgamesh Epic and Old Testament Parallels*, pp. 211–16; Nikolainen, I, pp. 126–7; S. R. Driver and G. B. Gray, *Job*, pp. 171–4; H. H. Rowley, *The Faith of Israel*, pp. 164–5; Cazelles in *S.O.*, IV, p. 117.

26 Cf. Lods, *Les prophètes*, p. 385; Pfeiffer, *op. cit.*, p. 707.
27 *Job* xxi. 23–6.
28 xxxviii–xli. 'Le poème n'offre pas de solution au problème posé: . . . il se dégage du poème une leçon de résignation à ignorance, en présence de la puissance formidable et de la sagesse qui apparaissent dans les merveilles de l'univers', Lods, *Les prophétes*, p. 385. Cf. P. Humbert in *Wisdom in Israel and in the Ancient Near East* (ed. M. Noth and D. Winton Thomas), pp. 157–8.
29 xliii. 7–17.
30 Cf. W. A. Irwin in the *Intellectual Adventure of Ancient Man* (ed. H. & H. A. Frankfort), pp. 273ff.; Brandon, *Man and his Destiny*, pp. 129ff. The theme of innocent suffering and ultimate divine vindication in the celebrated *Servant Sagas* (*Isaiah* xlii. 1–4; xlix. 1–6; l. 4–9; lii. 13–liii. 12) cannot be evaluated in this connection, since the identification of the Servant as a person or as Israel remains an enigma, despite detailed analysis and interminable discussion. Cf. H. H. Rowley, 'The Servant of the Lord in the Light of Three Decades of Criticism', in *The Servant of the Lord and Other Essays on the Old Testament*, pp. 3–93.
30a As, for example, in *Ecclesiasticus*, xliv. 9–14. Cf. *Man and his Destiny*, pp. 145–6.
31 *Ezekiel* xxxvii. 7–10. Cf. Cooke, *Ezekiel*, pp. 397, 399–400; Cazelles in *S.O.*, IV, p. 113: 'Voici que l'action de Yahvé passe la mort'.
32 xxxvii. 11–14. Cf. Nikolainen, I, p. 130; J. A. MacCulloch in *E.R.E.*, V, p. 378a.
33 Cf. *Man and his Destiny*, pp. 117–18, 137–8.
33a The date of *Ezekiel* continues to be a problem: cf. Pfeiffer, *Introduction to Old Testament*, pp. 527–9; Rowley, *Men of God*, pp. 198ff.
34 On the significance of the Maccabaean revolt see W. O. E. Oesterley, *History of Israel*, II, pp. 217–27; M. Noth, *History of Israel*, pp. 359–68.
35 II *Macc.* xii. 40: *hierōmata tōn apo Iamneias eidōlōn*. Cf. A. Kamphausen in *Die Apokryphen und Pseudepigraphen* (ed. E. Kautzsch), I, p. 112, n. b.
36 xii. 41–2.
37 xii. 43–4. Cf. Charles, *Critical History*, pp. 275–6.
38 Cf. E. Schürer, *Geschichte des jüdischen Volkes im Zeitalter Jesu Christi*, III, pp. 359–64; R. H. Pfeiffer, *History of New Testament Times*, pp. 514–16.
39 *Daniel* xii. 1–2.
40 Cf. R. H. Charles, *The Revelation of St John*, I, p. 84; A. Jeremias in *E.R.E.*, II, p. 794b; L. Koep in *R.A.C.*, II, 726–7.

41 Pp. 29ff.

42 Cf. Nikolainen, I, p. 140; Ed. Meyer, *Ursprung und Anfänge des Christentums*, II, p. 179; Charles, *Critical History*, pp. 211–13.

43 Cf. Charles, *Critical History*, pp. 137–8.

44 *Daniel* xii. 3. It is possible that the idea derives from Iran, where the Fravashis, i.e. the *manes*, were connected with the stars; cf. J. H. Moulton in *E.R.E.*, VI, p. 118a. For ancient Egyptian evidence see H. Bonnet, *Reallexikon*, p. 74a.

45 Cf. *Daniel* vii. 1ff.; xii. 1ff. Cf. J. Barr in *Peake's Commentary*², 524a–h, 528g–h; Charles, *Critical History*, pp. 126–7; H. H. Rowley, *The Faith of Israel*, p. 168: 'In this passage from Daniel (i.e. xii. 2), what is in mind is physical life in this world, side by side with those who had not passed through death, as we have found in certain passages also in the New Testament'.

46 E.g. *Daniel* vii. 19–27. Cf. Pfeiffer, *Introduction to the Old Testament*, pp. 777–8.

47 vii. 9–10. Oesterley and Robinson, *Hebrew Religion*, pp. 348–9, would see Iranian influence in the 'fiery stream' that flows before the Ancient of Days. Cazelles rightly remarks: 'Il faut reconnaître qu'encore ici, le Jugement solennel est plus un jugement sur les vivants que sur les morts, mais on est bien proche d'un jugement sur les morts qui fixera leur destinée dans l'Au-Delà'. (*S.O.*, IV, p. 122.) It is interesting to note, for future reference, that in *Daniel* v. 27, the idea of weighing occurs in passing judgment on Belshazzar: 'Tekel, you have been weighed in the balances (*mǒ'z^enēy'*) and found wanting'.

48 This section dates from about 100 BC: cf. Pfeiffer, *History of New Testament Times*, pp. 75, 76; Schürer, III, pp. 190–2, 200; C. Beer in *Apok. u. Pseudepig.* (ed. E. Kautzsch), II, p. 232; R. H. Charles, *The Book of Enoch*, pp. xiii–xv; F. Martin, *Le Livre d'Hénoch*, p. xcv.

49 *Enoch*, XXI. Cf. Charles, *Critical History*, pp. 213–15; Martin, *op. cit.*, pp. xxix–xxxi.

50 A variant reading has : 'The spirits of the bodies of the dead'; cf. Martin, p. 58, n. 4; Beer, *op. cit.*, II, p. 252, n. f. Cf. Charles, *Critical History*, pp. 241–2.

51 XXII. 3–4: trans. R. H. Charles, *Book of Enoch*, pp. 47–8; see also his renderings in *Apocrypha and Pseudepigrapha*, II, p. 203, and *Critical History*, p. 216. Cf. Beer, II, p. 252; Martin, pp. 58–9.

52 XXII. 9–14: trans. Charles, *Book of Enoch*, pp. 48–9: cf. Beer, II, pp. 252–3; Martin, pp. 59–62. See also Charles, *Critical History*, pp. 216–18.

52a In a later portion of *Enoch* (XXXVII–LXXI), known as the *Parables* or *Similitudes of Enoch*, dating possibly about 100–80 BC, a process of judgment or assessment is described: And the Lord of Spirits placed the Elect One on a throne of glory. And he shall judge all the works of the holy above

in the Heaven, And in the balance shall their deeds be weighed (LXI. 8).
Cf. Martin, p. 127 (8).

53 For Egyptian concern about water in the next world cf. A. Parrot, *Le 'Refrigerium' dans l'au-delà*, pp. 84–130, 168: 'l'influence égyptienne nous apparaît possible, d'autant qu'on la retrouve encore dans la littérature extra-canonique avec le livre d'Henoch'. Beer, II, p. 253, n. d, sees in this passage an explanation of the request of the rich man in the Dives and Lazarus passage.

53a XXII. 10.

54 Cf. E. A. W. Budge, *From Fetish to God in Ancient Egypt*, pp. 365–6. See also fig. 3.

55 See pp. 12ff.

56 See pp. 110ff.

57 Cf. Pfeiffer, *History of New Testament Times*, pp. 76, 78.

58 LI. 1–2: trans. Charles, *Book of Enoch*, p. 69; cf. Beer, II, p. 265, Martin, pp. 103–4, see also pp. xxxiv–xxxvii. See also *Enoch*, LXI. 8–LXIII. 12.

59 Cf. Charles, *Critical History*, pp. 86–8; Ch. Guignebert, *Le monde juif vers le temps de Jésus*, pp. 163–8; G. von Rad in *J.S.S.*, IV (1959), pp. 97–108.

60 Cf. Charles, *Critical History*, pp. 260–6; Guignebert, p. 185; S. Mowinckel, *He That Cometh*, pp. 358–9.

61 *Jubilees* V. 13–14: cf. E. Littmann in *Apokryphen u. Pseudepigraphen* (ed. E. Kautzsch), p. 49. Cf. Cazelles in *S.O.*, IV, p. 124.

62 Cf. Schürer, II, pp. 533–6.

63 Cf. A. Dupont-Sommer, *Les écrits esséniens découvertes près de la Mer Morte*, pp. 179–81; Y. Yadin, *The Scroll of the War of the Sons of Light against the Sons of Darkness*, pp. 3–5, 242; H. W. Huppenbauer, *Der Mensch zwischen zwei Welten*, pp. 112–15.

64 Cf. M. Hengel, *Die Zeloten*, pp. 308–18; S. G. F. Brandon, *Jesus and the Zealots*, pp. 50–1, 112.

65 Cf. Pfeiffer, *History of New Testament Times*, pp. 326–9; Schürer, III, pp. 380–1.

66 *Wisdom*, iv. 20–v. 2.

67 vi. 5–8: 'The author speaks of a Last Judgment without telling us whether it modified the state of the deceased, and, if so, how. It would even seem that the Judgment (like Armageddon) is a Jewish tradition incongruously superimposed on the Greek notion that the souls go to their eternal rewards and punishments after death', Pfeiffer, *op. cit.*, pp. 339–40. See pp. 338–42.

68 See Josephus' account of his early life in his *Life*, 7–12. Cf. G. Ricciotti, *Flavio Giuseppe*, I, pp. 1–42, 121–3; F. J. Foakes Jackson, *Josephus and the Jews*, pp. 3ff.

69 *Jewish Antiquities*, xviii. 14. Cf. Schürer, II, pp. 391–2; Brandon, *Man and his Destiny*, pp. 146–7.

The Judgment of the Dead

70 Mark xiii. 18–27 (and synoptic parallels); Acts xxiii. 6–9.

71 Pp. 83ff.

72 Cf. Nikolainen, I, pp. 173–8.

73 Cf. Pfeiffer, *History of New Testament Times*, pp. 81–6; W. O. E. Oesterley in *New Commentary*, Part II, pp. 32a, 33b; Charles, *Critical History*, pp. 338, 347.

74 II (IV) *Esdras* vii. 78–80 (R.V.). Cf. Nikolainen, I, p. 168; H. Gunkel in *Apok. u. Pseudepig.*, II, p. 374.

75 II (IV) *Esdras* vii. 81–7 (R.V.).

76 vii. 88–99 (R.V.). Cf. Charles, *Critical History*, pp. 350–3.

76a Nikolainen, I, p. 169, rightly observes: 'Die Lehre vom Zwischenzustand dient in erster Linie dem Vergeltunsgedanken. Zugleich ist aber auch die Bedeutung der Auferstehung geringer geworden, und die klar durch-geführte, kraftvoll auf religiöse Vorstellungen konzentrierte Anthropologie des A.T. ist verloren gezangen'.

77 vii. 104, 105 (R.V.). Cf. Gunkel, *op. cit.*, II, p. 330.

78 See pp. 103ff.

79 vii. 32–8 (R.V.). On the relation of this so-called *Ezra Apocalypse* to the *Shalatiel Apocalypse* see Charles, *Critical History*, pp. 338–9; Oesterley in *New Commentary*, Part II, p. 37a; Pfeiffer, *op. cit.*, p. 81. Cf. Schürer, II, p. 81; Gunkel, *op. cit.*, II, pp. 337–9.

80 See pp. 111ff.

80a Although dating after AD 70, II (IV) *Esdras* represents the Jewish *Weltan-schauung* that preceded the catastrophic destruction of Jerusalem. On the continuance of a Jewish apocalyptist tradition, threatening Rome with divine judgment for the destruction of the Temple, see A. Peretti, *La Sibilla babilonese nella propaganda ellenistica*, pp. 467ff.

81 *Berakhoth* IV, ii. (Fol. 28b), trans. in *Der babylonische Talmud* (ed. L. Goldschmidt), I, pp. 124–5.

82 *Aboth*, 4–229 trans. H. Danby, *The Mishnah*, p. 455.

83 Pp. 8ff.

84 *Exodus* xx. 4. On 'Yahweh's jealousy' see J. Pedersen, *Israel*, III–IV, p. 620.

IV   Graeco-Roman Culture

1 Cf. R. Cohen, *La Grèce et l'Hellénisation du monde antique*, pp. 27–43; G. Huxley in *The Birth of Western Civilization* (ed. M. Grant), pp. 41b–42b, 47a–50a; Lord William Taylour, *The Mycenaeans*, pp. 21–6.

2 Cf. G. Glotz, *La civilisation égéenne*, pp. 445–52; C. Picard, *Les religions préhelléniques*, pp. 285–6; A. W. Persson, *The Religions of Greece in Pre-historic Times*, pp. 125–52; R. W. Hutchinson, *Prehistoric Crete*, p. 23.

3 Cf. L. A. Stella in *Numen*, V (1958), pp. 18–57; Taylour, p. 63; Hutchinson, p. 231.

4   Cf. J. Chadwick in *Antiquity*, XXXIII (1959), pp. 269–78; Hutchinson, pp. 70–3.

5   Cf. Picard, *Les religions préhelléniques*, pp. 205–6; J. Charbonneaux in *H.G.R.*, II, p. 20; Hutchinson, pp. 228–31.

6   Cf. Charbonneaux, II, pp. 20–1; S. Alexiou in *I.L.N.*, vol. 237 (1960), p. 226, fig. 8; E. O. James, *The Cult of the Mother Goddess*, p. 132.

7   A similar view is suggested by the evidence of tombs of the same period found at Ugarit (Ras Shamra): cf. C. F. A. Schaeffer, *The Cuneiform Texts of Ras Shamra-Ugarit*, p. 47. For evidence of a similar import coming from Mesopotamia and Palestine cf. S. G. F. Brandon, *Man and his Destiny in the Great Religions*, pp. 72, 110–12.

8   For illustrations see *H.G.R.*, II, pp. 16–17; M. Rostovtzeff, *A History of the Ancient World*, I, Plate LII, 4; *C.A.H.*, vol. of plates, I, p. 203; M. P. Nilsson, *The Minoan-Mycenaean Religion and its Survival in Greek Religion*, p. 427, fig. 196; *Geschichte der griechischen Religion*[1], I, Tafel, 10; *Bilderatlas zür Religionsgeschichte*, 7, Lieferung, 89–91. It is wise to inspect these earlier photographs, since the sarcophagus, now in the museum at Herakleion, has been restored to show the object as indubitably a boat. Ed. Meyer, *Geschichte des Altertums*, II[1], p. 202, n. 1, thought that the object, in the original state in which the sarcophagus was found, could equally represent an elephant's tusk. Cf. Nilsson, *Gesch. d. griech. Rel.*[2], I, p. 327, n. 1. Despite the question of the justification of the restoration, the object seems to have represented a boat. For coloured photographs of the restored state of the scene see S. Marinatos and M. Hirmer, *Crete and Mycenae*, Plates XXVII, XXIXA, pp. 151–2.

9   *Works and Days*, 169–73.

10   τοῖσιν Κρόνος ἐμβασιλεύει (*ib.* p. 169; cf. Loeb ed. of Hesiod, p. 14, n. 1).

11   Cf. H. J. Rose, *Handbook of Greek Mythology*, pp. 43–5; F. Schwenn, *Die Theogonie des Hesiodos*, pp. 127–30; Nilsson, *Minoan-Mycenaean Religion*, p. 536; *Gesch. d. griech. Religion*, I, pp. 484–5; Picard, pp. 117–18; Brandon, *Creation Legends of the Ancient Near East*, pp. 172–3.

12   Thirteen ministrants, male and female, are shown employed in various ritual acts. Cf. Marinatos and Hirmer, p. 40.

13   Picard, pp. 164, 201, thinks that the fact that many ossuaries were sited close to the sea-shore also indicates that the Cretans thought of the abode of the dead as lying across the sea.

14   Others are just recorded to have perished in battle at Thebes and Troy (*Works and Days*, pp. 161–6).

15   *Odyssey* IV, 561–9; see pp. 83ff.

16   Cf. Picard, pp. 172–3; V. B. Brunelli, *L'Eroico omerico*, p. 8; L. Gernet and A. Boulanger, *Le génie grec dans la religion*, pp. 102–5; Rose, *Handbook*, p. 80.

17   *Odyssey* IV, 573–5.

18 See below, pp. 81ff.

19 Cf. Picard, pp. 201, 202; W. K. C. Guthrie, *The Greeks and their Gods*, p. 290.

20 See below, p. 83. Cf. A. R. Burn, *Minoans, Philistines and Greeks*, pp. 29, 31; Rose, *Handbook*, p. 85; J. Harrison, *Prolegomena to the Study of Greek Religion*, p. 610; E. Rohde, *Psyche*, I, pp. 77, n. 1; 81, n. 2; 310, n. 1.

21 Cf. Burn, pp. 27–31.

22 *Works and Days*, 171. Cf. A. Lesky, *Thalatta*, pp. 70ff.

23 Cf. Picard, pp. 289–90.

24 Cf. Brandon, *Creation Legends*, Plate X.

25 Cf. Picard, p. 290; 'Les balances des tombes mycéniennes et autres, décorées parfois du symbole du papillon (*psyché*), prouvent en tout cas la persistence d'une eschatologie déjà minoenne'. Cf. Nilsson, *Minoan-Mycenaean Religion*², pp. 34–6, 46; E. Wüst in *P.W.*, XXIII, 2 (1957), 1446, who suggests that they may have only a domestic significance, since they were found in graves where women and infants were buried.

26 XXII, 209–11: καὶ τότε δὴ χρύσεια πατὴρ ἐτίταινε τάλαντα, ἐν δ'ἐτίθει δύο κῆρε τανηλεγέος Θανάτοιο, τὴν μὲν Ἀχιλλῆος, τὴν δ'Ἑκτορος ἱπποδάμοιο.
On the so-called *psychostasia*, see Additional Note, pp. 96–7.

27 Cf. Nilsson, *Gesch. d. griech. Religion*², I, pp. 328–9; H. L. Lorimer, *Homer and the Monuments*, p. 99, n. 6; Wüst in *P.W.*, XXIII, 2, 1444–5, 1446; L. Kretzenbacher, *Die Seelenwaage*, pp. 31–2, 35–6.

28 Cf. G. E. Mylonas, *Eleusis and the Eleusinian Mysteries*, pp. 287–316.

29 Cf. Picard, pp. 244–5; Mylonas, pp. 15–20.

30 Cf. *O.C.D.*, p. 666b; Mylonas, pp. 238, 284.

31 *Hymn to Demeter*, 480–2; see also Sophocles, *Frag.*, 719 (Dindorf); Pindar, *Frag.*, 102. Cf. Rohde, *Psyche*, I, pp. 278–300; V. Magnien, *Les Mystères d'Éleusis*, pp. 36–52; Mylonas, pp. 267, 284–5.

32 Cf. Rohde, I, pp. 287–8, 312: 'Nicht das bürgerliche oder moralische, das "geistliche" Verdienst allein entscheidet'.

33 Cf. Brandon, *Man and his Destiny*, pp. 160–5.

34 Cf. R. B. Onians, *The Origins of European Thought*, pp. 23–40, 44, 94–6, 109–10, 118–20, 481; Nilsson, *Gesch. d. griech. Relig.*², I, pp. 193, n. 1, 194; L. Gernet in *Anthropologie religieuse* (ed. C. J. Bleeker), pp. 55–6.

35 See *Odyssey* XI, 204–22. Cf. Onians, pp. 94–5; Rohde, II, p. 141, n. 2; Nilsson, I², pp. 195–7. On Hades see Rohde, I, pp. 9–11, 307–14; *O.C.D.*, p. 401a–01b.

36 According to *Odyssey* X, 494–5, only the blind seer Teiresias had been permitted to retain self-consciousness; the rest of the dead 'flit about as shadows' (τοὶ δὲ σκιαὶ ἀίσσουσιν).

37 See pp. 51ff., 57ff.

38 See *Odyssey* XI, 36ff. Cf. Rose, *Handbook*, pp. 78–9; D. Page, *History and the Homeric Iliad*, pp. 303–4, 326, n. 8.

38a Cf. Rohde, I, pp. 49ff., 303–4.

39 *Odyssey* X, 488–95, XI, 100ff.

40 See the account of the Assyrian prince Kumma's visit to the underworld in *A.N.E.T.*, pp. 109ff. See also above p. 51.

41 *Odyssey* XI, 51–84, 150ff.

42 XI, 36–41; trans. A. T. Murray, Loeb ed. Homer's *Odyssey*, I, p. 389.

43 XI, 152–3. Cf. Rohde, pp. 56–9; Guthrie, *The Greeks and their Gods*, pp. 277–9.

44 XI, 482–6.

45 XI, 487–91; trans. A. T. Murray, Loeb ed., I, p. 421.

45a Cf. Brunelli, pp. 166–7; Burn, pp. 257–8.

46 XI, 568–71; trans. A. T. Murray, *op. cit.*, I, p. 427.

47 Cf. Burn, pp. 29–30. On legends about the fate of Kronis cf. Rose, *Handbook*, p. 45.

48 XI, 563: νεκύων κατατεθνηώτων.

49 XI, 570.

50 Cf. G. Glotz and R. Cohen, *Histoire grecque*, I, pp. 122–4. See above p. 8.

51 Cf. Onians, pp. 59–61.

52 The Annunaki seemed to have exercised in a similar rôle in the Mesopotamian underworld: cf. J.-M. Aynard in *S.O.*, IV, pp. 91. 92. See above p. 52.

53 XI, 576–81; trans. S. H. Butcher and A. Lang. On Tityos and his crime cf. Rose, *Handbook*, pp. 81. 139.

54 XI, 582–92; trans. S. H. Butcher and A. Lang.

55 Cf. Rose, *Handbook*, p. 81; Harrison, *Prolegomena*, pp. 606–7; Burn, pp. 143, 150; A. W. Mair in *E.R.E.*, XI, p. 551b.

56 XI, 593–600. Sisyphus incurred his punishment by outwitting Death, whom Zeus had sent out to fetch him, because he had betrayed Zeus' intrigue with Aigina. Cf. Rose, *Handbook*, pp. 270, 294; Harrison, *Prolegomena*, pp. 807–9

56a Cf. Rohde, I, pp. 61–2.

57 *Odyssey* XI, 29, 49.

58 Cf. Brandon, *Man and his Destiny*, pp. 168ff., and the references there given.

59 See the representations of *keres* or souls of the dead given by Harrison, *Prolegomena*, p. 43 (fig. 7), p. 166 (fig. 16), p. 616 (fig. 164). See also the interesting depictions of the dead on a mummy shroud of the Graeco-Roman period reproduced by S. Morenz, 'Das Werden zu Osiris' in *Forschungen und Berichte*, I (1957), Staatliche Museen zu Berlin, pp. 54, 55.

60 *C.I.A.*, I, 442; trans. F. M. Cornford, *Greek Religious Thought from Homer to the Age of Alexander*, p. 235. The absorption of the *psyche* into the

aithēr (air) might mean that it was incorporated into a divine substance (cf. G. S. Kirk and J. E. Raven, *The Presocratic Philosophers*, p. 150); but it could scarcely imply immortality, i.e. in the normal sense, as Guthrie suggests (*Greeks and their Gods*, pp. 262–3; *In the Beginning*, pp. 50–2). Cf. J. Burnet in *E.R.E.*, XI, p. 741, n. 1; P. Wheelwright, *Heraclitus*, pp. 48–9.

61 See J. W. Mackail, *Select Epigrams from Greek Anthology*, p. 161 (xxxiii); see also sections xi and xii. Cf. Rohde, II, pp. 393–6; Nilsson, *Gesch. d. griech. Relig.*, II, p. 221; F. Cumont, *After-Life in Roman Paganism*, pp. 6–19; J. Carcopino, *Aspects mystiques de la Rome païenne*, pp. 221, 228–35; I. A. Richmond, *Archaeology and the After-life in Pagan and Christian Imagery*, pp. 25–8.

61a On the horrific conceptions of death in popular belief see A. Dieterich, *Nekyia*, pp. 46–62.

62 Cf. A. Rostagni, *Storia della letteratura latina*, pp. 145–52; R. D. Hicks in *E.R.E.*, VIII, p. 190(1), p. 192(5), p. 193(9).

63 He clearly states his intention of showing how groundless is the fear of Hades (Acheron), III, 31ff.

64 III, 862–6; trans. W. H. D. Rouse, Loeb ed. of Lucretius, *De rerum natura*, pp. 231, 233.

65 III, 981–3; trans. Rouse, Loeb ed. of Lucretius, p. 238.

66 III, 992–4: *quem volucres lacerant atque exest anxius angor aut alia quavis scindunt cuppedine curae.*

67 III, 995–1002.

68 III, 1003–10. These maidens, pursuing for ever their futile task in Hades, are generally identified with the Danaids, the daughters of Danaos, who murdered their husbands on their wedding night (cf. *Der kleine Pauly*, I, 1379–80). The identification raises several problems which have been much debated. According to the evidence of a painting of Polygnotus (see below), of Plato (*Gorgias*, 493), and of certain vase-paintings (cf. Harrison, *Prolegomena*, figs. 164, 165), the idea of water-carriers in Hades was originally connected with the fate of those uninitiated into the mysteries, either the Eleusinian or Orphic, and not with the myth of the Danaids: cf. Rohde, I, pp. 326–9; Harrison, *Prolegomena*, pp. 613–23; Guthrie, *Orpheus and Greek Religion*, pp. 161–2; A. Dieterich, *Nekyia*, p. 76; Rose, *Handbook*, pp. 82, 272; Nilsson, *The Mycenaean Origin of Greek Mythology*, pp. 64–8; J. Carcopino, *La basilique pythagoricienne*, pp. 275–6, 291.

69 *hic Acherusia fit stultorum denique vita* (III, 1023).

70 *Frogs*, 145ff.; cf. W. B. Stanford, *Aristophanes: the Frogs*, pp. 83–4; Guthrie, *Orpheus*, pp. 160–1; V. Macchioro, *Zagreus: studi intorno all'orfismo*, p. 450. See p. 88.

71 'Homère parle pour la Grèce', Gernet et Boulanger, p. 236; cf. Guthrie, *The Greeks and their Gods*, p. 278.

72 *Republic*, I, 330D–31A; trans. A. D. Lindsay (Everyman ed. of *The Republic*, p. 4). Cf. Harrison, *Prolegomena*, p. 613.

73 II, 363C–D; trans. Cornford, *Greek Religious Thought*, pp. 195–6.

74 Cf. Guthrie, *Orpheus*, pp. 12, 191, n. 2.

75 *Frogs*, 145–59, 273–7, 313–35: cf. Stanford, pp. 85–6, 100–1. 'Solche, die falsch geschworen, den eigenen Vater geschlagen, das Gastrecht verletzt haben, lässt (in den "Fröschen") Aristophanes dort unten "im Schlamm liegen", eine Strafandrohung, die ursprünglich orphische Privatmysterien den Ungeweihten in Aussicht stellten, auf moralische Verschuldung übertragend', Rohde, I, p. 313; see also pp. 315–16.

76 *Apology*, 41A. On Aiakos cf. *Kleine Pauly*, I, 152; on Triptolemus cf. G. Méautis, *Les dieux de la Grèce et les mystères d'Éleusis*, pp. 115–18; Mylonas, pp. 20–1; Guthrie, *Orpheus*, pp. 135, 187.

77 *Gorgias*, 493B: οὗτοι ἀθλιώτατοι ἂν εἶεν οἱ ἀμύητοι, καὶ φοροῖεν εἰς τὸν τετρημένον πίθον ὕδωρ ἑτέρῳ τοιούτῳ κοσκίνῳ.
On the close connection between Orphism and Pythagoreanism see Guthrie, *Orpheus*, pp. 216–19. Cf. Carcopino, *La basilique pythagoricienne*, pp. 285–8.

78 Cf. Rohde, I, pp. 317–19; Macchioro, *Zagreus: studi intorno all'orfismo*, pp. 451–2.

79 Cf. Harrison, *Prolegomena*, pp. 599–613; Macchioro, *Zagreus*, pp. 453–8; Guthrie, *Orpheus*, pp. 187–91.

80 Cf. N. Turchi, *Fontes Historiae Mysteriorum Aevi Hellenistici*, pp. 25–31; Nilsson, *Gesch. d. griech. Relig.*², I, pp. 684–7; Guthrie, *Orpheus*, pp. 82–3; Macchioro, pp. 249–50; I. M. Linforth, *The Arts of Orpheus*, pp. 359–64.

81 *Phaedrus*, 245–50. Cf. L. Robin, *La pensée grecque et les origines de l'esprit scientifique*, pp. 244–6; Guthrie, *Orpheus*, pp. 164–8; A.-J. Festugière, *La révélation d'Hermès Trismégiste*, III, pp. 78–80, who rightly remarks: 'Maintenant on notera qu'il n'est pas question ici de jugement divin ou de châtiment: c'est par une sorte de necessité physique que l'âme qui n'a pu suivre descend ici-bas' (p. 79).

82 Cf. W. Jaeger, *The Theology of the Early Greek Philosophers*, p. 80; Nilsson, *Gesch. d. griech. Relig.*², I, p. 195; E. R. Dodds, *The Greeks and the Irrational*, pp. 138–9.

83 Frag. 117, Diogenes Laertius viii. 77, in Kirk-Raven, *Presocratic Philosophers*, p. 354(476).

84 *Dirges*, frag. 133, trans. Cornford, *Greek Religious Thought*, p. 64. Cf. Rohde, II, p. 211, n. 2, who explains 'in the ninth year' in terms of the period of exile and expiation for murder. The 'primal woe' (παλαιοῦ πένθεος), for which expiation has to be paid to Persephone, Rohde (p. 208, n. 2) interprets as 'die alte Schuld der Seele', and suggests that

Pindar is thinking in terms of expiation for blood-guiltiness. See also Jaeger, p. 87; Linforth, pp. 346–8; Guthrie, *Orpheus*, p. 165.

85 Empedocles, frag. 115 (Hippolytus, *Ref.* vii, 29 and Plutarch, *de exilio*, 17, 607C), in Kirk-Raven, pp. 351–2(471). Cf. Rohde, II, pp. 165, n. 2, 178–182; Jaeger, pp. 144–5, 147–8.

86 *Phaedrus*, 248–9. Cf. Rohde, II, p. 276, n. 4; Guthrie, *Orpheus*, pp. 164–5.

87 249; trans. J. Wright. (87a) Cf. Macchioro, pp. 437–43.

88 Cf. Harrison, *Prolegomena*, pp. 572–4; Macchioro, pp. 261–77; Guthrie, *Orpheus*, pp. 171–2; Rohde, II, pp. 217–22; Nilsson, *Gesch. d. griech. Relig.*, II, p. 226.

89 Trans. by G. Murray in J. Harrison, *Prolegomena*, pp. 667–9. Cf. Turchi, p. 37; Macchioro, pp. 283–4; Guthrie, pp. 173–5.

90 Cf. Dodds, *The Greeks and the Irrational*, pp. 150, 151. On the significance of the Hindu and Buddhist doctrines of reincarnation cf. Brandon, *Man and his Destiny*, pp. 319ff., 337ff.

91 Cicero, *De Rep.*, VI, 26, 28: '*Namque eorum animi qui se corporis voluptatibus dediderunt . . . impulsuque libidinum deorum et hominum iura violaverunt, corporibus elapsi circum terram ipsam volutantur . . .*' See Dante, *Divina Commedia*, *Inferno*, Canto V.

92 Cf. Carcopino, *La basilique pythagoricienne*, pp. 17–75, 160, 161, n. 1, 288, 384–5; A. Grenier, *Les religions étrusque et romaine*, pp. 203–4, 226.

93 Cf. Carcopino, pp. 274, 290–1. A similar refinement of metempsychosis as a retributive process is set forth in the Hermetic literature: cf. *Poimandres*, X, 19–21; XII, 3–7; in *Corpus Hermeticum* (ed. A. D. Nock and A.-J. Festugière), I, pp. 122–4, 175–7.

94 *Aeneid*, VI, 756ff. Cf. W. Warde Fowler, *The Religious Experience of the Roman People*, p. 409.

95 *Aeneid*, VI, 703–15. F. Altheim, *History of Roman Religion*, p. 300, believes that the Latin poet Ennius (*c.* 200 BC) taught metempsychosis.

96 VI, 739–51; trans. H. Rushton Fairclough, Loeb ed. of Virgil, I, pp. 557, 559.

97 *Republic*, X, 616; trans. A. D. Lindsay (Everyman Library ed. of *The Republic*, p. 320). On the cosmological significance of Tartarus cf. Brandon, *Creation Legends*, pp. 169, 170, n. 2, 173.

98 *Aeneid*, VI, 540: '*hic locus est, partis ubi se via finditur in ambas*'. Virgil here follows an ancient tradition, possibly of Pythagorean or Orphic origin, of two ways confronting the dead, one leading to beatitude, the other to torment. According to Plato (*Republic*, X, 614C), in the curious vision of Er, anonymous judges sat in the middle, giving judgment on the dead (δικαστὰς δὲ μεταξὺ τούτων καθῆσθαι); the just were ordered to take the right road, which ascended to heaven, the unjust went by the left way, which led downward. Cf. Rohde, II, p. 220, n. 4; Cumont, *After-Life in Roman Paganism*, pp. 151–2.

99 VI, 557–8.

100 VI, 566–69; trans. Fairclough, Loeb ed., I, p. 545.

101 VI, 571–617. Among traditional sufferers Virgil mentions Ixion, who tried to seduce Hera, and was punished by being bound to a burning wheel which revolves eternally: cf. Rose, Handbook, p. 256.

102 Cf. H. W. Fowler and F. G. Fowler, The Works of Lucian of Samosata, I, pp. vii–xiv.

103 In op. cit., I, p. 163(15). According to Plato, Gorgias, 523C–E, both the judges and the judged are stripped naked in Hades to ensure that justice will not be deflected by any pre-mortem considerations.

104 Dialogues of the Dead, XXV, in op. cit., I. p. 147.

105 Cf. M. R. James, The Apocryphal New Testament, pp. 505ff.

106 A. Dieterich, Nekyia: Beiträge zur Erklärung der neuentdeckten Petrus-apokalypse (Leipzig, 1893; 2nd ed., 1913), pp. 195–213. Cf. Nilsson, Greek Folk Religion, p. 119. Dieterich's thesis has recently been much strengthened by the evidence of what seems to have been an Orphic Katabasis, preserved on a papyrus now at Bologna: cf. R. Turcan in R.H.R., 150 (1956), pp. 136–72.

107 F. Cumont, After-Life in Roman Paganism, pp. 173–4.

108 Cf. Brandon, Creation Legends, p. 165.

109 Lucian in his tractate Menippus depicts the procedure at the court of Minos in terms of contemporary judicial practice. One particularly curious feature of his account is that he imagines that each person's shadow will act as the prosecuting witness at the post-mortem judgment (cf. op. cit., I, p. 162). The judges' action in Plato's myth of Er is too vaguely described to permit any useful conclusion to be drawn as to their procedure (see note 98 above). Two epitaphs in the Greek Anthology connect Minos respectively with retribution and assessment: cf. Loeb ed. of The Greek Anthology, II, 268, 596.

110 Cf. Gernet and Boulanger, Le génie grec dans la religion, pp. 514–17. It is not without significance that in the later fourth century AD, when a kind of 'official catechism for the Roman Empire' was drawn up by Sallustius, both a post-mortem judgment and the transmigration of souls were included. The reasons given for the judgment after death are vague, and no reference is made to divine sanction for the doctrine: 'Souls are punished when they have gone forth from the body, some wandering among us, some going to hot and cold places of the earth, some harassed by Spirits (δαίμονες). Under all circumstances they suffer with the irrational part of their nature, with which they have sinned. For its sake there subsists that shadowy body which is seen about graves, especially the graves of evil livers' (Sallustius, On the Gods and the World, XIX: trans. G. Murray in Five Stages of Greek Religion).

111 Cf. A. de Ridder et W. Deonna, *L'art en Grèce*, pp. 323-7; T. von Scheffer, *Die Kultur der Griechen*, Abb. 181-4; *C.A.H.*, vol. of plates II, pp. 64, 102-5.

112 Cf. Carcopino, *La basilique pythagoricienne*, p. 110, ill. VIII, IX; Harrison, *Prolegomena*, pp. 176-8 (of the earlier idea of the harpies as 'Snatchers').

113 The earlier tomb paintings recall the serene reticence of Greek sepulchral art; from the fourth century BC a more horrific imagery manifests itself: cf. A. Grenier, *Les religions étrusques et romaine*, p. 59; A. Hus, *The Etruscans*, pp. 107-8.

114 Cf. G. Dennis, *The Cities and Cemeteries of Etruria*, II, frontispiece and pp. 183-6; G. Bendinelli, *Compendio di storia dell'arte etrusca e romana*, figs. 146, 150, 151; A. Stenico, *Roman and Etruscan Painting*, 49; Richmond, *Archaeology and the After-Life in Pagan and Christian Imagery*, p. 21.

115 Cf. S. G. F. Brandon, 'The Personification of Death in Some Ancient Religions', in *B.J.R.L.*, 43 (1961), pp. 328-30. A similar tendency to concentrate upon the moment of death as the crucial moment of destiny occurs in Christianity: see below, p. 113.

116 *Divina Commedia*, *Inferno*, Canto I, 79ff. Cf. R. L. John, *Dante*, pp. 137, 190, 261.

117 The shades of the dead remained for ever in Hades. The only exception, according to Athenian popular belief, was that once a year, at the festival of the Anthesteria, the *kēres* revisted their former abodes, and food-offerings were set out for them: cf. Rohde, I, pp. 236-9; Harrison, *Prolegomena*, pp. 32-55; H. J. Rose, *Ancient Greek Religion*, pp. 79-80, 82.

118 Cf. Brandon, *History, Time and Deity*, pp. 85-96; see below, pp. 100ff., 139ff., 156ff.

V Christianity

1 The Nicene Creed properly so-called was issued in AD 325 by the Council of Nicaea; it embodied earlier formularies of belief, but was specifically concerned to define orthodox belief against Arianism. Cf. *D.C.C.*, pp. 952-3; J. N. D. Kelly, *Early Christian Creeds*, pp. 151-2.

2 This Creed probably dates between 381 and 428; cf. *D.C.C.*, 98-9; E. C. Ratcliff in *Liturgy and Worship* (ed. W. K. L. Clarke), pp. 280-1.

3 See *Galatians* i. 6-8; II *Cor.* xi. 3-4; cf. Brandon, *Fall of Jerusalem and the Christian Church*, pp. 54-73, 126-53; *Jesus and the Zealots*, pp. 152-4, 183, 184-8.

4 Cf. V. Taylor, *Formation of the Gospel Tradition*, pp. 168-89; Brandon, *Jesus and the Zealots*, pp. 149-50.

5 *Mark* i. 15. Cf. Ch. Guignebert, *Jésus*, pp. 394-5; M. Goguel, *Life of Jesus*, pp. 311-12.

6 Cf. Goguel, pp. 264-70.

Notes (Christianity)

7 Cf. E. Schürer, *G.J.V.*, II, pp. 496–553; R. H. Charles, *A Critical History of the Doctrine of a Future Life*, chs. vii–viii; S. Mowinckel, *He That Cometh*, pp. 261–450.

7a Cf. W. Förster, *Palestinian Judaism in New Testament Times*, p. 197.

8 *Mark* xii. 18–27; cf. V. Taylor, *Gospel according to St Mark*, pp. 480–4.

9 *Acts of Apostles* i. 6.

10 Cf. Schürer, II, 551–3; Mowinckel, pp. 393–9.

11 *Matthew* xxv. 31. Cf. E. Klostermann, *Das Matthäusevangelium*, pp. 204–5; R. Bultmann, *Die Geschichte der synoptischen Tradition*, pp. 130–1.

12 See pp. 73ff.

13 *Matthew* xxv. 32–4 (R.S.V.). The *Book of Enoch* provides some interesting parallels to the scene envisaged here: cf. lxi. 8; lxii. 2–3. In Palestine sheep are generally white and goats black. The title 'King' indicates that the Judge is the Messiah. On the magical significance of left and right cf. *Wörterbuch der Religion* (ed. A. Bertholet), p. 281. Cf. A. H. McNeile, *Gospel according to St Matthew*, pp. 368–9.

14 xxv. 40.

15 xxv. 41–5. Cf. Klostermann, pp. 206–7.

16 xxv. 46. Cf. H. Strack u. P. Billerbeck, *Kommentar z. N. T. aus Talmud u. Midrasch*, I, p. 985.

17 *Matthew* v. 29; cf. McNeile, pp. 64–5.

18 xiii. 30. The explanation given in verses 36–43 seems unnecessary and artificial; for its origin see Brandon, *Fall of Jerusalem*, pp. 234–6.

19 xiii. 41–3 (R.S.V.). Cf. Klostermann, pp. 123–4; T. W. Manson, *Teaching of Jesus*, pp. 128, 322.

19a Cf. Manson, pp. 285–308; Guignebert, *Jésus*, pp. 449–59; J. Klausner, *Jesus of Nazareth*, pp. 381–97.

20 This idea is clearly and vividly expressed in the oldest Christian apocalypse, namely, *Mark* xiii. 26–7. It is to be noted that where some form of judgment is envisaged in the Gospels, it is essentially in terms of an assessment of good and evil deeds: see Charles, *Critical History*, p. 394. Cf. Guignebert, pp. 483–7. The promise made by Jesus (probably from Q) in *Matt.* xix. 28 and *Luke* xxii. 30, that in the Messianic kingdom his twelve apostles would sit on thrones 'judging the twelve tribes of Israel' means in this context 'government': cf. Klostermann, pp. 158–9.

21 *Rev.* vi. 9–10. Cf. R. H. Charles, *The Revelation of St John*, I, pp. 171–2.

22 vii. 1–8. 'The 144,000 were Jews or Jewish-Christians in the original tradition', Charles, I, p. 193, see also pp. 188–201.

23 vii. 9.

24 vii. 14. Charles (*ib.*) thinks that the 'great multitude' and the 144,000 are identical: cf. N. Turner in *Peake's Commentary*[2], 919f. The words 'in the blood of Lamb' could mean either forgiveness of sins through faith in the sacrifice of Christ, or that the 'great multitude' were exclusively of

martyrs who had followed Christ in his vicarious martyrdom: cf. Charles, I, pp. 213–14.

25   vii. 15–17: cf. Charles, I, pp. 214–18.

25a Cf. Charles, I, pp. cxiii–cxiv, 140–3. However, the mixture of Jewish and Christian concepts even here should be noted, because the Lamb is also identified with the 'Lion of the tribe of Judah, the Root of David' (*Rev.* v. 5–6).

25b C. Charles, II, pp. 180–1; Turner in *Peake's Commentary*,[2] pp. 926a.

26   xx. 1–10. On the idea of the Millennial rule of Christ cf. Charles, *Critical History*, pp. 315, 324–7, 329–30, *Revelation of St John*, II, pp. 184, 456–7.

27   xx. 11–15 (R.S.V.).

28   xxi. 8. For the 'second death' as a Rabbinic expression cf. Charles, *Revelation of St John*, I, pp. 59–60.

29   Cf. Brandon in *B.J.R.L.*, 43 (1961), pp. 331–2.

30   The idea of the dead being judged on the testimony of written records had already found expression in *Daniel* vii. 10 and *Enoch* xc. 20. Cf. L. Koep in *R.A.C.*, II, 726–7.

31   Cf. M. Goguel, *La naissance du Christianisme*, pp. 296–9, 301–3; Mowinckel, *He That Cometh*, pp. 388–403.

32   Cf. Brandon, *Jesus and the Zealots*, pp. 13, 14, 151–4, 163–4, 182–5.

33   I *Corinthians* ii. 6–8. Cf. Bultmann, *Urchristentum im Rahmen der antiken Religionen*, pp. 211–12; H. Lietzmann, *An die Korinther I–II*, pp. 11–13; M. Dibelius in *R.A.C.*, I, 631–3 ('Archonten'); M. Werner, *Die Entstehung des christlichen Dogmas*, p. 238 (E.T., *Formation of Christian Dogma*, p. 95).

34   Cf. Brandon, *History, Time and Deity*, pp. 166–72.

35   *Romans* i. 18–ii. 12, iii. 9–20.

36   iii. 20, v. 6–21.

37   iii. 22–6; cf. W. Sanday and A. C. Headlam, *Epistle to the Romans*, pp. 87–8.

38   vi. 3–11 (R.S.V.). Cf. G. Wagner, *Das religionsgeschichtliche Problem von Römer 6*, 1–11, pp. 11–14, 16ff.; Goguel, *L'Église primitive*, pp. 321–4; K. Lake in *E.R.E.*, II, pp. 381b–82a; M. Eliade, *Traité d'histoire des religions*, pp. 174–5; H. J. Schoeps, *Paulus*, pp. 54, 112–14; R. Reitzenstein, *Die hellenistischen Mysterienreligionen*, pp. 258–62.

39   Cf. Brandon in *The Saviour God*, pp. 29–33; E. Dinkler in *R.G.G.*,[3] VI, p. 631a.

40   Cf. L. Duchesne, *Christian Worship*, pp. 308–16; M. Werner, *Die Entstehung des christlichen Dogmas*, pp. 420–1 (E.T., pp. 308–16). For representations of baptism in early Christian art see F. Grossi Gondi, *I Monumenti cristiani*, fig. 9, 72; P. du Bourguet, *Early Christian Painting*, ill. 102; M. Chatzidakis and A. Grabar, *Byzantine and Early Medieval Painting*, ill. 71, 101; J. Ainaud, *Romanesque Painting*, ill. 37, 129; F. van der

Meer and C. Mohrmann, *Atlas of the Early Christian World*, ill. 396–7, and p. 127; J. Z. Smith in *Hist. of Religions*, 5 (1966), pp. 217ff.

41 Cf. Goguel, *La naissance du Christianisme*, pp. 252–9; Bultmann, *Urchristentum*, pp. 219–22, in *N.T.S.*, I (1954), pp. 13–15; A. Schweitzer, *The Mysticism of Paul*, pp. 109–30; Brandon, *History, Time and Deity*, pp. 161–3.

42 I *Thess.* iv. 15 (R.S.V.).

43 The following are a selection of Paul's incidental references to God's judgment: *Rom.* i. 32, ii. 3, 16, iii. 19. Cf. J. Weiss, *Earliest Christianity*, II, pp. 540–3

44 I *Cor.* vi. 9–11 (R.S.V.).

45 *Galatians* v. 22–3.

46 *Rom.* iii. 23.

47 Cf. Brandon, *Fall of Jerusalem*, pp. 200–1 and Chapter xi.

48 *Mark* xiii. 26–7.

49 xiii. 30–1.

50 *Luke* xvii. 20–1. Cf. J. M. Creed, *Gospel according to St Luke*, pp. 218–19; E. Dinkler in *The Idea of History in the Ancient Near East* (ed. R. C. Dentan), pp. 196–7; Guignebert, *Jésus*, pp. 411–12.

51 *John* xvi. 5–14. Even more explicit repudiation of the traditional apocalyptic occurs in iii. 17, v. 24, xii. 31. Cf. C. H. Dodd, *The Interpretation of the Fourth Gospel*, pp. 404–5; Goguel, *La naissance*, p. 396; H. Conzelmann in *R.G.G.*[3], II, 1421.

52 Cf. Werner, *Die Entstehung des christlichen Dogmas*, pp. 667–702 (E.T., pp. 283–94).

53 *Hebrews* v. 14–16; vii. 24–5. Cf. F. F. Bruce in *Peake's Commentary*[2], 884f.; Dinkler in *Idea of History in Ancient Near East*, pp. 197–9; J. Mánek in *N.T.S.*, VI (1959–60), p. 51.

54 Cf. Werner, pp. 420–511, 636–66 (E.T., pp. 165–211, 269–82); J. F. Bethune-Baker, *Intro. to Early Hist. of Christian Doctrine*, pp. 356–75.

55 *Hebrews* vi. 1–3. Cf. S. C. Gayford in *A New Commentary of Holy Scripture*, II, p. 610b.

56 Cf. Brandon, *History, Time and Deity*, Chapter vi.

57 *Luke* xxiii. 43; cf. Creed, *St Luke*, pp. 287–8; Strack-Billerbeck, *Kommentar*, II, pp. 264ff.; G. Dalman, *Jesus-Jeshua*, pp. 198–201.

58 *Luke* xvi. 22ff.

59 xvi. 25–6.

60 According to Strack-Billerbeck, *Kommentar*, II, p. 227, the use of the expression 'Abraham's bosom' to denote a state of *post-mortem* felicity does not occur in early Rabbinical literature. The story which C. G. Montefiore (*Rabbinic Literature and Gospel Teachings*, pp. 357–60) cites as a Rabbinic illustration does not constitute a real parallel to the Lukan parable.

61 See above, pp. 43ff. The idea that the dead are thirsty and seek refreshment is typically Egyptian: cf. A. Parrot, Le 'Refrigerium' dans l'au-delà,
pp. 126–30, 166–7. Cf. Creed, St Luke, pp. 209–10; A. T. Olmstead,
Jesus in the Light of History, pp. 175–7; P. D. Scott-Moncrieff, Paganism
and Christianity in Egypt, pp. 46–51; H. Idris Bell, Cults and Creeds in
Graeco-Roman Egypt, p. 14; K. Grobel in N.T.S., X (1964), pp. 373–
382.

62 Cf. J. A. Fischer, Studien zum Todesgedanken in der alten Kirche, I, pp. 226–
315; A. Stuiber, Refrigerium Interim: die Vorstellungen vom Zwischenzustand und die frühchristliche Grabeskunst, p. 201; A. Schmidt-Clausing,
'Fegfeuer' in R.G.G.³, II, 892–4; K. Kirk, The Vision of God, pp. 286,
513 (O); A. Harnack, History of Dogma, II, pp. 377–8, III, p. 189, n. 1;
I. A. Richmond, Archaeology and the After-Life in Pagan and Christian
Imagery, pp. 49–50.

63 Cf. D.C.C., p. 1018b.

64 Cf. J. A. MacCulloch in E.R.E., V, p. 390a–b; G. G. Coulton, Five
Centuries of Religion, I, pp. 73–7.

65 De Visione Bernoldi (Pat. Lat., cxxv, 1115f.). Cf. J. A. MacCulloch,
Medieval Faith and Fable, p. 189; P. Dearmer, The Legend of Hell, pp. 61–6,
109–10.

66 See Purgatorio, Canto, X, XIII, XXV. Cf. G. G. Coulton, Medieval
Panorama, pp. 217–19. See Domenico di Michelino's fresco of Dante and
his Divina Commedia: cf. The Flowering of the Middle Ages (ed. J. Evans),
pp. 324–5; Cocagnac, Le jugement dernier dans l'art, p. 23.

67 Cf. Harnack, History of Dogma, VI, pp. 260–3. 'Purgatory ... became a
normal stage in the heavenward progress of all redeemed Christians,
except those whose penitential exercises, whether before or after
absolution, had been so exhaustive as to appear a sufficient substitute',
Kirk, Vision of God, p. 514. See also Coulton, Five Centuries of Religion,
III, pp. 283, 285–91.

68 Cf. S. Morenz, Die Geschichte vom Joseph dem Zimmermann, pp. 23–34, 96,
101, 112. See also M. R. James, Apocryphal New Testament, p. 84.

69 xxi. 1–2, in Morenz, pp. 16–17.

70 xxii. 1–2, in Morenz, p. 18.

71 xxii. 3, in Morenz, p. 19, see also pp. 66–8.

72 xxiii. 2–4, in Morenz, p. 19, see also pp. 68–70.

73 On the importance of death-bed confession and absolution in this connection see Kirk, Vision of God, pp. 511–13.

74 Cf. A. Malraux, The Metamorphosis of the Gods, pp. 344–5, 346–50;
J. Huizinga, The Waning of the Middle Ages, pp. 144–5. See also H.G.R.,
IV, ill. p. 59. The sculptured depiction of the legend of St Theophilus at
Souillac shows how even a pact with the Devil could be annulled at
death by divine intervention, in this case by the Virgin: cf. E. Mâle, L'art

religieux du XIIe siècle en France, p. 371, see also pp. 433–4; H. Focillon, *The Art of the West in the Middle Ages*, I, Plate III.

75 'Nearly all men believed more or less passively during life, and very actively on their death-bed, that the last breath would decide for them between an eternity of unspeakable torment or of unimaginable bliss: moreover, that the main deciding factor would be a man's belief in the Church doctrines and his reception of the Church's last formal rites', Coulton, *Five Centuries of Religion*, III, p. 16; see Chapters II and III. Cf. T. S. R. Boase in *The Flowering of the Middle Ages*, pp. 235–6, see also ill. on pp. 205–7, 223, 234.

76 On the incorporation of the belief into credal formularies cf. Kelly, *Early Christian Creeds*, pp. 378–83.

77 Cf. F. Loofs in *E.R.E.*, IV, pp. 654a–63a; Harnack, *History of Dogma*, III, p. 188, n. 3; *D.C.C.*, pp. 391–2; Guignebert, *Jésus*, p. 657; C. Clemen, *Religionsgeschichtliche Erklärung des Neuen Testsments*, pp. 92–3.

78 Cf. Loofs, *op. cit.*, pp. 660b–61b.

79 Cf. M. Simon, *Hercule et le Christianisme*, pp. 112–15.

80 Cf. J. Kroll, *Gott und Hölle*, p. 9; Brandon in *B.J.R.L.*, 43 (1961), p. 332.

81 Trans. M. R. James, *Apocryphal New Testament*, p. 139 (Greek 2).

82 Epiphanius, *adv. haer.* XLVI, 5, 7ff. See E. A. W. Budge, *The Book of the Cave of Treasures*, pp. 149–50; Werner, *Entstehung*, p. 490 (E.T., p. 203). Cf. J. Ainaud, *Romanesque Art*, ill. 43 (Cathedral of Spoleto, dated 1187); G. Ferguson, *Signs and Symbols in Christian Art*, p. 50.

83 Cf. Brandon, *History, Time and Deity*, pp. 172, 194, 204.

84 *Purgatorio*, Canto IV. On the idea of Limbo (*limbus*) see A. Loofs in *E.R.E.*, IV, pp. 655a–56a; Harnack, *Hist. of Dogma*, VII, p. 262, n. 1.

85 Cf. Coulton, *Five Centuries of Religion*, I, pp. 442–5; *Infant Perdition in the Middle Ages* (Medieval Studies, No. 16).

86 It is interesting to note that in *Purgatorio*, Canto III, Dante is concerned to explain that his body casts a shadow while Virgil, whose body lies buried in Naples, is shadowless, thus implying that the dead are non-material; yet his vivid descriptions of the sufferings of Purgatory imply that the dead are physically sensuous.

87 Cf. James, *Apocryphal New Testament*, pp. 505–7; *D.C.C.*, p. 1050b.

88 Trans. James, *op. cit.*, pp. 508–10 (Akhmin Fragment, 21–2, 24, 30, 32).

89 It is interesting to note that the crime of foeticide or infanticide, which is punished here, was also thought to bear a *post-mortem* penalty in Orphic eschatology according to a papyrus fragment at Bologna; cf. R. Turcan in *R.H.R.*, 150 (1956), pp. 149–55.

90 Trans. James, *op. cit.*, pp. 515 (Gr. 26), 517 (Ethiopic version). In mediaeval representations of the sufferings of the damned in Hell, the torments were sometimes conceived in terms of current forms of torture; see, for example, the wheel, gallows, and boiling vat depicted in a fourteenth-

century bas-relief in the parish church at Tour-en-Bessin, Calvados (J. Fournée, *Le jugement dernier*, Planche XLVIII), and the breaking on the wheel, the torment of the grid-iron, and the boiling vat illustrated in *The Little Book of the Dying Man*, published at Augsburg, Sorg, about 1480. The text runs: 'This fourth figure telleth of the great and grievous pains which the devils inflict upon damned and lost souls' (see G. G. Coulton, *Medieval Panorama*, p. 712 and xi). For some other representative mediaeval depictions of Hell see *The Flowering of the Middle Ages* (ed. J. Evans), the ill. on pp. 227–9, 232, 256, 288–9.

91 Tertullian, *De testimonio animae*, IV (trans. C. Dodgson, Library of the Fathers, Tertullian, vol. I).

92 Cf. Harnack, *Hist. of Dogma*, II, pp. 377–8; Chr. Lenz in *R.A.C.*, I, 514–15.

93 Cf. Harnack, III, p. 189, n. 1; *R.A.C.*, I, 515–16.

94 According to F. Grossi Gondi (*I Monumenti cristiani*, p. 264), 'Il giúdizio particolare dell'anima (fu rappresentata) nella frequente scena dell'anima in figura di orante, che si appressa a Cristo in tribunale, circondato dai Sante'. He interprets the sarcophagus of Junius Bassus as representing 'Giúdizio dell'anima ed intercessione dai Santi' (p. 461, fig. 32); it is difficult to see his reason for so doing.

95 Cf. F. van der Meer and C. Mohrmann, *Atlas of the Early Christian World*, ill. 236; M. Gough, *The Early Christians*, Plate 73 and p. 262. See also C. F. Rogers, *The Fear of Hell*, p. 38, fig. 6. It is possible that the 'Reading Shepherd', depicted above a group of sheep and goats in the third century Hypogeum of the Aurelians, may represent the Last Judgment. Cf. J. Carcopino, *De Pythagore aux Apôtres*, pp. 154–5.

96 Cf. Fournée, pp. 62–3. On Manichaean eschatology see H.-C. Puech, *Le Manichéisme*, p. 84, in *H.G.R.*, III, p. 100, and the illustrations on pp. 93, 108, 110, 111; Geo. Widengren, *Mani and Manichaeism*, p. 67. See also the scene of the Last Judgment in the Church of the Virgin 'Panagia Chalkeon', Salonika: cf. M. Chatzidakis and A. Grabar, *Byzantine and Early Medieval Painting*, ill. 32, who date it for about 1030.

97 Cf. Fournée, pp. 65–7, 135, Planches II, XLVII, LV; D. Talbot Rice, *The Beginnings of Christian Art*, pp. 170–2, *Art of the Byzantine Era*, pp. 180–1; T. S. R. Boase in *The Flowering of the Middle Ages*, pp. 232–3. See plate 3.

98 Cf. E. Mâle, *L'art religieux du XIIe siècle en France*, pp. 406–19; see also pp. 176–82; Fournée, p. 63. For a Romanesque painting of the Last Judgment see J. Ainaud, *Romanesque Painting*, iii. 14 (Basilica of Sant'Angelo in Formis, *c.* 1100). Cf. Cocagnac, pp. 17, 19.

99 Cf. Mâle, *The Gothic Image*, pp. 1, 355–89; A. Katzenellenbogen, *The Sculptural Programs of Chartres Cathedral*, pp. 25, 67, 79–90; O. von Simson, *The Gothic Cathedral*, pp. 8, 110–11, 113–14, 182.

100 Cf. D. Grivot and G. Zarnecki, *Gislebertus, Sculptor of Autun*, Plates, B, G, H, I; Fournée, pp. 71–4. See e.g. the 'Dooms' at Beaulieu, Laon,

Chartres, Notre-Dame, Paris, Poitiers, Amiens, Reims, Coutances (glass). See plate 4.

101 These 'signs' are usually, besides the Cross, the Pillar of Flagellation, the Spear and Lance with Sponge. Cf. Fournée, pp. 85–90. See plate 5.

102 I alone dispose of all things and crown the just, Those who follow crime I judge and punish (Grivot and Zarnecki, p. 26).

103 On Gislebertus see the magisterial study of D. Grivot and G. Zarnecki, *Gislebertus, Sculptor of Autun*, pp. 13–14.

104 See Grivot and Zarnecki, Plates B and K. Cf. Fournée, pp. 97–102; J. A. MacCulloch in *E.R.E.*, V, pp. 390b–91a. The subject has been treated in monographs by M. P. Perry, 'On the Psychostasis in Christian Art' (*The Burlington Magazine*, XXII, 1912–13, and L. Kretzenbacker, *Die Seelenwaage* (Klagenfurt, 1958).

104a If the sculptured cross of Muiredach at Monasterboice, Co. Louth, is to be dated for 923, it provides the earliest extant depiction of the weighing of the soul by Michael. Cf. L. Stone, *Sculpture in Britain: the Middle Ages*, p. 27; M. and L. de Paor, *Early Christian Ireland*, pp. 147–9. See fig. 6.

105 *Sermo I. in vig. Pentecost.*

106 Vincent of Beauvais significantly quotes Chrysostom in his *Spec. hist. Epil.*, cxviii. According to Mâle (*The Gothic Image*, pp. 23ff., *Religious Art*, pp. 62ff.), the *speculum majus* of Vincent of Beauvais constituted a most influential encyclopaedia of the mediaeval *Weltanschauung*. See also Lactantius, *Divine Institutes*, B. VII. Cf. Perry, *op. cit.*, p. 104; Kretzenbacher, *op. cit.*, pp. 59–62.

107 For eschatological use of the idea see *Enoch* xli. 1: 'I saw ... how the actions of men are weighed in the balance'; cf. lxi. 8. See above 214, n. 47, n. 52a.

108 On the date and provenance of the work see M. R. James, *The Testament of Abraham*, pp. 7–29, 76. Cf. E. Wüst in *P.W.*, XXIII. 2 (1957), 1454; Kretzenbacher, *Die Seelenwaage*, pp. 56–8.

109 *Test. of Abraham*, XII. 10–15 (ed. James, p. 91).

110 XII. 19–25 (ed. James, p. 91).

111 XIII. 5 (ed. James, p. 93).

112 Cf. James, *op. cit.*, pp. 70–2; Kretzenbacher, p. 56.

113 I. 6, in Morenz, *Die Gesch. von Joseph d. Zimmermann*, p. 2, see also pp. 35, 126.

114 Cf. James, *op. cit.*, pp. 29–34; James, *Apocryphal New Test.*, p. 84; *D.C.C.*, p. 744a.

115 See below, p. 126. Kretzenbacher provides in his *Die Seelenwaage* sixty-five illustrations of the transaction from a wide variety of sources, the majority being of Christian origin.

116 *Rev.* xii. 7–8. Cf. Charles, *Revelation of St John*, I, pp. 323–4.

117 *Jude* i. 9. The passage about Michael is wanting from the extant version

of the *Assumption of Moses*, which is incomplete. Clement, Origen and other Christian writers testify to the existence of the passage: cf. Schürer, *G.J.V.*, III, pp. 217, 221-2.

118 XXIII. 4. Michael is joined by Gabriel in the task: cf. Morenz, *op. cit.*, pp. 66, 69.

119 For a survey on Early Christian references to Michael as the guardian of the dead cf. J. Michl in *R.A.C.*, V, 249-50 ('Michael bei Tod u. Gericht'). 'Dokiel' is explained as 'göttliche Feinheit, göttlicher Scharfsinn' (*ib.* 210). Cf. Mâle, *Gothic Image*, pp. 377-8; Kretzenbacher, pp. 82-91.

120 See Grivot and Zarnecki, Plate K and p. 27a; Mâle, *L'art religieux du XIIe siècle*, pp. 413-14. See the examples illustrated by Fournée, Planches XXVIII and XXIX; see also, as an English example, the Doom at Chaldon, Surrey (G. H. Cook, *The English Mediaeval Parish Church*, ill. 107), and the Ethiopic version printed in Coulton's *Five Centuries of Religion*, I, Plate 21(b). Cf. Perry, *op. cit.*, pp. 102-3; Kretzenbacher (the contest appears in most of the numerous illustrations).

121 See Grivot and Zarnecki, Plate K; note also St Michael's protective gesture in the Bourges Cathedral 'Doom'. See plate 5. Memling's triptych of the Last Judgment at Dantzig shows Michael in full plate armour.

122 The Autun 'Doom' (Grivot and Zarnecki, Plate L) has a small demon in the scale-pan. Fournée (p. 101) identifies the object weighed in the Bourges version as 'un masque affreux symbolise les mauvaises actions et les vices de l'âme'. A devil also clings like a monkey to the scale-pan concerned to make it heavier. Cf. Perry, pp. 209, 210, 215. Generally the good outweighs the evil. See plate 5.

123 Cf. Fournée, p. 101; Mâle, *Gothic Image*, p. 377.

124 E.g. in the glass at Coutances (Fournée, Planche XXVIII), and the paintings of the Last Judgment by Memling (at Dantzig) and Van der Weyden (at Beaune). Cf. Fournée, p. 98. Perry, p. 104, suggests that the two human figures personify the individual's good and bad deeds respectively. Cf. Kretzenbacher, pp. 144-69. See plate 8.

125 E.g. on a capital of Saint-Eutrope, Saintes, in Mâle, *L'art religieux du XIIe siècle*, p. 413, fig. 237. See also the interesting fourteenth century icon, now at Pisa, of St Michael with the scales (D. Talbot Rice, *Art of the Byzantine Era*, ill. 226), and the stained glass panel in the Victoria and Albert Museum (100 *Masterpieces: Early Christian and Medieval*, no. 88). Kretzenbacher gives many other examples.

126 Cf. Fournée, pp. 99-100; Kretzenbacher, pp. 157-61.

127 E.g. it does not appear in the Dooms at Poitiers, Reims, St Denis, Beaulieu, Laon, or (in England) St Thomas, Salisbury. Its appearance in the Torcello Doom is allusive.

128 See Grivot and Zarnecki, Plates B, C, M; also plate 4 here.

129 Cf. H. Focillon, *The Art of the West in the Middle Ages*, II, ill. 75, 78 (Rampillon); Fournée, Planche LIV, LV, pp. 142–3; Boase in *The Flowering of the Middle Ages*, pp. 232b–35. It is interesting to note that Augustine (*Epistola* CLXXXVII) had some doubt about the location of 'Abraham's bosom'; but he concluded that it meant 'sedes beatorum'.

130 Cf. Grivot and Zarnecki, Plates B, K, L. See plate 4.

131 E.g. at Chartres, Poitiers, Amiens, Reims, Bamberg. See plates 5–7, 9.

132 The Autun Doom shows one case of torment, beyond that of the haling of the damned into Hell (but see n. 134 below). It is the nude figure of a woman whose breasts are being attacked by a serpent; she probably represents an adulteress (cf. Grivot and Zarnecki, Plate K). For some typical depictions of the torments of the damned in mediaeval Dooms see Fournée, Planches XLVI–L; to which may be added as an English specimen the Doom at Chaldon, Surrey (Cook, *English Mediaeval Parish Church*, ill. 107, pp. 198–9), and the 'Last Judgments' of Hieronymus Bosch (cf. J. Combe, *Jérome Bosch*, Planches 30, 31, 80, see also p. 36). Cf. G. G. Coulton, *Medieval Faith and Symbolism*, I, pp. 306–15. See n. 90 above. See plates 3–7, 9, and fig. 7.

133 'Thus shall rise again everyone who does not lead a sinful life,
    And endless light of day shall shine for him'
(Grivot and Zarnecki, p. 26b; see also Plate Q).

134 'Here let fear strike those whom earthly error binds,
    For their fate is shown by the horror of these figures'
(Grivot and Zarnecki, *ib.* and Plate Q). It is curious that among those resurrected to damnation three figures are depicted as already suffering torment: a man with a bag (of money?) is attacked by a snake, another is seized by two huge claw-like hands (see Grivot and Zarnecki, Plate P), and a woman has two serpents biting at her breasts (see n. 132).

135 *Genesis* iii. 24.

136 E.g. by Van der Weyden, Jean Provost, Frank Floris, Pierre Probus, Bernard van Orley (see Fournée, Planches X–XV), and Michelangelo's Sistine 'Last Judgment'.

137 See below, p. 129. In the frontispiece of the *Liber Vitae* of New Minster, Winchester, a demon threatens a soul with a written record, probably of his life.

138 Honorius of Autun, *Elucidarium*, cited by G. G. Coulton, *Medieval Faith and Symbolism*, I, p. 256; see also pp. 257–8, referring to the Doom in Basle Cathedral (*c.* 1170), in which the resurrected blessed are dressing themselves, while the damned remain naked. Cf. K. Clark, *The Nude*, pp. 305–9, 394 (commenting upon the figures in Van der Weyden's and Memling's *Last Judgments* as 'more naked and defenceless', an interesting comparison is made with the photographs of Belsen).

139 Although women are always distinguished by their breasts, the genital organs of men are not regularly depicted. In his 'Last Judgment' and 'Garden of Delights' altarpiece, Hieronymus Bosch suggests sexual assault on women by serpents or demons (cf. Combe, *Jérome Bosch*, Planches 31, 97: 'La femme nue en proie à des reptiles, image ancienne et fréquente de la Luxure est, . . .', p. 63, n. 93). The depiction of a nude woman, whose breasts are attacked by serpents (sometimes by a toad) often occurs in mediaeval sculpture from the twelfth century; see examples at Moissac, Vézelay and Charlieu (Loire) illustrated by Mâle, *L'art religieux du XIIe siècle en France*, figs. 17, 216, 217. These figures may symbolize the punishment of luxury in Hell; according to Mâle, the idea 'semble être sortie de l'imagination monastique' (*op. cit.*, p. 374). However, this form of *post-mortem* punishment seems to have been an ancient conception. As we have already noted, in the *Apocalypse of Peter* the milk of women, who had killed their children, issuing from their breasts, turned into snakes (James, *Apoc. New Test.*, p. 506, citing Clement of Alexandria) and tormented the women and their husbands (see above, p. 117). The *Apocalypse of Paul*, which had great vogue in the West, also describes women (and men), hung head downwards in Hell and devoured by serpents – 'These are the women that beautified themselves with paints and unguents and went to church to ensnare men' (James, *Apoc. New Test.*, p. 545). See p. 252.

139a The late Doom of the Cathedral at Bern provides an exception to the rule by depicting two women respectively of the saved and the damned with children.

140 E.g. at Bourges, Reims, Rampillon (cf. Focillon, ill. 75–8), Autun (Grivot and Zarnecki, Plate Q).

141 At Reims and Bamberg the damned are clothed, the bishop having even his crozier (Reims) as he is led to the cauldron of Hell. See plate 9.

142 E.g. at Chartres, Notre Dame, Paris, Poitiers, Amiens. For this feature at Torcello, in a Byzantine idiom, cf. Kretzenbacher, p. 73.

143 Cf. Mâle, *Gothic Image*, pp. 370–2; Fournée, pp. 103–11.

144 A notable example occurs in the famous *Mappa Mundi* in Hereford Cathedral in the Doom-scene over the circle of the world; see *History Today*, XVI (1966), p. 682. An interesting Florentine example is in New York (cf. J. J. Rorimer, *The Cloisters*, ill. 41 and pp. 91–2). Even more significant is Ruben's painting of the Virgin and St Francis protecting the world from a vengeful Christ. See plate 6.

145 In Fournée, pp. 110–11. At the side of the figure of the interceding Virgin in the Hereford *Mappa Mundi* the similar verses are inscribed:

> Veici beu fiz mon piz dedeinz la quele chare preistes:
> E les mameleites dont leit de Virgin queistes:
> Eyez merci de trouz si com vos memes deistes
> Ke moi ont servi Kant Sauveresse me feistes.

(Regard, my Son, the flesh, of which Thou'rt made:
Behold the breasts on which Thou once was laid:
On all who worship us pray take:
Who me revere, me their Saviouress make.)

(Translation from the *Gentleman's Magazine*, 1863.)

146 Cf. J. R. H. Moorman, *Church Life in England in the Thirteenth Century*, pp. 74-5, 158, Plate III; Cook, *The English Mediaeval Parish Church*, pp. 196-7 (who notes that more than one hundred examples are known in England), ill. 97, 107; M. Rickert, *Painting in Britain: the Middle Ages*, pp. 203-4. Coulton, *Medieval Faith and Symbolism*, I, pp. 306-14. The 'Doom' was essentially an expression of mediaeval Christianity; its depiction naturally ended in countries affected by the Reformation, but it virtually ceased also in Roman Catholic countries, except on wayside shrines. Coulton (*op. cit.*, p. 314, n. 2) notes an example in painted glass dating about 1850 in St Remi-de-Troyes. For the survival of the idea of the weighing of souls in literature, art and folk-custom down to the twentieth century see Kretzenbacher, pp. 184-200, 208-23.

147 Cf. *D.C.C.*, p. 398b.

148 Cf. A. C. Cawley, *Everyman and Medieval Miracle Plays*, pp. 264-6. See also M. D. Anderson, *Drama and Imagery in English Medieval Churches*, pp. 125-30.

149 Cf. Cawley, *op. cit.*, pp. 198-203. See above pp. 100-1. On the eschatological significance of the parable of the Wise and Foolish Virgins in mediaeval art and drama cf. Anderson, pp. 30-2.

150 In Cawley, *op. cit.*, p. 210, ll. 103-10.

151 *Op. cit.*, pp. 233-4, ll. 913-19. Cf. Anderson, pp. 72-84.

152 Cf. R. Schott, *Michelangelo*, pp. 175, 178. Schott believes that the Sistine 'Last Judgment' marks a definitive change in Michelangelo's spiritual life. He sees in the work a 'silent renunciation of humanism', in which Michelangelo recognized that 'the much vaunted classical approach to life would ultimately promote vanity, deceit, pride and spiritual alienation from the source of divine wisdom' (pp. 182-3). Accordingly, he sees Michelangelo as 'a partisan of the Counter-Reformation and an unofficial collaborator of Tridentism' (*ib.*). According to C. de Tolnay, *Michelangelo*, V, *The Final Period*, 'With Michelangelo the static zonal structure of the hierarchies (of the mediaeval "Dooms") was abolished and the dramatic action of the Judgment became all important' ... 'In abolishing the traditional Last Judgment type, Michelangelo created a new dynamic unity whereby the event can be experienced in its dramatic entirety for the first time' (pp. 23, 24); see also pp. 49-50.

153 Note the skeletons among the resurrected on the right side of the painting (in Tolnay, *op. cit.*, Plates 14, 36, 37, 38); compare, e.g. the resurrection scene in the *Heures à l'usage de Paris*, dating from about *c.* 1450 (in

Fournée, Planche VIII); also the Last Judgments of Signorelli (Orvieto), Probus (Bruges) and van Orley (Anvers). Cf. Tolnay, p. 34.

154 Dante had been ferried over infernal river by Charon (*Inferno*, Canto III, 109–11). See Tolnay, Plates 15, 34.

155 Dante had also seen Minos in the Inferno (Canto XXI, 25–36). Cf. Tolnay, p. 42, Plates 15, 35.

156 Cf. Tolnay, pp. 37–8, 47–9; Clark, *The Nude*, pp. 61, 204.

157 Cf. E. G. Rupp in the *New Cambridge Modern History*, II, pp. 76–7.

158 Cf. D. P. Walker, *The Decline of Hell: Seventeenth Century Discussions oj Eternal Torment*, pp. 59ff.

159 Cf. F. Wendel, *Calvin*, p. 287.

160 *Commentary on Acts* 3.20, Opp., 48, 71, cited by Wendel, p. 287.

161 *Inst.*, III, 25, 10, in Wendel, p. 289. Cf. Dearmer, pp. 28–31.

162 Cf. Walker, *Decline of Hell*, pp. 239–40.

163 In Walker, p. 240.

164 Cf. Walker, pp. 35ff.

165 Cf. Walker, pp. 67ff.

166 Cf. Walker, pp. 61–2, 99–100, 103, 240.

167 Cf. Walker, pp. 66–7. For evidence of the continuance of the 'Hell-fire' tradition, in both Catholic and Protestant circles, into the nineteenth century see Dearmer, pp. 39–47, 121–7, Plate III; Rogers, pp. 18–22, 73–87, 95–7 and fig. 11.

168 Cf. *D.C.C.*, p. 67 ('Apocatastasis'), 325; Walker pp. 67–70, 262–3.

169 *Doctrine in the Church of England* (Report of the Commission on Christian Doctrine), p. 217.

170 *Op. cit.*, p. 218.

171 *Ib.*

172 *Op. cit.*, p. 219. Cf. J. P. Martin, *The Last Judgment*, pp. xiii–xvi.

VI Islam

1 *Qur'ān*, Surah LI, 50–1; trans. by R. Bell, *The Qur'ān*, II, pp. 533–4 (published by T. & T. Clark, Edinburgh, 1939).

2 *Qur'ān*, Surah XXII, 112; trans. Bell, I, p. 300.

3 Cf. D. S. Margoliouth, art. 'Mecca', in *E.R.E.*, VIII, pp. 511a–14b; E. Dermenghem, *Muḥammad and the Islamic Tradition*, pp. 7–10.

4 On the religion of pre-Islamic Arabia see generally G. Ryckmans, 'Les religions arabes préislamiques', in *H.G.R.*, IV; A. Jamme in *A.N.E.T.*, pp. 507b–08a; Th. Nöldeke, 'Arabs (Ancient)' in *E.R.E.*, I, pp. 659–73; G. Snouck-Hurgronje in *L.R-G.*, I, pp. 639–55; J. Finegan, *Archeology of World Religions*, pp. 461–85; Tor Andrae, *Mahomet: sa vie et sa doctrine*, pp. 11–29; W. E. N. Kensdale, *The Religious Beliefs and Practices of the Ancient South Arabians*, pp. 1–7.

5   Cf. Ryckmans in *H.G.R.*, IV, pp. 322, 331–2; Jamme in *A.N.E.T.*, p. 512b.

6   Cf. Ryckmans, *op. cit.*, pp. 309b, 310a, 323b (ill. pp. 523–5, 307); Finegan, pp. 478–9 (ill. 212–17); D. Kirkbride in *I.L.N.*, vol. 237 (1960), pp. 202–3; Nöldeke in *E.R.E.*, I, p. 672b; M. Gaudefroy-Demonbynes, *Mahomet*, p. 657.

7   Abū Dāwūd, *Sunna*, 16, trans. by A. J. Wensinck, *The Muslim Creed*, p. 108. Cf. W. M. Watt, *Free Will and Predestination in Early Islam*, pp. 19, 94.

8   Trans. by C. J. Lyall, *Translations of Ancient Arabian Poetry*, p. 114. Cf. R. A. Nicholson, *A Literary History of the Arabs*, p. 118; A. J. Arberry, *The Seven Odes*, p. 118.

9   Surah XLV, 23–4 (Bell, II, p. 505).

10   Cf. Nöldeke in *E.R.E.*, I, pp. 661b, 662a; Ryckmans in *H.G.R.*, IV, p. 311b.

11   Cf. W. M. Watt in *E.I.* (new ed.), III, pp. 94–5, *Free Will*, pp. 20–2, S. G. F. Brandon, *History, Time and Deity*, p. 55, see also pp. 39–43.

12   Cf. Watt, *Free Will*, p. 31, n. 23.

13   Cf. Tor Andrae, pp. 24–7; Finegan, pp. 482–3; H. A. R. Gibb, *Mohammedanism*, p. 38; D. B. Macdonald in *E.R.E.*, I, pp. 326a–27a; Nöldeke, *ib.* p. 664b.

14   On Muḥammad's knowledge of Judaism and Christianity cf. R. Bell, *The Origin of Islam in its Christian Environment*, *passim*; Tor Andrae, pp. 96ff.; E. Kellerhals, *Der Islam*, pp. 67–9.

15   Cf. Finegan, pp. 470–81.

16   Cf. Finegan, pp. 472–3.

17   Surah VII, 78–82. Cf. *Gen.* xix, 24f.: Biblical example of God's judgment.

18   Surah XXXIV, 15–16 (trans. Bell, II, p. 423). For references to other disasters in the *Qur'ān* see Surahs VII, 72–6, 83–100, LIV, 18–32.

19   See Surah XXIX, 61, 63, 65, 66. Cf. Tor Andrae, pp. 53–4; Dermenghem, pp. 20–1.

20   Cf. Tor Andrae, pp. 116ff.; Snouck-Hurgronje in *L.R-G.*, I, pp. 662ff.

20a   Surah XXXIII, 63 (trans. Bell, II, p. 418).

21   Surah XXXVII, 12–23 (trans. Bell, II, p. 443). It would appear that verses 21ff. are spoken by Allāh or the angels at the Judgment.

22   Bell (II, p. 644, n. 1) explains this statement as meaning 'to be made suitable – for the theophany'. D. Sourdel translates the verse as 'et écoutera son Seigneur, selon son devoir' (in *S.O.*, IV, p. 181).

23   Surah LXXXIV, 1–12 (trans. Bell, II, pp. 644–5).

24   See pp. 29ff.

25   Trans. Bell, I, p. 198. The idea of a written record of men's deeds, in terms of which they will be judged at the Last Judgment, occurs in Christian eschatology and is graphically presented in *Rev.* XX, 12. Cf. R. H. Charles, *The Revelation of St John*, I, p. 84, II, p. 194; see above p. 103.

26 Surah XXI, 48.

27 Surah CI, 5–8. Bell (II, p. 674) translates verse 6: 'But as for him whose balances are light, his mother shall be hāwiya', i.e. 'childless', which he interprets (n. 6) as implying that the man will perish, but in view of verses 7–8 he takes the term as a designation for Hell. Sourdel in *S.O.*, IV, p. 184, thinks that the idea of the weighing of the soul is more likely to derive from Mazdean than from Christian tradition; he does not, however, give his reason for this. In view of the close relations between Arabia and Abyssinia during this period (cf. C. Brockelmann, *History of the Islamic Peoples*, p. 3; E. Ullendorff, *The Ethiopians*, pp. 54–7), it would seem likely that the eschatological imagery of Ethiopian Christianity would have been known in Arabia. Ethiopian Christianity derived from Egypt; it may also be noted that representations of the Osirian weighing of the heart were to be seen at Meroë, in the Sudan (cf. E. A. W. Budge, *Osiris and the Egyptian Resurrection*, I, plate facing p. 344). See also the interesting Ethiopian picture of the Madonna and Child at Vienna (Völkerkundemuseum), in which the infant Christ holds a pair of scales: cf. L. Kretzenbacher, *Die Seelenwaage*, Abb. 52. No Iranian depiction of the *psychostasia* is known.

28 Surah LXIX, 13–18 (trans. Bell, II, p. 601).

29 According to Sourdel (in *S.O.*, IV, p. 185, n. 2), 'L'Esprit apparaît ici comme un interprète de Dieu'. Cf. Surah XVII, 87.

30 Surah LXXVIII, 38 (trans. Bell, II, p. 631).

31 Surah L, 19–20 (trans. Bell, II, p. 529). Cf. Sourdel in *S.O.*, IV, p. 185.

32 See Surahs XXVI, 10; LXXIV, 49.

33 Surah LIII, 26–7 (trans. Bell, II, p. 541, who regards verse 27 as a later addition to verse 26).

34 Surah XVIII, 29–30 (trans. Bell, I, p. 277).

35 Surah XXXVII, 39–47 (trans. Bell, II, p. 444); see also Surah LVI, 12–39. Cf. Tor Andrae, pp. 56–7, 187–9; I. F. Wood in *E.R.E.*, XI, p. 850a; G. Wiet in *H.G.R.*, IV, pp. 352–4.

36 Surah XXII, 20–21 (trans. Bell, I, p. 319).

37 Surah IV, 59 (trans. Bell, I, p. 78).

37a On Muḥammad's conception of human nature see Brandon, *Man and his Destiny in the Great Religions*, pp. 245–7. Cf. A. Schimmel in *Anthropologie religieuse* (ed. C. J. Bleeker), pp. 140, 143–6; I. F. Wood in *E.R.E.*, XI, p. 849b.

38 Surah LVI, 46–56 (trans. Bell, II, 555–6). On Christian and Jewish sources of Muḥammad's eschatology see Tor Andrae, pp. 82–91. Cf. F. Refoulé, in *R.H.R.*, 163 (1963), pp. 46–7.

38a Bell (I, p. 299, n. 4) can find no adequate explanation of this expression. Cf. J. Rodwell's note 3 in his trans. of *The Koran* (Everyman Library ed.), p. 100. According to Mauloi Muhammad Ali, *The Holy Qur-án*, p. 636,

n. 1601A, 'The word may also signify *blind*, in reference to the guilty being raised up blind on the resurrection day'.

39 Surah XX, 102–4 (trans. Bell, I, pp. 299–300).

40 Surah XVIII, 18 (trans. Bell, I, p. 275). On the legend of the Seven Sleepers, in its various Christian and Islamic forms, see J. Guidi in *E.R.E.*, XI, pp. 428a–30b.

41 'Lorsqu'à la mort l'homme est rappelé auprès d'Allah, il tombe dans un état d'inconscience absolue, de sommeil profond et sans rêves. Mahomet n'a jamais dit où se trouvent les âmes qu'Allah a rappelées à lui, ni si elles sont anéanties ou si elles subsistent virtuellement', Tor Andrae, pp. 57–8. Cf. Sourdel in *S.O.*, IV, p. 187. Those who were killed 'in the way of Allah' were 'alive with their Lord', Surah III, 163.

42 Surah XXV, 9 (trans. Bell, II, p.429). It is interesting to compare Mauli Muhammad Ali's rendering of this verse, *The Holy Qur-án*, p. 714.

43 Surah XXXII, 13 (trans. Bell, II, p. 406). Cf. Surahs VI, 125; VII, 17; XXX, 28; XXXVII, 85.

44 See Surah XCIII, 6–8.

45 e.g. *Isaiah* vi. 9–10; *Mark* iv. 1–12; *Matt.* xiii. 1–15; *Luke* viii. 4–10. Of the malevolent activity of Satan, to which there are many references in the *Qur'ān* see Gaudefroy-Demombynes: 'En permettant à Satan de séduire les hommes, Dieu a fait de lui son instrument', *Mahomet*, p. 351. Cf. W. M. Watt, *Muḥammadat Mecca*, pp. 101–9.

46 It is concisely stated in the *shahāda* or profession of faith: 'There is but one God, Muḥammad is the Apostle of God'; see also Surah IV, 135. Cf. M. Soualah, *L'Islam*, p. 39.

47 Muḥammad called his faith *Islām*, because the Arabic verb *aslama* (its participle being *muslim*), expresses the idea of submission to a supreme will: cf. Snouck-Hurgronje in *L.R-G.*, I, p. 658.

48 See Surah LIII, 27. Cf. J. W. Bowker in *J.S.S.*, XI (1966), pp. 69–82.

49 Bokhāri, *Tawḥīd*, Chapter 24, in *S.O.*, IV, pp. 189–90.

50 Cf. Sourdel in *S.O.*, IV, pp. 190–1.

51 Surah XXXVII, 23; I, 6.

52 See below, pp. 153ff. Cf. G. A. Frank Knight in *E.R.E.*, II, p. 852b.

53 Bokhāri, *Tawḥīd*, Chapter 24, in *S.O.*, IV, p. 189.

54 The most notable examples occur in ancient Egyptian religion: cf. J. Vandier, *La religion égyptienne*, pp. 91–3; E. A. W. Budge, *From Fetish to God in Ancient Egypt*, pp. 368–79.

55 Cf. Snouck-Hurgronje in *L.R-G.*, I, pp. 724–7; Sourdel in *S.O.*, IV, pp. 194–5.

56 In *S.O.*, IV, p. 194: 'Il faut croire aussi à la trompette du Jugement dernier. Cette trompette est une corne dans laquelle soufflera Isrāfil.'

57 Trans. Bell, II, p. 517.

58 Sourdel in *S.O.*, IV, p. 188, thinks that 'cette figure dans de si nombreuses

traditions qu'on peut se demander si Mohammad n'avait pas, de son vivant, prêché doctrine de ce genre'. Cf. R. Eklund, *Life between Death and Resurrection according to Islam*, pp. 77–8.

59 The names of these two angels first appear in the collection of Tirmidhi (*Janâiz*, Chapter 70).

60 Cf. Sourdel in *S.O.*, IV, p. 204, n. 15.

61 The *qibla* is the prescribed direction, i.e. towards the Sacred Mosque of Mecca, to which the faithful turn themselves to worship.

62 This hypostatization of the deceased's deeds in the form of a woman doubtless derives from Iranian tradition: cf. Brandon, *Man and his Destiny*, pp. 284–5.

63 In *S.O.*, IV, pp. 197–8. On the interrogation by Munkar and Nakīr as an article of belief see Wensinck, *The Muslim Creed*, pp. 129, 164–5, 268, in *E.I.*, III, pp. 724a–25a; D. B. MacDonald, *The Development of Muslim Theology, Jurisprudence and Constitutional Theory*, pp. 305, 311; R. Ekland, *Life between Death and Resurrection according to Islam*, pp. 5–6, 50–2, 58–60; *S.O.*, IV, pp. 192, 202.

64 Cf. Sourdel in *S.O.*, IV, p. 200.

65 Cf. S. Lane-Poole in *E.R.E.*, IV, pp. 501b–02a.

66 Cf. Sourdel in *S.O.*, IV, pp. 201–2; A. S. Tritton, *Islam*, pp. 136–7. On the question of the eternal character of the punishment in hell see the review of sectarian opinion given by Eklund, pp. 87–92.

67 Cf. Wensinck, pp. 47–9, 184, 233; E. Sell in *E.R.E.*, V, p. 696b, in *E.R.E.*, XI, p. 149b; Tritton, *Islam*, pp. 42–3.

VII Iran

1 Zoroaster was the Greek rendering of the name. Cf. J. Duchesne-Guillemin, *Zoroastre*, pp. 7ff.

2 H. B. Henning, *Zoroaster: Politician or Witch Doctor?*, p. 41, gives three possible dates for Zoroaster's life: 630–553, 628–551, 618–541 BC. Cf. J. Finegan, *Archeology of World Religions*, pp. 77–83; C. F. Whitley in *Numen*, IV (1957), pp. 215–27; R. N. Frye, *The Heritage of Persia*, pp. 29–30.

3 The *Gāthās*, i.e. 'hymns' or 'songs' are embodied in the *Yasna*, a liturgical work. Cf. J. H. Moulton, *Early Zoroastrianism*, pp. 8–21; R. C. Zaehner, *The Dawn and Twilight of Zoroastrianism* (abbrev. *D.T.Z.*), pp. 25, 28ff.; W. Eilers in *R.G.G.³*, I, 797–800; A. W. Williams Jackson in *E.R.E.*, II, p. 268; J. Duchesne-Guillemin, *The Hymns of Zarathustra*, pp. 23–7.

4 Cf. Moulton, *Early Zoroastrianism*, p. 118; Henning, pp. 45–8; Zaehner, *D.T.Z.*, p. 35ff. M. Molé in *R.H.R.*, CLXII (1962), p. 50, is critical of the tendency to regard Zoroaster as a kind of Semitic prophet: 'Le ritual prime le dogme et la personnalité du Prophète fondateur n'est pas au premier plan'; see also pp. 55–6, 61, 182–3.

5 Cf. Zaehner, *D.T.Z.*, pp. 62ff.

5a According to Molé, *op. cit.*, p. 182, 'les *Gāthā* sont, dès l'origine, le texte d'un office de la fête du changement du temps'; cf. p. 72.

6 *Yasna*, xlv. 2–7; trans. J. H. Moulton in *Early Zoroastrianism*, pp. 370–1. For other trans. see Duchesne-Guillemin, *Zoroastre*, pp. 227–8, *The Hymns of Zarathustra*, pp. 93–5.

7 On these entities see Geo Widengren in *Numen*, I (1954), p. 23; Duchesne-Guillemin, *Zoroastre*, pp. 57–80, 146–7; G. Dumézil, *Naissance d'Archanges*, pp. 57–98.

8 See *Yasna*, l. 6.

9 See n. 7 above.

10 Cf. L. H. Mills in *S.B.E.*, XXXI, p. 30, n. 5; H. Güntert, *Der arische Weltkönig und Heiland*, p. 347; Moulton pp. 134–6, 144–5.

11 Cf. Zaehner, *D.T.Z.*, pp. 70–2, 78, 119–20; Duchesne-Guillemin, *Zoroastre*, pp. 152–3; Henning, pp. 35ff.

12 Cf. V. G. Childe, *The Aryans*, pp. 36–40; Ed. Meyer, *Geschichte des Altertums*, I, 2, pp. 896–902; E. Herzfeld, *Zoroaster and his World*, II, pp. 721–37; R. Ghirshman, *Iran*, pp. 73ff.; Frye, pp. 16–24; W. Culican, *The Medes and Persians*, pp. 18–21.

13 Cf. Zaehner, *D.T.Z.*, pp. 39–40; Frye, pp. 19–21, 24–7.

14 Cf. Widengren, *Hochgottglaube im alten Iran*, p. 252; Duchesne-Guillemin, *Zoroastre*, pp. 87–8, 105; Zaehner, *D.T.Z.*, pp. 66–8.

15 Cf. Dumézil, *Mitra-Varuna*, pp. 83–5; Zaehner, *Hinduism*, pp. 35–42.

16 Cf. Brandon, *History, Time and Deity*, pp. 32ff., 37ff.

17 Cf. Brandon, *Man and his Destiny in the Great Religions*, pp. 261–3, 267–8, 271–3.

18 Cf. Brandon, *Creation Legends of the Ancient Near East*, pp. 195–6.

19 Cf. Zaehner, *D.T.Z.*, pp. 71, 99–100; Widengren in *Numen*, I (1954), p. 28.

20 Cf. Widengren, *op. cit.*, p. 23; Duchesne- Guillemin, *Zoroastre*, pp. 57–80 146–7; Dumézil, *Naissance d'Archanges*, pp. 57–98.

21 *Yasna*, xxx. 2–5; trans. Moulton in *Early Zoroastrianism*, pp. 349–50; Geldner in *R-G.L.*, p. 324; Duchesne-Guillemin, *Hymns of Zarathustra*, pp. 103–5; Zaehner, *D.T.Z.*, p. 42.

22 Cf. Duchesne-Guillemin, *Zoroastre*, p. 157; Brandon, *Man and his Destiny*, pp. 277–8.

23 *Yasna*, xlvi. 10–11; trans. Moulton in *Early Zoroastrianism*, p. 329. For other trans. cf. Geldner in *R-G.L.*, p. 329; Duchesne-Guillemin, *Hymns of Zarathustra*, p. 79; Molé in *S.O.*, IV, pp. 147–8. The exact meaning of 'Karapan' and 'Kavis' are unknown. According to Molé (*S.O.*, IV, p. 174), 'il s'agit sans doute de princes et de prêtres adversaires de la religion proclamée dans les Gâthâ'. Duchesne-Guillemin translates 'Karapans' as 'Les sacrificateurs', and 'Kavis' as 'les princes-sorciers' (*Zoroastre*, p. 215). Moulton, p. 357, n. 46, regards the two words as denoting respectively the priests and the

chieftains of the *daēvayasna*, who were Zoroaster's opponents. Cf. Henning, p. 45; A. Christensen, *Le Zoroastrisme de la Perse antique*, pp. 25–35; Frye, p. 38; Zaehner, *D.T.Z.*, p. 37.

24 *Yasna*, li. 12–13; trans. by M. Henning from Duchesne-Guillemin's rendering in his *Hymns of Zarathustra*; for the original French see his *Zoroastre*, p. 277. Cf. Geldner in *R-G.L.*, pp. 333–4; Moulton, p. 386; Molé in *S.O.*, IV, p. 148.

24a Cf. Duchesne-Guillemin, *Zoroastre*, pp. 273–4.

25 G. A. F. Knight in *E.R.E.*, II, p. 854a.

26 *Yasna*, xlvi. 17, in Moulton, p. 166, see also p. 376. Cf. J. D. C. Pavry, *The Zoroastrian Doctrine of the Future Life*, pp. 53–4.

27 *Vedevdāt*, xix. 29. Cf. Molé in *S.O.*, IV, p. 157; Pavry, p. 64; Widengren, *Hochgottglaube*, p. 267, in *Numen*, I (1954), pp. 35–6; Zaehner, *Zurvan: a Zoroastrian Dilemma*, p. 275 (A. 1).

28 See below, p. 261.

29 Zaehner in *B.S.O.A.S.*, XVII/2 (1955), p. 247; cf. *D.T.Z.*, p. 56.

30 Below, pp. 158ff.

31 In *B.S.O.A.S.*, XVII/2 (1955), p. 247.

32 Cf. Duchesne-Guillemin, *Zoroastre*, pp. 89–93; Zaehner, *D.T.Z.*, p. 69.

33 Cf. H. Bonnet, *Reallexikon*, p. 146b–47; see also above 6ff., 33ff. Cf. G. Sergi in *E.R.E.*, IV, p. 473a; F. Cumont, *After-Life in Roman Paganism*, pp. 64–9.

34 Cf. Molé in *S.O.*, IV, pp. 152–3, in *R.H.R.*, CLXII (1962), pp. 155–85; N. Söderblom, *La vie future d'après la Mazdéisme*, pp. 14–15; Pavry, pp. 96–7; Widengren in *Numen*, I (1954), pp. 54–9; G. A. F. Knight in *E.R.E.*, II, pp. 852–54b.

35 Cf. Molé in *R.H.R.*, XLXII (1962), pp. 50, 55–6, 62, 182.

36 Cf. Widengren in *Numen*, I (1954), p. 32; Söderblom, p. 9; Duchesne-Guillemin, *Zoroastre*, p. 158, in *Anthropologie religieuse* (ed. C. J. Bleeker), p. 97; L. C. Casartelli in *E.R.E.*, XI, p. 744; H. S. Nyberg, *Die Religionen des alten Iran*, pp. 127ff.

37 Cf. Widengren, in *op. cit.*, p. 33; Duchesne-Guillemin in *op. cit.*, pp. 101–4; Moulton, pp. 263–5; I. Gershevitch, *The Avestan Hymn to Mithra*, pp. 242–3.

38 In *R.H.R.*, CLVII (1960), p. 170; in *S.O.*, IV, p. 147.

39 *Yasna*, xxx. 4, xlv. 7. Cf. Zaehner, *D.T.Z.*, pp. 56–7.

40 *Yasna*, xxx. 7; trans. Moulton, p. 350. Cf. Duchesne-Guillemin, *Hymns of Zarathustra*, p. 107.

41 *Yasna*, li. 9; trans. Moulton, p. 385. Cf. Geldner in *R-G.L.*, p. 333; Duchesne-Guillemin, *Hymns of Zarathustra*, p. 143.

42 Cf. Brandon, *History, Time and Deity*, pp. 83–4.

43 See below, p. 163.

44 Above, pp. 110ff.

45 See below, p. 162.

46 Cf. Dumézil, *Les dieux des Indo-Européens*, pp. 17, 18; Moulton, pp. 163–4, 350, n. 4, 378, n. 7; Widengren in *Numen*, I (1954), p. 23.

47 Cf. Herzfeld, II, pp. 747–8; Widengren, *op. cit.*, pp. 56–7; C. Huart, *La Perse et la civilisation iranienne*, pp. 161–2.

48 Cf. Brandon, *Man and his Destiny*, pp. 276–7.

49 For recent treatments see Zaehner, *D.T.Z.*, pp. 62ff.; Molé, 'Une histoire du mazdéisme est-elle possible?', in *R.H.R.*, CXLII (1962), pp. 45ff., 161ff.

50 Cf. Zaehner, *D.T.Z.*, pp. 63–78, 154ff.

51 Cf. Zaehner, *Zurvan*, pp. 35ff., *D.T.Z.*, pp. 175ff.

52 Cf. Molé in *S.O.*, IV, p. 162; Zaehner, *D.T.Z.*, pp. 193–4, *Zurvan*, p. 26.

53 In *D.T.Z.*, pp. 302–5. For another translation cf. Molé in *S.O.*, IV, pp. 162–5.

54 See the passage from the *Greater Bundahishn*, given by Zaehner, *Zurvan*, p. 199; 'From it the straight path of the Cinvat Bridge reaches to man on earth which for the blessed widens to the breadth of nine spears' length ... but for the damned becomes as a razor's edge, and they fall to hell'. Molé (*S.O.*, IV, p. 153) translates a pertinent passage from the *Saddar Bundehesh*: 'L'ésprit des Gâthâs devient comme un mur grand comme le monde et se dresse au milieu du pont Tchinvad, ne permet pas à l'âme de tomber dans les mains d'Ahriman et d'aller en enfer, mais intercède pour elle de façon à ce qu'elle soit punie sur place, au pont Tchinvad et ne tombe pas en enfer'.

55 *Yasna*, xlvi. 11. Cf. Duchesne-Guillemin, *Symbolik des Parsismus*, pp. 20–1; Frye, p. 285, n. 28.

56 See pp. 45ff., 84ff., 93ff., 116ff.

57 It would appear that the just have to endure punishment commensurate to whatever evil they may have done: cf. Edv. Lehmann in *R-G.L.*, II, pp. 251–2; Zaehner, *D.T.Z.*, p. 305.

58 Cf. Brandon, *History, Time and Deity*, pp. 141ff.

58a Ohrmazd is the Parsi name for Ahura Mazdah, deriving from the Pahlavi 'Auharmazd': cf. A. J. Carnoy in *E.R.E.*, IX, p. 566b.

59 Cf. Zaehner, *D.T.Z.*, pp. 263ff.

60 L. H. Gray in *E.R.E.*, VIII, p. 104b.

61 Sōshyans means 'Saviour': cf. Zaehner, *D.T.Z.*, pp. 58–9.

62 Gâyômard was the Primal Man in Iranian mythology: cf. S. S. Hartmann, *Gayōmart: Étude sur le syncrétisme dans l'ancien Iran*, pp. 37–44; Duchesne-Guillemin, *Ormazd et Ahriman*, pp. 49, 112; Güntert, *Der arische Weltkönig u. Heiland*, pp. 346–7; Zaehner, *D.T.Z.*, pp. 72, 128, 130.

63 Trans. E. West, *S.B.E.*, V, pp. 120ff. Cf. Molé in *S.O.*, IV, pp. 172–3; Zaehner, *D.T.Z.*, pp. 308ff.

64 See the passage from the *Saddar Bundehesh* given by Molé, *op. cit.*, p. 173.

65 See above, pp. 112ff.

66 According to West, *op. cit.*, p. 125, n. 3, a meteor strikes the earth.

67 *Bundahishn*, xxx. 20. Cf. Zaehner, *D.T.Z.*, p. 318; Pavry, p. 53.

68 *Bundahishn*, xxx. 23–6; trans. West, *op. cit.* This restoration of the dead to what was deemed an agreeable age of life is reminiscent of the presentation of the resurrected dead in the mediaeval Christian 'Doom', which we have noted. The statement that the resurrected dead will have no sexual intercourse may be compared with the similar qualification in the *Gospel of Mark* xii. 25.

69 E.g. in the eschatologies of Judaism, Christianity, and Islam.

70 Cf. Zaehner, *D.T.Z.*, p. 308. The idea may be compared with that of Origen's concept of the *apocatastasis*: see above, pp. 118, 133ff.

VIII   *Hinduism and Buddhism*

1 See pp. 89ff.

1a Cf. S. Radhakrishnan in 2500 *Years of Buddhism* (ed. P. V. Bapat), pp. xi.ff.

2 *Saṃsāra* ('stream') is aptly described by R. C. Zaehner, *Hinduism*, p. 45, as 'the endless flux of matter in ever-recurring cyclic time'.

3 Cf. S. G. F. Brandon, *Man and his Destiny in the Great Religions*, pp. 315–16, 321–3, where references are given.

4 Cf. L. Renou, *Religions of Ancient India*, pp. 10–12; A. A. Macdonell, *History of Sanskrit Literature*, pp. 40ff.; A. L. Basham, *The Wonder that was India*, pp. 30–8, 39ff., 386–7. On the Aryan invasion of India cf. S. Piggott, *Prehistoric India*, pp. 244ff.; M. Wheeler, *Civilizations of the Indus Valley and Beyond*, pp. 73, 78–83, 96ff.; R. L. Raikes in *Antiquity*, XXXIX (1965), pp. 196–203; H. P. Sullivan in *History of Religions*, 4 (1964), pp. 115–25.

5 Cf. Renou, pp. 12–21; Zaehner, *Hinduism*, pp. 22–40.

5a There were, of course, other aspects of sacrifice, as presented in the Vedic texts (cf. A. F. F. Hillebrant in *E.R.E.*, XII, pp. 796a–97a); but the principle of *do ut des* seems to be fundamental; cf. A. A. Macdonell in *E.R.E.*, XII, p. 611a–b; see also G. van der Leeuw, *La Religion*, pp. 342–4.

6 Cf. Zaehner, *Hinduism*, pp. 35–42; J. Gonda, *Die Religionen Indiens*, I, pp. 73–9; G. Dumézil, *Les dieux des Indo-Européens*, pp. 12, 42, 66.

7 Cf. H. Oldenberg, *Die Religion des Vedas*, p. 299.

8 Cf. H. D. Griswold, *Religion of the Rigveda*, pp. 322–5; J. Dowson, *Classical Dictionary of Hindu Mythology*, pp. 373–5; Oldenberg, pp. 280–8; H. de Wilman-Grabowska in *Asiatic Mythology*, pp. 107 (fig. 4), 116.

9 Cf. Zaehner, *Dawn and Twilight of Zoroastrianism*, pp. 132–4.

10. Cf. Oldenberg, pp. 543–7; Renou, p. 28.

11 *Rig-Veda*, X, 14, X, 15, 8–10, see also *Artharvaveda*, III, 28, 5; VI, 120, 3. Cf. J. Varenne in *S.O.*, IV, pp. 216, 228.

12 Cf. Varenne in *S.O.*, IV, pp. 214–15, 216–20; Renou, p. 28.

13 *Rig-Veda*, X, 14, 10, 11.

14 Cf. Varenne in *S.O.*, IV, p. 216; P. Deussen, *Philosophy of the Upanishads*, p. 319.

15 *Rig-Veda*, X, 14, 8. K. F. Geldner comments: 'Wörtlich: das Geopferte und Gespendete' (in *R-G.L.*, p. 137, n. 4). Cf. Geldner, *Der Rig-Veda* (Harvard Oriental Series, Cambridge, Mass.), III, p. 143.

16 *Rig-Veda*, VII, 104.3. Cf. Oldenberg, p. 538, n. 4.

17 *Rig-Veda*, VII, 104.17; see also IV, 5.5. Cf. *R-G.L.*, p. 148; Deussen, p. 322; Geldner, *Der Rig-Veda* (*H.O.S.*), I, p. 424, II, p. 275.

18 *Taitt. ĀR.*, VI, 5, 13, in Oldenberg, p. 541. Cf. Renou, p. 75; see also L. S. S. O'Malley, *Popular Hinduism*, pp. 10–11.

19 *S'atapathabr.*, 12, 9, 1, 1, in *R-G.L.*, p. 145. Cf. Deussen, p. 325. This reference was apparently overlooked by A. Foucher in his reply to Miss M. Phillips Perry, stating that in 'Indian antiquity' Yama was not associated with the weighing of souls: cf. *The Burlington Magazine*, XXII (1912–13), p. 95b.

20 I, 41–3, in *R-G.L.*, pp. 148–50. Cf. Deussen, pp. 324ff.

21 Cf. S. Konow in *L.R-G.*, II, pp. 72, 74; Deussen, p. 326; Gonda, I, pp. 197, 206.

22 See above, p. 46.

23 Cf. Macdonell, *History of Sanskrit Literature*, pp. 29–39.

24 Cf. Brandon, *Man and his Destiny*, pp. 308, 312–16.

25 *Rig-Veda*, X, 14.12. Cf. Geldner, *Rig-Veda* (*H.O.S.*), III, p. 144.

26 Cf. Varenne in *S.O.*, IV, pp. 216–18.

26a *Rig-Veda*, IX, 113.7–11. Cf. Geldner, *Rig-Veda* (*H.O.S.*), III, pp. 119–20.

27 It is impossible to assign exact dates to ancient Indian literature: cf. S. Radhakrishnan, *The Principal Upaniṣads*, p. 22; Basham, pp. xix, 242.

28 Cf. Radhakrishnan, *op. cit.*, pp. 22, 147; Basham, p. 242; Deussen, pp. 2–8.

29 Cf. S. K. Chatterji in *The Vedic Age* (ed. R. C. Majumdar), p. 151; J. Filliozat in *L'Anthropologie religieuse* (ed. C. J. Bleeker), pp. 109–11; Deussen, pp. 324–7; R. Garbe in *E.R.E.*, XII, pp. 434a–35b.

30 *Bṛh. Up.*, VI, 2.15; trans. S. Radhakrishnan in *The Principal Upaniṣads*, p. 314.

31 The 'fire of man' and the 'fire of woman' signify sexual intercourse, which is the immediate cause of rebirth: see *Bṛh. Up.*, VI, 2.12, 13. Cf. K. M. Panikhar in *The Kama Sutra of Vatsyayana*, trans. R. Burton and F. F. Arbuthnot, pp. 45–6; Deussen, pp. 333–4.

32 *Bṛh. Up.*, VI, 2.16; trans. Radhakrishnan, *op. cit.*, pp. 314–15.

33 Cf. Konow in *R-G.L.*, II, pp. 74–5; Deussen, p. 335; *Das System des Vedânta*, pp. 392–5; Zaehner, *Hinduism*, pp. 76–7.

34 Deussen, *Philosophy of Upanishads*, pp. 333, 336, thinks that the extant text incorporates two traditions, of which one is older.

35 *Bṛh Up.*, III, 2.13; trans. Radhakrishan, *op. cit.*, p. 217. Cf. *R-G.L.* (K. F. Geldner), p. 189; R. E. Hume, *The Thirteen Principal Upanishads*, p. 110.

36 Cf. C. R. Lanman, *A Sanskrit Reader*, p. 140a.

37 Cf. S. Dasgupta, *History of Indian Philosophy*, I, pp. 21–2, 25–7, 54–7; Zaehner, pp. 77–80.

38 *Bṛh. Up.*, IV, 4, 5–6; trans. Radhakrishnan, *op. cit.*, 272–3; Cf. Hume, pp. 140–1; *R-G.L.* (Geldner), p. 199; Deussen, *Philosophy of Upanishads*, pp. 328–32.

39 Cf. Gonda, I, pp. 200–3; Dasgupta, I, pp. 46–8; Konow in *L.R-G.*, II, pp. 70–1, 76–7; Radhakrishnan, *op. cit.*, pp. 95–104.

40 Cf. Dasgupta, I, pp. 58–61; Deussen, *Philosophy of Upanishads*, pp. 74–9; *Das System des Vedânta*, pp. 57–8; Zaehner, pp. 64–74, 80ff.

41 *Ch. Up.*, V, 10.7; trans. Radhakrishnan, *op. cit.*, p. 433. The 'Brāhmin', 'Kṣatriya', 'Vaiśya' are designations of the three higher classes of the Hindu caste system. A 'Caṇḍāla' is an 'untouchable': cf. Basham, pp. 144–5.

42 *Bṛh. Up.*, IV, 4.6.

43 See *Ch. Up.*, III, 14.3–4. Cf. Zaehner, pp. 51–74, and n. 38 above.

44 The most explicit statement about *māyā* in the classical *Upanishads* is in the late *Praśna Up.*, I, 16. The view of the empirical world implied in the *Upanishads* is, however, that connoted by *māyā*. Cf. P. D. Devanandan, *The Concept of Māyā*, pp. 56, 61; Radhakrishnan, *op. cit.*, p. 89; Dasgupta, I, p. 50; Deussen, *Philosophy of Upanishads*, pp. 228–39, *Das System des Vedânta*, p. 372, and n. 121.

45 Cf. Deussen, *Philosophy of Upanishads*, pp. 74, 77, 158–9; Gonda, I, pp. 209, 311; Radhakrishnan, pp. 87–90; Zaehner, pp. 96–104.

46 Cf. Brandon, *History, Time and Deity*, pp. 101–5.

47 'this is the self of mine within the heart; this is *Brahman*. Into him, I shall enter, on departing hence' (*Ch Up.*, II, 14.4).

48 *Brahman* is the impersonal ground or principle of reality, and the relation of the individual to Brahman was equally an impersonal, though an essential, one. Cf. Zaehner, pp. 61ff.

49 Cf. Zaehner, pp, 105–33; Renou, pp. 46ff.

50 On the so-called *bhakti-mārga* as a way of salvation cf. Konow in *R-G.L.*, II, pp. 148–9, 150–69; G. A. Grierson in *E.R.E.*, II, pp. 539a–51; Dasgupta, I, pp. 437–43, 549–52.

51 *Bhagavadgītā*, II, 71, 72; trans. F. Edgerton, *The Bhagavad Gītā*, I, pp. 29, 31.

52 *Vana Parvan*, 182, in *S.O.*, IV, p. 224. Cf. Zaehner in *The Saviour God*, pp. 218–25.

53 Cf. E. J. Thomas, *History of Buddhist Thought*, pp. 71, 72; E. Conze, *Buddhist Thought in India*, p. 48; Radhakrishnan in *2,500 Years of Buddhism*, pp. viii–xii.

54 Cf. Brandon, *Man and his Destiny*, pp. 337–43, where detailed references are given.

55 Cf. H. Oldenberg, *Buddha: sein Leben, seine Lehre, seine Gemeinde*, pp. 333, 335; Conze, *Buddhist Thought in India*, pp. 69–79; Thomas, pp. 121–4; Dasgupta, I, pp. 108–9; H. Günther, *Das Seelenproblem im älteren Buddhis-*

mus, pp. 150–1, 156–7; T. R. V. Murti, *The Central Philosophy of Buddhism*, pp. 47–50.

56 *Cūla-kammavibhanga-s.*, *Majjhima*, iii. 202; trans. E. J. Thomas, *Early Buddhist Scriptures*, p. 128.

57 Cf. E. Conze, *Buddhist Scriptures*, pp. 222–4.

58 Trans. Conze, *Buddhist Scriptures*, pp. 224–5. For other Buddhist conceptions of Hell cf. C.-H. Marchal in *Asiatic Mythology*, pp. 199–200 (Cambodia), and S. Eliséev in *op. cit.*, pp. 429–30 (Japanese); see also below, pp. 184ff., 191ff.

59 A rendering by Professor Conze drawn from three versions, in his *Buddhist Scriptures*, pp. 229–30. Cf. the translation given by W. Y. Evans-Wentz, *The Tibetan Book of the Dead*, pp. 165–9.

60 See the *Alagadūpama-s.*, *Majjhima*, i. 135; trans. Thomas, *Early Buddhist Scriptures*, pp. 108–9. Cf. Thomas, *History of Buddhist Thought*, pp. 117–18; Conze, *Buddhism*, pp. 93ff., *Buddhist Thought in India*, pp. 59–69.

61 Cf. L. de la Vallée Poussin in *E.R.E.*, II, 739a–53b, VIII, pp. 333b–34b; Konow in *L.R-G.*, II, pp. 126–9; Conze, *Buddhism*, pp. 125–30.

62 Cf. de la Vallée Poussin in *E.R.E.*, II, pp. 256b–61a; E. Frauwallner in *Anthropologie religieuse* (ed. E. J. Bleeker), p. 132; Conze, *Buddhism*, pp. 146–7, *Buddhist Scriptures*, pp. 232–6.

63 Cf. Thomas, *History of Buddhist Thought*, p. 191; Conze, *Buddhism*, pp. 153–4.

64 According to tradition, at his Enlightenment, the Buddha recalled all his former existences: cf. Thomas, *The Life of Buddha as Legend and History*, p. 67. On the idea of 'Store-Consciousness' see Conze, *Buddhism*, pp. 168–70.

IX China

1 Cf. D. H. Smith in *Numen*, V (1958), pp. 167–8; H. O. H. Stange in *Anthropologie religieuse* (ed. C. J. Bleeker), p. 138. Burial customs and symbols on painted pottery of the Neolithic period attest the existence of primitive forms of religious belief and practice. Cf. W. Watson, *Early Civilization in China*, pp. 29, 33, 44, 45ff.; *Ancient China before the Han Dynasty*, pp. 44, 57ff.; J. Finegan, *Archeology of World Religions*, pp. 318–329; C. Hentze, *Tod, Auferstehung, Weltordnung (Das mythische Bild im ältesten China, in den grossasiatischen und zirkumpazifischen Kulturen)*, Textband, pp. 28–9, 35, 37, 100–2.

2 Cf. Smith, *op. cit.*, p. 168.

3 Cf. Smith, in *Numen*, IV (1957), pp. 177–8, V (1958), pp. 169–70; J. Needham, *Science and Civilisation in China*, II, p. 227 (Table II, No. 58).

4 Cf. M. Granet, *La pensée chinoise*, pp. 391–2; W. G. Walshe in *E.R.E.*, IV, p. 450b; H. H. Dubs, *The Works of Hsüntze*, pp. 235–44; Smith in *Numen*, V, p. 169.

5 Cf. H. Maspero, *Les religions chinoises*, pp. 51–2; Smith in *Numen*, V, p. 172.

6 Cf. Granet, *La pensée chinoise*, pp. 116–19, 126 128ff.; Fung Yu-Lan, *A History of Chinese Philosophy*, I, pp. 32, 356, 395; Needham, II, pp. 273–8; A. Forke, *Die Gedankenwelt des chinesischen Kulturkreises*, pp. 106–13.

7 Cf. Smith in *Numen*, V, p. 173.

8 Cf. Granet, *La pensée chinoise*, p. 399, *Chinese Civilization*, p. 324.

9 Cf. Smith in *Numen*, V, pp. 173–5; Granet, *La religion des Chinois*, pp. 66–7; *La pensée chinoise*, pp. 397–401; A. Waley, *The Way and its Power*, pp. 28–9; Brandon, *Man and his Destiny in the Great Religions*, pp. 356–8, 360–1.

10 *Li Chi, Chi Yi*, sec. 2; trans. E. R. Hughes, *Chinese Philosophy in Classical Times* (Everyman's Library, published by J. M. Dent and Sons Limited), pp. 278–9. Cf. Smith in *Numen*, V, p. 175; J. J. M. de Groot, *Religion in China*, p. 12.

11 Cf. N. Vandier-Nicolas in *S.O.*, IV, pp. 233–6.

12 Cf. *Man and his Destiny*, pp. 357–8.

13 M. Granet, *Chinese Civilization*, p. 172; *La religion des Chinois*, pp. 22–4. Cf. O. Franke in *L.R-G.*, I, pp. 196–9; J. J. L. Duyvendak, *Tao Te Ching*, p. 133, note; E. R. and H. Hughes, *Religion in China*, p. 15.

14 Cf. Smith in *Numen*, IV, pp. 200–1; Granet, *La religion des Chinois*, pp. 65–6, *Chinese Civilization*, pp. 176–9.

15 Cf. Granet, *Chinese Civilization*, pp. 334–5; L. Wieger, *A History of the Religious Beliefs and Philosophical Opinions in China*, pp. 101, 122–3; W. G. Walshe in *E.R.E.*, III, p. 730a–b.

16 Cf. Vandier-Nicolas in *S.O.*, IV, pp. 233, 236. See n. 34 below.

17 Cf. H. Maspero, *Le Taoïsme*, pp. 83–4, 85ff., *Les religions chinoises*, pp. 53–4, 61–3; Franke in *L.R-G.*, I, pp. 204–5; Needham, II, 139–54.

18 The soul is imagined as wandering to one of the four points of the compass. Thus it is addressed, if it goes southwards:

O Ame, reviens! Dans la région méridionale il ne faut pas t'arrêter! Les Fronts-Tatoués et les Dents-Noires offrent de la chair humaine en sacrifice,
Et avec les os ils se font du bouillon.
C'est le pays des viperes et des serpents et des pythons larges de cent lieues.

Rappel de l'Ame, trans. H. Maspero in *Les religions chinoises*, p. 51. See n. 5 above, and p. 179.

19 *Lun Yü (Analects)*, XI, 11; trans. in Fung Yu-Lan, I, p. 58. Cf. H. G. Creel. *Confucius and the Chinese Way*, p. 115; Hughes, *Chinese Philosophy*, p. 15.

20 XIX, 9.14; trans. H. H. Dubs, *The Works of Hsüntze*, p. 227, see p. 235. Cf. Dubs, *Hsüntze, the Moulder of Ancient Confucianism*, pp. 137–42; Fung Yu-Lan, I, p. 349.

21 *Chuang-tzŭ*, 18; trans. in Fung Yu-Lan, I, p. 237.

22 Cf. C. Eliot, *Hinduism and Buddhism*, III, pp. 244–65; Franke in *L.R-G.*, I, pp. 229–36; Maspero, *Les religions chinoises*, pp. 197–211.

23 Cf. Vandier-Nicolas in *S.O.*, IV, pp. 236, 238; Maspero, *Les religions chinoises*, pp. 65, 75–83: 'A lutter l'un contre l'autre, Bouddhisme et le Taoïsme avaient usé leurs forces; chacun fut assez puissant pour empêcher le triomphe de l'autre, mais non pour assurer son propre triomphe" (p. 83). On the Confucian reaction cf. Liu Wu-Chi, *A Short History of Confucian Philosophy*, pp. 138–9, 175. 'Le Confucianisme est resté plus vivant, sinon comme système religieux, au moins comme système de direction de vie; mais ce n'est que dans un milieu relativement restreint, celui des Lettrés', Maspero, *Les religions chinoises*, p. 111. See also Needham, II, pp. 402–20, 490–3.

24 Cf. Maspero, *Les religions chinoises*, pp. 111ff.; Franke in *L.R-G.*, I, pp. 255ff.; Wieger, pp. 731ff.

25 Cf. Maspero, *Les religions*, pp. 117–18; in *Asiatic Mythology*, pp. 263–71, fig. 5 on p. 261.

26 Cf. Maspero in *Asiatic Mythology*, pp. 266–7, 278–88; Vandier-Nicolas in *S.O.*, IV, p. 239. The 'Great Emperor of the Eastern Peak' (Tᶜai-yo ta-ti), administered the earth and mankind as a kind vicegerent of the Jade Emperor. This deity was originally the god of Tᶜai-shan, a sacred mountain near Shantung, where the dead were believed to gather and from where souls went forth to be born. Cf. Maspero, *Les religions*, pp. 119–20.

27 Cf. Vandier-Nicolas in *S.O.*, IV, pp. 238–9.

28 Cf. Vandier-Nicolas, *op. cit.*, pp. 240–1, 253, n. 7, 9, 11, 254, n. 22; Maspero in *Asiatic Mythology*, pp. 364, 375.

29 Cf. Smith in *Numen*, V, pp. 175–6; Maspero, *Les religions*, p. 130.

30 The most desirable fate after death seems to be that returning directly, unpunished, to this world (see below). The desire to go directly to the heaven of Amitābha did not mean aspiration for Nirvāṇa; cf. pp. 176, 187.

31 Cf. Maspero, *Les religions*, pp. 130–1, in *Asiatic Mythology*, pp. 282–8, 371–2.

32 Maspero in *Asiatic Mythology*, p. 371.

33 Maspero in *op. cit.*, p. 287, fig. 23, p. 372.

34 It is possible that some primitive idea of a *post-mortem* chastisement arose out of the cult of the god of Tᶜai-shan (see n. 26 above). 'Der Gott des Tᶜai schan, der die Amtsbezeichnung "Fürst vom Bereich des Tᶜai schan" (Tᶜai schan fu kün) führt, erhält, ganz wie ein irdischer Grosswürdenträger, seine Unterbeamten, Diener und Rangabzeichen. In seinem Gerichtshofe waltet er seines Amtes und erkennt den abgeschiedenen Seelen ihr Mass an Lohn und Strafe zu,' Franke in *L.R-G.*, I, p. 222. The God of Walls and Moats was in effect the local representative of the Great Emperor of the Eastern Peak.

35 Cf. Vandier-Nicolas in *S.O.*, IV, p. 245. See p. 187 below.

36 Maspero in *op. cit.*, p. 373.

37 Cf. Maspero in *op. cit.*, p. 364; Vandier-Nicolas, p. 243; Wieger, p. 615.

38 According to popular superstitution, the same fate befell those who accidentally died as befell suicides. Taoist and Buddhist authorities opposed this belief.

39 Maspero in *op. cit.*, p. 365; Vandier-Nicolas, p. 244.

40 Maspero in *op. cit.*, p. 364; Vandier-Nicolas, *ib.*

41 Maspero, *ib.*

42 Maspero, *ib.*

43 E.g. see Wieger, pp. 358, 360. See above p. 229, n. 90.

44 See Maspero in *op. cit.*, pp. 365–8, figs. 79, 80, 81; Wieger, pp. 356–63.

45 Cf. Maspero in *op. cit.*, p. 363, fig. 78; Vandier-Nicolas, pp. 238–9.

46 Cf. Maspero, *Les religions*, pp. 131–2, in *Asiatic Mythology*, pp. 363–4.

47 Cf. Maspero in *Asiatic Mythology*, p. 366 and fig. 79.

48 See Wieger, p. 362; Maspero in *op. cit.*, p. 368; Vandier-Nicolas, p. 244.

49 See Maspero in *op. cit.*, p. 368, fig. 82; Vandier-Nicolas, p. 250. This 'broth of oblivion' recalls the river of Lethe in Orphic eschatology: cf. p. 92 above.

50 Cf. Maspero in *op. cit.*, pp. 368, 375; Wieger, p. 364.

51 Cf. Maspero in *op. cit.*, pp. 374–5; Vandier-Nicolas, p. 245.

52 Cf. Maspero in *op. cit.*, pp. 378–81.

53 Cf. Maspero in *op. cit.*, pp. 375–9; Vandier-Nicolas, pp. 246–51. Kuan-yin was the Chinese name for Avalokiteśvara: cf. E. J. Thomas, *History of Buddhist Thought*, p. 189, n. 1; see p. 176 above.

54 Cf. Maspero in *op. cit.*, p. 374.

55 See above n. 49.

56 See above pp. 172–3.

57 The Bodhisattva Ti-tsang, whose Sanskrit name was Kshitigarbha, was supposed to have been commissioned by the Jade Emperor as the 'Instructor of the Regions of Darkness', to succour the damned. Cf. Maspero in *op. cit.*, pp. 375, 377.

X Japan

1 Cf. K. Florenz, *Die historischen Quellen der Shinto-Religion*, pp. vi–ix; S. Eliséev in *Asiatic Mythology*, p. 386.

2 Cf. J. N. Takasaki in *2,500 Years of Buddhism*, pp. 70–3; K. Florenz in *L.R-G.*, I, pp. 349–68.

3 Cf. J. E. Kidder, *Japan before Buddhism*, pp. 90ff., 131–2; J. Finegan, *Archeology of World Religions*, pp. 421–5.

4 Cf. Eliséev in *op. cit.*, p. 386; Florenz in *L.R-G.*, I, p. 267; Finegan, pp. 425–6.

5 Cf. Kidder, p. 132.

6 *Kojiki*, 1, 2, in Florenz, *Quellen*, p. 11 ("'Einladener Herr" und "Einla-

dendes Weib", vom Verbum *izanafu* "einladen, auffordern"', p. 11, n. 8). Cf. Florenz in *L.R-G.*, I, pp. 276–7.

7 *Kojiki*, I, 7, 9, in Florenz, *Quellen*, pp. 19, 21–2. Another name for the underworld was the 'Root-land'. 'Das *Yomi*-oder *Yomo-tsu-kuni*, "Land der Finsternis", *Ne no kuni*, "Wurzelland", *Soko no kuni*, "Bodenland",' Florenz in *L.R-G.*, I, p. 274. Florenz thinks that the similarity between *Yomi* and *Yama*, the Indian ruler of the underworld, is accidental (*Quellen*, p. 21, n. 1). W. G. Aston suggests that, 'In the old times Yomi was probably only a sufficiently transparent metaphor for the grave' (in *E.R.E.*, XI, p. 464a). R. Sieffert in *S.O.*, IV, p. 258, believes that the conception of *Yomi* combines two traditions, one native and the other Chinese.

8 *Kojiki*, I, 9, in Florenz, *Quellen*, pp. 22–3.

9 *Kojiki*, I, 9–10, in Florenz, *Quellen*, pp. 23–6.

10 *Yomo tsu Oho-kami*. In the concluding dialogue between Izanagi and Izanami, the latter declares that she will cause a thousand men to die each day. Izanagi counters her threat to exterminate mankind by saying that he will cause one thousand five hundred to be born each day. It would seem that some ancient aetiological myth is involved here, accounting for death and the maintenance of the race. Cf. Florenz in *L.R-G.*, I, pp. 275–6; R. Sieffert in *S.O.*, IV, pp. 258–9.

11 'Den Gedanken einer Belohnung oder Bestrafung im Jenseits kennt der Shinto nicht; diese Vorstellung ist erst durch den Buddhismus nach Japan verpflanz worden,' Florenz in *L.R-G.*, I, p. 276. Cf. S. Eliséev in *Asiatic Mythology*, p. 387; Sieffert in *S.O.*, IV, p. 259.

12 Cf. Kidder, pp. 79–84, 104–10.

13 Cf. Sieffert in *S.O.*, IV, pp. 283–4; M. Revon in *E.R.E.*, I, p. 457a.

14 The custom was practised in China: cf. W. Watson, *Early Civilization in China*, pp. 49–50.

15 Cf. Revon in *E.R.E.*, I, pp. 455a–57b; Aston in *E.R.E.*, XI, p. 464a; Kidder, pp. 85–6.

16 Cf. M. Anesaki in *E.R.E.*, VIII, p. 37b. Anesaki thought that there is evidence of a primitive conception of 'double souls'; but he admitted that the evidence is very obscure (p. 38b).

17 Cf. A. Lloyd in *E.R.E.*, IV, p. 485a–b; see above p. 178.

18 Cf. Florenz in *L.R-G.*, I, pp. 385–93; Eliséev in *Asiatic Mythology*, p. 416; Takasaki in 2,500 *Years of Buddhism*, pp. 131–3.

19 Cf. Florenz in *L.R-G.*, I, pp. 387–90; Eliséev in *op. cit.*, pp. 416, 420–2.

20 Cf. Eliséev in *op. cit.*, pp. 416–17, 424–5, 428; Sieffert in *S.O.*, IV, p. 262.

21 Cf. Eliséev in *op. cit.*, pp. 416–17, 429; see also the plate facing p. 416 and figs. 30, 31. See plate 12 here.

22 See the references in preceding note.

23 Cf. Eliséev in *op. cit.*, pp. 432–4; Sieffert in *S.O.*, IV, pp. 274–5.

24 Cf. Sieffert in *op. cit.*, pp. 274–7, who cites one instance of Jizô's offering himself to bear the penalty in the place of the condemned one.

25 Cf. Sieffert, pp. 278–81.

26 Cf. Sieffert, p. 281: 'La passion du joueur (*Bakuchi*) intrigue fort, elle aussi, l'innocent juge des Enfers. Il se fait donc expliquer les règles du jeu par le pécheur et bientôt s'y laisse prendre.'

27 E.g. see E. Mâle, *L'Art religieux du XIIe. siècle en France* (Paris, 1953⁶), pp. 433–4; M. D. Anderson, *Drama and Imagery in English Medieval Churches* (Cambridge, 1963), pp. 171–7.

28 Cf. Sieffert, p. 282.

29 Cf. Anesaki in *E.R.E.*, VIII, p. 39b; H. Dumoulin, *A History of Zen Buddhism*, pp. 187–97, 240–1; D. T. Suzuki, *An Introduction to Zen Buddhism*, pp. 38–40; W. Gundert, 'Die Behandlung eschatologischer Fragen im Zen-Buddhismus', in *X. Internationaler Kongress für Religionsgeschichte* (1960), pp. 109–11.

30 *Op. cit.*, p. 41.

Addendum to p. 234, n. 139

The curious depiction in the mediaeval Dooms of serpents biting the breasts of women may derive from another tradition than that suggested above. In the folklores of many peoples the idea occurs of serpents sucking women's breasts; the idea probably stems from the serpent's love of milk. Cf. *E.R.E.*, XI, p. 410b.

BIBLIOGRAPHY

Introduction

BERTHOLET, A. *Wörterbuch der Religionen*, Stuttgart, 1952.
BREUIL, H. *Quatre cents siècles d'art pariétal (les cavernes ornées de l'Age de Renne)*, Montignac, 1954.
BREUIL, H. et LANTIER, R. *Les hommes de la Pierre Ancienne*, Paris, 1951.
BRANDON, S. G. F. *Man and his Destiny in the Great Religions*, Manchester University Press, 1962.
CLARK, G. *World Prehistory*, Cambridge, 1961.
GIEDION, S. *The Eternal Present: the Beginnings of Art*, Oxford, 1962.
HAWKES, J. *Prehistory*, vol. I (Part One), of *History of Mankind* (published by the International Commission for a History of the Scientific and Cultural Development of Mankind), London, 1963.
JAMES, E. O. *Prehistoric Religion*, London, 1950.
KENYON, K. M. 'Neolithic Portrait Skulls from Jericho', *Antiquity*, XXVII (1953).
KÜHN, H. *Die Felsbilder Europas*, Zürich/Wien, 1952.
LAMING, A. *Lascaux*, E. T., Harmondsworth, 1959.
MAINAGE, T. *Les religions de la Préhistoire: l'age paléolithique*, Paris, 1925.
MARINGER, J. *Vorgeschichtliche Religion (Religionen im steinzeitlichen Europa)*, Einseideln, 1956).
The Gods of Prehistoric Man, E.T., London, 1960.
MELLAART, J. 'Earliest of Neolithic Cities: the Third Season of Excavations at Anatolian Chatal Huyuk. Part I in *I.L.N.*, 1 February 1964; Part II in *I.L.N.*, 8 February 1964. *Earliest Civilisations of the Near East*, London, 1965.
PITTIONI, R. *Die urgeschichtlichen Grundlagen der europäischen Kultur*, Wien, 1949.
TYLOR, E. B. *Primitive Culture*, 2 vols., London, 1927 (1871).
WERNERT, P. 'Le culte des crânes à l'époque paléolithique', in *H.G.R.*, tome I.
WINDELS, F. *The Lascaux Cave Paintings*, London, 1949.

I Ancient Egypt

ALLEN, T. G. *The Egyptian Book of the Dead*, University of Chicago Press, 1960.
Ancient Near Eastern Texts relating to the Old Testament (ed. J. B. Pritchard), Princeton University Press, 2nd ed., 1955. Egyptian texts translated by J. A. Wilson.

ANTHES, R. *The original meaning of m3ʿḫrw* in *J.N.E.S.*, XIII (1954).

'Egyptian Theology of the Third Millennium BC', in *J.N.E.S.*, XVIII (1959).

BELL, H. I. *Cults and Creeds in Graeco-Roman Egypt*, Liverpool, 1953.

BONNET, H. *Reallexikon der ägyptischen Religionsgeschichte*, Berlin, 1952.

BOYLAN, P. *Thoth, the Hermes of Egypt*, Oxford, 1922.

BRANDON, S. G. F. *Man and his Destiny in the Great Religions*, Manchester University Press, 1962.

Creation Legends of the Ancient Near East, London, 1963.

'The Ritual Technique of Salvation in the Ancient Near East', in *The Saviour God* (ed. S. G. F. Brandon, Manchester University Press, 1963).

'A Problem of the Osirian Judgment of the Dead', in *Numen*, V (Leiden, 1958).

History, Time and Deity, Manchester University Press, 1955.

BREASTED, J. H. *The Development of Religion and Thought in Ancient Egypt*, London, 1912.

Ancient Records of Egypt, vol. I, Chicago, 1906.

The Dawn of Conscience, New York, 1935.

DE BUCK, A. *The Egyptian Coffin Texts*, vols. I–VII, Chicago Univ. Press 1935–61.

BUDGE, E. A. W. *The Book of the Dead: Facsimile of the Papyrus of Ani*, British Museum, 2nd ed., 1894.

The Book of the Dead: the Papyrus of Ani, 2 vols., London/New York, 1913.

The Book of the Dead (The Chapters of the Coming Forth by Day), 3 vols., London, 1898; also trans. only, 2nd ed., London, 1953.

Osiris and the Egyptian Resurrection, 2 vols., London, 1911.

The Mummy, Cambridge, 1925.

From Fetish to God in Ancient Egypt, Oxford, 1934.

CAPART, J. 'Ra, Juge des Morts', in *C.E.*, IV (1939).

Thebes: the Glory of a Great Past, E.T., London, 1926.

ČERNÝ, J. *Ancient Egyptian Religion*, London, 1952.

DESROCHES-NOBLECOURT, C. 'Les religions égyptiennes', in *H.G.R.*, I (1948).

Dictionary of Egyptian Civilization, ed. G. Posener, E.T., London, 1962.

DONADONI, S. *La religione dell'antico Egitto*, Bari, 1959.

DRIOTON, E.-VANDIER, J. *L'Égypte*, 2nd ed., Paris, 1946.

EDWARDS, I. E. S. *The Pyramids of Egypt*, Harmondsworth, 1947.

ERMAN, A. *Die Religion der Aegypter*, Berlin/Leipzig, 1934.

The Literature of the Ancient Egyptians, trans. and ed. A. M. Blackman, London, 1927.

Aegypten, neu bearbeitet von H. Ranke, Tübingen, 1923.

FRANKFORT, H. *Kingship and the Gods*, University of Chicago Press, 1948.

Ancient Egyptian Religion, New York, 1948.

GARDINER, A. *Egyptian Grammar*, Oxford, 1927.

Egypt of the Pharaohs, Oxford, 1961.

'Ethics and Morality (Egyptian)', in *E.R.E.*, VIII (1915).

Bibliography

GREVEN, L. *Der Ka in Theologie und Königskult der Aegypter des alten Reiches*, Glückstadt, 1952.

GRIFFITH, F. L. *Stories of the High Priests of Memphis*, Oxford, 1900.

HAMANN, R. *Aegyptische Kunst*, Berlin, 1944.

HORNUNG, E. 'Die Verurteilten des ägyptischen Totengerichtes', in *X. Internationaler Kongress für Religionsgeschichte* (Marburg, 1960).

JUNKER, H. *Pyramidenzeit (Das Wesen der altägyptischen Religion)*, Zürich, 1949.

KEES, H. *Totenglauben und Jenseitsvorstellungen der alten Aegypter*, 2 Aufl., Berlin, 1956.

Aegypten, Lieferung 10, in *R-G.L.*, 2 Aufl. (1928).

LANGE, K. and HIRMER, M. *Egypt*, E.T., London, 1956.

LEFEBVRE, G. *Le tombeau de Pétosiris*, 2 tomes, Cairo, 1923-4.

MASPERO, G. *Les contes populaires de l'Égypte ancienne*, 4th ed., Paris, 1911; E.T., *Popular Stories of Ancient Egypt*, London, 1915.

MAYSTRE, CH. *Les déclarations d'innocence (Livre des morts*, Chapitre 125), Institute francais d'archéologie orientale. Recherches d'archéologie, de philologie et d'histoire, tome 8, Cairo, 1937.

MERCER, S. A. B. *The Religion of Ancient Egypt*, London, 1949.

The Pyramid Texts, 4 vols., New York, 1952.

The Literary Criticism of the Pyramid Texts, London, 1956.

MONTET, P. *Eternal Egypt*, E.T., London, 1964.

MORENZ, S. *Aegyptische Religion*, Stuttgart, 1960.

Die Zauberflöte, Münster/Köln, 1952.

Die Geschichte von Joseph dem Zimmermann (Texte u. Untersuchungen z. Gesch. d. altchr. Literatur, hrg. W. Eltester u. E. Klostermann, Bd. 56), Berlin, 1951.

'Das Werden zu Osiris', in *Staatliche Museen zu Berlin: Forsuchungen und Berichte*, I, 1957.

MORET, A. *Au temps des Pharaons*, Paris, 1912.

PIANKOFF, A. *Le 'Coeur' dans les textes égyptiennes*, Paris, 1930.

The Shrines of Tut-Ankh-Amen, New York, 1962.

PORTER, B. and MOSS, R. L. B. *Topographical Bibliography of Ancient Egyptian Hieroglyphic Texts, Reliefs, and Paintings*, II, Oxford, 1929.

ROEDER, G. *Die aegyptischen Religion in Texten und Bilden*, Band I (*Die aegyptische Götterwelt*), Zürich, 1959. Band IV (*Der Ausklang der aegyptischen Religion mit Reformation, Zauberei, und Jenseitsglauben*), 1961.

Urkunden zur Religion des alter Aegypten, Jena, 1923.

SAINTE FARE GARNOT, J. 'Les formules funéraires des stèles égyptiennes', in *H.G.R.*, I (1948).

SANDER-HANSEN C. E. *Der Begriff des Todes bei den Aegyptern*, Copenhagen, 1942.

SCHOTT, S. *Mythe und Mythenbildung im alten Aegypten*, Leipzig, 1945.

SCHWEITZER, U. *Das Wesen des Ka im Diesseits und Jenseits der alten Aegypter*, Glückstadt, 1956.

SCOTT-MONCRIEFF, P. D. *Paganism and Christianity in Egypt*, Cambridge, 1913.

SETHE, K. *Die altägyptischen Pyramidentexte*, 4 Bände, 2. Aufl., Hildesheim, 1960.

Übersetzung und Kommentar zu den altägyptischen Pyramidentexten, 4 Bände, n.d.

Urkunden des Alten Reichs, Band I, Leipzig, 1903.

Aegyptische Lesestücke, Leipzig, 1928.

SPELEERS, L. *Les textes des pyramides égyptiennes*, 2 tomes, Bruxelles, 1923-4.

SPIEGEL, J. *Die Idee vom Totengericht in der aegyptischen Religion*, Glückstadt, 1935.

'Die religionsgeschichtliche Stellung der Pyramidentexte', in *Orientalia*, XXII (1955).

Das Werden der altägyptischen Hochkultur, Heidelberg, 1953.

SUYS E. *Vie de Petosiris, grand prêtre de Thot à Hermopolis*, Bruxelles, 1927.

THAUSING, G. *Der Auferstehungsgedanke in ägyptischen religiosen Texten*, Leipzig, 1943.

VANDIER, J. *La religion égyptienne*, Paris, 1949.

WILSON, J. A. *The Culture of Ancient Egypt*, University of Chicago Press, 1966.

YOYOTTE, J. 'Le jugement des morts dans l'Égypte ancienne', in *Sources orientales*, IV, Paris, 1961.

ZANDEE, J. *Death as an Enemy according to Ancient Egyptian Conceptions*, Leiden, 1960.

II   Ancient Mesopotamia

Ancient Near Eastern Texts relating to the Old Testament, ed. J. B. Pritchard, 2nd ed., Princeton University Press, 1955. Sumerian texts trans. by S. N. Kramer; Babylonian texts trans. by E. A. Speiser.

AYNARD, J.-M. 'Le jugement des morts chez les Assyro-Babyloniens', in *Sources orientales*, IV (Paris, 1961).

BRANDON, S. G. F. 'The Epic of Gilgamesh: a Mesopotamian Philosophy', in *History Today*, XI, London, 1961.

Man and his Destiny in the Great Religions, Manchester University Press, 1962.

Creation Legends of the Ancient Near East, London, 1963.

CASTELLINO, G. 'Le sorti del re nell'Aldilà secondo un testo di Urnammu di Ur', in *Atti dell'VIII Congresso internazionale di Storia delle Religioni* (1955), Firenze, 1956.

'Urnammu, three Religious Texts', Z.A., LII (1957).

CHILDE, V. G. *New Light on the Most Ancient East*, London, 1953.

CONTENAU, G. *Les divinations chez les Assyriens et les Babyloniens*, Paris, 1940.

DHORME, ED. *Choix de textes religieux assyro-babyloniens*, Paris, 1907.

Les religions de Babylonie et Assyrie, Paris, 1945.

EBELING, T. *Tod und Leben nach den Vorstellungen des Babylonier*, Berlin/Leipzig, 1931.

FISH, T. 'Some Ancient Mesopotamian Traditions concerning Men and Society', in *B.J.R.L.*, vol. 30 (1946).

'The Zu Bird', in *B.J.R.L.*, vol. 31 (1948).

Bibliography

FRANKFORT, H. *The Birth of Civilization in the Near East*, London, 1954.
Kingship and the Gods, Chicago University Press, 1948.

GADD, C. J. *Ideas of Divine Rule in the Ancient East* (Schweich Lectures, 1945), London, 1948.

HEIDEL, A. *The Gilgamesh Epic and Old Testament Parallels*, 2nd ed., Chicago University Press, 1949.

JACOBSEN, T. in *The Intellectual Adventure of Ancient Man* (ed. H. and H. A. Frankfort), Chicago University Press, 1946.

JASTROW, M. *Some Aspects of Religious Belief and Practice in Babylonia and Assyria*, New York, 1911.

JEAN, C.-F. *La religion sumérienne (d'après les documents sumériens antérieurs à la dynastie d'Isin (−2186)*, Paris, 1931.

JENSEN, P. *Das Gilgamesh-Epos in der Weltliteratur*, Band I, Strasbourg, 1906.

JEREMIAS, F. 'Semitische Völker in Vorderasien', in *L.R.-G.*, I, 4 Aufl. (1925).

KRAUS, F. R. 'Altmesopotamisches Lebensgefühl', in *J.N.E.S.*, XIX (1960).

KRAMER, S. N. *Sumerian Mythology*, Philadelphia, 1944.
From the Tablets of Sumer, Colorado, 1956.
'Mythology of Sumer and Akkad', in *Mythologies of the Ancient World* (ed. S. N. Kramer), New York, 1961.

LAMBERT, W. G. *Babylonian Wisdom Literature*, Oxford, 1960.

LANGDON, S. H. 'Death and Disposal of Dead (Babylonian)', in *E.R.E.*, IV (1911).
'Babylonian Wisdom', in *Babylonica* (ed. Ch. Virolleand), t. VII, Paris, 1922–3.

DE LIAGRE BÖHL, F. M. TH. 'Das Menschenbild in babylonischer Schau', in *Anthropologie religieuse* (ed. C. J. Bleeker), Leiden, 1955.

MALLOWAN, M. E. L. *Early Mesopotamia and Iran*, London, 1965.

MEISSNER, B. *Babylonien und Assyrien*, Band II, Heidelberg, 1925.

MOORGAT, A. *Tammuz: der Unsterblichkeitsglaube in der altorientalischen Bildkunst*, Berlin, 1947.

PARROT, A. *Archéologie mesopotamienne*, I, Paris, 1946.
Le 'Refrigerium' dans l'au-delà, Paris, 1937.

SAGGS, H. W. F. *The Greatness that was Babylon*, London, 1962.

THOMPSON, R. C. *Devils and Evil Spirits of Babylonia*, vol. I, London, 1903.

UNGNAD A. *Die Religion der Babylonien und Assyrer*, Jena, 1921.

WISEMAN, *Cylinder Seals of Western Asia*, London, n.d.

WOOLLEY, L. *Excavations at Ur*, London, 1955.

III   Hebrew Religion

Die Apokryphen und Pseudepigraphen des Alten Testaments (ed. E. Krautzsch), 2 Bände, Tübingen, 1900.

BEYERLIN, W. *Herkunft und Geschichte der ältesten Sinaitraditionen*, Tübingen, 1961.

Biblisch-historiches Handwörterbuch (ed. Bo Reicke u. L. Rost), 3 Bände, Göttingen, 1962.

BRANDON, S. G. F. *Man and his Destiny in the Great Religions*, Manchester University Press, 1962.

Creation Legends of the Ancient Near East, London, 1963.

History, Time and Deity, Manchester University Press, 1965.

Jesus and the Zealots, Manchester University Press, 1967.

BUDGE, E. A. W. *From Fetish to God in Ancient Egypt*, Oxford, 1934.

CAZELLES, H. 'Le jugement des morts en Israël', in *Sources orientales*, IV (Paris, 1961).

CHARLES, R. H. *A Critical History of the Doctrine of a Future Life*, 2nd ed., London, 1913.

The Revelation of St John (International Critical Commentary), 2 vols., Edinburgh, 1920.

The Book of Enoch, London, 1921.

COOKE, G. A. *Ezekiel* (International Critical Commentary), Edinburgh, 1936.

DHORME, ED. *Les religions de Babylonie et d'Assyrie*, Paris, 1945.

DRIVER, S. R. and GRAY, G. B. *Job* (International Critical Commentary), Edinburgh, 1921.

DUPONT-SOMMER, A. *Les écrits esséniens découvertes près de la Mer Morte*, Paris, 1959.

FOHRER, G. *Das Buch Jesaja*, I, Zürich/Stuttgart, 1960.

GUIGNEBERT, CH. *Le monde juif vers le temps de Jésu*, Paris, 1935.

HEIDEL, A. *The Gilgamesh Epic and Old Testament Parallels*, Chicago University Press, 2nd ed., 1949.

HENGEL, M. *Die Zeloten*, Leiden, 1961.

HUMBERT, P. 'Le modernisme de Job', in *Wisdom in Israel and the Ancient Near East* (ed. M. Noth and D. Winton Thomas), Leiden, 1955.

HUPPENBAUER, H. W. *Der Mensch zwischen zwei Welten*, Zürich, 1959.

IRWIN, W. A. *The Intellectual Adventure of Ancient Man* (ed. H. and H. A. Frankfort), Chicago University Press, 1946.

JACKSON, F. J. FOAKES. *Josephus and the Jews*, London, 1930.

JEREMIAS, A. 'Book of Life', in *E.R.E.*, II (1909).

JOHNSON, A. R. *The Vitality of the Individual in the Thought of Ancient Israel*, University of Wales Press, Cardiff, 1949.

KOEP, L. 'Buch IV (himmlisch)', in *R.A.C.*, II (1954).

LODS, A. *Israël: des origines au milieu du VIII. siècle*, Paris, 1932.

Les prophètes d'Israël et les débuts du Judaïsme, Paris, 1935.

MacCULLOCH, J. A. 'Eschatology', in *E.R.E.*, V (1912).

MARTIN, F. *Le Livre d'Hénoch* (traduit sur le texte éthiopien), Paris, 1906.

MEYER, ED. *Ursprung und Anfänge des Christentums*, 3 Bände, Stuttgart/Berlin, 1921–3.

The Mishnah, trans. H. Danby, Oxford, 1933.

Bibliography

MOWINCKEL, S. *He That Cometh*, E.T., Oxford, 1956.

A New Commentary of Holy Scripture, ed. C. Gore, H. L. Goudge, A. Guillaume, 2 vols., London, 1929.

NIKOLAINEN, A. T. *Der Auferstehungsglauben in der Bibel und ihrer Umwelt*, 2 Bände, Helsinki, 1944.

NOTH, M. *The History of Israel*, E.T., 2nd ed., London, 1960.

OESTERLEY, W. O. E. and ROBINSON, T. H. *Hebrew Religion*, London, 1930.

An Introduction to the Old Testament, London, 1937.

A History of Israel, vol. II, Oxford, 1932

PARROT, A. *Le 'Refrigerium' dans l'au-delà*, Paris, 1937.

Peake's Commentary on the Bible, ed. M. Black and H. H. Rowley, London, 1962.

PEDERSEN, J. *Israel: its Life and Culture*, I–IV, in 2 vols., Copenhagen and London, 1926, 1940.

PERETTI, A. *La Sibilla babilonese nella propaganda ellenistica*, Firenze, 1943.

PFEIFFER, R. H. *Introduction to the Old Testament*, ed. 1948, London.

History of New Testament Times (with an Introduction to the Apocrypha), New York, 1949.

PIDOUX, G. 'L'homme dans l'Ancien Testament', in *Anthropologie religieuse* (ed. C. J. Bleeker), Leiden, 1955.

VON RAD, G. 'The Origin of the Concept of the Day of Yahweh', in *J.S.S.*, IV (1959).

RICCIOTTI, G. *Flavio Giuseppe*, vol. I, Torino, 1936.

ROWLEY, H. H. *From Joseph to Joshua* (Schweich Lectures, 1948), London, 1950.

The Faith of Israel, London, 1956.

The Servant of the Lord and Other Essays on the Old Testament, London, 1952.

Men of God: Studies in Old Testament History and Prophecy, London, 1963.

SCHÜRER, E. *Geschichte des jüdischen Volkes im Zeitalter Jesu Christi*, 3 Bände, 3 u. 4 Aufl., Leipzig, 1898–1901.

Der babylonische Talmud (ed. L. Goldschmidt), Band I, Berlin, 1930.

WILDBERGER, H. *Jahwes Eigentumsvolk*, Zürich, 1960.

YADIN, Y. *The Scroll of the War of the Sons of Light against the Sons of Darkness*, Oxford, 1962.

IV   Graeco-Roman Culture

ALTHEIM, F. *A History of Roman Religion*, E.T., London, 1938.

ARISTOPHANES, *The Frogs*—see under Stanford, W. B.

BENDINELLI, G. *Compendio di storia dell'arte etrusca e romana*, Milan, 1931.

BRANDON, S. G. F. *Man and his Destiny in the Great Religions*, Manchester University Press, 1962.

Creation Legends of the Ancient Near East, London, 1963.

'The Personification of Death in some Ancient Religions', in *B.J.R.L.*, 43 (1961).

BRUNELLI, V. B. *L'Eroico omerico*, Padua, 1941.

BURN, A. R. *Minoans, Philistines and Greeks*, London, 1930.

BURNET, J. 'Soul (Greek)', in *E.R.E.*, XI (1920).

CARCOPINO, J. *Aspects mystiques de la Rome païenne*, Paris, 1942.
La basilique pythagoricienne de la Porte Majeure, Paris, 1943.

CHADWICK, J. 'Minoan Linear A', in *Antiquity*, XXXIII (1959).

CHARBONNEAUX, J. 'La religion égéene préhellénique', in *H.G.R.*, II (Paris, 1948).

COHEN, R. *La Grèce et l'hellénisation du monde antique*, Paris, 1948.

CORNFORD, F. M. *Greek Religious Thought from Homer to the Age of Alexander*, London, 1923.

Corpus Hermeticum, text and trans., A. D. Nock and A.-J. Festugière, 4 tomes, Paris, 1945–54.

CUMONT, F. *After-Life in Roman Paganism*, New York, 1959 (1922).

DENNIS, G. *The Cities and Cemeteries of Etruria*, 2 vols., London, 1907.

Der Kleine Pauly, I, Stuttgart, 1964.

DIETERICH, A. *Nekyia: Beiträge zur Erklärung der neuentdeckten Petrusapokalypse*, 2 Aufl., Leipzig/Berlin, 1913.

DODDS, E. R. *The Greeks and the Irrational*, University of California Press, 1963.

EMPEDOCLES, see under Kirk, G. S. and Raven, J. E.

FESTUGIÈRE, A.-J. *La révélation d'Hermès Trismégiste*, 4 tomes, Paris, 1950–54.

FOWLER, W. WARDE, *The Religious Experience of the Roman People*, London, 1911.

GERNET, L. 'L'Anthropologie dans la religion grecque', in *Anthropologie religieuse* (ed. C. J. Bleeker), Leiden, 1955.

GERNET, L. et BOULANGER, A. *Le génie grec dans la religion*, Paris, 1932.

GLOTZ, G. *La civilisation égéene*, Paris, 1937.

GLOTZ, G. et COHEN, R. *Histoire grecque*, I (Des origines aux guerres médiques), Paris, 1938.

Greek Anthology. trans. and ed., W. R. Paton, Loeb Classical Library, vol. II, London, 1939.

GRENIER, A. *Les religions étrusque et romaine*, Paris, 1948.

GUTHRIE, W. K. C. *Orpheus and Greek Religion*, 2nd ed., London, 1952.
The Greeks and their Gods, London, 1950.
In the Beginning (Some Greek views on the origins of life and early state of man), London, 1957.

KIRK, G. S. and RAVEN, J. E. *The Presocratic Philosophers*, Cambridge, 1960.

KRETZENBACHER, L. *Die Seelenwaage (Zur religiösen Idee vom Jenseitsgericht auf der Schicksalswaage in Hochreligion, Bildkunst, und Volksglaube)*, Klagenfurt, 1958.

HARRISON, J. *Prolegomena to the Study of Greek Religion*, 3rd ed., New York, 1955.

Bibliography

HESIOD, *The Homeric Hymns and Homerica*, Loeb Classical Library, trans. and ed. H. G. Evelyn White, London, 1914.

HICKS, R. D. 'Lucretius', in *E.R.E.*, VIII (1915).

HOMER, *The Iliad*, 2 vols., trans. and ed. A. T. Murray, Loeb Classical Library, London, 1932.

The Odyssey, 2 vols., trans. and ed. A. T. Murray, Loeb Classical Library, London, 1938.

HUS, A. *The Etruscans*, E.T., London, 1961.

HUTCHINSON, R. W. *Prehistoric Crete*, Harmondsworth, 1962.

HUXLEY, G. 'The Genesis of Greece', in *The Birth of Western Civilization* (ed. M. Grant), London, 1964.

JAEGER, W. *The Theology of the Early Greek Philosophers*, Oxford, 1948.

JAMES, E. O. *The Cult of the Mother Goddess*, London, 1959.

JAMES, M. R. *The Apocryphal New Testament*, Oxford, 1926.

JOHN, R. L. *Dante*, Wien, 1946.

LINFORTH, I. M. *The Arts of Orpheus*, University of California Press, 1941.

LORIMER, H. L. *Homer and the Monuments*, London, 1950.

LUCIAN, *The Works of Lucian of Samosata*, trans. and ed. H. W. Fowler and F. G. Fowler, 4 vols., Oxford, 1939 (1905).

LUCRETIUS, *De rerum natura*, trans. and ed. W. H. D. Rouse, Loeb Classical Library, London, 1947.

MACCHIORO, V. *Zagreus; studi intorno all'orfismo*, Firenze, 1930.

MACKAIL, J. W. *Select Epigrams from the Greek Anthology*, London, 1925.

MAGNIEN, V. *Les Mystères d'Éleusis*, Paris, 1950.

MAIR, A. W. 'Sin (Greek)', in *E.R.E.*, XI (1920).

MARINATOS, S. and HIRMER, M. *Crete and Mycenae*, London, 1960.

MÉAUTIS, G. *Les dieux de la Grèce et les mystères d'Éleusis*, Paris, 1959.

MEYER, ED. *Geschichte des Altertums*, II, 1, Stuttgart/Berlin, 1928.

MORENZ, S. 'Das Werden zu Osiris', in *Forschungen und Berichte*, I (1957), Staatliche Museen zu Berlin.

MURRAY, G. *Five Stages of Greek Religion*, London, 1935.

MYLONAS, G. E. *Eleusis and the Eleusinian Mysteries*, Princeton University Press, 1961.

NILSSON, M. P. *Geschichte der griechischen Religion*, München, Band I^1 (1941), I^2 (1955), Band II (1950).

The Minoan-Mycenaean Religion and its survival in Greek Religion, 2nd ed., Lund, 1950.

Greek Folk Religion, New York, 1961.

ONIANS, R. B. *The Origins of European Thought about the Body, the Mind, the Soul, the World, Time and Fate*, Cambridge, 1951.

The Oxford Classical Dictionary, Oxford, 1949.

PAGE, D. *History and the Homeric Iliad*, University of California Press, 1963.

PICARD, C. *Les religions préhelléniques*, Paris, 1948.

PINDAR, see under Cornford, F. M.

PLATO, *The Republic*, ed. J. Adam, Cambridge, 1900.

Gorgias, ed. and trans. W. R. M. Lamb, Loeb Classical Library, London, 1946.

RICHMOND, I. A. *Archaeology and the After-life in Pagan and Christian Imagery* (Riddell Memorial Lectures, University of Durham), London, 1950.

DE RIDDER, A. et DEONNA, W. *L'art en Grèce*, Paris, 1924.

ROBIN, L. *La pensée grecque et les origines de l'esprit scientifique*, Paris, 1928.

ROHDE, E. *Psyche: Seelencult und Unsterblichkeitsglaube der Griechen*, 2 Bände, Freiburg, 1898.

ROSE, H. J. *A Handbook of Greek Mythology*, London, 1928.

Ancient Greek Religion, London, 1948.

ROSTAGNI, A. *Storia della letteratura latina*, 11th ed., Verona, 1942.

ROSTOVTZEFF, M. *A History of the Ancient World*, I, Oxford, 1945.

SCHAEFFER, C. F. A. *The Cuneiform Texts of Ras Shamra-Ugarit* (Schweich Lectures, 1936), London, 1939.

VON SCHEFFER, T. *Die Kultur der Griechen*, Königsberg, 1938.

SCHWENN, F. *Die Theogonie des Hesiodos*, Heidelberg, 1934.

STANFORD, W. B. *Aristophanes: the Frogs*, 2nd ed., London, 1963.

STELLA, L. A. 'La religione greca nei testi miceni', in *Numen*, V (Leiden, 1958).

STENICO, A. *Roman and Etruscan Painting*, E.T., London, 1963.

TAYLOUR, LORD WILLIAM, *The Mycenaeans*, London, 1964.

TURCAN, R. 'La catabase orphique du papyrus de Bologne', in *R.H.R.*, 150 (1956).

TURCHI, N. *Fontes Historiae Mysteriorum Aevi Hellenistici*, Roma, 1923.

VIRGIL, *Aeneid*, trans. and ed. H. Rushton Fairclough, Loeb Classical Library, London, 2 vols., London, 1953.

WHEELWRIGHT, P. *Heraclitus*, Princeton University Press, 1959.

WÜST, E. 'Psychostasie (Seelenwägung)', in *P.W.*, XXXIII.2 (1957).

V Christianity

AINAUD, J. *Romanesque Painting*, E.T., London, 1963.

ANDERSON, M. D. *Drama and Imagery in English Medieval Churches*, Cambridge, 1963.

BELL, H. IDRIS. *Cults and Creeds in Graeco-Roman Egypt*, Liverpool University Press, 1953.

BETHUNE-BAKER, J. F. *An Introduction to the Early History of Christian Doctrine*, London, 1903.

BOASE, T. S. R. 'King Death: Mortality, Judgment, and Remembrance', in *The Flowering of the Middle Ages* (ed. J. Evans), London, 1966.

DU BOURGUET, P. *Early Christian Painting*, E.T., London, 1965.

BRANDON, S. G. F. *The Fall of Jerusalem and the Christian Church*, 2nd ed., London, 1957.

Bibliography

'The Personification of Death in Some Ancient Religions', in *B.J.R.L.*, 43 (1961).

History, Time and Deity, Manchester University Press, 1965.

Jesus and the Zealots, Manchester University Press, 1967.

'The Ritual Technique of Salvation in the Ancient Near East', in *The Saviour God* (ed. S. G. F. Brandon), Manchester University Press, 1963.

BUDGE, E. A. W. *The Book of the Cave of Treasures*, London, 1927.

BULTMANN, R. *Die Geschichte der synoptischen Tradition*, 3 Aufl., Göttingen, 1957.

Urchristentum im Rahmen der antiken Religionen, Zürich, 1949.

'History and Eschatology in the New Testament', in *N.T.S.*, I (1954).

CARCOPINO, J. *De Pythagore aux Apôtres*, Paris, 1956.

CAWLEY, A. C. *Everyman and Medieval Miracle Plays* (Everyman Library), London, 1956.

CHARLES, R. H. *A Critical History of the Doctrine of a Future Life*, 2nd ed., London, 1913.

The Revelation of St John (International Critical Commentary), 2 vols., Edinburgh, 1920.

CHATZIDAKIS, M. and GRABAR, A. *Byzantine and Early Medieval Painting*, E.T., London, 1965.

CLARK, K. *The Nude: A Study of Ideal Art*, London, 1960.

CLEMEN, C. *Religionsgeschichtliche Erklärung des Neuen Testaments*, Giessen, 1924.

COMBE, J. *Jérome Bosch*, Paris, 1946.

CONZELMANN, H. 'Jesus Christus', in *R.G.G.*, 3 Aufl., III (1959).

COOK, G. H. *The English Mediaeval Parish Church*, London, 1954.

COULTON, G. G. *Five Centuries of Religion*, 4 vols., Cambridge, 1923–50.

Medieval Panorama, Cambridge, 1938.

Infant Perdition in the Middle Ages (Medieval Studies, No. 16), London, 1922.

Medieval Faith and Symbolism, New York (being Part I of *Art and the Reformation*, Cambridge, 1953).

CREED, J. M. *The Gospel according to St Luke*, London, 1929.

DALMAN, G. *Jesus-Jeshua*, E.T., London, 1929.

DEARMER, P. *The Legend of Hell: an Examination of the Idea of Everlasting Punishment*, London, 1929.

DIBELIUS, M. 'Archonten', in *R.A.C.*, I (1950).

DINKLER, E. 'Earliest Christianity', in *The Idea of History in the Ancient Near East* (ed. R. C. Dentan), Yale University Press, 1955.

'Taufe II. Im Urchristendum', in *R.G.G.*, 3 Aufl., VI (1962).

Doctrine in the Church of England (The Report of the Commission on Christian Doctrine appointed by the Archbishops of Canterbury and York in 1922), London, 1938.

DODD, C. H. *The Interpretation of the Fourth Gospel*, Cambridge, 1954.

DUCHESNE, L. *Christian Worship: its Origin and Evolution*, E.T., London, 1927.

ELIADE, M. *Traité d'histoire des religions*, Paris, 1949.

FERGUSON, G. *Signs and Symbols in Christian Art*, New York, 1961.

FISCHER, J. A. *Studien zum Todesgedanken in der alten Kirche*, I, München, 1954.

The Flowering of the Middle Ages (ed. J. Evans), London, 1966.

FOCILLON, H. *The Art of the West in the Middle Ages*, E.T., 2 vols., London, 1963.

FÖRSTER, W. *Palestinian Judaism in New Testament Times*, E.T., Edinburgh, 1964.

FOURNÉE, J. *Le jugement dernier (Essai d'exégèse d'une oeuvre d'art: le vitrail de la cathédrale de Coutances)*, Paris, 1964.

GOGUEL, M. *The Life of Jesus*, E.T., London, 1933.

La naissance du Christianisme, Paris, 1946.

L'Église primitive, Paris, 1947.

GOUGH, M. *The Early Christians*, London, 1961.

GRIVOT, D. and ZARNECKI, G. *Gislebertus, Sculptor of Autun*, London, 1961.

GROBEL, K. '. . . Whose Name was Neves', in *N.T.S.*, X (1964).

GROSSI GONDI, F. *I Monumenti cristiani*, Roma, 1923.

GUIGNEBERT, CH. *Jésus*, Paris, 1947 (1933).

HARNACK, A. *History of Dogma*, 3rd ed., E.T., vols. I–VII, New York, 1961.

HUIZINGA, J. *The Waning of the Middle Ages*, E.T., New York, n.d.

JAMES, M. R. *The Apocryphal New Testament*, Oxford, 1926.

The Testament of Abraham (Texts and Studies, vol. II), Cambridge, 1892.

KATZENELLENBOGEN, A. *The Sculptural Programs of Chartres Cathedral*, New York, 1959.

KELLY, J. N. D. *Early Christian Creeds*, London, 1950.

KIRK, K. *The Vision of God*, London, 1950 (1931).

KLAUSNER, J. *Jesus of Nazareth*, E.T., London, 1929.

KLOSTERMANN, E. *Das Matthäusevangelium*, 2 Aufl., Tübingen, 1927.

KOEP, L. Buch IV (himmlisch), in *R.A.C.*, II (1954).

KRETZENBACHER, L. *Die Seelenwaage (Zur religiösen Idee vom Jenseitsgericht auf der Schicksalwaage in Hochreligion, Bildkunst und Volkglaube*, Klagenfurt, 1958.

KROLL, J. *Gott und Hölle*, Leipzig/Berlin, 1932.

LAKE, K. 'Baptism (Early Christian)', in *E.R.E.*, II (1909).

LENZ, CHR. 'Apokatastasis', in *R.A.C.*, I (1950).

LIETZMANN, H. *An die Korinther, I–II*, 2 Aufl., Tübingen, 1923.

Liturgy and Worship (ed. W. K. L. Clarke), London, 1932.

LOOFS, F. 'Descent to Hades (Christ's)', in *E.R.E.*, IV (1911).

MacCULLOCH, J. 'Eschatology', in *E.R.E.*, V (1912).

Medieval Faith and Fable, London.

MÂLE, E. *L'art religieux du XIIIe siècle en France*, Paris, 1922.

The Gothic Image, E.T., London, 1961.

Religious Art from the Twelfth to the Eighteenth Century, E.T., New York, 1965.

Bibliography

MALRAUX, A. *The Metamorphosis of the Gods*, E.T., London, 1960.

MANSON, T. W. *The Teaching of Jesus*, Cambridge, 1935.

MÁNEK, J. 'The Biblical Concept of Time and our Gospels', *N.T.S.*, VI (1959–60).

MCNEILE, A. H. *The Gospel according to St Matthew*, London, 1952 (1915).

VAN DER MEER, F. and MOHRMANN, C. *Atlas of the Early Christian World*, E.T., London/Edinburgh, 1958.

MICHL, J. 'Engel VII (Michael)', in *R.A.C.*, V (1962).

MOIR, A. L. 'The World Map', in *History Today*, XVI (1966), London.

MONTEFIORE, C. G. *Rabbinic Literature and Gospel Teachings*, London, 1930.

MOORMAN, J. R. H. *Church Life in England in the Thirteenth Century*, Cambridge, 1955.

MOWINCKEL, S. *He That Cometh*, E.T., Oxford, 1958.

MORENZ, S. *Die Geschichte vom Joseph dem Zimmermann (Texte u. Untersuchungen z. Gesch. d. altchr. Literatur*, hrg. W. Eltester u. E. Klostermann, Bd. 56), Berlin, 1951.

A New Commentary of Holy Scripture, ed. C. Gore, H. L. Goudge, A. Guillaume, 2 vols., London, 1929.

OLMSTEAD, A. T. *Jesus: in the Light of History*, New York, 1942.

The Oxford Dictionary of the Christian Church (ed. F. L. Cross), London, 1958.

DE PAOR, M. and L. *Early Christian Ireland*, London, 1958.

PARROT, A. *Le 'Refrigerium' dans l'au-delà*, Paris, 1937.

Peake's Commentary on the Bible, 2nd ed., M. Black and H. H. Rowley, London/ Edinburgh, 1962.

PERRY, MARY PHILIPPS. 'On the Psychostasis in Christian Art', in *The Burlington Magazine*, XXII (1912–13).

PUECH, H.-C. *Le Manichéisme*, Paris, 1949.

'Le Manichéisme', in *H.G.R.*, III (1947).

REITZENSTEIN, R. *Die hellenistischen Mysterienreligionen*, Stuttgart, 1956.

RICE, D. TALBOT, *The Beginnings of Christian Art*, London, 1957.

Art of the Byzantine Era, London, 1963.

RICHMOND, I. A. *Archaeology and the After-Life in Pagan and Christian Imagery* (The Riddell Memorial Lectures, Durham University), London, 1950.

RICKERT, M. *Painting in Britain: the Middle Ages*, Harmondsworth, 1954.

ROGERS, C. F. *The Fear of Hell as an Instrument of Conversion*, London, 1939.

RORIMER, J. J. *The Cloisters, the Building and the Collection of Medieval Art in Fort Tryon Park*, Metropolitan Museum of Art, New York, 1963.

RUPP, E. G. 'Luther and the German Reformation to 1529', in *The New Cambridge Modern History*, II, Cambridge, 1958.

SANDAY, W. and HEADLAM, A. C. *The Epistle to the Romans* (International Critical Commentary), Edinburgh, 1900.

SCHMIDT-CLAUSING, A. 'Fegfeuer', in *R.G.G.*, 3 Aufl., II (1958).

SCHOEPS, H. J. *Paulus; die Theologie des Apostels im Lichte der jüdischen Religions-geschichte*, Tübingen, 1959.

SCHOTT, R. *Michelangelo*, E.T., London, 1963.

SCHÜRER, E. *Geschichte des jüdischen Volkes im Zeitalter Jesu Christi*, 3 Bände, Leipzig, 1898–1901.

SCHWEITZER, A. *The Mysticism of Paul*, E.T., London, 1931.

SCOTT-MONCRIEFF, P. D. *Paganism and Christianity in Egypt*, Cambridge, 1913.

SIMON, M. *Hercule et le Christianisme*, Paris, 1955.

VON SIMSON, O. *The Gothic Cathedral*, London, 1956.

STONE, L. *Sculpture in Britain: the Middle Ages*, Harmondsworth, 1955.

STRACK, H. und BILLERBECK, P. *Kommentar zum Neuen Testament aus Talmud und Midrasch*, 4 Bände, Munich, 1922–8.

STUIBER, A. *Refrigerium Interim: die Vorstellungen vom Zwischenzustand und die frühchristliche Grabeskunst*, Bonn, 1957.

TAYLOR, V. *The Formation of the Gospel Tradition*, London, 1945.

The Gospel according to St Mark, London, 1952.

TERTULLIAN, *De testimonio animae*, trans. C. Dodgson, in The Library of the Fathers, Tertullian, vol. I, Oxford, 1842.

Testament of Abraham (Greek text), see under James, M. R.

DE TOLNAY, C. *Michelangelo. V. The Final Period*, Princeton University Press, 1960.

TURCAN, R. 'La catabase orphique du papyrus de Bologne', in *R.H.R.*, 150 (1956).

Victoria and Albert Museum: 100 *Masterpieces, Early Christian and Mediaeval*, 1930.

WAGNER, G. *Das religionsgeschichtliche Problem von Römer*, 6, 1–11, Zürich, 1962.

WALKER, D. P. *The Decline of Hell: Seventeenth Century Discussions of Eternal Torment*, London, 1964.

WEISS, J. *Earliest Christianity*, E.T., 2 vols., New York, 1959.

WENDEL, F. *Calvin*, E.T., London, 1965.

WERNER, M. *Die Entstehung des Christlichen Dogmas*, 2 Aufl., Bern/Tübingen, 1941.

The Formation of Christian Dogma, E.T., by S. G. F. Brandon, London, 1957.

WIDENGREN, GEO. *Mani and Manichaeism*, E.T., London, 1965.

Wörterbuch der Religion (ed. A. Bertholet), Stuttgart, 1952.

VI Islam

ANDRAE, TOR, *Mahomet: sa vie et sa doctrine*, Paris, 1945.

ARBERRY, A. J. *The Seven Odes: the first Chapter in Arabic Literature*, London, 1957.

Bibliography

BELL, R. *The Qur'ān* (*Translated, with a critical arrangement of the Surahs*), 2 vols., Messrs. T. and T. Clark, Edinburgh, 1937–9.

The Origin of Islam in its Christian Environment, London, 1926.

BOWKER, J. W. 'Intercession in the Qur'ān and the Jewish Tradition', in *J.S.S.*, XI. (1966).

BRANDON, S. G. F. *Man and his Destiny in the Great Religions*, Manchester University Press, 1962.

History, Time and Deity, Manchester University Press, 1965.

BROCKELMANN, C. *History of the Islamic Peoples*, E.T., London, 1950.

EKLUND, R. *Life between Death and Resurrection according to Islam*, Uppsala, 1941.

FINEGAN, J. *Archeology of World Religions*, Princeton University Press, 1952.

GAUDEFROY-DEMONBYNES, M. *Mahomet*, Paris, 1957.

GIBB, H. A. R. *Mohammedanism*, London, 1949.

GUIDI, J. 'Seven Sleepers', in *E.R.E.*, XI (1920).

KELLERHALS, E. *Der Islam* (*seine Geschichte, seine Lehre, sein Wesen*), Basel, 1945.

KENSDALE, W. E. N. *The Religious Beliefs and Practices of the Ancient South Arabians*, Ibadan University Press, 1955.

KNIGHT, G. A. FRANK, 'Bridge', in *E.R.E.*, II (1909).

KRETZENBACHER, L. *Die Seelenwaage*, Klagenfurt, 1958.

LANE-POOLE, S. 'Death and Disposal of the Dead (Muhammadan)', in *E.R.E.*, IV (1911).

LYALL, C. J. *Translations of Ancient Arabian Poetry*, London, 1885.

MACDONALD, D. B. *The Development of Muslim Theology, Jurisprudence and Constitutional Theory*, London, 1903.

'Allah', in *E.R.E.*, I (1908).

MARGOLIOUTH, D. S. 'Mecca', in *E.R.E.*, VIII (1915)

MAULI MUHAMMAD ALI, *The Holy Qur-ān* (containing the Arabic text with translation and commentary), 2nd ed., Lahore, 1920.

NICHOLSON, R. A. *A Literary History of the Arabs*, London, 1914 (1907).

NÖLDEKE, TH. 'Arabs (Ancient)', in *E.R.E.*, I (1908).

Qur'ān, see under Bell, R.

REFOULÉ, F. 'Immortalité de l'âme et resurrection de la chair', in *R.H.R.*, 163 (1963).

RODWELL, J. *The Koran* (Everyman Library), London, 1924.

RYCKMANS, G. 'Les religions arabes préislamiques', in *H.G.R.*, IV (1947).

SCHIMMEL, A. 'Zur Anthropologie des Islams', in *Anthropologie religieuse* (ed. C. J. Bleeker), Leiden, 1955.

SELL, E. 'Faith (Muslim)', in *E.R.E.*, V (1912).

'Sin (Muslim)', in *E.R.E.*, XI (1926).

SNOUCK-HURGRONJIE, G. 'Der Islam', in *L.R-G.*, I (1925).

SOUALAH, M. *L'Islam et l'evolution de la culture arabe*, Alger, 1935.

SOURDEL, D. 'Le jugement des morts dans l'Islam', in *Sources orientales*, IV (1961).

TRITTON, A. S. *Islam*, London, 1951.

ULLENDORFF, E. *The Ethiopians*, London, 1960.

WATT, W. M. *Free Will and Predestination in Early Islam*, London, 1948.

Muḥammad at Mecca, Oxford, 1953.

'Dahr', in *E.I.* (new ed.), II, pp. 94–5.

WENSINCK, A. J. *The Muslim Creed*, Cambridge, 1932.

WIET, G. 'La religion islamique', in *H.G.R.*, IV (1947).

WOOD, I. F. 'State of the Dead (Hebrew, Muhammadan)', in *E.R.E.*, XI (1920).

VII Iran

BRANDON, S. G. F. *Man and his Destiny in the Great Religions*, Manchester University Press, 1962.

Creation Legends of the Ancient Near East, London, 1963.

History, Time and Deity, Manchester University Press, 1965.

Bundahishn, trans. E. W. West, in *S.B.E.*, V (Pahlavi Texts), Oxford, 1880.

CARNOY, A. J. 'Ormazd', in *E.R.E.*, IX (1917).

CASARTELLI, L. C. 'Soul (Iranian)', in *E.R.E.*, XI (1920).

CHILDE, V. G. *The Aryans: a Study of Indo-European Origins*, London, 1926.

CHRISTENSEN, A. *Le Zoroastrisme de la Perse antique*, Copenhagen, 1928.

CULICAN, W. *The Medes and Persians*, London, 1965.

CUMONT, F. *After-Life in Roman Paganism*, New York, 1959 (1922).

DUCHESNE-GUILLEMIN, J. *Zoroastre*, Paris, 1948.

The Hymns of Zarathustra, E.T., London, 1952.

'L'homme dans la religion iranienne', in *Anthropologie religieuse* (ed. C. J. Bleeker), Leiden, 1955.

Symbolik des Parsismus, Stuttgart, 1961.

DUMÉZIL, G. *Naissance d'Archanges*, Paris, 1945.

Mitra-Varuna (Essai sur deux représentations indo-européennes de la souveraineté), Paris, 1948.

Les dieux des Indo-Européens, Paris, 1952.

EILERS, W. 'Avesta', in *R.G.G.*, 3 Aufl., I (1957).

FINEGAN, J. *Archeology of World Religions*, Princeton University Press, 1952.

FRYE, R. N. *The Heritage of Persia*, London, 1962.

GELDNER, K. F. 'Die zoroastrische Religion (das Avesta)', in *R-G.L.* (1908).

GERSHEVITCH, I. *The Avestan Hymn to Mithra*, Cambridge, 1959.

GHIRSCHMAN, R. *Iran*, Harmondsworth, 1954.

GRAY, L. H. 'Death and Disposal of Dead' (Ancient Persian Rites), in *E.R.E.*, IV (1911).

GÜNTERT, H. *Der arische Weltkönig und Heiland*, Halle, 1923.

HARTMANN, S. S. *Gayōmart: étude sur le syncrétisme dans l'ancien Iran*, Uppsala, 1953.

Bibliography

HENNING, W. B. *Zoroaster: Politician or Witch-Doctor?* (Ratabai Katrak Lectures, 1949), Oxford, 1951.

HERZFELD, E. *Zoroaster and his World*, 2 vols., Princeton University Press, 1947.

HUART, C. *La Perse et la civilisation iranienne*, Paris, 1925.

JACKSON, A. W. WILLIAMS, 'Avesta', in *E.R.E.*, II (1909).

KNIGHT, G. A. F. 'Bridge', in *E.R.E.*, II (1909).

LEHMANN, EDV. 'Die Perser', in *R-G.L.*, II (1925).

MEYER, ED. *Geschichte des Altertums*, I, 2, Stuttgart/Berlin, 1913.

MOLÉ, M. 'Une histoire du mazdéisme est-elle possible? Notes et remarques en marge d'un ouvrage récent', in *R.H.R.*, 162 (1962).

'Le jugement des morts dans l'Iran pré-islamique', in *Sources orientales*, IV (1961).

MOULTON, J. H. *Early Zoroastrianism*, London, 1913.

NYBERG, H. S. *Die Religionen des alten Iran*, Leipzig, 1938.

PAVRY, J. D. C. *The Zoroastrian Doctrine of the Future Life*, New York, 1929.

SERGI, G. 'Death and Disposal of the Dead (Greek)', in *E.R.E.*, IV (1911).

SÖDERBLOM, N. *La vie future d'après la Mazdéisme*, Paris, 1906.

WHITLEY, C. F. 'The Date and Teaching of Zarathustra', in *Numen*, IV (Leiden, 1957).

WIDENGREN, GEO, 'Stand und Aufgaben der iranischen Religionsgeschichte', in *Numen*, I (1954), II (1955).

Hochgottglaube im alten Iran, Lund, 1938.

ZAEHNER, R. C. *Zurvan: a Zoroastrian Dilemma*, Oxford, 1955.

'Postscript to Zurvān', in *B.S.O.A.S.*, XVII/2 (1955).

The Dawn and Twilight of Zoroastrianism, London, 1961.

Hinduism, London, 1962.

Zend-Avesta (Venîdâd), Part III, trans. J. Darmesteter, in *S.B.E.*, IV, Oxford, 1880.

Zend-Avesta (The *Yasna* etc.), trans. L. H. Mills, in *S.B.E.*, XXX, Oxford, 1887.

VIII Hinduism and Buddhism

BASHAM, A. L. *The Wonder that was India*, London, 1954.

BRANDON, S. G. F. *Man and his Destiny in the Great Religions*, Manchester University Press, 1962.

History, Time and Deity, Manchester University Press, 1965.

CONZE, E. *Buddhist Thought in India*, London, 1962.

Buddhist Scriptures, Harmondsworth, 1959.

Buddhism: its Essence and Development, Oxford (Cassirer), 1957 (1951).

DASGUPTA, S. *A History of Indian Philosophy*, I, Cambridge, 1922.

DEUSSEN, P. *Das System des Vedānta*, Leipzig, 1883.

The Philosophy of the Upanishads, E.T., Edinburgh, 1906.

DEVANANDAN, P. D. *The Concept of Maya*, London, 1950.

DOWSON, J. *A Classical Dictionary of Hindu Mythology*, 7th ed., London, 1950.

DUMÉZIL, G. *Les dieux des Indo-Européens*, Paris, 1952.

EDGERTON, F. *The Bhagavad Gītā*, 2 vols., Harvard University Press, 1952.

EVANS-WENTZ, W. Y. *The Tibetan Book of the Dead*, 3rd ed., London, 1957.

FILLIOZAT, J. 'L'apport de l'étude des religions de l'Inde à la science de l'homme', in *Anthropologie religieuse* (ed. C. J. Bleeker), Leiden, 1955.

FRAUWALLNER, E. 'Die Anthropologie des Buddhismus', in *Anthropologie religieuse* (ed. C. J. Bleeker), Leiden, 1955.

GARBE, R. 'Transmigration (Indian)', in *E.R.E.*, XII (1921).

GELDNER, K. F. *Der Rig-Veda, aus den Sanskrit ins Deutsche übersetzt* (Harvard Oriental Series), vols. I–IV, Cambridge, Mass., 1951-7.

'Die Religionen der Inder (Vedismus und Brahmanismus)', in *R-G.L.*, (1908).

GONDA, J. *Die Religionen Indiens*, I: *Veda und älterer Hinduismus*, Stuttgart, 1960.

GRIESSON, A. 'Bhakti-Màrga', in *E.R.E.*, II (1909).

GRISWOLD, H. D. *The Religion of the Rigveda*, Oxford, 1923.

GÜNTHER, H. *Das Seelenproblem im älteren Buddhismus*, Konstanz, 1949.

HILLEBRANT, A. F. F. 'Worship (Hindu)', in *E.R.E.*, XII (1921).

HUME, R. E. *The Thirteen Principal Upanishads*, Oxford, 1921.

The Kama Sutra of Vatsyayana, trans. R. Burton and F. F. Arbuthnot, London, 1963.

KONOW, S. 'Die Inder', in *L.R-G.*, II, 4 Aufl., 1925.

LANMANN, C. R. *A Sanskrit Reader*, Harvard University Press, 1927.

VAN DER LEEUW, G. *La religion dans son essence et ses manifestations*, Paris, 1948.

MACDONELL, A. A. *A History of Sanskrit Literature*, London, 1928.

'Vedic Religion', in *E.R.E.*, XII (1921).

MARCHAL, C.-H. 'The Mythology of Indo-China and Java', in *Asiatic Mythology*, E.T., London, 1932.

MURTI, T. R. V. *The Central Philosophy of Buddhism, a study of the Madhyanka System*, London, 1955.

OLDENBERG, H. *Die Religion des Vedas*, 2 Aufl., Berlin/Stuttgart, 1917.

Buddha: sein Leben, seine Lehre, seine Gemeinde, 5 Aufl., Stuttgart/Berlin, 1906.

O'MALLEY, L. S. S. *Popular Hinduism*, Cambridge, 1935.

PIGGOTT, S. *Prehistoric India*, Harmondsworth, 1950.

RADHAKRISHNAN, S. *The Principal Upaniṣads*, London, 1953.

RAIKES, R. L. 'The Mohenjo-daro Floods', in *Antiquity*, XXXIX (1965).

RENOU, L. *Religions of India*, London, 1953.

SULLIVAN, H. P. 'A Re-Examination of the Religion of the Indus Civilization', in *History of Religions*, 4 (Chicago University Press, 1964).

THOMAS, E. J. *The History of Buddhist Thought*, 2nd ed., London, 1951.

Early Buddhist Scriptures, London, 1935.

2,500 Years of Buddhism (ed. P. V. Bapat), Publications Department, Government of India, 1959.

DE LA VALLÉ POUSSIN, L. 'Bodhisattva', in *E.R.E.*, II (1909).

Bibliography

VARENNE, J. 'Le jugement des morts dans l'Inde', in *Sources orientales*, IV (1961).
The Vedic Age, ed. R. C. Majumdar, London, 1951.
WHEELER, M. *Civilizations of the Indus Valley and Beyond*, London, 1966.
DE WILMAN-GRABOWSKA, H. 'Brahmanic Mythology', in *Asiatic Mythology*, E.T., London, 1932.
ZAEHNER, R. C. *Hinduism*, London, 1962.
The Dawn and Twilight of Zoroastrianism, London, 1961.

IX   China

BRANDON, S. G. F. *Man and his Destiny in the Great Religions*, Manchester University Press, 1962.
CREEL, H. G. *Confucius and the Chinese Way*, New York, 1949.
DUBBS, H. H. *The Works of Hsüntze*, London, 1928.
Hsüntze (the Moulder of Ancient Confucianism), London, 1928.
DUYVENDAK, J. J. L. *Tao Te Ching (The Book of the Way and its Virtue)*, London, 1954.
ELIOT, C. *Hinduism and Buddhism*, vol. III, London, 1954 (1921).
FINEGAN, J. *Archeology of World Religions*, Princeton University Press, 1952.
FORKE, A. *Die Gedankenwelt des chineschen Kulturkreises*, München/Berlin, 1927.
FRANKE, O. 'Die Chinesen', in *L.R-G.*, 4 Aufl., I (1925).
FUNG YU-LAN, A History of Chinese Philosophy, E.T., I, London, 1937.
GRANET, M. *Le pensée chinoise*, Paris, 1950 (1934).
La religion des Chinois, 2nd ed., Paris, 1951.
Chinese Civilization, E.T., London, 1930.
DE GROOT, J. J. M. *Religion in China*, New York, 1912.
HENTZE, C. *Tod, Auferstehung, Weltordnung (das mythische Bild im ältesten China, in den grossasiatischen und zirkumpazifischen Kulturen*, Textband, Zürich, 1955.
HUGHES, E. R. *Chinese Philosophy in Classical Times* (Everyman Library), London, 1942.
HUGHES, E. R. and H. *Religion in China*, London, 1950.
MASPERO, H. 'The Mythology of Modern China', in *Asiatic Mythology*, E.T., London, 1932.
Les religions chinoises, Paris, 1950.
Le Taoïsme (being tomes I and II of the *Mélanges posthumes sur les religions et l'histoire de la China*), Paris, 1950.
NEEDHAM, J. (with WANG LING), *Science and Civilisation in China*, vol. II, Cambridge, 1956.
SMITH, D. H. 'Chinese Concepts of the Soul', in *Numen*, V (1958), Leiden.
'Divine Kingship in Ancient China', in *Numen*, IV (1957), Leiden.
STANGE, H. O. H. 'Die Religion des alten China (in anthropologischer Hinsicht)', in *Anthropologie religieuse* (ed. C. J. Bleeker), Leiden, 1955.

THOMAS, E. J. *A History of Buddhist Thought*, 2nd ed., London, 1951.

VANDIER-NICOLAS, N. 'Le jugement des morts en Chine', in *Sources orientales*, IV (1961), Paris.

WALEY, A. *The Way and its Power*, London, 1934.

WALSHE, W. G. 'Communion with the Dead (Chinese)', in *E.R.E.*, III (1910). 'Death and Disposal of Dead (Chinese)', in *E.R.E.*, IV (1911).

WATSON, W. *Ancient China before the Han Dynasty*, London, 1961. *Early Civilization in China*, London, 1966.

WIEGER, L. *A History of the Religious Beliefs and Philosophical Opinions in China*, E.T., Hsien-Lsien Press, 1927.

X Japan

ANESAKI, M. 'Life and Death (Japanese)', in *E.R.E.*, VIII (1915).

ASTON, W. G. 'Shinto', in *E.R.E.*, XI (1920).

DUMOULIN, H. *A History of Zen Buddhism*, E.T., London, 1936.

ELISÉEV, S. 'The Mythology of Japan', in *Asiatic Mythology*, E.T., London, 1932.

FINEGAN, J. *The Archeology of World Religions*, Princeton University Press, 1952.

FLORENZ, K. *Die historischen Quellen der Shinto-Religion*, Göttingen, 1919. 'Die Japaner', in *L.R-G.*, 4 Aufl., I (1925).

GUNDERT, W. 'Die Behandlung eschatologischer Fragen im Zen-Buddhismus', in *X. Internationaler Kongress für Religionsgeschichte* (Marburg, 1960), Kommissionsverlag, Marburg, 1961.

KIDDER, J. E. *Japan before Buddhism*, London, 1959.

LLOYD, A. 'Death and Disposal of the Dead (Japanese)', in *E.R.E.*, IV (1911).

REVON, M. 'Ancestor-Worship (Japanese)', in *E.R.E.*, I (1908).

SIEFFIERT, R. 'De quelques représentations du jugement des mort chez les Japonais', in *Sources orientales*, IV (1961), Paris.

SUZUKI, D. T. '*An Introduction to Zen Buddhism*', London, 1959.

TAKASAKI, J. N. in *2,500 Years of Buddhism* (ed. P. V. Bapat), Publications Department, Government of India, 1959.

Addenda

BLEEKER, C. J. 'Die Idee des Schicksals in der altägyptischen Religion', in *Numen*, II (1955).

COCAGNAC, A.-M. *Le jugement dernier dans l'art*, Paris, 1955.

DRIOTON, E. 'La religion égyptienne', in *Les religions de l'orient ancien* (Coll: 'Je sais - je crois'), Paris, 1957.

LACROIX, P. *Military and Religious Life in the Middle Ages and the Renaissance* (E.T.), 1874, repr. 1964, New York (fig. 393, from a twelfth-century MS now destroyed, provides an interesting example of the incident discussed on p. 234, n. 139: the serpent is identified with the 'worm that dieth not').

Bibliography

LESKY, A. *Thalatta: der Weg der Griechen zum Meer*, Wien, 1947.

MARTIN, J. P. *The Last Judgment, in Protestant Theology from Orthodoxy to Ritschl*, Edinburgh, 1963.

MORET, A. *Le Nil et la civilisation égyptienne*, Paris, 1926.

SMITH, J. Z. 'The Garments of Shame', in *History of Religions*, vol. 5 (1966), Chicago University Press.

INDEX OF SOURCES

(References to the notes are shown in brackets)

II   Ancient Mesopotamia

III   Hebrew Religion

IV Graeco-Roman Culture

Index of Sources

Papiro Bolognese, no. 3	223 (106), 229 (89)
Pindar, *Frag.*	102: 218 (31)
Dirges	frag. 133: 221 (84)
Plato, *Apology*	41A: 221 (76)
Gorgias	493: 220 (68)
	493B: 221 (77)
	523C–E: 223 (103)
Phaedrus	245–50: 221 (81)
	248–9: 222 (86)
Phaedrus	245–50: 221 (81)
	248–9: 222 (86)
Republic	I. 330D–31A: 221 (72)
	II. 363C–D: 221 (73)
	X. 614C: 222 (98)
	616: 222 (97)
Poimandres (*Corpus Hermeticum*)	X. 19–21: 222 (93)
	XII. 3–7: 222 (93)
Sallustius, *On the Gods and the World*	XIX: 223 (110)
Sophocles, *Frag.*	719: 218 (31)
Virgil, *Aeneid*	VI. 540: 222 (98)
	557–8: 223 (99)
	566–9: 223 (100)
	571–617: 223 (101)
	703–15: 222 (95)
	739–51: 222 (96)
	756ff.: 222 (94)

V   Christianity

Acts	i. 6: 225 (9)
Acts of Pilate	114–15
L'Advocacie Nostre-Dame	129
Apocalypse of Peter	116–17
Augustine, *Epistola*	CLXXXVII: 233 (129)
Calvin, *Commentary on Acts* 3.20	Opp. 48.71: 236 (160)
	Inst. III. 25.10: 236 (161)
I *Cor.* ii. 6–8: 226 (33)	
iii. 13–16: 112	
vi. 9–11: 227 (4)	
Dante, *Inferno*	XXI. 25–36: 236 (155)
Purgatorio	III: 229 (86)
	IV: 229 (84)
	X, XIII, XXV: 228 (66)

VI Islam

IX   China

X   Japan

INDEX OF MODERN AUTHORS

INDEX OF NAMES AND SUBJECTS

293

Date Due